Alec Reid has been producing *With Great Pleasure* for two and a half years, taking over the series from the late Brian Patten. He joined the BBC in 1961 and has produced for all four national radio networks in a wide variety of departments, from sound archives to religion, talks, documentaries and drama.

Alec Reid won the International Ondas Award in Spain for a musical version of Oscar Wilde's *The Selfish Giant*, and has written two further musicals for radio performance as well as producing records for Harrap and Penguin Educational. He is also responsible for producing the weekly Radio 4 programme, *Time for Verse*.

He lives in Bristol, and is married with two young sons.

# *WITH GREAT PLEASURE*

## *Volumes I and II*

*An Anthology of Poetry and Prose from the BBC Radio 4 Programme*

EDITED BY ALEC REID

*By arrangement with BBC Publications, a division of BBC Enterprises Limited*

ARROW BOOKS

Arrow Books Limited
20 Vauxhall Bridge Road, London SW1V 2SA

An imprint of Random Century Group

London Melbourne Sydney Auckland
Johannesburg and agencies throughout
the world

*With Great Pleasure, Volume I* first published
in Great Britain by Hutchinson 1986

*With Great Pleasure, Volume II* first published
in Great Britain by Hutchinson 1988

First published in this collected edition by Arrow 1989
by arrangement with BBC Publications, a division of
BBC Enterprises Limited



Photoset by Rowland Phototypesetting Limited
Bury St Edmunds, Suffolk
Printed in Great Britain by
The Guernsey Press Co. Limited
Guernsey, Channel Islands

ISBN 0 09 965940 9

# *WITH GREAT PLEASURE*

*Volume I*

# *CONTENTS*

# ACKNOWLEDGEMENTS

*Going, Going* reprinted by permission of Faber and Faber Ltd from 'High Windows' by PHILIP LARKIN
*A Lament for Moira McCavendish* and *A Ballad of Investiture 1969* reprinted by permission of John Murray (Publishers) Ltd from 'Collected Poems' by JOHN BETJEMAN
*But Murderous* by STEVIE SMITH from 'The Collected Poems of Stevie Smith' published by Penguin Modern Classics, reproduced by permission of James MacGibbon
*Waste* and *Billy* by HARRY GRAHAM from 'Ruthless Rhymes for Heartless Homes' published by E. J. Arnold Ltd
*The Thousandth Man* by RUDYARD KIPLING from 'Rudyard Kipling's Verse' reproduced by permission of A. P. Watt Ltd on behalf of The National Trust and Macmillan London Ltd
Extract from *Advice to a Lecturer* by MICHAEL FARADAY reproduced by courtesy of the Royal Institution
Extract from *Beginning Again* by LEONARD WOOLF reproduced by permission of the author's Estate and Chatto & Windus: The Hogarth Press
*Eight O' Clock* and extract from *A Shropshire Lad* from 'Collected Poems' by A. E. HOUSEMAN reproduced by permission of The Society of Authors (as the literary representative of the Estate of A. E. Houseman) and Jonathan Cape Ltd
*The Thirty-Ninth Rose* by ERIC WALTER WHITE published privately 1977 and reproduced by permission of Sarah White
*The Psychology of Shakespeare* from 'The State of Psychiatry' by AUBREY LEWIS reproduced by permission of Routledge & Kegan Paul Ltd
*To Hedli* from '85 Poems' by LOUIS MACNEICE published by Faber and Faber Ltd and reproduced by permission of David Higham Associates Ltd
*Her Triumph, The Pity of Love* and *September 1913* by W. B. YEATS reproduced by permission of A. P. Watt Ltd on behalf of Michael Yeats and Macmillan London Ltd

*A Marginal Gloss on the Death of Irish* © AIDAN CARL MATTHEWS reproduced by permission of the author
Extract from *The Life of the Caterpillar* by JEAN FABRÉ published by Hodder & Stoughton Ltd and reprinted by permission of Hughes Massie Ltd
*The Cicada* © LAWRENCE DURRELL from 'Collected Poems' reprinted by permission of Faber and Faber Ltd
*Letter to a Publisher* by SYLVIA TOWNSEND WARNER reprinted by permission of the author's Estate and Chatto & Windus: The Hogarth Press
*The Naming of Cats* reprinted by permission of Faber and Faber Ltd from 'Old Possum's Book of Practical Cats' by T. S. ELIOT
*Letter from a Girl to her Aunt* reprinted by permission of Methuen & Co from 'Post-Bag Diversions' ed. E. V. LUCAS
*That Music Stuff* from 'Dancing in the Streets' © CLIFFORD HANLEY reprinted by permission of Curtis Brown Ltd
Extract from *How to be a Doctor* reprinted by permission of The Bodley Head Ltd from 'Literary Lapses' by STEPHEN LEACOCK
*On Gout* by A. P. HERBERT reprinted by permission of A. P. Watt Ltd on behalf of Lady Herbert
*How Long, O Lord . . .* © KEITH WATERHOUSE from 'Waterhouse at Large' published by Michael Joseph and reprinted by permission of David Higham Associates Ltd
*Death of the Bird* © Professor A. D. HOPE reprinted by permission of Angus & Robertson (U.K.) Ltd
*The Coast Norfolk* by FRANCES CORNFORD reprinted by permission of Professor C. F. Cornford
Extract from *The Initials in the Heart* by LAURENCE WHISTLER reprinted by permission of John Murray (Publishers) Ltd
*The Physicians Prayer* by SIR ROBERT HUTCHISON Bt reproduced by permission of Sir Peter Hutchison Bt
*Cargoes*, Extract from *Good Friday* and Extract from *Right Royal* by JOHN MASEFIELD reprinted by permission of The Society of Authors as the literary representative of the Estate of John Masefield
*The Fossils* from 'The Carnival of the Animals' © OGDEN NASH reproduced by permission of Curtis Brown Ltd
*Suicide in the Trenches* by SIEGFRIED SASSOON reprinted by permission of George Sassoon

# FOREWORD

This book celebrates 'With Great Pleasure', a programme which has been running successfully for over fifteen years on Radio 4. A person, generally prominent in the arts or in public life, presents in some hall, theatre or studio, a selection of his or her favourite poetry and prose. Reading the items to the assembled audience are an actor and actress.

On the face of it nothing could be simpler, but it is often the simplest ideas that need the most careful thought. In a less unjust world it would not be me compiling this anthology, but my predecessor, the late Brian Patten, a gifted and much loved producer with the BBC in Bristol. Although the series came into existence in 1970 every programme was produced by a different person and it tended to be somewhat untidy in form, with some presenters both introducing and reading the whole selection – a feat which few could bring off with any conviction – and others with just one actor of the same sex reading with them, leading in the end to a sameness of sound little different from the solo performances. It was Brian in the mid 1970s who – along with his assistant Margaret Bradley, now a producer in her own right – took the whole thing over, lent it a style and ensured its continuing popularity. It is a programme in which people like to be invited to appear. After all, the chance to share a lifetime's reading, a lifetime's enthusiasms is almost irresistible. The shock comes sometimes when the presenter realises that the well-remembered poem is not, after all, remembered word for word, that the novel which changed his life contains no passage that can be lifted to stand on its own, and did he, in any case, want to re-read the whole thing just then? Many a time I have been told, 'Well, it was great fun, but I never realised it would be such hard work.' By telling you this, I have no wish to discourage potential contributors – the other side of the coin is that the actual recording tends to be extremely pleasurable for all concerned. Whenever possible we go to some town or village with which the presenter is connected, where he or she was brought up, say, or where he or she has laid down roots. In consequence the local audience is generally warmly disposed towards the participants. It is invidious to single out individual programmes, so in citing Sir Peter Pears' programme as illustration of the latter point I do so because the recording took place only last week and it is uppermost in my mind. The affection the audience in the Jubilee Hall at Aldeburgh had for him raised the temperature of a chilly January day by several degrees. This of course added to the pleasure of the evening for him and for us, and, ultimately, for the listener at home.

There have now been well over 160 programmes and of course over the years a number of items have proved popular with both presenters and listeners. Indeed, tactful negotiation occasionally has to take place to ensure that the same poem does not occur more than once in the same series. One of the more requested items, not included in this anthology, is Rupert Brooke's 'The Old Vicarage, Grantchester', and for the sake of the audience I have to limit its appearance to no more than once every couple of series or so. In general, however, there are no restrictions as to choice placed on the presenters. After all, we are inviting them to share with us what has given *them* most pleasure.

In selecting for this book I was placed in somewhat of a dilemma. Should I concentrate on the items most often included on the air? I decided in the end not to make that the basis for selection, if only on the grounds that they are almost certainly readily available elsewhere and you probably already have them. At the same time there would be no point in making the book totally unrepresentative of the series as a whole. So how about a 'Best Of . . . ?' Totally impossible as the book would then almost certainly be over 160 programmes long! I realised in the end that I was in a uniquely favoured position, in that whereas the people I invite to take part are constrained by the almost impossible task of having to distil a lifetime's reading into forty-five minutes, I have been given the equivalent of eighteen hours or so to present from the programmes pieces that I have particularly enjoyed and which in very many cases were new discoveries for me. Some pieces that I have included also because every time they are broadcast we receive dozens of letters from people requesting information as to where it is possible to obtain a copy. I will be pleased to direct them to this volume.

I have made a point also of including some items which have rarely if ever been published, for instance a piece of Chaucer discovered by a colleague of Sir Lawrence Bragg's and included in his programme, or a letter of proposal to one of Steve Race's ancestors which must have been totally resistible at the time and which is now totally charming and funny.

As its producer, the programme provides me with opportunities to meet many of those whom I have admired and enjoyed in their public capacities and to get to know them a little better as people. It is a privileged position and I am grateful for it. It is with great pleasure that I share it with you.

Alec Reid
January 1986

# *KINGSLEY AMIS*

## *1980*

*The affability, the fondness for whisky and the insistence on the correct use of language and pronunciation, these were to be expected. What did surprise me was Kingsley Amis's relish for sending himself up. In the break between the rehearsal and the recording of 'With Great Pleasure' we conducted a spoof interview for an April Fool programme I was producing for Radio 3. It concerned a non-existent poet called Brian Alexander (an amalgam of my name and that of the writer, Brian Sibley) who was purported after one of his readings to have thrown the distinguished novelist, who had happened to be in the audience, down the stairs. With remarkable generosity of spirit, Amis agreed to take part in the 'documentary' and to analyse Alexander's appeal. Entering into the spirit of the thing, he looked at the poems, which were in fact slightly improved adolescent verses of Brian's, and said to me, 'Well, which of my lines do you want me to take – "I really don't go much for all this modern rubbish" or "It's good to see someone struggling with traditional forms these days"?' He then proceeded to deliver a shrewd and extremely funny extempore review.*

Let's begin with a poem I came across as a schoolboy. It showed me two things: one, that poetry could be as exciting as Louis Armstrong, whose works I was discovering at about the same time, and two, that poetry wasn't remote and high-flown, or needn't be; it could be very much of the time and place I was living in. Later I found that the poet, Francis Thompson, was a bad guy, that he was sentimental and sensationalist and anyway out of fashion. Later still I forgot all that and saw that although 'The Kingdom of God' wasn't the greatest poem in the world, as I'd once thought, it was pretty good for all that. The very well-known phrase that comes in the middle is Thompson's invention as far as I know.

## *The Kingdom of God*

FRANCIS THOMPSON

O world invisible, we view thee,
O world intangible, we touch thee,
O world unknowable, we know thee,
Inapprehensible, we clutch thee.

Does the fish soar to find the ocean,
The eagle plunge to find the air –
That we ask of the stars in motion
If they have rumour of thee there?

Not where the wheeling systems darken,
And our benumbed conceiving soars! –
The drift of pinions, would we hearken,
Beats at our own clay-shuttered doors.

The angels keep their ancient places; –
Turn but a stone, and start a wing!
'Tis ye, 'tis your estranged faces,
That miss the many-splendoured thing.

But (when so sad thou canst not sadder)
Cry; – and upon thy so sore loss
Shall shine the traffic of Jacob's ladder
Pitched betwixt Heaven and Charing Cross.

Yea, in the night, my Soul, my daughter,
Cry, – clinging Heaven by the hems;
And lo, Christ walking on the water,
Not of Gennesaret, but Thames!

One man who was completely out in my schooldays and later, out in a bigger way than Thompson could ever have been, was Tennyson. No insult was too big for him: he was hypocritical, superficial, smug, patriotic (a deadly sin), stupid and, worst of all, Victorian. That was a long time ago; it's interesting to see how that word 'Victorian' has changed from being a term of abuse to denoting envious approval, so that people talk about the Victorian values of stability and domesticity. Anyway, Victorian or not, and I think not in a lot of ways, Tennyson was a poet of stupendous natural talent: not even Keats surpassed him in that. He said of himself that other men had written better poetry than his, but none had written poetry that sounded better. Correct. Here's one of the songs from his verse play, *The Princess*:

## *Come Down O Maid*

ALFRED, LORD TENNYSON

'Come down, O maid from yonder mountain height:
What pleasure lives in height (The shepherd sang)
In height and cold, the splendour of the hills?
But cease to move so near the Heavens, and cease
To glide a sunbeam by the blasted Pine,
To sit a star upon the sparkling spire;
And come, for Love is of the valley, come,
For Love is of the valley, come thou down
And find him; by the happy threshold, he,
Or hand in hand with plenty in the maize,
Or red with spirted purple of the vats,
Or foxlike in the vine; nor cares to walk
With Death and Morning on the silver horns,
Nor wilt thou snare him in the white ravine,
Nor find him dropt upon the firths of ice,
That huddling slant in furrow-cloven falls
To roll the torrent out of dusky doors:
But follow; let the torrent dance thee down
To find him in the valley; let the wild
Lean-headed Eagles yelp alone, and leave
The monstrous ledges there to slope, and spill
Their thousand wreaths of dangling water-smoke,
That like a broken purpose waste in air:
So waste not thou; but come; for all the vales
Await thee; azure pillars of the hearth

Arise to thee; the children call, and I
Thy shepherd pipe, and sweet is every sound,
Sweeter thy voice, but every sound is sweet;
Myriads of rivulets hurrying through the lawn,
The moan of doves in immemorial elms,
And murmuring of innumerable bees.'

I was lucky enough to be a contemporary of Philip Larkin at Oxford and have never quite recovered from my surprise at finding that that beer-drinking, jazz-loving breaker of college rules was also a most sensitive and exquisite poet, in the true senses of those terms. He didn't always write in that mood or that style; he had a tougher, more direct manner, well illustrated in a poem he wrote on a commission from the Department of the Environment, if you can believe such a thing. It was first published about fifteen years ago, and since then things have certainly gone the way he said they would.

### *Going, Going*

PHILIP LARKIN

I thought it would last my time –
The sense that, beyond the town,
There would always be fields and farms,
Where the village louts could climb
Such trees as were not cut down;
I knew there'd be false alarms

In the papers about old streets
And split level shopping, but some
Have always been left so far;
And when the old parts retreat
As the bleak high-risers come
We can always escape in the car.

Things are tougher than we are, just
As earth will always respond
However we mess it about;
Chuck filth in the sea, if you must:
The tides will be clean beyond.
– But what do I feel now? Doubt?

Or age, simply? The crowd
Is young in the M1 cafe;
Their kids are screaming for more –
More houses, more parking allowed,
More caravan sites, more pay.
On the business page, a score

Of spectacled grins approve
Some takeover bid that entails
Five per cent profits (and ten
Per cent more in the estuaries): move
Your works to unspoilt dales
(Grey area grants)! And when

You try to get near the sea
In summer . . .

It seems, just now,
To be happening so very fast;
Despite all the land left free
For the first time I feel somehow
That it isn't going to last,

That before I snuff it, the whole
Boiling will be bricked in
Except for the tourist parts –
First slum of Europe: a role
It won't be so hard to win,
With a cast of crooks and tarts.

And that will be England gone,
The shadows, the meadows, the lanes,
The guildhalls, the carved choirs.
There'll be books; it will linger on
In galleries; but all that remains
For us will be concrete and tyres.

Most things are never meant.
This won't be, most likely: but greeds
And garbage are too thick strewn
To be swept up now, or invent
Excuses that make them all needs.
I just think it will happen soon.

No programme of writings that give me pleasure would be anything else but disastrously incomplete without something by John Betjeman. In a time when so many public figures are monsters or frauds it was nice to come across one who thoroughly deserved his popularity. He's probably the last poet to have commanded anything like a mass audience in the manner of Tennyson, whom he greatly admired and whose work had something in common with his own, mastery of sound, for example. Where Betjeman was quite different, indeed unique, was his ability to move from something pleasantly light, even comic, to painful emotions like grief and remorse, and to do it quite smoothly, without any noticeable change of key. So in the next poem, *A Lament for Moira McCavendish*, we begin in a spirit of gentle fun and then find ourselves plunged into sorrow and a sense of loss; very characteristic of this splendid poet.

## *A Lament For Moira McCavendish*

JOHN BETJEMAN

Through the midlands of Ireland I journeyed by diesel
  And bright in the sun shone the emerald plain;
Though loud sang the birds on the thorn-bush and teasel
  They could not be heard for the sound of the train.

The roll of the railway made musing creative:
  I thought of the colleen I soon was to see
With her wiry black hair and grey eyes of the native,
  Sweet Moira McCavendish, Acushla Machree.

Her brother's wee cabin stands distant from Tallow
  A league and a half, where the Blackwater flows,
And the musk and potato, the mint and the mallow
  Do grow there in beauty, along with the rose.

'Twas smoothly we raced through the open expansion
  Of rush-covered levels and gate-lodge and gate
And the ruined demesne and the windowless mansion
  Where once the oppressor had revelled in state.

At Castletownroche, as the prospect grew hillier,
  I saw the far mountains to Moira long-known
Till I came to the valley and townland familiar
  With the Protestant church standing locked and alone.

O vein of my heart! upon Tallow Road Station
  No face was to greet me, so freckled and white;
As the diesel slid out, leaving still desolation,
  The McCavendish ass-cart was nowhere in sight.

For a league and half to the Blackwater river
  I tramped with my bundle her cabin to see
And herself by the fuchsias, her young lips a-quiver
  Half-smiling, half-weeping a welcome to me.

Och Moira McCavendish! the fangs of the creeper
  Have struck at the thatch and thrust open the door;
The couch in the garden grows ranker and deeper
  Than musk and potato which bloomed there before.

Flow on, you remorseless and salmon-full waters!
  What care I for prospects so silvery fair?
The heart in me's dead, like your sweetest of daughters,
  And I would that my spirit were lost on the air.

*Readers: Judi Dench, Tim Pigott-Smith*

*Full Selection:*
*The Kingdom of God*, FRANCIS THOMPSON
*Come Down O Maid*, ALFRED, LORD TENNYSON
*Going, Going*, PHILIP LARKIN
*Don't Miss This*, PETER SIMPLE
*The Runnable Stag*, JOHN DAVIDSON
*The Cuirassiers of the Frontier*, ROBERT GRAVES
*Act of Faith*, IRWIN SHAW
*A Lament for Moira McCavendish*, JOHN BETJEMAN
*Exposure*, WILFRED OWEN
*That Hideous Strength*, C. S. LEWIS
*The Gods of the Copybook Headings*, RUDYARD KIPLING
*Right Ho, Jeeves*, P. G. WODEHOUSE
*Fancy's Knell*, A. E. HOUSMAN
*The Rolling English Road*, G. K. CHESTERTON

# *LINDSAY ANDERSON*

## *1984*

*He won't remember the first time we met. It was during 1973 in the stalls of the Royal Court Theatre. As a producer attached to Radio Four's arts magazine programme, 'Kaleidoscope', I was sent to report on the Court's plans for the forthcoming season. As I was about to leave, I saw Lindsay Anderson standing on his own and, full of youthful enthusiasm – 'Kaleidoscope' was at that time a very new programme – asked if I might interview him. After looking me up and down for what seemed a considerable time, he finally said 'Ah well, I suppose you could do with a leg-up in your career.' That early impression of waspishness was for me totally dispelled on our second meeting, for the recording of 'With Great Pleasure', He was relaxed and friendly, full of professional courtesy and genuine warmth. It turned out to be one of the most enjoyable of any of the series I have worked on to date, and not just because the evening ended with all of us drinking on the lawns of Balliol College at midnight.*

It is impossible to start on a programme of this kind without asking oneself 'Why?' I mean why did I, for instance, let myself in for it? Vanity and self display of course enter into it, but also the desire to share, to let people know about some works that have been a part of one's thinking and which perhaps they don't know and will enjoy, or be affected by too.

It may well be my classical background – I did Latin and Greek as a schoolboy and in fact came up to this very university, though not to Balliol, but to Wadham round the corner, on classics –

returning to Oxford from the war I'm afraid I lapsed into English literature – but I have still clung, I hope, to the classical ideas of lucidity, directness of communication, clarity of thought; and these are the qualities I like in poetry. I am not good at modern, should I say contemporary, poetry but the modern poets I like tend to be quirky, like Stevie Smith for instance. Here is a characteristic piece of hers in caustic common sense rather than whimsical mood.

### *But Murderous*

STEVIE SMITH

A mother slew her unborn babe
In a day of recent date
Because she did not wish him to be born in a world
Of murder and war and hate
'Oh why should I bear a babe from my womb
To be broke in pieces by the hydrogen bomb?'

I say this woman deserves little pity
That she was a fool and a murderess
Is a child's destiny to be contained by a mind
That signals only a lady in distress

And why should human infancy be so superior
As to be too good to be born in this world?
Did she think it was an angel or a baa-lamb
That lay in her belly furled?

Oh the child is the young of its species
Alike with that noble, vile, curious and fierce
How foolish this poor mother to suppose
Her act told us aught that was not murderous

(As, item, That the arrogance of a half-baked mind
Breeds murder; makes us all unkind.)

I have to admit that with the years my attitude to my fellow men has grown more sardonic. They are really a rum lot. I don't think of myself as cynical – cynics prefer to think of themselves as realists – but I do have to admit to being unable to read a newspaper today or watch the news on television without a certain amount of revulsion. There is a verse that expresses the feeling perfectly by Walter Raleigh, not *the* Sir Walter Ralegh, but an Edwardian literatus.

### *I Wish I Loved the Human Race*

WALTER RALEIGH

I wish I loved the human race
I wished I loved its silly face
I wish I loved the way it walks
I wish I loved the way it talks
And when I'm introduced to one
I wish I thought what jolly fun.

In this mood I am fond of repeating to myself a selection of Harry Graham's *'Ruthless Rhymes for Heartless Homes'*. They provide a healthy tonic, I think, against conventional sentimentalism. Here are two of my favourites.

### *Waste*

HARRY GRAHAM

I had written to Aunt Maud
Who was on a trip abroad
When I heard she'd died of cramp
Just too late to save the stamp.

### *Billy*

Billy, in one of his nice new sashes
Fell in the fire and was burned to ashes
Now, although the room grows chilly
I haven't the heart to poke poor Billy.

Ah yes, rhymers, scepticism, cynicism – call it anything you like – is dangerously attractive. I know one has to be careful or it slips into facility, but in a world so full of falsity, realism is surely beneficial as well as attractive.

It's a commonplace that as we get older we become more conservative, ever more reactionary. When I was young in the heady days of post-war Britain, I suppose I could be called an idealist, though hopeful was really a better word. I was certainly labelled an angry young man, and even a socialist. I wore a leather jacket and that was enough to label you a Brechtian. Well in fact I would never have called myself a socialist because I have always been too sceptical of centralised power. I've certainly found, and still find, a lot to be angry about, but I had great sympathy with the aristocratic ideal, with the sense of individual moral responsibility that goes with it and its mistrust of facile egalitarianism. Not fashionable. This brings me to another writer I'm always fond of dipping into and like to carry around with me. Henry Frederick Amiel was a Swiss-French intellectual and literatus whose sixty years of life spanned the middle of the last century. He wrote a journal, a chronicle of reflections and observation which was once celebrated, and which now no one seems to have read or heard of. *Amiel's Journal* is full of wisdom, the kind of wisdom I've been talking about. Not fashionable. Here for instance are some remarks of his on equality. Could it be called the twentieth century heresy?

## *Amiel's Journal*

The modern leveller, after having done away with conventional inequalities, with arbitrary privilege and historical injustice, goes still further and rebels against the inequalities of merit, capacity and virtue. Beginning with a just principle he develops it into an unjust one. Inequality may be as true and as just as equality; it depends on what you mean by it, but this is precisely what nobody cares to find out. All passions dread the light and the modern zeal for equality is a disguised hatred which tries to pass itself off for love.

And the continuation . . .

Liberty, equality; bad principles, the only true principle for humanity is justice. And justice towards the feeble becomes necessarily protection or kindness.

'Liberty, equality; bad principles.' It would take some courage to say that on television today, or maybe even on radio. Only Enoch Powell at his best, I suppose could have got away with it. Here is another reflection from Amiel which I think provides a very direct and necessary comment on the characteristics of contemporary sophistication, what Amiel calls cultivated society, and this was written I suppose about a hundred years ago.

If ignorance and passion are the foes of popular morality, moral indifference is the malady of the cultivated classes. The modern separation of enlightenment and virtue, of thought and conscience, of the intellectual aristocracy from the honest and vulgar crowd is the greatest danger that can threaten liberty. Our cynics and railers are mere egotists who stand aloof from the common duty and are of no service to society against any ill that may attack it. Their cultivation consists in having got rid of feeling, and thus they fall further and further away from true humanity and approach nearer to the demonical nature. What was it that Mephistopheles lacked? Not intelligence certainly, but goodness.

I'd like to leave you with a quotation to identify if you can. Who said, and where, and why, 'We go further. I am well and happy.'?

*Readers: Jill Bennett, Frank Grimes*

*Full Selection:*
*The Municipal Gallery Revisited*, W. B. YEATS
*But Murderous*, STEVIE SMITH
*Autumn Journal, Section IX*, LOUIS MACNEICE
*I Wish I Loved the Human Race*, SIR WALTER A. RALEIGH
*Waste*, HARRY GRAHAM
*Billy*, HARRY GRAHAM
*On the Birth of His Son* from ARTHUR WALEY'S translation of 170 Chinese poems
*The Scholar Recruit*, PAO CHAO from above
*Sailing Homeward* from above
*Out of Africa*, KAREN BLIXEN
*Amiel's Journal*
*God Is an Englishman*, DONALD BORNE
*Brief Quotations* from JOHN DONNE, JOYCE CAREY, HENRY FIELDING, JEAN JACQUES ROUSSEAU, JOHN KEATS, KAREN BLIXEN and YURI GAGARIN
*The Memoirs of Shostakovitch*

Poem from *The Farm*, DAVID STOREY
*Prater Violet*, CHRISTOPHER ISHERWOOD
*Red River Valley* (song)

# *JEFFREY ARCHER*

## *1984*

*At the time of writing, Jeffrey Archer had put aside for a time his career as a novelist to become deputy chairman of the Conservative Party. For the press it seemed as if it had suddenly become the Glorious Twelfth with Jeffrey as chief grouse. My own first impression of him was of an amiable, even kind man possessed of a pushy intelligence. There was on occasion a surprising element of self-deprecation. That may have been calculated, but what wasn't – and it made me warm to him further – was the revelation that he had included Kipling's 'The Thousandth Man' in appreciation of a friend who had stood by him during the worst of his financial troubles.*

I have often heard it said that young people introduced to Shakespeare don't enjoy it because they either meet up with it too young or fail to appreciate its value. One of the great privileges I had at school was being taught by a man called Alan Quilter, now the Headmaster of Wells Cathedral School in Somerset, where I come from. He instilled in me a love of Shakespeare from a very young age. This piece I have chosen is one that shook me when I was young; it is of Richard II showing that he is the king. I couldn't believe that any man believed he would be a god or above all men, but this speech leaves one in absolutely no doubt.

## *Richard II*

WILLIAM SHAKESPEARE

K. RICHARD. (To Northumberland)
We are amaz'd; And thus long have we stood
To watch the fearful bending of thy knee,
Because we thought ourself thy lawful king:
And if we be, how dare thy joints forget
To pay their awful duty to our presence?
If we be not, show us the hand of God
That hath dismiss'd us from our stewardship;
For well we know, no hand of blood and bone
Can gripe the sacred handle of our sceptre,
Unless he do profane, steal or usurp.
And though you think that all, as you have done,
Have torn their souls by turning them from us,
And we are barren and bereft of friends;
Yet know, my master, God omnipotent,
Is mustering in his clouds on our behalf
Armies of pestilence; and they shall strike
Your children yet unborn and unbegot,
That lift your vassal hands against my head
And threat the glory of my precious crown.
Tell Bolingbroke, – for yond methinks he stands, –
That every stride he makes upon my land
Is dangerous treason: he is come to ope
The purple testament of bleeding war;
But ere the crown he looks for live in peace,
Ten thousand bloody crowns of mothers' sons
Shall ill become the flower of England's face,
Change the complexion of her maid-pale peace
To scarlet indignation, and bedew
Her pastures' grass with faithful English blood.

When I came to live in London, I took a great interest in the theatre and there are certain plays that remain fixed in my memory. I remember Laurence Olivier's *Long Day's Journey Into Night*, I remember Alan Badel's *Kean* and I also remember my introduction to *The Relapse* by John Vanbrugh: Donald Sinden's performance, at the Royal Shakespeare Company when it was at the Aldwych, of the marvellous part of Lord Foppington, a character I always thought of as rather courageous as well as just being fun, as indeed were the women that surrounded him.

## *The Relapse*

JOHN VANBRUGH

AMANDA. Nay, I love a neat library, too; but 'tis, I think, the inside of the book should recommend it most to us.
LORD FOPPINGTON. That, I must confess, I am nat altogether so fand of, Far to mind the inside of a book, is to entertain one's self with the forced product of another man's brain. Naw I think a man of quality and breeding may be much better diverted with the natural sprauts of his own. But to say the truth, madam, let a man love reading never so well, when once he comes to know this tawn, he finds so many better ways of passing the four-and-twenty hours, that 'twere ten thousand pities he should consume his time in that. Far example, madam, my life; my life, madam, is a perpetual stream of pleasure, that glides through such a variety of entertainments, I believe the wisest of our ancestors never had the least conception of any of 'em. I rise, madam, about ten a-clack. I don't rise sooner, because 'tis the worst thing in the world for the complexion; nat that I pretend to be a beau; but a man must endeavour to look wholesome, lest he make so nauseous a figure in the side-bax, the ladies should be compelled to turn their eyes upon the play. So at ten a-clack, I say, I rise. Naw, if I find 'tis a good day, I resalve to take a turn in the Park, and see the fine women; so huddle on my clothes, and get dressed by one. If it be nasty weather, I take a turn in the chocolate-haus: where, as you walk, madam, you have the prettiest prospect in the world; you have looking glasses all round you. – But I'm afraid I tire the company.
BERINTHIA. Not at all. Pray go on,
LORD FOPPINGTON. Why then, Ladies, from thence I go to dinner at Lacket's, where you are so nicely and delicately served, that, stap my vitals, they shall compose you a dish no bigger than a saucer, shall come to fifty shillings. Between eating my dinner (and washing my mauth, ladies) I spend my time, 'till I go to the play; where 'till nine a-clack, I entertain myself with looking upon

the company, and usually dispose of one hour more in leading 'em aut. So there's twelve of the four-and-twenty pretty well over. The other twelve, madam, are disposed of in two articles: in the first four I toast myself drunk, and in t'other eight I sleep myself sober again. Thus, ladies, you see my life is an eternal round O of delights.

I have always been moved by the poet and writer Rudyard Kipling, probably because my father was a soldier and the great traditions he stood for I think are still worth standing for today. It's a nice touch that Alec (McCowen) is actually playing Kipling here at the Mermaid theatre. He told me that many people have written to him and asked him why he left this great poem out – to which he replied again and again that it would have been an eight or nine-hour performance if he had included everything that everybody wanted. None the less it is still a magnificent poem; it's called 'The Thousandth Man' and in it we see everything we expect from our closest friends.

### *The Thousandth Man*

RUDYARD KIPLING

One man in a thousand, Solomon says,
Will stick more close than a brother.
And it's worth while seeking him half your days
If you find him before the other.
Nine hundred and ninety-nine depend
On what the world sees in you,
But the Thousandth Man will stand your friend
With the whole round world agin you.

'Tis neither promise nor prayer nor show
Will settle the finding for 'ee.
Nine hundred and ninety-nine of 'em go
By your looks, or your acts, or your glory.
But if he finds you and you find him,
The rest of the world don't matter;
For the Thousandth Man will sink or swim
With you in any water.

You can use his purse with no more talk
Than he uses yours for his spendings,
And laugh and meet in your daily walk
As though there had been no lendings.
Nine hundred and ninety-nine of 'em call
For silver and gold in their dealings;
But the Thousandth Man he's worth 'em all,
Because you can show him your feelings.

His wrong's your wrong, and his right's your right,
In season or out of season.
Stand up and back it in all men's sight –
With *that* for your only reason!
Nine hundred and ninety-nine can't bide
The shame or mocking or laughter,
But the Thousandth Man will stand by your side
To the gallows-foot – and after!

*Readers: Judi Dench, Alec McCowen*

*Full selection:*
*Matilda, Who Told Lies, and Was Burned to Death*, HILAIRE BELLOC
*Burial of Sir John Moore after Corunna*, CHARLES WOLFE
*Richard II, Act III, Scene II*, WILLIAM SHAKESPEARE
*Inaugural Address of President Kennedy*, J. F. KENNEDY
*Romeo and Juliet, Act IV, Scene III*, WILLIAM SHAKESPEARE
*The Relapse*, JOHN VANBRUGH
*The American Constitution, (Declaration of Independence) 1776*
*The Prodigy*, HERMAN HESSE
*Call for The Dead*, JOHN LE CARRÉ
*The Old Vicarage, Grantchester*, RUPERT BROOKE
*London Telephone Directory A–D*
*The Sensible Thing*, F. SCOTT FITZGERALD
*Arthur Wellard (1902–1980)*, HAROLD PINTER
*A Midsummer Night's Dream*, WILLIAM SHAKESPEARE

# *DAVID BELLAMY*

## *1981*

*Bellamy's joy in life virtually leaps from the page. It seems wholly appropriate that when including a poem of Rupert Brooke's, he should choose 'The Great Lover', a celebration of the senses. With such joy is linked, inevitably, energy. Many of the hosts of 'With Great Pleasure' select a passage from the Bible, usually something to do with peace and understanding; in Bellamy's case it was the parable of the talents. As a teacher he sees his responsibility as helping a student find what is relevant to him or her: 'When somebody finds what is relevant to them, they find their talent and off they go.' He finds some amusement that his talent should have been that of a naturalist: 'I wish I could have sung tenor, or been as good as Nureyev in the ballet – that would have been a talent.' Another talent he possesses, he didn't mention directly, that of professional communicator, but he used it effectively in the programme to put the case for what springs from his love of his surroundings, that of conservation.*

I can't think of anything which would give me more pleasure than to sit on a beautiful, sunny summer's evening in a place like the Bowes Museum, which is ultra-Victorian, and be read all my favourite poems and prose by two extremely talented people. And I really am a Victorian at heart; I always think I was born about a hundred years too late. But I must also add that I'd like to have been an 'up-market' Victorian: I'd like to have been the guy who actually built this place, rather than perhaps the guy who had to work out there.

First memories of the countryside: and the first countryside I knew was deep in the heart of Surrey, a little place called Spring Pond, and it was so private and so exciting that I didn't really want anybody else to know where it was. But there was a pond there, fed by a spring. My big brother and I used to build rafts, we would go across it on those rafts, and it was the whole world. And there at the end of the pond were some rhododendrons – you could go behind the rhododendrons and you could have been anywhere; it was to me total excitement. It was exploring a cool, wet, green, wonderfully smelling world, that damp and thrilling smell that we living out in the country here all know so well, but then I didn't.

And I can well remember going collecting whortleberries or bilberries or windberries, they have so many different common names. I used to go with my Granny and she was the best berry-picker of the lot. Along she would go and all her bag would be full and my mouth would be full and I wouldn't have very many in my bag at all.

I remember one day she turned round – we were in deep bracken – and she was holding an adder in her hand, and she said, 'What a pretty stick', and then realised. That is the magic of the countryside, because if you know what you are doing then you are safe, and if you don't know what you are doing you do it with complete naivety and I'm quite sure you're still safe. That snake knew just as well as I did that Granny was a townsperson, that she didn't really know what she was doing.

So, Spring Pond Cottage – my first look at the countryside, my first real adventure, one of the first things I really learned to love. It brings me to my favourite poet, Rupert Brooke, and his poem 'The Great Lover'.

## *The Great Lover*

RUPERT BROOKE

These I have loved:
White plates and cups, clean gleaming,
Ringed with blue lines; and feathery, faery dust;
Wet roofs, beneath the lamp-light; the strong crust
Of friendly bread; and many-tasting food;
Rainbows; and the blue bitter smoke of wood;

And radiant raindrops couching in cool flowers;
And flowers themselves, that sway through sunny hours,
Dreaming of moths that drink them under the moon;
Then, the cool kindliness of sheets, that soon
Smooth away trouble; and the rough male kiss
Of blankets; grainy wood; live hair that is
Shining and free; blue-massing clouds; the keen
Unpassioned beauty of a great machine;
The benison of hot water; furs to touch;
The good smell of old clothes; and others such –
The comfortable smell of friendly fingers,
Hair's fragrance, and the musty reek that lingers
About dead leaves and last year's ferns . . .
And washen stones, gay for an hour; the cold
Graveness of iron; moist black earthen mould;
Sleep; and high places; footprints in the dew;
And oaks; and brown horse-chestnuts, glossy-new;
And new-peeled sticks; and shining pools on grass; –
All these have been my loves. And these shall pass,
Whatever passes not, in the great hour,
Nor all my passion, all my prayers, have power
To hold them with me through the gate of Death.
They'll play deserter, turn with the traitor breath,
Break the high bond we made, and sell Love's trust
And sacramented covenant to the dust.
– Oh, never a doubt but, somewhere, I shall wake,
And give what's left of love again, and make
New friends, now strangers . . .
But the best I've known
Stays here, and changes, breaks, grows old, is blown
About the winds of the world, and fades from brains
Of living men, and dies.
Nothing remains.

O dear my loves, O faithless, once again
This one last gift I give; that after men
Shall know, and later lovers, far-removed,
Praise you, 'All these were lovely'; say, 'He loved'.

I can't think of anything in that poem which I don't myself love, that I haven't a great love for. He mentions it all. I tried to sit down and think of other things and put in other lines, which is pretty terrible when you're looking at a poet such as that. But one always must remember that Rupert Brooke gave his life in the War, gave his life to this thing which is the British Isles – I think more than anything that means most to me – this diversity, yet uniformity. Let's go perhaps to my favourite poem of all, 'The Old Vicarage, Grantchester', which is about the Cambridgeshire landscape. In it he says he's speaking from Germany where he's serving in the army:

> Here tulips bloom as they are told;
> Unkempt about those hedges blows
> An English unofficial rose.

And that's it: we still have an unofficial countryside, a countryside which criss-crosses and holds together this highly productive machine on which we so depend. And as long as that semi-natural web-matrix is there, Britain will stay the same – productive, and looked after.

A great conflict has been raging with me in the last few years because I have had more and more letters saying 'how can you talk about evolution and also say you are a Christian?' I must have had three thousand letters during the running of 'Botanic Man' on television saying I was a wicked man – 'Bellamy and Attenborough are cast on the anvil of the Devil. If it wasn't for men like these our churches would be full to overflowing', that sort of thing. I want to state why I can believe in both. I believe in God and it doesn't matter whether it's our God, there are plenty of other Gods worshipped just as religiously and fervently and with just as much devotion across this world of ours. But God created a law – a law which governs the interaction between matter and energy. Einstein showed us that they were both but two forms of the same thing. Once that law, which basically says that wherever there is energy, wherever there is potential it will be used, had been created – evolution had to happen. This whole complex thing had to happen, reaping the benefit of this planet Earth. Man has been set aside from all the other products of evolution not by the power of conscious thought, because whales and dolphins and I'm sure certain other organisms share that with us, but by free will.

And it is by the exercise of free will that we may disobey that law of the universe. We needn't use everything which is there; we can conserve; we can put things away for the future. Conservation is the sensible utilisation of natural resources. If we choose that we will survive. If we don't do that we will join other groups of animals that have taken too much – that have obeyed the law and not had the purposeful thing of free will. We will join them; we will follow them to extinction, to self-destruction.

## *The Shaping of Progress* from *The Human Experiment*

W. GRAHAM SMITH

Men are the only conscious organising agents on this planet. If they are to perform this function satisfactorily, shaping progress rather than following where events blindly lead, then it is essential that we as individuals should understand the more important principles that underlie the behaviour of the world in which we live. These principles have been made known gradually by the collective efforts of mankind, largely as a result of the progress of science; some of them and their approximate interrelations have been noted in the present book. Unless individual men and women come to know the feel of the nature of things in this kind of way, and to apply this understanding, then we cannot hope to develop our world to good purpose, not least because it is a single interacting whole. At present however most of us are scarcely aware of the principles involved, and still less of their implications. It is argued that it is essential that we should modify our cultural approach in general, and our educational system in particular, with a view to overcoming this deficiency. Its accomplishment would involve changes in our outlook, in our forms of social organisation, in our relation to plants and animals, and to our environment as a whole. We would find ourselves able in due course to bring all these to interact with one another in a harmonious way and so produce a global setting that was essentially self-regulating and stable and would provide a healthy base that could support virtually infinite further qualitative growth. Progress along such lines would be broadly to the benefit of all men and women living on this planet; it is a goal towards which we can all work without conflict of interest, whatever our race or circumstances, in our conjoint endeavour to enable the creative potential inherent in the Universe to attain a full expression here on Planet Earth.

Can it be done? The answer is yes. And I will tell you why. Because somewhere in this mess we call the end of the twentieth century there are decent human beings trying to get out. The meek shall inherit the earth – if the meek don't get out pretty soon and become vociferous it is not going to be worth inheriting.

The next piece was an entry to a competition in the magazine *The Living Countryside*, and it was project No.6 in which the entrants were asked to define a project in their own area which would improve the environment. A ten-year-old little girl:

At our shopping parade there is a small area of grass which could be very nice because it has a seat on it – old people could sit there. But people walk across the grass and wear it out and so it gets dirty and water-logged, people leave litter, sweet papers, silver paper and old paper bags. I think there should be a small fence round the grass and a litter bin and perhaps a tree should be planted, I think this might be possible by sending a letter such as 'Dear Sir, we are very concerned about the state of our corner. Is it possible that we can arrange to meet you to discuss how we can make improvements? Yours sincerely.'

That doesn't sound very important does it? But here is the letter that came with it:

Dear Sir, this notebook will arrive too late to be included in the competition. However, the child's brothers wish you to see her notebook and she herself would have wanted me to send it to you. Emily completed her notebook while in the last stages of terminal cancer. She persevered every week looking forward to each new issue of the magazine to see what that week's project contained. We got a bit stuck on project Number 5, because the only tree she could see from her bed was a very old gnarled plum. Similarly in Number 6, she could no longer get out of bed so sent her Daddy off to take photos of the small patch of grass. By the time we got to the last page she could no longer see what she was writing. The little notebook represents enormous courage and endurance by a child who was passionately fond of plants and wildlife and I felt you should all see it. I enclose a stamped addressed envelope for its return as it is very precious. Emily died a fortnight ago.

Now if there are children like that, and there are many – all over the world I meet people with that sort of caring knowledge – we can make it work.

*Readers: Michele Dotrice, Dinsdale Landen*

*Full Selection:*
*Swallows and Amazons,* ARTHUR RANSOME
*The Way Through the Woods,* RUDYARD KIPLING
*The Great Lover,* RUPERT BROOKE
*The Naturalist on the Amazon,* H. W. BATES
*The Parable of the Talents*
*The Way that I Went,* ROBERT LLOYD PRAEGER
*The Courtship of the Yonghy-Bonghy-Bo,* EDWARD LEAR
*The Mind in the Waters,* J. MACINTYRE
*Genesis 1:26*
*The Teacher,* LESLIE PINCKNEY HILL
*The Shaping of Progress,* W. GRAHAM SMITH (From *The Human Experiment*)
Competition Letters
Chocolate Button Advertisement

# ALAN BENNETT

## 1977

*For all his delight in humour and pleasure in entertaining, his stylish analysis of the nature of programmes such as 'With Great Pleasure', much of Alan Bennett's selection appeared to highlight some of the sad resonances of English life, a sense of energy wasted: 'Diary of a Nobody', Auden's 'Musée des Beaux Arts', Stevie Smith's 'Not Waving But Drowning' and Philip Larkin's 'The Whitsun Weddings' where after the excitement and the conspiracy of women 'there swelled/A sense of falling . . .' Perversely the final impression is not of a pessimistic view of England or of mere nostalgia, but of a sort of weary optimism, as if under all the emotional dust the polish on the drawing-room furniture still shines.*

I am being entertained.

My host sits me down, puts on a record and says, coyly, 'I think you're going to like this'.

I fix on my face an expression of what I hope will pass for appreciation. I even shake my head slowly as though granted a revelation of such beauty it's unbearable. Meanwhile he sits back with a look of immense self-satisfaction watching the spell work what he imagines is its old magic.

It can be pre-Columbian flute music. It can be Elton John. Either way it is a nightmare.

And I don't want to do that to you. I am not saying with each of the items I have chosen 'You'll like this. I do,' so much as 'I am the sort of person who likes this.' It is a form of self-revelation, even self-indulgence. It's a bit of a striptease. This was very well put by Kenneth Grahame, the author of *Wind in the Willows*.

You must please remember that a theme, a thesis, a subject, is in most cases little more than a sort of clothes line on which one pegs a string of ideas, quotations, allusions and so on, one's mental undergarments of all shapes and sizes, some probably fairly new, but most rather old and patched; and they dance and sway in the breeze and flap and flutter, or hang limp and lifeless, and some are ordinary enough, and some are of a rather private and intimate shape and rather give the owner away and show up his or her own peculiarities.

That is my side of it. Your side of it is summed up in a remark by Florence Nightingale.

What it is to be read aloud to. The most miserable exercise of the human intellect. It is like lying on one's back with one's hands tied and having liquid poured down one's throat.

When it comes to reading I am easily put off. I am put off a book if too many people like it. I am put off a book if some people like it too much.

Lewis Carroll is a case in point, Tolkien another. Both to some extent *picketed* by their admirers. I have never managed to read Wodehouse because I'm depressed by the enthusiasm of the people who do.

I am sure this is foolish and a failing on my part, but I'm also sure with books you're more likely to have a love-affair after a casual pick-up than after an 'I'm sure you two are going to get on like a house on fire' sort of introduction.

A book chooses its readers as a play chooses its audience. Fashion has something to do with it, but it's not fashion alone. Somewhere a voice is calling and if the wrong people respond it puts me off the author. I do not read his book. I do not see his play.

I am sure this applies to myself too and indeed when I sit in the audience at one of my own plays I often feel that's not where I belong. Had I not written it I probably shouldn't have gone to see it.

The public are often more interested in an author's life than in his or her work. Certainly this is true of Virginia Woolf and perhaps not so surprising since her novels are short on plot and without much humour. Her life on the other hand had plenty of both.

## *Beginning Again, an Autobiography of the Years 1911–1918*

LEONARD WOOLF

Virginia and I were married on Saturday, August 10, at St Pancras Register Office in a room which, in those days, looked down into a cemetery. In the ceremony before a Registrar one makes no promise 'to love and to cherish, till death us do part, according to God's holy ordinance', but in the St Pancras Office, facing the window and looking through it at the tombstones behind the Registrar's head, one was, I suppose appropriately, reminded of the words 'till death us do part'. Apart from the tombstones, our wedding ceremony was provided with an element of comic relief (quite unintended) characteristic of the Stephens.

In the middle of the proceedings Vanessa (Virginia's sister) interrupted the Registrar, saying: 'Excuse me interrupting; I have just remembered: we registered my son – he is two years old – in the name of Clement, and we now want to change his name to Quentin. Can you tell me what I have to do?' There was a moment of astonished silence in the room as we all looked round sympathetically and saw the serious, slightly puzzled look on Vanessa's face. There was a pause while the Registrar stared at her with his mouth open. Then he said severely: 'One thing at a time, please, Madam.'

*Readers: Alan Bennett, Phyllida Law*

*Full Selection:*
*Fetching Cows*, NORMAN MACCAIG
*The Diary of a Nobody*, GEORGE and WEEDON GROSSMITH
*Denton Welch: A Selection from His Published Works* edited by JOCELYN BROOKS
*Musée des Beaux Arts*, W. H. AUDEN

*Beginning Again, an Autobiography of the Years 1911–1918,* LEONARD WOOLF
*Period Piece,* GWEN RAVERAT
*The Whitsun Weddings,* PHILIP LARKIN
*Not Waving But Drowning,* STEVIE SMITH
*Bleak House,* CHARLES DICKENS
*Goodbye to the Villa Piranha,* FRANCIS HOPE

# *SIR JOHN BETJEMAN*

## *1979*

*As Sir John is far and away the most requested modern poet, there is hardly an edition of 'With Great Pleasure' that does not include one of his poems, it was only a matter of time before my predecessor, Brian Patten, asked him to present his own selection. I met him a number of times whilst I was a studio manager, notably for the recordings of the Poetry Proms which were produced by George MacBeth and which featured Jill Balcon and Gary Watson as readers. My favourite memory, however, is of one of Sir John's programmes on the English Hymnal, produced by Religious Broadcasting. Assorted senior members of that department were fussing about in the studio, making a great display of welcome. Sir John let this continue for a while, but I could see he was amused. Suddenly he said, 'I say, do you think we could have some gin?', and produced a fiver from his trouser pocket. It was ten o'clock in the morning. There was much embarrassment, during which he was prevailed upon to put away his money and the boss left, sending a secretary in search of an off-licence. Sir John, the producer, the other studio manager and I then set about recording the programme which didn't take very long, though long enough for the gin to arrive. We were all sitting round the table, neat gin in paper cups, when Sir John produced a book, 'Have you seen the new edition of Hardy? It's frightfully good.' He then proceeded to read us a great many of the poems. It made for a delightful morning – after all, not many jobs allow the possibility of a pleasant couple of hours being read Hardy by the Poet Laureate. The remainder of the gin (there wasn't much) was finally locked away in a cupboard somewhere in the bowels of Religious Broadcasting.*

Desmond McCarthy, I think it was, said that he was once staying in a country house and Hardy was a fellow guest, and Hardy was very quiet and when they went for a walk McCarthy said, 'Why are you so quiet, don't you like these people?' And Hardy said, 'Oh, I like them, but I don't trust them.'

'Why don't you trust them?'

'I think they'll steal my plots,' Hardy said.

Hardy, apparently, set great store by his plots.

## *Her Second Husband Hears Her Story*

THOMAS HARDY

'Still, Dear, it is incredible to me
    That here, alone,
You should have sewed him up until he died,
And in this very bed. I do not see
How you could do it, seeing what might betide.'

'Well, he came home one midnight, liquored deep –
    Worse than I'd known –
And lay down heavily, and soundly slept:
Then, desperate driven, I thought of it, to keep
Him from me when he woke. Being an adept

'With needle and thimble, as he snored, click-click
    An hour I'd sewn,
Till, had he roused, he couldn't have moved from bed,
So tightly laced in sheet and quilt and tick
He lay. And in the morning he was dead.

'Ere people came I drew the stitches out,
    And thus 'twas shown
To be a stroke.' – 'It's a strange tale!' said he.

'And this same bed?' – 'Yes, here it came about.'
'Well, it sounds strange – told here and now to me.

'Did you intend his death by your tight lacing?'
'O, that I cannot own.
I could not think of else that would avail
When he should wake up, and attempt embracing.' –
'Well, it's a cool queer tale!'

It most certainly is.

I can see how Ezra Pound was probably right when he said that Hardy's novels were really compressed into his poems.

And now we go to Cambridge, because the Lord of Language, for me, is Alfred Tennyson. And 'In Memoriam' I think contains his most beautiful poems. He was a Lincolnshire man, east coast and there's one little piece I want to recite 'cos I can remember it, which gives you the east coast. 'As when the crest of some slow arching wave, heard at midnight upon that table shore drops flat. And after the great waters break, whitening for half a league, and thin themselves far over sands, marbled with moon and cloud, from less and less to nothing.'

I didn't tell the artistes I was going to put that little bit in. And it was you who brought it out in me.

But now Tennyson's love was for Cambridge, where he was brought up at Trinity.

## *In Memoriam*

ALFRED, LORD TENNYSON

I past beside the reverend walls
In which of old I wore the gown;
I roved at random thro' the town,
And saw the tumult of the halls;

And heard once more in college fanes
The storm their high-built organs make,
And thunder-music, rolling, shake
The prophet blazon'd on the panes;

And caught once more the distant shout,
The measured pulse of racing oars
Among the willows; paced the shores
And many a bridge, and all about

The same gray flats again, and felt
  The same, but not the same; and last
  Up that long walk of limes I past
To see the rooms in which he dwelt.

It was in Trinity College, Cambridge, that Housman, the poet, was a Fellow. He's said to have started a speech there in Trinity Hall with these words: 'In this hall Wordsworth was once drunk and Fawson – that was a very famous scholar – was once sober. A better poet than Fawson, a better scholar than Wordsworth, I stand before you today betwixt and between.'

I love that; it's a very typical piece of Cambridge pedantry. The other side of Housman comes out in his poems, particularly in their 1890 melancholy and sound of words.

Here is Housman at his most summery and luxuriant.

## *A Shropshire Lad*

A. E. HOUSMAN

On the idle hill of summer,
  Sleepy with the flow of streams,
Far I hear the steady drummer
  Drumming like a noise in dreams.

Far and near and low and louder
  On the roads of earth go by,
Dear to friends and food for powder,
  Soldiers marching, all to die.

By Jove! You can't forget Housman, his power, also his use of words and of the sound of chimes and bells in this extraordinary piece – and I may say Housman was never hanged.

## *Eight O' Clock*

A. E. HOUSMAN

He stood, and heard the steeple
  Sprinkle the quarters on the morning town.
One, two, three, four, to market-place and people
  It tossed them down.

Strapped, noosed, nighing his hour,
He stood and counted them and cursed his luck;
And then the clock collected in the tower
Its strength, and struck.

The next piece is by, Eric Walter White, a Bristolian-born poet, who lived latterly in Islington. It's about the death of his wife, Dodo.

### *The Thirty-Ninth Rose*

ERIC WALTER WHITE

*In Memoriam Edith Dorothy White (Dodo)*
*16 October 1909 – 1 July 1977*

Thirty-nine roses for thirty-nine summers.
The first summer started late;
The last one was broken . . .

When we knew you had only five months –
Or was it six or seven? – to live,
How the days went scurrying by!
No one could tell what the next day would bring.
When I saw you look in the mirror,
I wondered if you were thinking
Is this the last time I shall look
In this mirror to do my hair
And renew my make-up?
When I saw you climb with increasing difficulty
The stairs from the hall to the floor above,
I wondered if you were thinking
Is this the last time I shall have strength enough
To climb this staircase to go to bed?
When I sat by your bedside and saw
Your eyes open and recognise me,
I wondered if you were thinking
Is this the last time I shall see his features?
But I tried to conceal these thoughts from you
Lest my eyes betray me;
And when the moment came,
It was Sarah who saw you for the last time still alive.
And I who saw you for the first time dead.

I remember how courageously
You fought with the dark angel during those last weeks –
How beneath the sheet your limbs thrashed out,
Trying to ward off the incarcerating mesh
Of the iron maiden of cancer.
It was as if under the implacable glare of ringside lights
Your agony was featured
In a canvas by Francis Bacon.
Who that saw them can forget your agonies? –
The agony of being shifted on to a new pile of pillows:
The agony of the new position:
The agony of the parched tongue;
The agonies from which there seemed to be
No deliverance except through drugs.
And yet there were still occasions when you found
The right touch at the right moment 'marvellous'.

You always hated the voyeur;
But in this succesion of agonies
I found I could not keep away from your bedroom,
I could not, not look at what was happening.
But so as not to disturb you with my glance
I would stand outside the room
And peep through the crack between door and jamb.
Forgive me!
How far have you travelled
Since I entered your bedroom a short while ago
And saw you had just died?
The shadow of this eclipse had already spread over your
features.
And your skin had the beauty of a waxen mask.
My first thought was that you had stopped
While Sarah and I continued to live.
But later I saw that it was we who had stopped
While you were bound on an unknown voyage
Towards an uncharted goal.
. . . The petals from the thirty-ninth rose
Have fallen upon your shroud;
And now the long loneliness begins.

Thank Goodness that there's such good language written and that we've got poets today who can move us deeply.

*Readers: Richard Briers, Eleanor Bron*

*Full Selection:*
*19th Century Railway Carriages*, HAMILTON ELLIS
*Isaac Watts' Divine and Moral Songs*
*The Diary of a Nobody*, GEORGE and WEEDON GROSSMITH
*Vitae Summa Brevis Spem Nos Vetat Incohare Longam*, ERNEST DOWSON
*Her Second Husband Hears Her Story*, THOMAS HARDY
*In Memoriam*, ALFRED, LORD TENNYSON
*A Shropshire Lad*, A. E. HOUSMAN
*Eight O'Clock*, A.E. HOUSMAN
*Pain*, ELIZABETH JENNINGS
*The Thirty-Ninth Rose*, ERIC WALTER WHITE
*The Trees*, PHILIP LARKIN
*Meditation on The A 30*, JOHN BETJEMAN
*Mr Sponge's Sporting Tour*, ROBERT SURTEES
*In a Little Wadi*, MICHAEL DUGDALE
*Christmas* JOHN BETJEMAN

# SIR LAWRENCE BRAGG

## 1970

*It is a commonplace, I suppose, that whilst there may be many engineers who play the violin, there are few violinists who have any notion of how to build a bridge. Certainly it is true that the majority of people who work in the arts, myself included, have only the haziest knowledge of matters technical and scientific. Nevertheless, this distinguished scientist obviously felt a need to take note of criticism from that quarter: 'It is very well known to our arts colleagues, who never cease to remind us about it, that (a) scientists have hardly any human or artistic feelings at all and (b) that they are quite inarticulate, quite helpless at explaining even such feelings as they have.' However, he did not have the slightest difficulty in including items by Robert Browning, Jane Austen, Sir Arthur Conan Doyle, E. M. Forster, Virginia Woolf and Tolstoy amongst those which had given him great pleasure. Nevertheless, perhaps in order to redress the balance, I have chosen from his programme pieces by two scientists, the second of whom, though, is generally reckoned to be the province of students of English Literature rather than that of budding physicists.*

The art of lecturing, of talking about science, has always fascinated me, and Faraday was a great exponent of it. As well as being a very great scientist, probably our greatest scientist since Newton, he was well-known for his talks. His biographer, Bence Jones, said of him: 'His manner was so natural that the thought of any art in his lecturing never occurred to anyone'. Yet these notes show how intensely he studied this art.

## *Advice to a Lecturer*

MICHAEL FARADAY

A lecturer should appear easy and collected, undaunted and unconcerned, his thoughts about him and his mind clear for the contemplation and description of his subject. His action should be slow, easy and natural, consisting principally in changes in the posture of the body, in order to avoid the air of stiffness or sameness that would be otherwise unavoidable.

His whole behaviour should evince a respect for his audience, and he should in no case forget that he is in their presence.

Some lecturers choose to express their thoughts extemporaneously immediately as they should occur to the mind, whilst others previously arrange them and draw them forth on paper.

But although I allow a lecturer to write out his matter, I do *not* approve of his reading it – at least, not as he would a quotation or extract. He should deliver it in a ready and free manner, referring to his book merely as he would to copious notes, and not confining his tongue to the path there delineated but digress as the circumstances may demand or localities allow.

A lecturer falls deeply beneath the dignity of his character when he descends so low as to angle for claps and ask for commendation. Yet I have even seen a lecturer at this point.

I have heard him causelessly condemn his own powers. I have heard him dwell for a length of time on the extreme care and niceness that the experiment he will make requires.

I have heard him hope for indulgence when no indulgence was wanted, and I have heard him declare that the experiment cannot fail from its beauty, its correctness and its application, to gain the approbation of all.

I feel this last is perhaps a little too hard, and I haven't quite got a clear conscience about it. I'm not sure I haven't sometimes angled for claps and commendations. But the main reason for my including those notes is that I think they reveal something of Faraday's greatness.

And now as a scientist I must choose for you something from a scientific paper. The author is explaining how to make a scientific instrument – a sort of large protractor, with scales around the edge and strings going from pins near the middle. And the purpose of it is to find the position of the planets and sun and moon in the sky at any given date. This is how he starts:

In the name of the god pitos & merciable the largere pt thow makest this instrument/ the largere ben thi chef deuisions/ the largere pt ben tho deuisions/ in hem may ben mo smale fraccions/ 'euere the mo of smale fraccions the ner the trowthe of thy conclusions/ tak ther fore a plate of metal or elles a board pt be smothe shaue/ by leuel/ & euene polised of which whan it is rownd (by compas)/ the hole diametre shal contene .72. large enches or elles .6. fote of mesure/ the whiche rownd bord fot it shal nat werpe ne Krooke/the eggs of (the) circumference shal be bownde wt a plate of yren in maner of a karte whel./ this bord yif the likith may be vernissed or elles glewed wt perchemyn for honestyte tak thanne a cercle of metal pt be .2. enche of brede/ this cercle wole I clepe the lymbe of myn equatorie pt was compowned the yer of crist .1392. complet the laste meridie of decembre.

That treatise was apparently never published, that is to say, copied by professional scribes, because of course there was no printing at that time. It is a draft, obviously in the author's own handwriting, with his corrections and emendations written all over it. Now the story about it is as follows: When I was at the Cavendish, I had a young man, a historian of science, Derek Price, working for me on the Cavendish archives; there's a wonderful lot of letters from various professors there. He was working on the letters of our first professor, Clerk Maxwell, and he was in Peterhouse library, where he was getting a lot of his information. He asked the librarian at Peterhouse library whether he had any old scientific documents, just on spec. as it were. The librarian turned up one which had been in the library for about three hundred years. It was ascribed in the catalogue to a man called Bredon.

Now Price knew enough about the history of science to know that Bredon had been dead for a long time in 1392, which was the date of this document. He read it, got more and more suspicious – the book had been bound with big leather thongs sometime in the Middle Ages, and he asked for leave to unbind the thongs because they covered up the margins. In the margins he found what was pretty obviously the name of the author, Chaucer – Geoffrey Chaucer of the Canterbury Tales.

He checked this by going up to the record office where they have the files where Chaucer was a kind of Civil Servant. They said that they had so many files that it would take far too long to go through them all. Price said that he knew the writing so well and that if they would only let him flip through them he would recognise it. To cut a long story short, one appeared and he said, 'I think this looks like it'. They opened it and it was an authorisation for someone to act in Chaucer's place in an office while Chaucer was absent on a mission in France, signed 'Chaucer' – with the signature absolutely identical with the one in the manuscript. So it's pretty well clinched – it's all right.

Chaucer was an excellent amateur astronomer. He wrote a book called *The Astrolabe* and in it he promised another book on the planets. This must be the draft for it which never appeared in print. Chaucer never finished it or corrected it before his death.

My pleasure in this treatise is partly, I'm afraid, an ignoble one. I can't help chortling a little that it should be left to a scientist to discover the only known manuscript in Chaucer's handwriting. Just think of the excitement if he'd discovered another draft for an unpublished Canterbury Tale. But as well as that I think I have a more creditable pleasure in it – the fascination of seeing how six hundred years ago the scientific author set forth his ideas in English.

*Readers: Hugh Dickson, Olive Gregg*

*Full Selection:*
*Advice to a Lecturer*, MICHAEL FARADAY
*Home Thoughts from Abroad*, ROBERT BROWNING
*Emma*, JANE AUSTEN
*How to Make a Scientific Instrument*, GEOFFREY CHAUCER
*The Hound of the Baskervilles*, ARTHUR CONAN DOYLE
*Aspects of the Novel*, E. M. FORSTER
*The Death of the Moth*, VIRGINIA WOOLF
*Anna Karenina*, LEO TOLSTOY

# *MELVYN BRAGG*

## *1981*

*The selection of items for a programme like 'With Great Pleasure' inevitably leads in the end to a sort of autobiography. If 'you are what you eat', then clearly, if you are a thinking person, you are also what you read. What you choose to remember defines you further, so it's not surprising that on occasion presenters of the programme reveal more about themselves than they sometimes realise. This was not the case, I think, with this subject. Daunted by the enormous number of books that he had clearly remembered with affection, he decided to offer an anthology of writings about the area in which he grew up, Cumbria and the Lake District.*

After the middle of the eighteenth century, the writers and illustrators began to pile on to the new stage coaches coming up from London, bowl along the new turnpike roads and discover enough interest in what they found here to have their records printed and published back in London. Before the end of the century, and before Wordsworth came back to his birthplace, there were many guides, engravings and prints galore about this 'barren and frightful' place as Defoe had described it. The one-armed Joseph Budworth was a typical gossipy traveller of his time – he came for a fortnight and, like all good travellers, he didn't fail to leave an account of what he ate.

## *Dinner at Grasmere*

JOSEPH BUDWORTH

After as good and well-dressed a dinner, at Robert Newton's, as a man could wish, we set out to surmount the steep ascent of Helm Crag; but the dinner was so cheap, I must mention what it consisted of:

Roast pike, stuffed,
A boiled fowl,
Veal-cutlets and ham,
Beans and bacon,
Cabbage,
Peas and potatoes,
Anchovy sauce,
Parsley and butter,
Plain butter,
Butter and cheese,
Wheat bread and oat cake,
Three cups of preserved gooseberries, with a bowl of rich cream in the centre;
For two people, at ten-pence a head.

And that, remember, just before they set out to climb the Fell! Budworth, incidentally, unwittingly caused a local tragedy when he praised the beauty of the daughter of an inn-keeper to such effect that tourists and poets made special journeys to come and see her and a bigamist turned up to marry her. Then he abandoned her – and later was hanged in Carlisle Castle.

It's interesting that, at the time, so little had been written over hundreds of years, in detail, about landscape. And people coming here, and people from here, were about to do a great deal to change that. Because William and Dorothy Wordsworth came back to live in Dove Cottage at Grasmere, a few miles from Cockermouth where they'd been born.

William is a mountain of a poet, but I'd like to start with some of his most mysterious and very gentle short verses on Lucy.

## *Lucy Poems*

WILLIAM WORDSWORTH

Strange fits of passion have I known:
And I will dare to tell,
But in a Lover's ear alone,
What once to me befell.

When she I loved looked every day
Fresh as a rose in June,
I to her cottage bent my way,
Beneath an evening-moon.

Upon the moon I fixed my eye,
All over the wide lea;
With quickening pace my horse drew nigh
Those paths so dear to me.

And now we reached the orchard-plot;
And, as we climbed the hill,
The sinking moon to Lucy's cot
Came near, and nearer still.

What fond and wayward thoughts will slide
Into a Lover's head:
'Oh mercy!' to myself I cried,
'If Lucy should be dead!'

She dwelt among the untrodden ways
  Beside the springs of Dove,
A Maid whom there were none to praise
  And very few to love:

A violet by a mossy stone
  Half hidden from the eye!
Fair as a star, when only one
  Is shining in the sky.

She lived unknown, and few could know
  When Lucy ceased to be;
But she is in her grave, and oh,
  The difference to me!

A slumber did my spirit seal;
I had no human fears;
She seemed a thing that could not feel
  The touch of earthly years.

No motion has she now, no force;
She neither hears nor sees,
Rolled round in earth's diurnal course
  With rocks and stones and trees!

Whether those poems were directly inspired by his sister, Dorothy, or not, the fact is that from the 1790s until the end of his life Wordsworth was deeply helped by his sister. As he said: 'She gave me eyes, she gave me ears and humble cares and delicate fears.'

She had a passion for the details of nature and of daily life, which very often started off a poem and not infrequently seems to have been almost a first draft. Here she is writing about what became a famous walk.

## *Daffodils at Gowbarrow Park*

DOROTHY WORDSWORTH

Thursday, 15th April 1802

It was a threatening, misty morning, but mild. We set off after dinner from Eusemere. Mrs Clarkson went a short way with us, but turned back. The wind was furious and we thought we must have turned back. We first rested in the large boathouse, then under a furze bush opposite Mr Clarkson's. Saw the plough going in the field. The wind seized our breath. The lake was rough. There was a boat by itself floating in the middle of the bay below Water Millock. When we were in the woods beyond Gowbarrow Park, we saw a few daffodils close to the waterside. We fancied that the lake had floated the seeds ashore and that the little colony had so sprung up. But as we went along there were more and yet more; and, at last, under the boughs of the trees, we saw that there was a long belt of them along the shore, about the breadth of a country turnpike road.

I never saw daffodils so beautiful. They grew among the mossy stones, about and about them. Some rested their heads upon these stones, as on a pillow, for weariness; and the rest tossed and reeled and danced, and seemed as if they verily laughed with the wind that blew upon them over the lake. They looked so gay, ever glancing, ever changing. The wind blew directly over the lake to them. There was here and there a little knot, and a few stragglers higher up; but they were so few as not to disturb the simplicity, unity, and life of that one busy highway.

And here is what Wordsworth himself made of it in a poem that, once upon a time, most school children used to know by heart:

## *Daffodils*

WILLIAM WORDSWORTH

I wandered lonely as a cloud
That floats on high o'er vales and hills,
When all at once I saw a crowd,
A host, of golden daffodils;
Beside the lake, beneath the trees,
Fluttering and dancing in the breeze.

Continuous as the stars that shine
And twinkle on the Milky Way,
They stretched in never-ending line
Along the margin of a bay;
Ten thousand saw I at a glance,
Tossing their heads in sprightly dance.

The waves beside them danced, but they
Out-did the sparkling waves in glee;
A poet could not but be gay,
In such a jocund company:
I gazed – and gazed – but little thought
What wealth the show to me had brought.

For oft, when on my couch I lie
In vacant or in pensive mood,
They flash upon that inward eye
Which is the bliss of solitude;
And then my heart with pleasure fills,
And dances with the daffodils.

John Ruskin, Arthur Ransome and Beatrix Potter are just three of the many writers whose childhood visits, particularly to the southern lakes, affected their lives and brought them back here to live out most of their adult years. Beatrix Potter's diary can be compared with Dorothy Wordsworth's journals in the richness and contentment that they both found in such an apparently circumscribed place and life,

## *Extract from Windermere 1895*

BEATRIX POTTER

Saturday, August 10th

In afternoon went with pony up Troutbeck and put it up at the Mortal Man, which looks a very nice little inn. Papa and I walked up Nanny Lane and got over a stile into the heather, sweet and heavy with honey. There was a thunder haze, no view, but very peaceful, except that the stone walls were covered with flying-ants.

There was an old shepherd half way up the side of Troutbeck, much bent and gesticulating with a stick. He watched the collie scouring round over stone walls, coming close past us without taking the slightest notice. Four or five sheep louped over a wall at least three feet high, on our right, and escaped the dog's observation, whereupon the ancient shepherd – a mere speck in the slanting sunlight down the great hillside, this aged Wordsworthian worthy – awoke the echoes with a flood of the most singularly bad language. He gesticulated and the dog ran round on the top of the dykes, and some young cattle ran down with their tails in the air. We passed him sitting on a wall as we came down, a pleasant, smiling old fellow. We asked him which was Ill Bell, and he leant over the wall – 'ye'll perceive I'm rather hard of hearing' – then we heard that the prize pup at Kelso Show was named 'Sandy Walker'.

*Readers: Joan Bakewell, Ronald Herdman.*

*Full Selection:*
*Barren and Frightful,* DANIEL DEFOE (From A Tour Through the Whole Island of Great Britain)
*Dinner at Grasmere,* JOSEPH BUDWORTH (From 'A Fortnight's Ramble to the Lakes' Third Edition, 1810)
*Mountains as Picturesque Objects,* WILLIAM GILPIN (From Observations Relative Chiefly to Picturesque Beauty in the Mountains and Lakes of Cumberland and Westmorland)
*Lucy Poems,* WILLIAM WORDSWORTH
*Daffodils at Gowbarrow Park,* DOROTHY WORDSWORTH (From Grasmere Journal)
*Daffodils,* WILLIAM WORDSWORTH
*Trance and Delight,* SAMUEL TAYLOR COLERIDGE
*Light and Shade at Grasmere and Rydale,* DOROTHY WORDSWORTH (From Grasmere Journal)
*Meeting with Wordsworth,* THOMAS DE QUINCEY
*A Merry Meet,* JOHN KEATS (From The Life and Letters of John Keats by Lord Houghton)
*The Lazy Tour of Two Idle Apprentices,* CHARLES DICKENS (From The Wilds of Carrock)
*How They Lived at Wastdale Head,* HARRIET MARTINEAU (From A Complete Guide to the English Lakes)
*Some Celebrated Wrestlers,* WILLIAM LITT (From Wrestliana)
*D'Ye Ken John Peel,* JOHN GRAVES
*It's Nobbut Me,* JOHN RICHARDSON
*Windermere 1895,* BEATRIX POTTER
*Like a Little Doll,* ELIZABETH A. M. ROBERTS and 'MRS N. O. 4'
*Sea to the West,* NORMAN NICHOLSON
*Intimations of Immortality from Recollections of Early Childhood,* WILLIAM WORDSWORTH

# *JAMES CAMERON*

## *1975*

*James Cameron was a familiar figure in the sixth floor corridors of Broadcasting House whence he visited the office of whichever Archive Features Department producer was working with him at the time on a series of beautifully presented programmes for which the archive material was often merely the peg to enable him to continue to debate his view of the world. A lifetime spent as a journalist had left him not cynical but wise and warm, shot through with a sometimes acerbic common sense. I remember sitting with him on a canal-boat moving slowly past the Snowdon bird house at London Zoo. He was talking into camera – it was some television producer's idea of the perfect setting for Cameron to expound on the joys of the coming week on BBC1. Admiring the grace with which he carried out this trivial task and seeing his frail form set against the colourful, rare birds, it was easy to wonder which in fact was the endangered species.*

I don't know why I became so obsessed with the Elizabethans. Of course I do know why: they were meat and drink to any young man trying to learn the riches and resources of the English language, who jumped into the deep end, at the period when they weren't ashamed to be sentimental, and romantic, and even baroque. Though it's still a bit of a mystery to me how that particular sixteenth century produced such a fantastic flowering, how so many marvellous people were writing marvellous things all, as it were, at the same time. Lots of people think I am pretty square about my idolatry of John Donne, for example, but I am besotted by him. When I first came to London I lived in a sort of chambers that were alleged to have been the attics of his house – you know that John Donne was Vicar of Lincoln's Inn. All I knew then was that it was very handy for Fleet Street. But my John Donne kick has lasted forty years. The first present my wife ever gave me was a splendid, expensive Nonesuch Edition of Donne. It was very perceptive, since my own one had broken its back years before.

> 'Now that thou hast lov'd me one whole day,
> Tomorrow when thou leav'st, what wilt thou say?
> Wilt thou then antedate some new-made vow?
> Or say that now
> We are not just those persons which we were?
> Or that oaths made in reverential fear
> Of love, and his wrath, any may forswear?
> Vain lunatic, against these scapes I could
> Dispute, and conquer, if I would;
> Which I abstain to do,
> For by tomorrow, I may think so too.'

He really was a hell of an old Vicar, this John Donne, a real old Reverend Rake. Nevertheless he left something that I think is one of the most tremendous love poems in the world.

> 'When I died last – and dear, I die
> As often as from thee I go,
> Though it be but an hour ago,
> And Lovers' hours be full of eternity,
> I can remember yet, that I
> Something did say, and something did bestow;
> Though I be dead, which sent me, I should be
> Mine own executor and legacy.
>
> I heard me say, Tell her anon,
> That my self (that is you, not I)
> Did kill me, and when I felt me die,
> I bid me send my heart, when I was gone;
> But I alas could find there none,

When I had ripp'd me, and search'd where hearts did lie;
It killed me again, that I who still was true,
In life, in my last Will should cozen you.

Yet I found something like a heart,
But colours it and corners had,
It was not good, it was not bad,
It was entire to none, and few had part.
As good as could be made by art
It seem'd; and therefore for our losses sad
I meant to send this heart instead of mine.
But oh, no man could hold it, for 'twas thine.'

Possibly because I work in a context so different, so much coarser and more hasty and immediate, these sixteenth century cadences fill me with such nourishment and love and envy.

I like the anonymous poets of the Bible as much as I dislike, shall I say, Hymns Ancient and Modern. Obviously an enormous volume of poetry has come out of the need of man to come to terms with the supernatural, the Creator, religion, whatever it may be – not necessarily Christian; look at the vast epic poetry of the Hindus or the Hebrews – presumably because when he was faced with a problem like that, man felt he had to adopt a special literary formula, and it came out as poetry. Naturally. For me, I'm obliged to say, when it's theological it's beyond me and when it's pietistic I leave it alone. A very few men have been accepted and embraced by both the Church and the poets, and I would suggest that by far and away the most sincere and interesting of these is Gerard Manley Hopkins, who became a Jesuit in the last century. I don't know whether many people read Hopkins now but for a very long time he, more than most poets, was examined and analysed and argued about, not so much for his religious content (which was agonisingly deep) but for his poetic *technicalities*, the elaborations of his word-patterns, his craftsman's innovations, the so-called 'sprung rhythms' and so on. He was a great questioner of everything, from religious dogma to traditional verse forms. Even as a small schoolboy in Highgate he could write a very cheeky little couplet: 'A little sickness in the air, From too much fragrance everywhere.'

Some people have hinted that Hopkins was a poet despite his priesthood. I simply wouldn't know, but I do know that for years and years I've carried in my head one verse of his, written as a priest who trusts his God, but can still argue with him – *Justus quidem tu es, Domine, si disputem tecum . . .*

### *Thou Art Indeed Just, Lord*

GERARD MANLEY HOPKINS

Thou art indeed just, Lord, if I contend
With thee; but, Sir, so what I plead is just.
Why do sinners' ways prosper? and why must
Disappointment all I endeavour end?

Were thou my enemy, O thou my friend,
How would'st thou worse, I wonder, than thou dost
Defeat, thwart me? Oh, the sots and thralls of lust
Do in spare hours more thrive than I that spend,

Sir, life upon thy cause. See, banks and brakes
Now, leavèd how thick! lacèd they are again
With fretty chervil; look, and fresh wind shakes

Them; birds build – but not I build; no, but strain
Time's eunuch, and not breed one work that wakes.
Mine, O thou lord of life, send my roots rain.

What writer in the world hasn't known the agony of that dilemma? Surely only one poet has ever confessed that he had dried up, and expressed it in words that showed, so abundantly, that he hadn't – a pretty serious lesson for any writer, great or little. Though not an easy one to learn.

*Readers: Clive Merrison, Margaret Robertson, John Samson*

*Full Selection:*
*Defence of Poesie*, SIR PHILIP SYDNEY
*Now That Thou Hast Lov'd Me*, JOHN DONNE
*When I Died Last*, JOHN DONNE
*The Merchant of Venice, Act V*, WILLIAM SHAKESPEARE
*Essay on Wilfred Owen*, DYLAN THOMAS
*Exposure*, WILFRED OWEN
*It Seemed That Out of Battle I Escaped*, WILFRED OWEN

*The Watch*, FRANCES CORNFORD
*Passage from Ecclesiastes*
*Thou Art Indeed Just, Lord*, GERARD MANLEY HOPKINS
*A Highland Fisherman Asking God Why He Should Not Fish on Sunday* anon Gaelic, translated into Latin by ARTHUR JOHNSON, English translation anon
*The Napoleon of Notting Hill*, G. K. CHESTERTON
*The Robin*, JOHN CLARE
*Letter from Lady Montague to The Countess of Pomfret in March 1739*
*Father, Forget Not*, ELINOR JENKINS
*Verse on Tombstone*, MARTIN ELGINBRODDE
*A Song*, JOHN DONNE

# CHARLES CAUSLEY

## 1977

*At the time of writing, Charles Causley had just been awarded the CBE. Let us hope that it is merely the first step to greater honours for this fine poet and Cornishman. A sense of pride in his origins permeated the programme, not a sense of place and people only, but a feel for myth, the idea that every stone could and does tell a story, a story simple enough for children, which somehow contains a look into the darker recesses of adult consciousness.*

It was Noel Coward who remarked on the potency of what he called cheap music, and for those of us who go through life as book worms – or as a book anaconda in my case – I think the same is true of literature. The sort of reading that's given me the greatest pleasure, the most lasting blow to the senses, isn't necessarily a spectacularly fine piece of writing by a great writer. A lot depends on who we were, and even where we were, when we first read it.

The very first poem I remember hearing at my primary school I've always thought a masterpiece, and dearly wish I'd written it myself. It's a murder ballad; author: anon. I should also tell you that I was madly in love with the infant teacher who read it to us. I can see her now: tall, calm amid the smells and squalls of the baby class; a pre-Raphaelite beauty, with cool, marble hands and soft brown hair hanging below her shoulders.

As for the poem itself, I had no idea that – in varying European forms – it perhaps had its origins in Scandinavian myth and the death of Balder, the god of light, or that it's believed by some to be an allegorical account of the murder of William Rufus in the New Forest in the year 1100, as well as – a bit nearer our own time – an ironic tale of the end of the career, in the eighteenth century, of Sir Robert Walpole.

I enjoyed – and enjoy – the poem as a poem about the death of that bold and independent bird the robin.

One little point about the verse:

Who'll toll the bell?
I said the Bull,
Because I can pull . . .

How often have you seen him depicted as a farmyard bull, of massive animal architecture? I'm certain we should really see a bird here, the bullfinch, for all the other creatures in the poem are small ones: sparrow, beetle, fly, fish, linnet and so on.

*Who Killed Cock Robin*

Who killed Cock Robin?
I, said the sparrow,
With my bow and arrow,
I killed Cock Robin.

Who saw him die?
I, said the Fly,
With my little eye,
I saw him die.

Who caught his blood?
I, said the Fish,
With my little dish,
I caught his blood.

Who'll make the shroud?
I, said the Beetle,
With my thread and needle,
I'll make the shroud.

Who'll dig his grave?
I, said the Owl,
With my pick and shovel,
I'll dig his grave.

Who'll be the parson?
I, said the Rook,
With my little book,
I'll be the parson.

Who'll be the clerk?
I, said the Lark,
If it's not in the dark,
I'll be the clerk.

Who'll carry the link?
I, said the Linnet,
I'll fetch it in a minute,
I'll carry the link.

Who'll be chief mourner?
I, said the Dove,
I mourn for my love,
I'll be chief mourner.

Who'll carry the coffin?
I, said the Kite,
If it's not through the night,
I'll carry the coffin.

Who'll bear the pall?
We, said the Wren,
Both the cock and the hen,
We'll bear the pall.

Who'll sing the psalm?
I, said the Thrush,
As she sat on a bush,
I'll sing a psalm.

Who'll toll the bell?
I, said the Bull,
Because I can pull,
I'll toll the bell.

All the birds of the air
Fell a-sighing and a-sobbing,
When they heard the bell toll
For poor Cock Robin.

*Poor* Cock Robin. How skilfully that anonymous author calls forth our sympathy for the fabled bird that was believed to spread leaves over not only the Babes in the Wood, but over all lost and dead travellers! An animal poem I didn't hear at school – though if I had, I know I'd have loved it – was written by a Cornish poet who was also a Cornish miner. John Harris was born the eldest of ten children, at Six Chimneys Cottage in Camborne, in the year 1820. His father was a miner and small farmer, and at the age of ten John was put to work dressing copper ore at the giant Dolcoath mine. By the time he was twelve years old, he was working underground. He continued as a miner for a quarter of a century more, at a time when the average age of miners at death in many parts of Cornwall ranged from twenty to thirty.

John Harris was a compulsive writer, quite undeterred by poverty. If he hadn't got any paper, he wrote his poems on tiles and roof-slates, on his fingernails, on iron wedges in the mine, even inside his hat. When he ran out of ink, he made his own out of blackberry juice. The poem I've chosen is a piercingly sharp, as well as infinitely tender evocation of a childhood experience I'm sure almost everyone shares: the funeral of a little creature who was not only a valuable working member of a poor family of those days, a provider of food for the pot, but also a dearly loved pet – in this case, a ferret. The actors in this drama of the last rites are all children.

## *The Burial*

JOHN HARRIS

Will's ferret was buried this morn:
  When Samuel came down from his bed,
He whisper'd, with aspect forlorn,
  'O Kitty, Will's ferret is dead.'

And Kitty soon told it to Mark,
  And Mark to the rest of his clan
We sorrow'd with visages dark,
  As if we were mourning a man.

'Come, Ann, let us lay her to rest,
  And you must prepare us a bier:
We will heap the cold earth on her breast,'
  And we wiped from our eyelids a tear.

So Ann made a coffin so small,
  Of cast-off brown paper and thread:
This served for a shroud and a pall, –
  False trappings, unknown to the dead.

And Samuel was sexton and clerk,
  And Benjamin bearer so brave,
While Kitty, and Jacob, and Mark
  Soon bore her away to the grave.

My mother was curious enow,
  And so she came softly behind,
Well pleased with her children, I trow,
  Who to the poor brute were so kind.

'Neath the hawthorn its grave was dug deep,
  With sharp-pointed pickaxe and spade,
Lie down, little ferret, and sleep
  On the couch that affection has made.

At the age of thirty-seven, Harris was rescued from a life of labour in the mines to become a kind of itinerant scripture-reader, and he went on to produce fifteen or sixteen collections of verse altogether.

The poet Percy Bysshe Shelley was drowned at the age of thirty while sailing in the Italian Gulf of Spezia in the summer of 1822. He had, no doubt still has, many detractors, both as a poet and a person. But his friend, the Cornishman Edward John Trelawney once said, significantly, 'To know an author personally is too often but to destroy the illusion created by his works . . .' and that, 'Shelley was a grand exception to this rule'. And Lord Byron called him 'the best and most benevolent of men; they hooted him out of his country like a mad dog, for questioning a dogma.'

My feelings about that sweet natured, unselfish, immensely courageous poet are by no means all sad ones. One of his earliest – and one of his best – biographers was Thomas Jefferson Hogg: the friend and exact contemporary – he was born in 1792 – who was sent down from Oxford after the furore created by the publication of the poet's famous pamphlet called 'The Necessity of Atheism'. Like Edward John Trelawney, Hogg produces a marvellously vivid portrait of Shelley. Here, for instance, is the poet with his books, and, a little later, being pursued by another poet, Robert Southey, who wants to read his latest work to him. Shelley, at this time, is aged twenty and living in Keswick in Cumberland.

## *Shelley at Home*

THOMAS JEFFERSON HOGG

Shelley . . . was always reading; at his meals a book lay by his side, on the table, open. Tea and toast were often neglected, his author seldom; his mutton and potatoes might grow cold; his interest in a work never cooled. He invariably sallied forth, book in hand, reading to himself, if he was alone; if he had a companion, reading aloud. He took a volume to bed with him, and read as long as his candle lasted; he then slept – impatiently no doubt – until it was light, and he recommenced reading at the early dawn . . . In consequence of this great watching, and of almost incessant reading, he would often fall asleep in the daytime – dropping off in a moment – like an infant. He often quietly transferred himself from his chair to the floor, and slept soundly on the carpet, and in the winter upon the rug, basking in the warmth like a cat, and like a cat his little round head was roasted before a blazing fire. If anyone humanely covered the poor head to shield it from the heat, the covering was impatiently put aside in his sleep . . .

Southey was addicted to reading his terrible epics – before they were printed – to anyone who seemed to be a fit subject for the cruel experiment. He soon set his eyes on the newcomer, and one day having effected the capture of Shelley, he immediately lodged him securely in a little study upstairs, carefully locking the door upon himself and his prisoner and putting the key in his waistcoat pocket. There was a window in the room it is true, but it was so high above the ground that Baron Trenck himself would not have attempted it.

'Now you shall be delighted,' Southey said: 'but sit down.'

Poor Bysshe sighed, and took his seat at the table. The author seated himself opposite, and placing his MS on the table, before him, began to read slowly and distinctly. The poem, if I mistake not, was 'The Curse of Kehama'. Charmed with his own composition the admiring author read on, varying his voice occasionally, to point out the finer passages and invite applause. There was no commendation; no criticism; all was hushed. This was strange. Southey raised his eyes from the neatly written MS: Shelley had disappeared. This was still more strange. Escape was impossible; every precaution had been taken, yet he had vanished. Shelley had glided noiselessly from his chair to the floor, and the insensible young Vandal lay buried in profound sleep underneath the table.

*Readers: William Squire, Margot van der Burgh*

*Full Selection:*
*Cock Robin* trad
*The Burial*, JOHN HARRIS
*Reticent*, D. M. THOMAS
*A Cornish Anthology. Billy Bray: Miner, Evangelist*, ed. A. L. ROWSE
*After Billy Bray*, JACK CLEMO
*The Aboriginals*, RONALD TAMPLIN
*The Unicorn in the Garden*, JAMES THURBER
*Shelley at Home*, THOMAS JEFFERSON HOGG
*Ozymandias*, P. B. SHELLEY

*Mrs Malone,* ELEANOR FARJEON
*Framed in a First-Storey Winder* anon from 'Strange to Tell' ed. D. SAUNDERS

# PROFESSOR ANTHONY CLARE

## 1985

*The rehearsal had finished early and everybody involved had a couple of hours to kill. This can sometimes be a difficult time, with the discovery that whilst the members of the group may be perfectly friendly and amiably disposed towards one another, they actually have very little in common other than the purpose for which they were assembled. Under such circumstances conversation is frequently desultory, books are produced, one person takes a walk, another phones his agent until suddenly it's time for the recording, the audience is appreciative, it's gone well and in the euphoria that follows we all get on swimmingly and exchange telephone numbers. That wasn't the case on this occasion. The conversation flowed in that two hours. It became clear that the interviewing style Anthony Clare employs for 'In the Psychiatrist's Chair' isn't solely a professional technique, but arises from his genuine interest and concern for people and their well-being. A man of gentle humour, he confessed 'I became almost suicidal in my search for a selection that makes me laugh. It was the surfeit not the shortage that almost killed me.' In the end he settled on Tom Sharpe 'partly because I still remember my father-in-law being rendered speechless with laughter one Christmas reading "Wilt".' For the rest, included in his immaculately written script, aside from Joyce and Yeats, perhaps predictable choices from an Irishman, were pieces which reflected his professional, and therefore humanitarian, concerns. At the end of the evening he drove everybody home.*

Faced with the near-impossibility of selecting pieces for this programme, I have chosen pieces of prose and poetry which, in addition to giving me pleasure and provocation, are in some way linked with elements in my own life, usually people. My own love for and interest in literature are due, in great part, to my wife who is better read and certainly far more literate than I can ever hope to be, and a Jesuit teacher at my day school in Dublin, a hater of set texts and smelly orthodoxies who struggled manfully to introduce a scruffy gaggle of boys to the glorious repository of English literature. He was not, however, very fond of my next choice despite the fact that the Jesuits educated him too.

I only really discovered what it is like to be a Dubliner when I left Dublin, first to spend a year as a newly-qualified intern in America and later, and more permanently, when I crossed the Irish sea to work in London. My trip to the US was purely pragmatic – I wanted to marry my wife. Irish hospitals, unlike American ones, did not provide married quarters for their junior staff – like the church, they regarded sexual activity, even of the marital and therefore approved sort, as a most regrettable distraction and I suspect that some senior Irish physicians of the time would have shared Freud's view, a man they otherwise abhorred, that much of the good things man gets up to are sublimations of unexpressed sexual needs. To this day I cherish towards the United States the most intense and confused feelings. I am appalled by the brashness and entranced by the energy. It is fashionable for British observers to dismiss America as adolescent, but then there is something geriatric about current British preoccupations with the past and in contrast to the dynamism of New York, London has all the trappings of an admittedly well-appointed museum.

In the 1960s and 1970s, the formative years of my life, termed by Tom Wolfe 'The Purple Decades' there was a revival of charismatic religion, a phenomenon common to Western society but, of course, at its most flamboyant across the Atlantic. For my own part, such little sympathy as I have with charismatic faith is due in part to several summers spent in Assisi in Umbria, a heavenly paradise of a place where not only is Francis buried, but my namesake, St Clare too. Incidentally, did you know that St Clare is the patron saint of television? It is, as you might expect of such matters, a most fitting choice in that once while in her cell at the convent of San Damiano she heard and saw mass underway at the distant church of St Francis of Assisi – the first recorded occurrence of dual transmission and, to date, the only one without elaborate equipment – indeed without any equipment!

Another namesake of whom I am proud – although sadly we are in no way related – is John Clare, the nineteenth century poet. Clare, the son of a poor labourer, wrote some of the most lyrical poetry of his time. He suffered a severe mental breakdown as a young man and spent the rest of his life in a mental hospital. During his stay he wrote an intensely moving poem which to this day remains one of the clearest statements of the enormity that is mental illness and it is for this reason and the fact that it is a lovely creation that I have chosen 'Written in Northampton County Asylum'.

### *Written in Northampton County Asylum*

JOHN CLARE

I am! yet what I am who cares, or knows?
  My friends forsake me like a memory lost.
I am the self-consumer of my woes;
  They rise and vanish, an oblivious host,
Shadows of life, whose very soul is lost,
  And yet I am – I live – though I am toss'd

Into the nothingness of scorn and noise,
  Into the living sea of waking dream,
Where there is neither sense of life, nor joys,
  But the huge shipwreck of my own esteem
And all that's dear. Even those I loved the best
Are strange – nay they are stranger than the rest.

I long for scenes where man has never trod –
  For scenes where women never smiled or wept –
There to abide with my Creator, God,
  And sleep as I in childhood sweetly slept,
Full of high thoughts, unborn. So let me lie, –
The grass below; above, the vaulted sky.

Perhaps it is because I am a doctor but for me the one real unanswerable question is not that of God's existence but suffering's.

I try and convince myself of its efficacy, that it cleanses, elevates, exalts and that only he who has suffered is privy to certain truths. Yet I am not convinced and most of the time I regard suffering as a barbarity and the fight to eliminate it the noblest and most worthwhile fight of all. There is now a rich literature on illness and suffering written from the inside as it were. One such creation is 'The Journal of a Disappointed Man and a Last Diary' written by W. N. P. Barbellion, who suffered a particularly malignant form of multiple sclerosis. Like so many sufferers Barbellion was, as his brother wrote, 'as greedy as a shark for life in the raw, for the whole of life' but, understandably, there were moments of intense, despairing gloom, moments captured in the remarkable diary which he kept regularly during the years before his death.

## *The Journal of a Disappointed Man and a Last Diary*

W. N. P. BARBELLION

*February 3rd*

Suffering does not only insulate. It drops its victim on an island in an ocean desert where he sees men as distant ships passing. I not only feel alone, but very far away from you all. But what is my suffering? Not physical pain. I have none. Pain brings clusters of one's fellows – a toothache is intelligible. But when I say I have grown tired of myself, have outlived myself, am unseasonable and 'mopy' like a doomed swallow in November, it is something that requires a John Galsworthy to understand. The world to me is but a dream or mock show; and we all therein but Pantalones and Anticks to my severe contemplations. This used to be a transitory impression that amused my curiosity. But it hurts and bewilders now that it has become the permanent complexion of my daily existence, when I long for real persons and real things. Tinsel and pictures are melancholy substitutes to anyone heart-hungry for the touch of real hands, and the sound of real voices. Acute mental pain at intervals seizes me with pincers and casts me helpless into the whirlpool – it may be W–'s despair, or the failure to find a home for me to go to. But there are spasms of reality, the momentary opening and closing of a shutter on Life. As soon as they are over, I at once relapse into the dull monotone of misery and picture-show.

I have not left my room since November 11th. I eat well, sleep well, am in possesion of all my higher faculties – those for feeling and thinking. But I can't get out.

I think sometimes folk do not come to see me because I am such a gruesome object. It is not pleasant to feel you are gruesome. I have outstayed my welcome. I know everyone will be relieved to hear of my death – no doubt for my sake, as they will eagerly point out, but also for their sake, as I believe. Yet now and then in selfish and ignoble moods, I, being an egotist, fancy I would like some loving hands to clutch at me, in a blind, ineffectual effort to save me in any condition if only alive.

*February 4th*
The last part of yesterday's entry was maudlin tosh – 'entirely foreign to my nature'. I hereby cancel it.

I intended to end my selection with Emily Dickinson, a poet who more than once concerned herself with medicine and madness. It was she who wrote:

Faith is a fine invention
For gentlemen who see;
But microscopes are prudent
In an emergency.

As fine a comment on the limits of belief and the usefulness of science as I know.

But my last choice is – Shakespeare. Having once seen Gielgud as Prospero, it can only be that great speech in which the mystery and abyss of existence is stared in the eye. Before it, an excerpt from a great psychiatrist, the late Sir Aubrey Lewis, one-time director of the Maudsley Hospital, where I trained and spent many happy years. Here is Lewis speculating on the character of Shakespeare.

## *The Psychology of Shakespeare*

AUBREY LEWIS

It may be accepted that in his early manhood, when witty talkers, young lovers and fiery adventurers predominated in his plays, Shakespeare himself was ardent and bold; later when deep and moral problems, the crudities and sufferings that sexuality entails, the humiliations imposed by the imperious body and its desires, the meaning of death, frustration and disillusionment – when these were the central themes of his plays, and the chief characters in them were powerful fathers and rulers who suffered defeat, we may, hesitantly, surmise that Shakespeare had himself an anguished maturity, to be succeeded at last by the relative serenity and renunciation which are expressed in *The Tempest*, his final play. There he had come to the time when he must break his magic staff and drown his book deeper than did ever plummet sound; he asked for solemn music, and he spoke his farewell nobly:

> Our revels now are ended. These our actors
> As I foretold you, were all spirits and
> Are melted into air, into thin air;
> And, like the baseless fabric of this vision,
> The cloud-capp'd towers, the gorgeous palaces,
> The solemn temples, the great globe itself,
> Yea, all which it inherit, shall dissolve,
> And, like this insubstantial pageant faded,
> Leave not a rack behind. We are such stuff
> As dreams are made on; and our little life
> Is rounded with a sleep.

*Readers: Andrew Sachs, Rosalind Shanks*

*Full Selection:*
*Journey of the Magi*, T. S. ELIOT
*The Dead*, JAMES JOYCE
*The Purple Decades*, TOM WOLFE
*Written in Northampton County Asylum*, JOHN CLARE
*The Plague*, ALBERT CAMUS
*The Second Coming*, W. B. YEATS
*Wilt*, TOM SHARPE
*Riders in the Chariot*, PATRICK WHITE
*The Journal of a Disappointed Man and a Last Diary*, W. N. P. BARBELLION

*The Psychology of Shakespeare,* AUBREY LEWIS
*Our Revels now are Ended* – from *The Tempest,* WILLIAM SHAKESPEARE

# RENE CUTFORTH

## 1970

*Rene Cutforth was a journalist of what is sometimes, wincingly, called the 'Old School' – a term of approbation generally, it is often used by an older person to underline the failings of a younger generation whilst being forgiving of those of the professional under discussion. Not being of Cutforth's generation, I can offer the opinion that in his case it does not seem totally unfair. It is rare nowadays to hear the news reported in a way that employs the English language in anything other than its most functional expression, as if words were merely nuts and bolts without the potential of being artists' materials. In fairness the ability to conjure up pictures in the mind with a clarity and emotional truth that rendered the invention of television superfluous was one given to few. As a young studio manager in the 1960s I can remember being faced in the studio with this, to me, elderly and slightly hungover man possessed of a voice which was the audible equivalent of malt whisky, and a face which looked as if it had been preserved in it. Apparently, he had been out of favour and giving him a small series of four programmes was a first attempt at rehabilitation. In charge of the proceedings was Francis 'Jack' Dillon, a distinguished Features producer who managed, well after retirement, to be barred from the BBC Club for disorderly behaviour! After recording the first programme, I rushed back to the office and demanded to be allocated to work on the rest of the series. I had never heard scripts as good. It wasn't until later that I learned that Cutforth had written them on rising from Jack's office floor after sleeping off the previous night's drinking. Certainly, by far the most substantial part of his edition of 'With Great Pleasure', recorded in the Concert Hall, Broadcasting House, was a paean of praise to a nearby public house.*

What I've chosen has, I hope, some bearing on the climate and the situation my friends and I find ourselves in. Particularly since most of them are about my age, with aerials of similar wavelengths and have had something to do with what I must be careful not to call 'the wireless'. But most of all because a great many of them have been through either the full course or the shorter course in Further Education at the George public house in Mortimer Street.

Since the George and its denizens is part of the theme of this programme I'll go on about it a bit. When I first pushed open the George's gloomy swing door in 1946, the interior could be described as austere.

It had, and still has, a good deal of rather overbearing mahogany and mirrors brassily inscribed with the names of forgotten drinks, Shrub for instance, and somebody's Entire, whatever that might mean.

The damp dun-coloured floor could have been made of stone or wood or almost anything, but it was in fact a piece of lino glued to the foundations with beer. There wasn't much light and the effect of the mahogany and the lights refracted through red and yellow bottles was rather like diving into a fruit cake stuffed with cherries and bits of candied peel. You would get mousetrap cheese and onions if you made a fuss but that was all the George had to offer in those days except the company.

It was crammed to bursting with poets and producers and actors in pursuit of the producers, and professors with Third Programme talks, and journalists from the Newsroom and people who described themselves as writers but talked so much in the George they never got round to putting anything down. Many of the members were idiosyncratic to the verge of eccentricity. There was the poet who at a certain stage in the evening rang his own telephone number to see if he was there; the brilliant writer who'd written nothing since the early part of the war and who stood with a silver-knobbed stick in one hand and a cigar in the other and claimed your undivided attention for hour after hour for an endless shouted fantasy about himself. There was the professor whose hobby in life was the punctuation of the poems of Pope. He collected the commas particularly. There was a Highland film producer, almost incomprehensible, who forced you by sheer pertinacity to join him in weeping for his poor old father. There were Welshmen in search of harmony and Irishmen in search of injustice.

It was said of the George that more books were conceived there which never came to delivery than in any other place on earth. But it was the poets, scratching and biting, who made the place. Every contemporary poet you'd ever heard of came in at one time or another, but chief of them all in the George in the fifties was Louis MacNeice, good poet, economical of speech, tall and saturnine and brooding over his Guinness.

Poets in those days were apt to give out from time to time a sort of cultural weather forecast, with observations about the prevailing wind and any compass bearings they had to offer. Auden could frighten you to death with a weather report, but no one was better at them then MacNeice. He told you exactly what it was that was rumbling about in a disquieting way at the back of your mind and since I want to remind you of the last great cataclysmic change in the weather which has made so much difference to our lives I am including the very last weather report that Louis MacNeice wrote in 1959, part of the dedication to his book *85 Poems*.

## *To Hedli* from *85 Poems*

LOUIS MACNEICE

Acting younger than I am and thinking older
I have buried so many stray moments in this volume
That I feel shrunk; as though those April answers
Had withered off their Question and now turning,
As the year turns, I bind up ghost and image
To give them, Hedli, to you, a makeshift present.

For having lived, and too much, in the present,
Askance at the coming gods, estranged from those older
Who had created my fathers in their image,

I stand here now dumbfounded by the volume
Of angry sound which pours from every turning
On those who only lately knew the answers.

So I lay my ear to the ground and no one answers
Though I know that the Word, like a bulb, is there, is present
And there the subterranean wheels keep turning
To make the world gush green when, we being older,
Others will be in their prime to drench a volume
In the full leaf of insight and bloom of image.

At one time I was content if things would image
Themselves in their own dazzle, if the answers
Came quick and smooth and the great depth and volume
Of the cold sea would wash me the chance present,
Bone or shell or message from some older
Castaway for whom there was no returning.

But now I am not content, the leaves are turning
And the gilt flaking from each private image
And all the poets I know, both younger and older,
Condemned to silence unless they divine the answers
Which our grim past has buried in our present
And which are no more than groped for in this volume.

Still at this point I tender you this volume
In hopes, my dearest, that your fingers turning
These pages may let fall, among those present,
Some greeting on my waifs and wraiths of image
And half-blind questions that still lack their answers,
Which lack grows no way less as I grow older.

Older and older. Which was the right turning?
Rhythm and image and still at best half answers
And at half volume. But take this; it is a present.

*Reader: Hugh Burden*

*Full Selection:*
*To Hedli,* LOUIS MACNEICE
*Cards of Identity,* NIGEL DENNIS

*To the Unknown Citizen*, W. H. AUDEN
*The Garden Party*, HILAIRE BELLOC
*The Love Song of J. Alfred Prufrock*, T. S. ELIOT
*Part XI of Amours de Voyage*, ARTHUR HUGH CLOUGH
*Scoop*, EVELYN WAUGH
*Lord Hippo*, HILAIRE BELLOC
*How the Kooks Crumble*, JAMES THURBER

# *DAVID DAICHES*

## *1985*

*It has been a pleasure of mine, over many years, to produce on location in the Scottish border country a number of Features, written and presented by Hugh Douglas, about authors who had had close connections with that part of the world – Robert Burns, John Buchan, James Hogg and Sir Walter Scott. Daiches, a distinguished academic, editor and critic made vivid contributions to the programmes on Hogg and Scott. He must have written and lectured on them many times, but on each occasion, as we sat in his Edinburgh house listening to him talking so ebulliently, it was as if he had just discovered a fresh and exciting new talent. We recorded his edition of 'With Great Pleasure' in Sir Walter Scott's house at Abbotsford, guests of Walter Scott's delightful great-great-great-great-great-grand-daughters, Jean and Patricia Maxwell-Scott. As so often before they made us warmly welcome. They must by now be used to the BBC paraphernalia, but they turned not a hair at the arrival of an audience of about thirty to be squeezed into the library. Many of them were members of Burns clubs and so on whom Hugh and I had met on previous trips and knew to be jolly and entertaining. And so they were, before and after the recording. During the performance, which they claimed to have enjoyed, they remained largely silent and straight-faced, taking their pleasure seriously. Nothing wrong with that of course; it's just that it's difficult to convey on tape that they are having a good time when they don't make a sound. And entertaining David's presentation certainly was. All his enthusiasm and joy when talking about his favourite writers would have been clear to the most distant listener at home.*

Let us move to the early eighteenth century, to a poem of melancholy, the elegant pensiveness of Matthew Prior. It's carefully chiselled down as a work of art. It is done with wit and done with a kind of stoical acceptance – life is like this; we civilised men know that people cling to life even after they have got nothing left; they may be poor, they may be ill, they may be better dead, but they cling to life and that is the lesson of history. It's almost as if the poem exists for the sake of the last line, 'Unwilling to retire, tho' weary'. It sums up the human condition as he sees it. The poem is called 'Written in the Beginning of Mezeray's History of France'. I've never read Mezeray's *History of France* and I don't think many people would have remembered it if Matthew Prior hadn't written in the fly-leaf.

## *Written in the Beginning of Mezeray's History of France*

MATTHEW PRIOR

Whate'er thy Countrymen have done,
By law and Wit, by Sword and Gun,
In Thee is faithfully recited:
And all the Living World, that view
Thy Work, give thee the Praises due:
At once Instructed and Delighted.

Yet for the Fame of all these Deeds,
What Beggar in the Invalides,
With Lameness broke, with Blindness smitten,
Wished ever decently to die,
To have been either Mezeray,
Or any Monarch He has written?

It strange, dear Author, yet it true is,
That down from Pharamond to Louis,
All covet Life, yet call it Pain;

All feel the Ill, yet shun the Cure:
Can Sense this Paradox endure?
Resolve me, Cambray or Fontaine.

The Man in graver Tragic known,
Tho' his best Part long since was done,
Still on the Stage desires to tarry:
And He who play'd the Harlequin,
After the Jest still loads the Scene,
Unwilling to retire, tho' weary.

Dr Johnson I think is the greatest epistolary in the history of literature. This is his letter to Lord Chesterfield. Lord Chesterfield had been asked by Johnson – or at least he'd tried to ask him but he didn't get any contact with him – to help him when he was working on his great dictionary. He didn't, but after the dictionary was finally completed after many years of solitary labour Chesterfield wrote two articles in a periodical, known as *The World*, praising it. And Johnson felt it was a bit belated.

This letter is generally taken to have marked the end of the age of patronage, the subsidising of literature by men of power and money to whom authors had to be subservient. Johnson put an end to that with a bang.

*Boswell's Johnson*

To the Right Honourable The Earl of Chesterfield. February 7, 1755.

My Lord,
I have lately been informed, by the proprietor of *The World*, that two papers, in which my Dictionary is recommended to the public, were written by your lordship. To be so distinguished is an honour, which being very little accustomed to favours from the great, I know not well how to receive, or in what terms to acknowledge.

When, upon some slight encouragement, I first visited your lordship, I was overpowered, like the rest of mankind, by the enchantment of your address, and could not forbear to wish that I must boast myself *Le vainqueur du vainqueur de la torte*: that I might obtain that regard for which I saw the world contending; but I found my attendance so little encouraged, that neither pride nor modesty would suffer me to continue it. When I had once addressed your lordship in public, I had exhausted all the art of pleasing which a retired and uncourtly scholar can possess. I had done all that I could; and no man is well pleased to have his all neglected, be it ever so little.

Seven years, my lord, have now passed since I waited in your outward rooms, or was repulsed from your door; during which time I have been pushing my work through difficulties, of which it is useless to complain, and have brought it, at last, to the verge of publication, without one act of assistance, one word of encouragement, or one smile of favour. Such treatment I did not expect, for I never had a patron before.

The shepherd in *Virgil* grew at last acquainted with Love, and found him a native of the rocks.

Is not a patron, my lord, one who looks with unconcern on a man struggling for life in the water, and, when he has reached ground, encumbers him with help? The notice which you have been pleased to take of my labours, had it been early, had been kind; but it has been delayed till I am indifferent, and cannot enjoy it; till I am solitary and cannot impart it; till I am known and do not want it. I hope it is no very cynical asperity not to confess obligations where no benefit has been received, or to be unwilling that the public should consider me as owing that to a patron which Providence has enabled me to do for myself. Having carried on my work thus far with so little obligation to any favourer of learning. I shall not be disappointed though I shall conclude it, if less be possible, with less; for I have been long wakened from that dream of hope, in which I once boasted myself with so much exultation.

My Lord, your lordship's most humble,
Most obedient servant,
Sam Johnson.

Terrific stuff. Johnson's wife had died while he was writing the dictionary hence that extraordinary three-fold thing: 'till I am indifferent, and cannot enjoy it; till I am solitary, and cannot impart it; till I am known and do not want it'. The way he spits that out! And the way he avoids having to sign himself 'your lordship's obedient servant': The time has long since passed 'in which I once boasted myself with so much exultation . . .', so he even gets out of the conventional compliment at the end.

And now I turn to something very different, an extract from Robert Louis Stevenson's unfinished masterpiece – he died in the middle of it – *Weir of Hermiston*. It is the book in which the father–son conflict which was so strong in all Stevenson's feelings and writings is most perfectly achieved in fiction. He had a great conflict with his own father whom he both dearly loved and bitterly quarrelled with on matters of religion. And again and again in his novels, in his letters, in his essays you get reflections of this, but he finally found the appropriate literary way of purging himself of this in the situation in *Weir of Hermiston*, in the relationship between the father, the tough judge – Scots speaking, he'd have nothing to do with the new-fangled English modes of speech – the old, traditional, stern, cruel, but just Scottish judge and his sensitive son of a sensitive and weak mother. Strong in his own way, but very differently from his father, the son in this conflict, in this dialogue, speaks English. The father speaks good old-fashioned Scots as they did so often on the bench in those days, at the very end of the eighteenth century. What happens is this Weir of Hermiston, the judge, the justice clerk, had sentenced to death a man called Duncan Jopp for sheep-stealing which was then a capital offence. The son, Archie, had been present at the court and was absolutely horrified at what he considered to be the glee with which his father hunted down this wretched man. And that evening at the Speculative Society, in Edinburgh, at the debate he opposed capital punishment, his mind full of the horror of his father's sentencing this wretched man to death. And then when he was publicly hanged shortly afterwards, he attended the hanging and was absolutely revolted. He cried out against what was happening even though he knew his father was responsible for it. When he gets home he finds that his father had heard about what he had done and this is an abridged version of the interview that takes place. The father speaking Scots, the son speaking English, the whole thing is done by the contrast of vowels you might almost say.

## *Weir of Hermiston*

ROBERT LOUIS STEVENSON

For a moment Hermiston warmed his hands at the fire, presenting his back to Archie; then suddenly disclosed on him the terrors of the Hanging Face.

'What's this I hear of ye?' he asked.

There was no answer possible to Archie.

'. . . I hear that at the hanging of Duncan Jopp – and, man! ye had a fine client there – in the middle of all the riffraff of the ceety, ye thought fit to cry out, "This is a damned murder, and my gorge rises at the man that haangit him."'

'No, sir, these were not my words,' cried Archie.

'What were yer words, then?' asked the judge.

'I believe I said, "I denounce it as a murder!"' said the son. 'I beg your pardon – a God-defying murder. I have no wish to conceal the truth,' he added, and looked his father for a moment in the face.

'There was nothing about your gorge rising, then?'

'That was afterwards, my lord, as I was leaving the Speculative. I said I had been to see the miserable creature hanged, and my gorge rose at it.'

'You're a young gentleman that doesna approve of caapital punishment,' said Hermiston. 'Weel, I'm an auld man that does. I was glad to get Jopp haangit, and for what would I pretend I wasna? You're all for honesty, it seems; you wouldn't even steik your mouth on the public street. What for should I steik mines upon the Bench, the King's officer, bearing the sword, a dreid to evil-doers, as I was from the beginning, and as I will be to the end! Mair than enough of it! Heedious! I never gave twa thoughts heediousness, I have no call to be bonny. I'm a man that gets through with my day's business, and let that suffice.'

The ring of sarcasm had died out of his voice as he went on, the plain words became invested with some of the dignity of the Justice-seat. 'It would be telling you if you could say as much,' the speaker resumed. 'But ye cannot. Ye've been reading some of my cases, ye say. But it was not for the law in them, it was to spy out your faither's nakedness, a fine employment in a son. You're splairging; you're running at lairge in life like a wild nowt to the Bar. You're not fit for it; no splairger is . . .'

'. . . Father, let me go to the Peninsula,' said Archie. 'That's all I'm fit for – to fight . . .'

'. . . I think not,' continued Hermiston. 'And I would send no man to be a servant to the King, God bless him! that has proved such a shauchling son to his own faither. You can splairge here on Edinburgh street, and where's the hairm? It doesna play buff on me! And if there were twenty thousand eediots like yourself, sorrow a Duncan Jopp would hang the fewer. But there's no splairging in a camp; and if you were to go to it, you would find out for yourself whether Lord Well'n'ton approves of caapital punishment or not. You a sodger!' he cried, with a sudden burst of scorn. 'Ye auld wife, the sodgers would bray at ye like cuddies!' As at the drawing of a curtain, Archie was aware of some illogicality in his position, and stood abashed. He had a strong impression, besides, of the essential valour of the old gentleman before him, how conveyed it would be hard to say . . .

'. . . I have no other son, you see,' said Hermiston. A bonny one I have gotten! But I must just do the best I can wi' him, and what am I to do? If ye had been younger, I would have wheepit ye for this rideeculous exhibeetion. The way it is, I have just to grin and bear. But one thing is to be clearly understood. As a faither, I must grin and bear it; but if I had been the Lord Advocate instead of the Lord Justice-Clerk, son or no son, Mr Erchibald Weir would have been in a jyle the night.'

*Readers: Iain Cuthbertson, Judy Cornwell*

*Full Selection:*
*Sun Rising*, JOHN DONNE
*Sonnet 116*, WILLIAM SHAKESPEARE
*A, B and C*, STEPHEN LEACOCK
*Mezeray's History of France*, MATTHEW PRIOR
*Musée des Beaux Arts*, W. H. AUDEN
*Boswell's Johnson*
*Pride and Prejudice*, JANE AUSTEN
*A slice of Wedding Cake*, ROBERT GRAVES

*Weir of Hermiston*, ROBERT LOUIS STEVENSON
*During Wind and Rain*, THOMAS HARDY
*The Sunlight on the Garden*, LOUIS MACNEICE

# *FRANK DELANEY*

## *1984*

*Frank Delaney is a clever man to have built such a good career out of what gives him such great pleasure, reading and talking about books. He helped create Radio 4's 'Bookshelf' programme, and presented it for its first five years, during which time he interviewed 1200 authors. It must have been a daunting workload, however enjoyable the reading may have been. Fortunately for him, he has one of those wonderful memories that can recall a phrase, read sometimes many years previously, exactly apposite to the subject in hand. His 'With Great Pleasure', recorded as part of the Lancaster Literary Festival, was the first I produced on taking over the series. It was very popular, both with the audience in the theatre and the audience at home. However I had the benefit of an extra show, the sight of Frank Delaney and the actor T. P. McKenna trying to outdo each other in miming the gaits of various characters commonly seen in the vicinity of Dublin pubs.*

Anybody with an Irish accent choosing is expected, obliged, to include the ineluctable William Butler Yeats – not mind you the 'Lake Isle of Innisfree', what Dr Leavis called 'that unfortunate poem' because it was anthologised so much. I've chosen as a beginning and an end as it were one short poem which is economical, but rich and final in what it says. It's Yeats at his best, I believe, on his best subject – love.

## *The Pity of Love*

W. B. YEATS

A pity beyond all telling
Is hid in the heart of love;
The folk who are buying and selling,
The clouds on their journey above,
The cold winds ever blowing,
And the shadowy hazel grove
Where mouse-grey waters are flowing,
Threaten the head that I love.

Given that Yeats never finally 'got it together' with Maud Gonne MacBride, his fellow Dublin men would say 'Ah sure, what would he know about it?' But there is a point in that poem; you see the point about the Irish is when we talk a lot we may actually say very little, but when we talk very little we may actually be saying a lot. This characteristic stems as much from language as from temperament. Yeats wrote entirely in English, to his regret, because the original Gaelic spoken in Ireland is at once marvellously obfuscating and lucid – ideal for poetry, and of course at the same time the exemplar of the living Celtic paradox. But unfortunately today that language, that Erse, has taken a pounding over the years and is now in danger of being beached by the tide of English language which sweeps over the island.

A young Irish poet called Aidan Carl Matthews packed the whole idea into a three line poem.

## *A Marginal Gloss on the Death of Irish*

AIDAN CARL MATTHEWS

The tide gone out for good,
Thirty-one words for seaweed
Whiten on the foreshore.

Thirty-one words for seaweed! How many words I wonder for love? Growing up in Ireland I always knew when love was taking place if, on a Sunday afternoon, when a couple walked out together, he, silently, but eloquently, was wheeling her bicycle.

When I was a small boy around the fat acres of County Tipperary, I was a voyeur. Love in all its forms interested me, the hope of seeing lovers kissing or even meeting was electric – and I didn't even know that I should tell it in confession.

There is a phrase that comes to mind which recalls an early ambition of mine. The phrase is in the second verse of 'Fern Hill' by Dylan Thomas, that Welshman who, if he had learnt to swim, could have been an Irishman. The line was 'And as I was green and carefree, famous among the barns'. I wanted to be famous among the barns, not as a lover because I was still terrified of the parish priest. I wanted to be famous as, perhaps, a legendary huntsman, or a farmer known for being a shrewd judge of cattle, or a ploughman with a straight eye and a steady hand.

I grew up in the province of Munster in the 1940s and '50s. The new nation of the south was poor, but hopeful and it was desperate for self knowledge and respectability. I am no huntsman, can't plough, was too poor to farm. But there was one way to become famous among the barns in those days, and that was to acquire a reputation for learning. A century before me a romantic and gaunt figure stalked the land whom I thought I might one day emulate. The poet Padraic Colum captured him.

### *A Poor Scholar of the Forties*

PADRAIC COLUM

My eyelids red and heavy are
With bending o'er the smouldering peat.
I know the Aeneid now by heart,
My Virgil read in cold and heat,
In loneliness and hunger smart;
  And I know Homer, too, I ween,
  As Munster poets know Ossian.

And I must walk this road that winds
'Twixt bog and bog, while east there lies
A city with its men and books;
With treasures open to the wise,
Heart-words from equals, comrade-looks;
  Down here they have but tale and song.
  They talk Repeal the whole night long.

'You teach Greek verbs and Latin nouns,'
The dreamer of Young Ireland said,

'You do not hear the muffled call,
The sword being forged, the far-off tread
Of hosts to meet as Gael and Gall –
    What good to us your wisdom-store
    Your Latin verse, your Grecian Lore?'

And what to me is Gael or Gall?
Less than the Latin or the Greek –
I teach these by the dim rush-light
In smoky cabins night and week.
But what avail my teaching slight?
    Years hence, in rustic speech, a phrase,
    As in wild earth a Grecian Vase!

But that poem, learned with joy in school, also aroused great conflicts in me. Political words those: 'Repeal' meant repeal of the Act of Union, the 'sword being forged' meant war, Gael and Gall Irish versus foreigner. Deep within my bones lay the old feelings for this strange green island I lived on, with its sense of the happy-grotesque. Yet my intake in print was all in the English language and usually emanating from England, though it would be too much of an exaggeration to say that I was becoming culturally English while remaining emotionally Irish. Coming as I did from a male-dominated society, the most exciting revelation I had in the five years of presenting 'Bookshelf' on Radio 4, that doughty son of the Home Service, was the manner in which writing by women had become so important at this point in the century. The list of authors whose books struck chords is a long list – earlier, Rebecca West, Elizabeth Bowen, Virginia Woolf, then Rosamund Lehmann, Storm Jameson followed by Iris Murdoch, Margaret Drabble, Elizabeth Jane Howard, Susan Hill, Judith Burnley, Edna O'Brien.

Their statements collectively, for me at any rate, put the labels on our society in a way in which we can all read them. In assessing the mood which their books created in me, and in the context of this anthology, I was looking for one simple way in which to consider their obvious solitary commitment to what they do. And I found it in the works of one of their predecessors.

## *Autumn*

CHRISTINA ROSSETTI

I dwell alone – I dwell alone, alone,
Whilst full my river flows down to the sea,
  Gilded with flashing boats
    That bring no friend to me:
O love-songs, gurgling from a hundred throats,
    O love-pangs, let me be.

Fair fall the freighted boats which gold and stone
    And spices bear to sea:
Slim, gleaming maidens swell their mellow notes,
    Love-promising, entreating –
    Ah! sweet, but fleeting –
  Beneath the shivering, snow-white sails.
Hush! the wind flags and fails –

Hush! they will lie becalmed in sight of strand –
  Sight of my strand, where I do dwell alone:
Their songs wake singing echoes in my land –
  They cannot hear me moan.

  One latest, solitary swallow flies
  Across the sea, rough autumn-tempest tost,
  Poor bird, shall it be lost?
Dropped down into this uncongenial sea,
    With no kind eyes
    To watch it while it dies,
  Unguessed, uncared for, free:
    Set free at last,
    The short pang past,
In sleep, in death, in dreamless sleep locked fast.

Mine avenue is all a growth of oaks,
    Some rent by thunder-strokes,
Some rustling leaves and acorns in the breeze;
    Fair fall my fertile trees,
That rear their goodly heads, and live at ease.

A spider's web blocks all mine avenue;
  He catches down and foolish painted flies,

That spider wary and wise.
Each morn it hangs a rainbow strung with dew
Betwixt boughs green with sap.
So fair, few creatures guess it is a trap:
I will not mar the web.
Tho' sad I am to see the small lives ebb.

It shakes – my trees shake – for a wind is roused
In cavern where it housed:
Each white and quivering sail,
Of boats among the water leaves
Hollows and strains in the full-throated gale;
Each maiden sings again –
Each languid maiden sings again –
Had lulled to sleep with rest of spice and balm.
Miles down my river to the sea
They float and wane,
Long miles away from me.
Perhaps they say: 'She grieves,
Uplifted, like a beacon, on her tower.'
Perhaps they say: 'One hour
More, and we dance among the golden sheaves.'
Perhaps they say: 'One hour
More, and we stand,
Face to face, hand in hand;
Make haste, O slack gale, to the looked-for land!'
My trees are not in flower,
I have no bower,
And gusty creaks my tower,
And lonesome, very lonesome, is my strand.

*Readers: Barbara Jefford, T. P. McKenna*

*Full Selection:*
*The Pity of Love,* W. B. YEATS
*A Marginal Gloss on the Death of Irish,* AIDAN CARL MATTHEWS
*Sonnet from The Portugese,* ELIZABETH BARRETT BROWNING
*Meeting at Night,* ROBERT BROWNING
*How to Grow a Wisteria,* EDNA O'BRIEN

*Windy Nights*, ROBERT LOUIS STEVENSON
*A Poor Scholar of the Forties*, PADRAIC COLUM
*Miss Knightsbridge*, CANDIDA LYCETT-GREEN
*Meeting Point*, LOUIS MACNEICE
*Autumn*, CHRISTINA ROSSETTI
*The Power and the Glory*, GRAHAM GREENE
*Ulysses*, JAMES JOYCE
*If You Ever Go to Dublin*, PATRICK KAVANAGH
*After-Meeting*, CHRISTY BROWN

# LORD DENNING

## 1981

*The generally wise, frequently controversial and always venerable figure of the Master of the Rolls possessed, on the evidence of this programme, a personality of great warmth and robust humour. His selection was wide-ranging, showing a strong preference for the classics of English literature: Wordsworth, Browning, Jane Austen, Dickens, Betjeman, Shakespeare, Masefield, Kipling and so on. If there were few surprises, no real quirkiness, that is not to say that in making his selection Lord Denning merely fell back on to a half-remembered introduction to literature from his schooldays. On the contrary, it is clear that throughout his programme the items and authors chosen were those that after a lifetime of reading he genuinely loved the best.*

This evening I am going to throw all the law books out of the window. I have left them in my library the other side of the river. They are not fit to be read aloud – or at all. We are going to read to you some works of literature. In doing so I shall be following the advice of Sir Walter Scott in his novel *Guy Mannering*. When the lay clerk went into the lawyer's chambers, he found the walls lined, not with law books but with books of history and literature – the great authors – and on the walls a portrait or two. The lawyer, pointing to the books of history and literature, says: 'These are my tools of trade. A lawyer without history of literature is a mechanic, a mere working mason; if he have some knowledge of these, he may venture to call himself an architect.'

So there – let's be architects, but first a little bit of prose of my own. I'm going to tell you of a letter which I received a little while ago from a student. He knew I was Master of the Rolls. This is what he wrote from International Students' House in London:

Dear Lord Denning,
I am an Indian citizen. I graduated in mechanical engineering in the University of London and was awarded a Master of Science degree. I feel I have the necessary qualifications, motivation, energy, drive and personality to begin a successful career in an automobile industry. I will ever remain grateful to you if you will kindly help me to begin my professional career with your company, the Rolls Royce Motor Company.

I notice we have the Vicar here. He might like another little story of mine. This is when a Lord Bishop went to the Temple Church in London, where the lawyers congregate and the acoustics are not at all good. The Verger said to the Bishop, 'Pray, my Lord, speak very clearly and distinctly because the agnostics here are terrible.'

I expect that all of you know from childhood – as I do – the charming piece by Leigh Hunt about Abou Ben Adhem. It was a favourite of my dear friend and great advocate, Norman Birkett. Lady Denning used to recite it too when she was young.

### *Abou Ben Adhem*

LEIGH HUNT

Abou Ben Adhem (may his tribe increase!)
  Awoke one night from a deep dream of peace,
And saw, within the moonlight in his room,
Making it rich, and like a lily in bloom,

An angel writing in a book of gold:-
Exceeding peace had made Ben Adhem bold,
And to the presence in the room he said,
'What writest thou?' – The vision rais'd its head,
And with a look made of all sweet accord,
Answer'd, 'The names of those who love the Lord.'
'And is mine one?' said Abou. 'Nay, not so,'
Replied the angel. Abou spoke more low,
But cheerly still; and said, 'I pray thee, then,
Write me as one that loves his fellow men.'
The angel wrote, and vanish'd. The next night
It came again with a great wakening light,
And show'd the names whom love of God had blest,
And lo! Ben Adhem's name led all the rest.

Some people have said that my style of writing is similar to that of Lord Macaulay. I don't think so myself, but if I have been influenced by it, it is quite unconscious. I have always admired his writing and particularly the passage in which he describes the trial of Warren Hastings, when he appeared before the House of Lords on a charge of corruption in India.

## *Warren Hastings' Trial*

LORD MACAULAY

Hastings advanced to the bar, and bent his knee. The culprit was indeed not unworthy of that great presence. He had ruled an extensive and populous country, and made laws and treaties, had sent forth armies, had set up and pulled down princes. And in his high place he had so borne himself, that all had feared him, that most had loved him, and that hatred itself could deny him no title to glory, except virtue. He looked like a great man, and not like a bad man. A person small and emaciated, yet deriving dignity from a carriage which, while it indicated deference to the court, indicated also habitual self-possession and self-respect, a high intellectual forehead, a brow pensive, but not gloomy, a mouth of inflexible decision, a face pale and worn, but serene, on which was written, as legibly as under the picture in the council-chamber at Calcutta, *Mens aequa in arduis*; such was the aspect with which the great proconsul presented himself to his judges.

Each year – early in May – I go to a beautiful set of almshouses in Greenwich. They were founded 400 years ago by my predecessor, the Master of the Rolls at that time. I preach a sermon to the elderly ones there, some older than me. But I am no good at sermons. It being a lovely spring day I sometimes recite to them the words of Robert Browning which express our springtime better than any.

## *Home Thoughts from Abroad*

ROBERT BROWNING

O to be in England
Now that April's there,
And whoever wakes in England
Sees, some morning, unaware,
That the lowest boughs and the brushwood sheaf
Round the elm-tree bole are in tiny leaf,
While the chaffinch sings on the orchard bough
In England – now!

And after April, when May follows,
And the whitethroat builds, and all the swallows!
Hark, where my blossom'd pear-tree in the hedge
Leans to the field and scatters on the clover
Blossoms and dewdrops – at the bent spray's edge –
That's the wise thrush; he sings each song twice over,
Lest you should think he never could recapture
That first fine careless rapture!
And though the fields look rough with hoary dew,
All will be gay when noontide wakes anew
The buttercups, the little children's dower
– Far brighter than this gaudy melon-flower.

I always enjoy Charles Dickens, especially *Pickwick Papers*, and the trial of Bardell against Pickwick. But I prefer the time when Mr Pickwick and Sam Weller took the London coach to Ipswich. They stayed at the Great White Horse. When they went to bed, Mr Pickwick got into a room with double beds which he thought was his own. He put on his night-cap and was about to get undressed when a person with a candle came in and sat down at a dressing-table. It was a four-poster bed – he slipped behind the curtains with his head just peeping out and looked out to see who was there.

## *Pickwick Papers*

CHARLES DICKENS

Mr Pickwick almost fainted with horror and dismay. Standing before the dressing-glass was a middle-aged lady, in yellow curl-papers, busily engaged in brushing what ladies call their 'back-hair'. However the unconscious middle-aged lady came into that room, it was quite clear that she contemplated remaining there for the night; for she had brought a rushlight and shade with her, which, with praiseworthy caution against fire, she had stationed in a basin on the floor, where it was glimmering away, like a gigantic lighthouse in a particularly small piece of water. 'Bless my soul,' thought Mr Pickwick, 'what a dreadful thing!'

'Hem!' said the lady; and in went Mr Pickwick's head with automaton-like rapidity.

'I never met with anything so awful as this,' thought poor Mr Pickwick, the cold perspiration starting in drops upon his night-cap. 'Never. This is fearful . . .'

'This matter is growing alarming,' reasoned Mr Pickwick with himself.

'I can't allow things to go on in this way. By the self-possession of the lady it is clear to me that I must have come into the wrong room. If I call out she'll alarm the house; but if I remain here the consequences will be still more frightful.'. . .

He shrank behind the curtains, and called out very loudly:

'Ha – hum!' . . .

'Gracious Heaven!' said the middle-aged lady, 'what's that?'

'It's – its – only a gentleman, Ma'am, said Mr Pickwick from behind the curtains.

'A gentleman!' said the lady with a terrific scream.

'It's all over!' thought Mr Pickwick.

'A strange man!' shrieked the lady . . .

'Ma'am,' said Mr Pickwick, thrusting out his head, in the extremity of his desperation, 'Ma'am . . .'

'Wretch,' said the lady, covering her eyes with her hands, 'what do you want here?'

'Nothing, Ma'am; nothing whatever, Ma'am;' said Mr Pickwick earnestly.

Mr Pickwick then tried to explain that he must have mistaken this bedroom for his own.

'If this improbable story be really true, sir,' said the lady, sobbing violently, 'you will leave it instantly.'

'I will, Ma'am, with the greatest pleasure,' replied Mr Pickwick.

'Instantly, sir,' said the lady.

'Certainly, Ma'am,' interposed Mr Pickwick very quickly. 'Certainly, Ma'am. I – I am very sorry, Ma'am,' said Mr Pickwick, making his appearance at the bottom of the bed, 'to have been the innocent occasion of this alarm and emotion; deeply sorry, Ma'am.'

The lady pointed to the door. One excellent quality of Mr Pickwick's character was beautifully displayed at this moment, under the most trying circumstances. Although he had hastily put on his hat over his night-cap, after the manner of the old patrol; although he carried his shoes and gaiters in his hand, and his coat and waistcoat over his arm; nothing could subdue his native politeness.

'I am exceedingly sorry, Ma'am,' said Mr Pickwick, bowing very low.

'If you are, sir, you will at once leave the room,' said the lady.

'Immediately, Ma'am; this instant, Ma'am,' said Mr Pickwick, opening the door, and dropping both his shoes with a crash in so doing.

'I trust, Ma'am,' resumed Mr Pickwick, gathering up his shoes, and turning round to bow again: 'I trust, Ma'am, that my unblemished character, and the devoted respect I entertain for your sex, will plead as some slight excuse for this.' – but before Mr Pickwick could conclude the sentence the lady had thrust him into the passage, and locked and bolted the door behind him.

*Readers: Jill Balcon, Paul Rogers*

*Full Selection:*
*Abou Ben Adhem*, LEIGH HUNT

*Speech in the House of Commons 4 June 1940*, WINSTON CHURCHILL
*Warren Hastings' Trial* from the essay by LORD MACAULAY
*Upon Westminster Bridge*, WILLIAM WORDSWORTH
*Home Thoughts from Abroad*, ROBERT BROWNING
*Pride and Prejudice*, JANE AUSTEN
*Pickwick Papers*, CHARLES DICKENS
*King Henry V – St Crispin's Day Speech*, WILLIAM SHAKESPEARE
*Diary of a Church Mouse*, JOHN BETJEMAN
*The Soldier*, RUPERT BROOKE
*The Brook*, ALFRED, LORD TENNYSON
*Pilgrim's Progress*, JOHN BUNYAN
*Sea-Fever*, JOHN MASEFIELD
*The Glory of the Garden*, RUDYARD KIPLING
*Say Not the Struggle Naught Availeth*, ARTHUR HUGH CLOUGH
*Macavity: the Mystery Cat*, T. S. ELIOT
*Forefathers*, EDMUND BLUNDEN
*Four Things a Man Must Learn to Do*, HENRY VAN DYKE

# GERALD DURRELL

## 1976

*Many years ago, reading for the first time 'My Family and Other Animals' had me rattling the chair with laughter. At the time I had not heard of Gerald Durrell, not known that he was a very funny man who took great pleasure in the idiosyncrasies not only of his fellow men, but of all creatures, so the laughter contained an element of delighted surprise. The humour he conveys is not a trivialising one that sees wild creatures as somehow cute, but an essential element in his sharing with the reader his excitement at what he sees around him: 'I, in the days of my youth, used to read avidly every travel book that came my way, and I'd read something called, you know, "Ninety Years in Tibet, with Sidelights on the Plant Life, Animal Life, Zoo Geography, Geology, Natives and their customs", and I'd read five hundred pages of this and I'd discover that this man had spent ninety years in Tibet and nothing funny had ever happened to him. So I swore to myself, having been bored by hundreds of these tomes, that if I ever wrote about travel I would try and write a little bit humorously.'*

I was brought up in Greece and I was mad on animals from the word go. My mother, who was a reasonably honest woman, once said to me that the first word I ever spoke was in fact 'zoo'. I have being saying it in terms of despair ever since.

When I lived in Greece I could keep pets and have fun. In that respect, the natural world was to me an open book, but I also had to read in order to explore it thoroughly and one of the very first people I read was the great French naturalist Jean Henri Fabre – an enormously important man in terms of my development, and indeed in terms of the development of natural history, because he was one of the first people who proved that you could examine the workings of creatures and interpret them in a poetical fashion in beautiful prose, which really meant something, so that you didn't have to be a scientist to appreciate what he was talking about.

## *The Life of the Caterpillar*

J. H. FABRE

Physical science is today preparing to give us wireless telegraphy, by means of Hertzian waves. Can the Great Peacock have anticipated our efforts in this direction? In order to set the surrounding air in motion and to inform pretenders miles away, can the newly hatched bride have at her disposal electric or magnetic waves, which one sort of screen would arrest and another let through? In a word, does she, in her own manner, employ a kind of wireless telegraphy? I see nothing impossible in this: insects are accustomed to invent things quite as wonderful.

I therefore lodge the female in boxes of various characters. Some are made of tin, some of cardboard, some of wood. All are hermetically closed, are even sealed with stout putty. I also use a glass bell-jar standing on the insulating support of a pane of glass.

Well, under these conditions of strict closing, never a male arrives, not one, however favourable the mildness and quiet of the evening. No matter its nature, whether of metal or glass, of wood or cardboard, the closed receptacle forms an insuperable obstacle to the effluvia that betrays the captive's whereabouts. A layer of cotton two fingers thick gives the same result. I place the female in a large jar, tying a shoot of wadding over the mouth by way of a lid. This is enough to keep the neighbourhood in ignorance of the secrets of my laboratory. No male puts in an appearance.

On the other hand, make use of ill-closed cracked boxes, or even hide them in a drawer, in a cupboard; and, notwithstanding this added mystery, the Moths will arrive in numbers as great as when they come thronging to the trellised cage standing in full view on a table. I have retained a vivid recollection of an evening when the recluse was waiting in a hat-box at the bottom of a closed wall-cupboard. The Moths arrived, went to the door, struck it with their wings, knocked at it to express their wish to enter. Passing wayfarers, coming no one knows whence across the fields, they well knew what was inside there, behind those boards.

We must therefore reject the idea of any means of information similar to that of wireless telegraphy, for the first screen set up, whether a good conductor or a bad, stops the female's signals completely. To give these a free passage and carry them to a distance, one condition is indispensable: the receptacle in which the female is contained must be imperfectly closed, so as to establish a communication between the inner and the outer air. This brings us back to the probability of an odour, though that was contradicted by my experiment with naphthaline.

Fabre had an enormous effect on me as a young naturalist at the age of seven to ten. I read him avidly and he led me, as it were, by the hand into the undergrowth to observe insects and to learn how to observe them in fact.

I lived a fairly unconventional life in Greece, one way and another. I was allowed to do and read pretty well anything that I liked, and I lived a very interesting life in the sense that I lived in two worlds; by virtue of the currency in those days we were what could be described as multi-millionaires, and the sort of society that we moved in were multi-millionaires, but at the same time all my friends were among the peasants, so I saw real poverty on the one hand, and riches on the other hand. And I also had a very eccentric family who had eccentric friends, and this again opened up new windows to me. I also had a series of very extraordinary tutors, because I didn't have any conventional training as far as education was concerned. Even now I have difficulty signing my name with a cross. But I had these remarkable tutors who discovered that the only way they could teach me, in fact, was to teach me through animals. Everything had to be geared to animals; if they wanted to teach me mathematics for example they had to work out things like: 'If it takes a caterpillar six weeks to eat one leaf, how long will it take forty-six caterpillars to . . .' You know, all that sort of stuff. And my family's approach to life was very astringent and, I think, unconventionally good from the point of view of somebody who's growing up. I remember my mother once saying, in terms of despair almost, 'Why is it that we always think other people are peculiar?' and my brother replying 'Because they are.'

I think that poets by and large are failed naturalists. They seem to see our kinship with nature much more clearly than the average novelist. You can read page after page of interminable kitchen-sink stuff, where so-and-so's sleeping with so-and-so or going out with so-and-so, or so-and-so's reacting with so-and-so, and they never have a sentence which tells you that there's a sparrow chirping on the roof; which rather gives you the feeling that everything is kitchen sink. Whereas the poets do take you out of that, and have a much sharper eye in putting us into our context. We tend to step out of our context now. We've stepped out of nature and we're pretending to be God, which is a rather dangerous thing to do, and the poets, I think, push us back into where we belong. Now John Donne, who's probably one of the most moving, the most virile of the English poets, uses with incredible effect in a love poem, of all things a small parasite as a symbol of love.

## *The Flea*

JOHN DONNE

Mark but this flea, and mark in this,
How little that which thou deny'st me is;
It suck'd me first, and now sucks thee,
And in this flea, our two bloods mingled be;
Thou know'st that this cannot be said
A sin, nor shame, nor loss of maidenhead,
  Yet this enjoys before it woo,
  And pamper'd swells with one blood made of two,
  And this, alas, is more than we would do.

Oh stay, three lives in one flea spare,
Where we almost, yea more than married are.
This flea is you and I, and this
Our marriage bed, and marriage temple is;
Though parents grudge, and you, we're met,
And cloister'd in these living walls of jet.
  Though use make you apt to kill me,
  Let not to that, self-murder added be,
  And sacrilege, three sins in killing three.

Cruel and sudden, hast thou since
Purpled thy nail, in blood of innocence?
Wherein could this flea guilty be,
Except in that drop which it suck'd from thee?
Yet thou triumph'st, and say's that thou
Finds't not thyself, nor me, the weaker now;
  'Tis true, then learn how false, fears be;
  Just so much honor, when thou yield'st to me,
  Will waste, as this flea's death took life from thee.

My brother suffered much at my hands when I was young. As far as animal life was concerned, he always seemed to be bearing the brunt of whatever pets I happened to have. He was always being pecked by magpies or having an owl descend on his head when he least expected it, or a scorpion fall out of a matchbox, that sort of thing. So he really was not a great lover of animal life. But even he, as a poet, can be good.

I must admit this, albeit reluctantly, and this very short poem by him contains, I think, some very lovely images.

*The Cicada*

LAWRENCE DURRELL

Transparent sheath of the dead cicada,
The eyes stay open like a dead Jap,
Financially no spongy parts to putrefy
Simply snap off the scaly integument of mica.
You could make a tiny violin of such a body,
Lanterns for elves, varnish into brooches
And wear by lamplight this transparent stare of noon,
In gold or some such precious allegorical metal,
Which spells out the dead wine which follows soon.

Even my brother has moments.

Actually I shouldn't be rude about him because he has always helped and encouraged me. In fact it was he that really wanted me to be a writer, and not get mixed up with animals. He was always encouraging me to write even when I was young, and he's always been very proud of any progress that I've made. People always think that because there are two writers in the family there must be some sort of rivalry between them, but in this particular instance there isn't. I just simply tell him that he writes great literature and I write books that people read . . .

*Readers: Geoffrey Collins, Anne Rosenfeld*

*Full Selection:*
*The Life of the Caterpillar*, J. H. FABRE
*A Naturalist's Voyage Around the World* CHARLES DARWIN
*Mariana*, ALFRED, LORD TENNYSON
*The Flea*, JOHN DONNE
*The Cicada*, LAWRENCE DURRELL
*Travels in West Africa*, MARY KINGSLEY
*Winnie the Pooh*, A. A. MILNE
*An Attractive Impediment*, PATRICK CAMPBELL
*The Journey's Echo*, FREYA STARK

# SEAN O'FAOLAIN

## 1970

*When a poet or other writer presents 'With Great Pleasure', he or she generally makes an honest attempt to be self-revealing and entertaining. It seldom, however, contains writing of the quality that made him or her famous in the first place. It would be unfair to expect it to do so. The style of the programme is deliberately informal, a conversation with the audience. Indeed the presenters frequently extemporise from notes rather than deliver a fully fledged script. Sean O' Faolain, however, managed to maintain informality whilst from the first sentence leaving us in no doubt we were in the presence of a mind of poetic drive and sinew.*

Of all the countless words that we may remember from our early reading I think the least interesting are those we remember most easily – words that lie on the surface of our minds, that can pop up as effortlessly as a piece of toast out of a toaster – apt quotations for any chance occasion. The words I would like to resurrect here are deeper rooted, pieces of prose or verse that were planted in me by experience that it takes a conscious effort to recall, words that have become so much part of my purely instinctive being that they're like past pastures and cuds chewed long ago by some old ruminant animal who lives in a perpetual Now.

I was born in Cork in 1900 which makes me a man of the twenties. Meaning the 1820s – like Yeats, our last romantic: Shelley, Keats, Byron and all that, on to the pre-Raphaelites, Blake, Matthew Arnold. In other words, I grew up simple, sensuous and passionate in a nineteenth-century country town, differing only in so far as Dublin was and still is a somewhat larger nineteenth-century country town. In Cork the green hills walked down into the streets and the Atlantic flowed into them, sometimes literally, yet leaving us all in our smoky little valley with just enough of the oppressiveness of city life to make us relish the beauty, the escape, the release of the surrounding countryside. So, even if Cork was not Oxford, or Paris or London, feverishly intellectual or breathlessly competitive, it was inevitable that I should fall in love with English pastoral poetry, as a very young man with The Scholar Gypsy's abjurations to fly from the feverish contact of the busy world whose 'mental strife, though it gives no bliss yet spoils our rest'.

## *The Scholar Gypsy*

MATTHEW ARNOLD

Then fly our greetings, fly our speech and smiles!
  – As some grave Tyrian trader, from the sea,
  Described at sunrise an emerging prow
Lifting the cool-hair'd creepers stealthily,
  The fringes of a southward-facing brow
    Among the Aegean isles;
And saw the merry Grecian coaster come,
  Freighted with amber grapes, and Chian wine,
  Green bursting figs, and tunnies steep'd in brine;
And knew the intruders on his ancient home.

The young light-hearted Masters of the waves;
  And snatched his rudder, and shook out more sail,
    And day and night held on indignantly
  O'er the blue Midland waters with the gale,
    Betwixt the Syrtes and soft Sicily,
      To where the Atlantic raves
Outside the Western Straits, and unbent sails
  There, where down cloudy cliffs, through sheets of foam,
  Shy traffickers, the dark Iberians come;
And on the beach undid his corded bales.

Like so much of nineteenth-century nature poetry – and how odd that phrase 'nature poetry' sounds today! – 'The Scholar Gypsy' had one great drawback for me. It evoked the scenery, the details of life, even the ethos of another civilisation. If Cork was not Arnold's Oxford, alas!, neither, alas, was his Oxfordshire my County Cork. The furniture of the poem kept it as remote from me as Russia. Inglenooked alehouses, mossy barns, maidens dancing around ancient elms in May, nightingales, dingles – I had to look up that word in a dictionary – 'the line of festal lights in Christ Church Hall'. If it is true that the most difficult thing for any youth to do is to see life with his own eyes, it's also true that he carries on the bridge of his nose clotted eye-filters bequeathed to him by his elders. Poetry like Arnold's, for me, at that time, was enchanting but it was also emollient, escapist and ultimately unrevealing.

My Book of Revelation – I still have it, the spine gone, the pages dog-eared and foxed – was Kuno Meyer's translations from the Old Irish. Here I found poetry that was recognisable in every detail, at its best particular, almost always dramatic and personal. The words 'I' and 'me' are all over Irish poetry. It is our ethnic tendency, perhaps, to dramatise; and it makes for objectivity; and it saves us from what T. S. Eliot thought one of the weaknesses of all nineteenth-century English poetry – its habit of ruminating self-indulgently.

Here are a few verses from the long poem 'King and Hermit' where simply in order that the poet may present his nature poem as a little one-act play, the king is made to ask the hermit why he is a hermit. And the hermit's answer is the poem.

### *King and Hermit*

Old Irish trans. KUNO MEYER

I have chosen a hut in the wood
Because nobody sees it but God,
Between a hazel and an ash,
With a tall pine over it.

The kindly coloured summer
Pours into my dish
Pignuts, leeks and marjoram,
Morning sweet and fresh.

My music is the humming
Of tiny bees and chafers,
Or the woodcock and the geese
Drumming through the rain,

When the winter wails
Through the woven wood,
And the clouded waterfalls
Dull the whooping swans.

Here, free from strife and fighting
I can praise the King, my God,
Who fills my wood
With everything that's good.

A simple, spare, concrete, intimate, ungeneralised close-up. With scores of such poems in my mind I could, under the carved arch of any ruined Romanesque churchlet, deep in docks, nettles, mallow, cowdung, neglect and tinkers' rags, blend myself into ancestral memories of my own people.

It was the same with love poems. For every youth every love poem was written specially for him and her alone. He turns every love poem into a mirror of his desire. I may have, in self-protection, laughed with my friends over Meredith's 'Love in a Valley'. In secret I adored it.

*Love in a Valley*
GEORGE MEREDITH

Shy as the squirrel and wayward as the swallow,
  Swift as the swallow along the river's light
Circleting the surface to meet his mirrored winglets
  Fleeter she seems in her stay than in her flight.
Shy as the squirrel that leaps among the pinetops,
  Wayward as the swallow overhead at set of sun,
She whom I love is hard to catch and conquer,
  Hard, but O the glory of the winning were she won!

Two dozen idyllic, dancing verses of it, mightily effective for the springtime of youth, but though its sentiments are unassailable, all passionate feeling is held off – like the swallow in that excellent image, 'circleting the surface to meet his mirrored winglets . . . along the river's light'. So that very soon, when hot desire fanned love to passion and, as all young men do at that stage, I was wondering what on earth to do about it all, I began to think it a carminative poem – that lovely adjective (in case you do not happen to know) simply means any medicine that lets the gas out of you.

Besides, Meredith, like Arnold, expected more stock responses than I, as an alien, could give to the inevitable red-roofed 'mossed old farmhouse', the cottage garden with its dainty tulips and lilies (tulips I might manage but lilies were beyond my means), the boys playing cricket on the village green, the white owl curving through the dusk, the doves among the fir trees that 'through the long noon coo, crooning through the coo'. These furnishings were all elements in an enviable tradition of civil living in an island that had not been invaded since William the Conqueror. They were, in Henry James's words about Nathaniel Hawthorne – a writer whose unfinished environment I was better fitted to understand – all part of 'the dense, richer, warmer European spectacle' that I would not share for many years to come.

'Love in the Valley' is a charming love poem but it is far removed from the wilder passions proper to our natural environment, our tradition, as the half-tamed barbarians that, at our best and worst, we so splendidly are.

After Nature and love my generation found its greatest release through political revolt. Politics and poetry, however, have never been fertile bedfellows, until, after the event, when the poet goes to bed with a memory or a ghost. I know that I read all Shelley's rebellious poetry during those troubled years. I remember being held up by a British patrol in Cork, on a bridge at midnight, and how the young lieutenant in charge drew from my pocket a small blue volume – which I still have. He flashed his torch on the title, *The Poems of Shelley*, returned it and with a faint smile said, 'Pass on!' I almost thought he was going to add, 'Friend'. I see that in this little volume I wrote the words *fine stuff* beside 'The Mask of Anarchy' and the 'Ode to Liberty'. They are certainly not part of my flower-garden today. If those poems are not in Wyndham Lewis's anthology of bad poetry, *The Stuffed Owl*, they should be.

## *I Met Murder on the Way*

P. B. SHELLEY

I met murder on the way –
He had a mask like Castlereagh –
Very smooth he looked and grim;
Seven bloodhounds followed him.

All were fat and well they might
Be in admirable plight,
For one by one and two by two
He tossed them human hearts to chew . . .

And the little children who
Around his feet played to and fro
Thinking every tear a gem
Had their brains knocked out of them . . .

Yeats was more suitable for us than Shelley but Yeats, unfortunately, did not publish his finest patriotic poems, such as 'Easter 1916' or 'Sixteen Dead Men', until 1921, but he did publish one blazing poem that we all knew in 1914 – following the death of his old Fenian friend John O'Leary and Jim Larkin's gallant but doomed Tramway Strike in 1913.

## *September 1913*

W. B. YEATS

What need you, being come to sense,
But fumble in a greasy till
And add the halfpence to the pence
And prayer to shivering prayer, until
You have dried the marrow from the bone?
For men were born to pray and save:
Romantic Ireland's dead and gone,
It's with O'Leary in the grave.

Yet they were of a different kind
The names that stilled your childish play,
They have gone about the world like wind,
But little time had they to pray
For whom the hangman's rope was spun.

And what, God help us, could they save?
Romantic Ireland's dead and gone,
It's with O'Leary in the grave.

Was it for this the wild geese spread
The grey wing upon every tide;
For this that all the blood was shed,
For this Edward Fitzgerald died,
And Robert Emmet and Wolfe Tone,
All that delirium of the brave?
Romantic Ireland's dead and gone,
It's with O'Leary in the grave.

Yet could we turn the years again,
And call those exiles as they were
In all their loneliness and pain,
You'd cry, 'Some woman's yellow hair
Has maddened every mother's son':
They weighed so lightly what they gave.
But let them be, they're dead and gone,
They're with O'Leary in the grave.

It may seem a strange wish to dine at journey's end with Pater and with Donne, and Daedalus. But in 'death's dream kingdom' as Eliot calls this world of ours, there are also many mansions and, like Keats, we must traverse them all, opening door after door, embracing all experience. It may be that what blends all these men together is the eternal note of sadness. And that was Arnold's phrase for Sophocles, who heard it long ago on the Aegaean, as Daedalus must have when he saw Icarus tumbling into the sea under the heat of the sun.

*Reader: Ray McAnally*

*Full Selection:*
*The Scholar Gypsy*, MATTHEW ARNOLD
*King and Hermit Old Irish* trans. KUNO MEYER
*Love in the Valley*, GEORGE MEREDITH

*I Cannot Tear Myself in Two*, TOMAS O'HUIGIN trans. FRANK O'CONNOR
*I Met Murder on the Way*, PERCY BYSSHE SHELLEY
*September 1913*, W. B. YEATS
*Easter 1916*, W. B. YEATS
*Marius the Epicurean*, PATER
*The Progresse of the Soul*, JOHN DONNE
*Portrait of the Artist as a Young Man*, JAMES JOYCE

# CHRISTOPHER FRY

## 1986

*As a schoolboy in the fifties and as an amateur actor in the sixties I grew up with Christopher Fry's verse plays and elegant translations of French playwrights. Both are still being performed constantly, both by amateurs and professional companies. Listening to a voice from the radio and imagining what that person behind it looks like frequently leads to astonishment on finding out that the speaker looks nothing like the figure imagined. So it was with Christopher Fry. Hearing his voice on the telephone and imagining someone rather tall and patrician, I was both surprised and delighted to find that he was shorter than I expected, with a genial appearance and manner, and looking at least fifteen years younger than his true age. His performance and hold of an audience were exemplary, for example taking care to laugh at jokes in the pieces – even though he knew them well and indeed had heard them a number of times in rehearsal – to encourage the audience to share in them more fully and hence laugh louder. It made for more pleasure for them and a better show for us. Although his place in the history of drama is assured, it seems he may have a further pleasure to offer. At the time of writing there is talk of a new play for radio.*

Faced with putting together half-an-hour's worth of prose and verse brought out all the indecision in me. After seventy years of reading, seventy hours wouldn't have seemed too much; so, to narrow the range of choice, I began by leaving out almost all of the big guns – no Shakespeare or Tolstoy or Keats and so forth – and many other pleasurable ones, Charles Lamb for instance (when did you last read him?) or Sir Thomas Browne or, eccentrically perhaps, Carlyle. But it's prodigal to spend time telling you what I haven't chosen. The choice in the end was governed by a vague sense of chronology, and partly by some slight linking ideas – journeying is one, and visiting another.

It's easy enough to know where to begin: we can start with my starting to learn to read, the first steps of a long journey to follow. The first lessons, of course, must have been of the Cat on the Mat kind; I don't remember anything about that. But then my Aunt Ada put before me her copy of *Pilgrim's Progress*, given to her by her father for Christmas 1865. First of all I feasted on the illustrations – one hundred and two of them, and marvellous they were – and then the serious matter of reading began.

Here, from the second part of the book, is the description of how Christiana and the children came to the Enchanted Ground. There is a note at the bottom of the page explaining that 'the mist and darkness of this stage are consistent with the spirit of the enchanted scene. Worldly pleasure waves her magic wand, and bids a cloud of misty incense to arise, and mysterious darkness to descend; and under these influences the soul is induced to sleep the deadly sleep of oblivion and forgetfulness.'

This is how John Bunyan describes it.

## *Pilgrim's Progress*

JOHN BUNYAN

By this time they were got to the Enchanted Ground, where the air naturally tended to make one drowsy: and that place was all grown over with briars and thorns, excepting here and there, where was an enchanted arbour, upon which if a man sits, or in which if a man sleeps, it is a question, say some, whether he shall ever rise or wake again in this world. Over this forest therefore they went, both one and another: Mr Great-heart went before, for that he was their guide, Mr Valiant-for-truth came behind, being rear-guard; for fear lest peradventure some fiend, or dragon, or giant, or thief, should fall upon their rear, and so do mischief. They went on here, each man with his sword drawn in his hand, for they knew it was a dangerous place. Also they cheered up one another, as well they could. Feeble-mind, Mr Great-heart commanded, should come up after him, and Mr Despondency was under the eye of Mr Valiant.

Now they had not gone far, but a great mist and darkness fell upon them all, so that they could scarce, for a great while, one see the other: wherefore they were forced for some time to feel for one another by words, for they walked not by sight. But any one must think that here was but sorry going for the best of them all; but how much worse was it for the women and children, who both of feet and heart were but tender. Yet so it was, that, through the encouraging words of him that led in the front, and of him that brought them up behind, they made a pretty good shift to wag along.

'They were forced for some time to feel for one another by words.' I suppose that is what writing is, what all human communication is. I think it's a malady of most writers to have the feeling from time to time that their publishers could be making a greater effort to push the sale of their books. So it's unexpected to find that when Sylvia Townsend Warner's publisher wrote lamenting that he hadn't sold more copies of some book of hers, she wrote that he should look at things differently.

## *From a Letter to Her Publisher*

SYLVIA TOWNSEND WARNER

I don't think four thousand copies such a wretched sale. You should try to take a longer view of it. If you had sold four thousand female kittens, for instance, you would think you had done marvels.

Now that we're on to the subject of what the poet Gray called 'the tabby kind', I wish we had time for William Cowper's 'Retired Cat' who:

Recumbent at her ease, ere long,

And lulled by her own humdrum song,
She left the cares of life behind . . .

But first in the Catalogue of poets is T. S. Eliot. I met him for the first time at almost exactly the time of the publication of *The Book of Practical Cats*. I know it was then because the 1939 war had just begun. I told him that I had thought of trying to join a Fire Brigade in London, but had a poor head for heights. 'You should specialise', he said, 'in basements.'

## *The Naming of Cats*

T. S. ELIOT

The Naming of Cats is a difficult matter,
It isn't just one of your holiday games;
You may think at first I'm as mad as a hatter
When I tell you, a cat must have THREE DIFFERENT NAMES.
First of all, there's the name that the family use daily,
Such as Peter, Augustus, Alonzo or James,
Such as Victor or Jonathan, George or Bill Bailey –
All of them sensible everyday names.
There are fancier names if you think they sound sweeter,
Some are for gentlemen, some for the dames:
Such as Plato, Admetus, Electra, Demeter –
But all of them sensible everyday names.
But I tell you, a cat needs a name that's particular,
A name that's peculiar, and more dignified,
Else how can he keep up his tail perpendicular,
Or spread out his whiskers, or cherish his pride?
Of names of this kind I can give you a quorum,
Such as Munkustrap, Quaxo, or Coricopat,
Such as Bombalurina, or else Jellyorum –
Names that never belong to more than one cat.
But above and beyond there's still one name left over,
And that is the name that you never will guess;
The name that no human research can discover –
But THE CAT HIMSELF KNOWS, and will never confess.
When you notice a cat in profound meditation,
A reason, I tell you, is always the same;
His mind is engaged in a rapt contemplation

Of a thought, of the thought, of the thought of his name;
His ineffable effable
Effanineffable
Deep and inscrutable singular Name.

W.H. Hudson was both a journeyer and a visitor. In 1900 he visited Chichester, near my present home, and took the darkest view of the city. He found it 'profoundly depressing'. 'The depression,' he says, 'is probably the malady commonly known as "the Chichesters" from which many persons who visit this town are said to suffer.' I hope and believe he would have a very different opinion now.

There's so much of his writing about England that would be a pleasure to include here – from *Hampshire Days*, or *A Shepherd's Life* or *Nature in Downland*; but I've chosen a piece from his first book, a novel, *The Purple Land*, in which the hero, leaving his wife behind in Montevideo, sets out on horse-back to ride to a place two hundred miles away. He comes to a long, low house thatched with rushes, and asks to lodge there for the night.

## *The Purple Land*

W. H. HUDSON

I was kindly received by a numerous family, consisting of the owner, his hoary-headed old mother-in-law, his wife, three sons, and five daughters, all grown up . . . Besides the people, there were dogs, cats, turkeys, ducks geese, and fowls without number. Not content with all these domestic birds and beasts, they also kept a horrid, shrieking paraoquet, which the old woman was incessantly talking to, explaining to the others all the time, in little asides, what the bird said or wished to say, or rather, what she imagined it wished to say. There were also several tame young ostriches, always hanging about the big kitchen or living-room on the look-out for a brass thimble, or iron spoon, or other little metallic *bonne bouche* to be gobbled up when no one was looking. A pet armadillo kept trotting in and out, in and out, the whole evening, and a lame gull perpetually wailing for something to eat – the most persistent beggar I ever met in my life.

The people were very jovial and rather industrious for so indolent a country. The land was their own, the men tended the cattle

. . . while the women made cheeses, rising before daylight to milk the cows . . . There were also several small children, belonging, I believe, to the daughters, notwithstanding the fact that they were unmarried. I was greatly amazed at hearing the name of one of these youngsters. Such Christian names as Trinity, Heart of Jesus, Nativity, John of God, Conception, Ascension, Incarnation, are common enough, but these had scarcely prepared me to meet with a fellow-creature named – well, Circumcision!

The most astounding journeys of the human being were those voyages into the unknown – the discovery, for example, of 'North and South Americay', as Arthur Hugh Clough rhymes them in an untitled poem. Clough, who had so much brilliance when he was at school at Rugby under Dr Arnold, died at the age of 42, before his gifts had borne all the fruit they promised. I have sometimes thought that in his 'Amours de Voyage' he may have given that hint of a verse-line which Eliot followed up in 'The Cocktail Party' and 'The Elder Statesman'.

In this piece he speaks for all of us in asking 'How in heaven's name did Columbus get over?'

## *How in Heaven's Name Did Columbus Get Over?*

ARTHUR HUGH CLOUGH

How in heaven's name did Columbus get over,
Is a pure wonder to me, I protest,
Cabot and Raleigh too, that well-read rover,
Frobisher, Dampier, Drake and the rest;
Bad enough all the same,
For them that after came;
But in great heaven's name,
How he should ever think
That on the other brink
Of this wild waste, terra firma should be,
Is a pure wonder, I must say, to me.

How a man should ever hope to get thither,
Even if he knew there was another side,
But to suppose he should come any hither,
Sailing straight on into chaos untried:
In spite of the motion,

Across the whole ocean,
To stick to the notion
That in some nook or bend
Of a sea without end,
He should find North and South America,
Was pure madness, indeed, I must say.

What if wise men had, as far back as Ptolemy,
Judged that the earth like an orange was round,
None of them ever said, Come along, follow me,
Sail to the West, and the East will be found.
Many a day before
Ever they'd come ashore
Of the San Salvador
Sadder and wiser men,
They'd have turned back again;
And that *he* did not, but did cross the sea,
Is a pure wonder, I must say, to me.

Tennyson's 'Ode on the Death of the Duke of Wellington' written while he was Poet Laureate moved me as a small boy. Over a century later there was another memorable laureate poem, John Betjeman's 'A Ballad of the Investiture 1969': and in it you will find the visiting, the journeying, the detail of historic event, and Betjeman's true voice, not a ceremoniously assumed one. The 'Harry' mentioned at the end of the first stanza is The Reverend H. A. Williams; at the time of the poem he was Fellow and Dean of the Chapel of Trinity College, Cambridge.

## *A Ballad of the Investiture 1969*

JOHN BETJEMAN

The moon was in the Cambridge sky
And bathed Great Court in silver light
When Hastings-Bass and Woods and I
And quiet Elizabeth, tall and white,
With that sure clarity of mind
Which comes to those who've truly dined,
Reluctant rose to say good-night;
And all of us were bathed the while
In the large moon of Harry's smile.

Then, sir, you said what shook me through
So that my courage almost fails:
'I want a poem out of you
On my Investiture in Wales.'
Leaving, you slightly raised your hand –
'And that,' you said, 'is a command.'
For years I wondered what to do
And now, at last, I've thought it better
To write a kind of rhyming letter.

Spring frocks, silk hats, at morning's prime,
One of a varied congregation
I glided out at breakfast time,
With Euston's Earl from Euston Station,
Through Willesden's bleak industrial parts,
Through Watford on to leafy Herts
Bound for a single destination.
Warwicks and Staffs were soaked in rain;
So was the open Cheshire plain.

The railway crossed the river Dee
Where Mary called the cattle home,
The wide marsh widened into sea,
The wide sea whitened into foam.
The green Welsh hills came steeply down
To many a cara-circled town –
Prestatyn, Rhyl – till here were we,
As mountains rose on either hand,
Awed strangers in a foreign land.

I can't forget the climbing street
Below Caernarvon's castle wall,
The dragon flag, the tramp of feet,
The gulls' perturbed, insistent call,
Bow-windowed house-fronts painted new,
Heads craning out to get a view,
A mounting tension stilling all –
And, once within the castle gate,
The murmuring hush of those who wait.

Wet banners flap. The sea mist clears.
Colours are backed by silver stone.
Moustached hereditary peers
Are ranged in rows behind the throne.
With lifted sword the rites begin.
Earl Marshal leads the victims in.
The Royal Family waits alone.
Now television cameras whirr
Like cats at last induced to purr.

You know those moments that there are
When, lonely under moon and star,
You wait upon a beach?
Suddenly all Creation's near
And complicated things are clear,
Eternity in reach!
So we who watch the action done –
A mother to her kneeling son
The Crown of office giving –
Can hardly tell, so rapt our gaze
Whether but seconds pass or days
Or in what age we're living.

You knelt a boy, you rose a man.
And thus your lonelier life began.

In 1936 or thereabouts my wife and I used to get great pleasure from an anthology of passages from letters written to E. V. Lucas, in a book he edited called *Post-Bag Diversions* – particularly from the only one not in fact written to him, but written by a young girl to her aunt. The War came, and we moved, and the book disappeared, and it took me fifty years to find it again. But it turned up at last a few months ago, and, turning to the letter, we got as much pleasure from it as we had done before. Unfortunately Lucas doesn't tell us the name of the girl, or the date of writing.

*Letter from a Girl to Her Aunt Telling of a Remarkable Experience at a Dinner Party:*
from 'Post-Bag Diversions' edited by E. V. LUCAS

I went in to dinner with a very shy young man – rather pretty he was, with a fair moustache. I made a very bad beginning because I took hold of the back of my chair and the top came off in my hand just as Mr Smith was beginning to say grace, and it so upset me that I dropped my roll straight into my soup with a splash. Then I couldn't make out the young man at all. He talked a great deal of slang but he didn't seem to want to take a ticket for our café chantant and he said he never danced, but I never thought he was a parson because of his ordinary evening dress and his moustache.

Then a terrible drama began. We were eating mince-pies and I suddenly looked and beheld Daddy tethered by a string leading from his mouth to the middle of the table. A bit of the table centre had frayed, a string had crossed his plate and Daddy had eaten the end with his mince-pie. I felt the shy young man was talking to me but I never heard a word he said, and I caught Mum's eye who was opposite. She saw it too and began to grow redder and redder . . .

Daddy in blissful ignorance was talking blithely to his neighbour and chewing mince-pie and string. Then he moved his head and the string caught the wine-glasses. They wobbled about; he looked rather worried – put them straight – and then of course they wobbled again. At last he began to think something was going wrong so he put a large piece of mince-pie out of his mouth and on to his plate and all was well. Then the maid took Daddy's plate away and the portion of mince-pie remained behind! It sat on the table in front of him. Mum and I were going through gymnastic feats to keep our faces straight. She was simply red in the face and the tears began to run down my cheeks. Then my dear Papa, still being blind to the awful situation, knocked the piece of mince-pie off the table on to his knee, thereby pulling the string so that a portion of the table centre jumped forward and the glasses hopped about. Then he continued his conversation and Mum and I were just beginning to calm down a bit when he suddenly pushed the table centre back and up flew the bit of mince-pie off his knee on to the table with a wild hop that nearly finished Mum and me off . . .

Finally I believe he cut the string but before that happened I was roused by the shy young man repeating over and over again: 'I don't know why you should laugh, I am sure. I shouldn't say I was a curate if I wasn't. I don't see why it's so funny.' All the time he was explaining he was a curate at St Thomas's I never heard a word. I was reduced to mopping my tears with my dinner-napkin and giving dreadful and unexpected gurgles and the more I tried to explain that I wasn't laughing at him the more certain he got that I was – so it never got settled at all. And Daddy never knew till we told him all about it driving home.

*Readers: Sarah Badel, Christopher Fry*

*Full Selection:*
*Pilgrim's Progress*, JOHN BUNYAN
*Ode on the Death of the Duke of Wellington*, ALFRED, LORD TENNYSON
*Love's Caution*, W. H. DAVIES
*Extract from a Letter to Her Publisher*, SYLVIA TOWNSEND WARNER
*Retired Cat*, WILLIAM COWPER
*The Naming of Cats*, T. S. ELIOT
*The Naming of Parts*, HENRY REED
*Little Dorrit*, CHARLES DICKENS
*The Purple Land*, W. H. HUDSON
*How in Heaven's Name Did Columbus Get Over*, ARTHUR HUGH CLOUGH
*Lord Jim*, JOSEPH CONRAD
*Frederick the Great*, THOMAS MANN
*A Ballad of the Investiture 1969*, JOHN BETJEMAN
*The Mayor of Casterbridge*, THOMAS HARDY
*The Later Years of Thomas Hardy*, F. E. HARDY
*A Luncheon*, MAX BEERBOHM
*Letter from a Girl to Her Aunt Telling of a Remarkable Experience at a Dinner Party* (From 'Post Bag Diversions' edited by E. V. Lucas)
*Divine Poems XIV*, JOHN DONNE
*Ecclesiastes*, 12

# *PROFESSOR ALAN GEMMELL*

## *1982*

*As a newly graduated botanist, Alan Gemmell applied for a Commonwealth Fellowship to the United States. When asked what sort of research he intended to do there, he replied 'I want to research on improving golf course greens.' A far cry, perhaps, from presenting 'Gardeners' Question Time', but it is a clear example of the good humour that has entertained millions of listeners through the years. The story of how he got that job too is told below. His account of how he made his choice for 'With Great Pleasure' is perhaps the most convincing of many I have read. 'Why they gave me pleasure I'm not awfully sure in some cases. In some I'm absolutely certain. In others I can rationalise and make up reasons why I like them, but some others I just like because they are. And I think always it's a mistake to look for inwardness in everything; simplicity is a virtue in itself.'*

Anybody who has been born in Glasgow – you can only be born in Glasgow once – always has a deep sentimental attachment to it. It is such a jolly, dirty, rough, drunken city, but it is full of a very kind set of people with a language of their own. If you listen to an interview of streetmen – passers-by in Glasgow streets – they need translating, half of them. And Glasgow has a sense of humour all its own. There are only two cities to my mind in Britain which one recognises as having real personalities. One is Glasgow and the other is Liverpool. They both are jolly, they both are dirty, but they have a warmth and humour about them which transcends the apparent disadvantages which physically they might suffer from.

To find a quotation about Glasgow is easy because there are lots of books which stress the rather dirty side of Glasgow, but I'd like to offer you an extract from a book called *Dancing in the Streets* by a tiny little man called Clifford Hanley, which explains one side of Glasgow life beautifully.

## *That Music Stuff*

CLIFFORD HANLEY

There is always a lot of singing in Glasgow, everybody does it. Burns songs, pop songs, folk songs, operatic songs, patriotic songs, all kinds of songs. But mostly, in terms of sheer bulk, passionately sentimental songs.

Every wedding in Glasgow proves that every family in Glasgow has at least one singing uncle, usually called Willie. The Uncle Willies tend to choose songs with a bit of tone, like 'Red, Red Rose', or the 'Rowan Tree'. Both of these are certain death to amateur singers, but they die happy and proud. They take pride in a good-going tremolo, produce very rolling r's, very broad a's, and o's and u's so narrow you could slice a cheese with them, and whatever the tempo, when they hit a good note fair and square, they hang on to it till they've milked it of every drop of passion.

Singing is not permitted by law in Glasgow pubs, because Glasgow understands the dangerous power of music, which inflames as readily as it soothes; especially as pub singers would always be liable to come up with 'The Wild Colonial Boy', or 'Ra Sash my Farra Wore', either of them guaranteed to spark off a crusade.

But buskers sing outside the pubs, and customers sing after they leave the pubs. They still cling to their ancient favourites, for instance:

> 'Ra pale mune wos raaaaaaaaaaaaaaaa-ising,
> Above rgrnmounte-e-e-e-e-e-ens . . .'

Or the song that is the Glasgow drunkard's national anthem, although Glasgow (and Will Fyffe) gave the rest of the world 'I belong to Glasgow' for the world's drinking parties. But

Glasgow's own choice is 'The Bonnie Wells o' Wearie', pronounced 'Rab Onie Wells a Wee-a-rie'. Glaswegians never sing this song sober because it is believed to bring on rain.

I left Glasgow and moved to live in the west coast town of Troon. In school we learnt a verse of poetry every night. We had to recite it the next day. You could walk round the school and through the windows of the classrooms you'd hear 'Gray's Elegy' being done, the curfew was tolling the knell in 4b or whatever it was. The main town on the west coast of Scotland, in my mind, is always Ayr, and I went to Ayr Academy, founded in the thirteenth century, a school with an enormous sense of tradition and history. The Romans were in Ayr, Wallace and Bruce started the wars against the English in Ayr. In fact, the only history I ever learnt was Scots history. I couldn't tell you the name of a single King or Queen of England apart from Edward the First because Scotland beat him at the battle of Bannockburn. But in Ayr there was another thing – Burns was born just outside Ayr. We were made to learn and got to like and love his poetry. He's difficult in some of his things, but to my mind he's the best lyric poet writer I've ever met. Practically all his words are monosyllables, and yet they convey thoughts that are very lovely, very deep. And one of the simplest and best is the one that Cliff Hanley mentioned.

## *A Red, Red Rose*

ROBERT BURNS

O my Luve's like a red, red rose,
 That's newly sprung in June;
O my Luve's like the melodie
That's sweetly played in tune.

As Fair art thou, my bonie lass,
 So deep in luve am I;
And I will love thee still, my Dear,
 Till a' the seas gang dry.

Till a' the seas gang dry, my Dear,
 And the rocks melt wi' the sun;
O I will love thee still, my Dear,
 While the sands o' life shall run.

And fare thee weel, my only Luve!
And fare thee weel, a while!
And I will come again, my Luve,
Tho' it were ten thousand mile!

When I went up to the University at Glasgow, I went up with the full intention of reading Honours Chemistry and becoming a school teacher. But across the road from us in Troon there lived a man called Daniel Grant O'Brien to whom I've always been grateful. He was an agriculturalist who worked in the Agricultural College at Auchincruive near Ayr who one day said to my mother, 'If Alan can get a good degree in Botany, I can get him a job.' This was at the time of the Depression, so when I came home from the University one day my mother met me at the door and said, 'You're not a chemist any more, you're a botanist.' When I was a boy at school I had always thought of Botany as a terribly feminine occupation, that it was to do with gathering flowers, that it was to do with everything that was gentle and Victorian. But then I got an interest in Natural History and I started reading Gilbert White. He wrote *The Natural History of Selborne* in 1788. He writes a lot about birds, but in one letter he writes to the Honourable Daines Barrington about botany, and it was this that made me decide to accept my mother's command. I had little option.

## *Letter to The Honourable Daines Barrington from Natural History and Antiquities of Selborne*

GILBERT WHITE

The standing objection to botany has always been, that it is a pursuit that amuses the fancy and exercises the memory, without improving the mind or advancing any real knowledge: and, where the science is carried no farther than a mere systematic classification, the charge is but too true. But the botanist that is desirous of wiping off this aspersion should be by no means content with a list of names, he should study plants philosophically, should investigate the laws of vegetation, should examine the powers and virtues of efficacious herbs, should promote their cultivation; and graft the gardener, the planter, and the husbandman, on the phytologist. Not that system is by any means to be thrown aside; without system the field of Nature would be a pathless wilderness: but system should be subservient to, not the main object of, pursuit.

Instead of examining the minute distinctions of every various species of obscure genus, the botanist should endeavour to make himself acquainted with those that are useful. You shall see a man readily ascertain every herb of the field, yet hardly know wheat from barley, or at least one sort of wheat or barley from another.

But of all sorts of vegetation the grasses seem to be most neglected; neither the farmer nor the grazier seem to distinguish the annual from the perennial, the hardy from the tender, nor the succulent and nutritive from the dry and juiceless.

The study of grasses would be of great consequence to a northerly and grazing kingdom. The botanist that could improve the sward of the district where he lived would be a useful member of society: to raise a thick turf on a naked soil would be worth volumes of systematic knowledge; and he would be the best commonwealth's man that could occasion the growth of 'two blades of grass where only one was seen before'.

Every gardener starts as a reluctant gardener and I did this. My father bade me do it, and being a dutiful obedient son, I half did it. But I've got to like it. After a bit of wandering I ended up in Manchester, at the University there, where I was a lecturer in the Botany Department. A fellow lecturer in the Botany Department, a man called Samson, was a charming man who smoked a pipe; he always knocked it out in the palm of his hands and then rubbed his hands over his face and by half past nine in the morning he had black stripes down his face. I remember him meeting me in the corridor one day and saying to me in all seriousness, 'You know, Alan, what's wrong with this University is that there are no eccentrics in it.' And there he was . . . But Samson was a very good botanist, especially a horticultural botanist, and he had been asked to participate in a new gardening programme that was starting in Manchester in 1947. He had participated in it for about a couple of years and then, probably thanks to his face, he was appointed to a chair of Botany in the University of Ebaden in West Africa. He was asked if he could suggest somebody who might replace him in 'Gardeners'

Question Time'. Now Samson was a Scotsman, and if you ask a Scotsman a question like that he's not going to suggest a Welshman or an Englishman, so he said, 'Now, there's a tall, handsome, dark-haired young man in the Department called Gemmell, try him.' So I started in 1949. And because it's been such a major part of life, I wondered what bit about gardening gave me the most pleasure, and I thought of the poems, as you all will do, about daffodils and daisies and 'Bavarian Gentians' and poems like that, and decided no, I won't have that. What I will have is an essay which was written by Francis Bacon in 1625 about gardens.

## *The Moral and Historical Works of Lord Bacon*
## *Chapter XLVI – of Gardens*

FRANCIS BACON

God Almighty first planted a garden; and, indeed, it is the purest of human pleasures; it is the greatest refreshment to the spirits of man; without which buildings and palaces are but gross handy-works; and as man shall ever see, that, when ages grow to civility and elegancy, men come to build stately, sooner than to garden finely; as if gardening were the greater perfection. I do hold it in the royal ordering of gardens, there ought to be gardens for all months in the year, in which, severally, things of beauty may be then in season.

And because the breath of flowers is far sweeter in the air (where it comes and goes, like the warbling of music), than in the hand, therefore nothing is more fit for that delight, than to know what be the flowers and plants that do best perfume the air. Roses, damask and red, are fast flowers of their smells; so that you may walk by a whole row of them, and find nothing of their sweetness; yea, though it be in a morning's dew. Bays, likewise, yield no smell as they grow, rosemary little, nor sweet marjoram; that which, above all others, yields the sweetest smell in the air, is the violet, especially the white double violet, which comes twice a year, about the middle of April, and about Bartholomew-tide. Next to that is the musk-rose; then the strawberry-leaves dying, with a most excellent cordial smell; then the flower of the vines, it is a little dust like the dust of a bent, which grows upon the cluster in the first coming forth; then the sweet-briar then wallflowers, which are very delightful to be set under a parlour or lower chamber window; then pinks and gilliflower; then the flowers of the lime-tree; then the honeysuckles, so they be somewhat afar off. Of bean-flowers I speak not, because they are field flowers; but those which perfume the air most delightfully, not passed by as the rest, but being trodden upon and crushed, are three; that is, burnet, wild thyme, and water-mints; therefore you are to set whole alleys of them, to have the pleasure when you walk or tread.

I've often wondered, because I was trained as a scientist, and have lived all my life as a scientist really, what is the peculiar attraction of gardens – why so many people do, and enjoy, gardening. I think it's a combination of a number of things: First of all it gives very ordinary people the power to create something that's beautiful out of bare soil. For those that are sedentary, it gives them physical exercise if they'll take advantage of it. It also has a marvellous thing about it that somehow or other, your mistakes in gardening are never permanent – if the thing dies you can try it again next year, in the same or in a different place, a different variety, you can plant it at a different time. Finally – I don't know if it's a combination of all these or if it's something quite different – constant working in the garden gives you what I hate to call 'a peace and a philosophy and a kind of mystic communion', which sounds terribly twee, but undoubtedly is true. This feeling about gardens is not mine alone – it's very very many people's and it was expressed in a dialogue which was written by Ralph Austen in 1676. It's a dialogue between the husbandman and the fruit trees in the orchard.

## *A Dialogue Between the Husbandman and Fruit-trees*

RALPH AUSTEN

HUSBANDMAN. Methinks ye swagger and are very brave this May morning, in your beautiful blossoms and green leaves. Whence had ye all this gallantry?

FRUIT-TREES. It pleased our bountiful Creator to bestow it upon us; but it is for thee, and for the sake of mankind which engageth thee, and all men, to acknowledge it, and to serve Him and praise Him with more cheerfulness. This is our language and lesson to all men, which every particular tree among us does daily speak aloud.

HUSBANDMAN. Ye have many visitors, frequently. Have you this familiar discourse with every one as we have at present, and as often as we are disposed?

FRUIT-TREES. Many people, of all sorts, come from time to time, and walk among us, and look upon us, and commend us for brave handsome trees, lovely and beautiful, especially when we are in our gallantries, full of beautiful blossoms and pleasant and wholesome fruits; and some greedily pluck us, and tear us, and sometimes break off some of our branches to get our fruits, and so go on their ways, but never speak a word with us, neither do they understand what we say to them . . .

HUSBANDMAN. Come, my friends, let us walk into this pleasant garden and have some further discourse with those innocent, harmless companions, the fruit-trees. They will bid us welcome and are still ready and at leisure to confer with us . . . But we must not forget what hath often been said concerning the way and the manner of their discourse with men: that it is not audible to the outward sense of hearing, in the sound of words, but always to the inward sense, the mind and understanding.

Scientists are thought to be strange people, and in many ways they are. And as a biologist, of course, I am a scientist, and science, especially biology, is a very rewarding exercise. You have the pleasure of doing experiments, you have the pleasure of explaining to people, you have a lot of frustration, but there's great happiness in it. Unfortunately scientists tend to be looked on by many of the population as people who are terribly hard, terribly based on material things, terribly rigid with little imagination. Having said that, probably the greatest biological scientist who ever lived was Darwin. He has been having a very bad press recently. He published his *Origin of Species*, in which he propounded his theory of evolution by natural selection, in 1859, and for a theory in science to last that length of time is not bad. In fact it's very good. Although his theory can be criticised and although Darwin can be criticised in many things, much of the criticism springs from the fact that he couldn't be expected to have had the knowledge then that we have now. It comes too from people who have never read his works and who have never really tried to understand them, and none of the critics has ever produced a theory which will match and encompass the things that the theory of evolution does.

But Darwin's publication started off an enormous religious controversy: people who believed in Darwin and thought Darwin was probably correct were tarred with a brush as being unfeeling, atheistic, unthinking clods.

If you read Darwin, you'll find a charm, you'll find a simplicity, you'll find a beauty of expression and you'll find a depth of feeling that somehow or other never gets into the ordinary conversation, and that's why I've chosen to end this selection of things I like with the last paragraph of *Origin of Species*.

## *Origin of Species*

CHARLES DARWIN

It is interesting to contemplate an entangled bank, clothed with many plants of many kinds, with birds singing on the bushes, with various insects flitting about, and with worms crawling through the damp earth, and to reflect that these elaborately constructed forms, so different from each other, and dependent on each other in so complex a manner, have all been produced by laws acting around us. These laws, taken in the largest sense, being Growth and Reproduction; Inheritance which is almost implied by reproduction; Variability from the indirect and direct action of the external conditions of life, and from use and disuse; a Ratio of Increase so high as to lead to a Struggle for Life, and as a consequence to Natural Selection, entailing Divergence of Character and the Extinction of less-improved forms. Thus, from the war of nature, from famine and death, the most exalted object which we are capable of conceiving, namely the production of the higher animals, directly follows. There is a grandeur in this view of life, with its several powers, having been originally breathed into a few forms or into one; and that, whilst this planet has gone cycling on according to the fixed law of gravity, from so simple a beginning endless forms most beautiful and most wonderful have been, and are being, evolved.

*Readers: Douglas Blackwell, John Cairney*

*Full Selection:*
*Disenchantment*, C. E. MONTAGUE
*That Music Stuff*, from *Dancing in the Streets* CLIFFORD HANLEY
*A Red, Red Rose*, ROBERT BURNS
*Seaside Golf*, JOHN BETJEMAN
*Letter to The Honourable Daines Barrington*, GILBERT WHITE
*A Drink with Something in It*, OGDEN NASH
*Prospice*, ROBERT BROWNING
*The Moral and Historical Works of Lord Bacon: XLVI*
*A Dialogue Between the Husbandman and Fruit-trees*, RALPH AUSTEN
*The Spring Was Late that Year*, VITA SACKVILLE-WEST
*When You Are Old*, W. B. YEATS
*Origin of Species*, CHARLES DARWIN

# *RICHARD GORDON*

## *1979*

*Medical fiction, hospital romances featuring stern-jawed doctors/specialists/anaesthetists/ and patients heroic in suffering, or wise old fellows in country practices and so on, have long been queue-jumpers in the best-seller lists. Doctor Richard Gordon's novels detailing some of the comic horror inherent in the day-to-day life of the medical profession came as a refreshing incision into the pulp. But wonderfully funny and entertaining though they were, he has been careful not to spend a lifetime merely churning out the same sort of stuff. Just as Dirk Bogarde, who starred so elegantly in* Doctor in the House *and other 'Doctor' films, went on to become a fine and subtle actor in a variety of character roles, so Gordon has written stronger, more serious novels, many with a medical background, to be sure, but which dig deeper into the personalities of the people he created. To the delight of the listeners, however, his selection for 'With Great Pleasure', recorded at St Bartholomew's Hospital, was chosen entirely with laughter in mind.*

I became a novelist entirely by mistake. I had got a job on the British Medical Journal. I went along there with the idea of starting a doctor's comic column, but the editor having a rather sharper sense of humour than I had, put me in charge of the Obituary Notices. I always claim that this was invaluable practice – it taught me how to write convincing fiction. Well unfortunately one week I killed a Doctor of Divinity by mistake. I won't bore you with the details, but it became necessary to put as much space between myself and the British Medical Journal as possible, so I ran away to sea – in comfort. I signed on as a ship's doctor aboard a cargo boat sailing from London to Australia. Now nobody told me before we started that we were going via Newfoundland, which is rather a long way round, you must admit. I mean I wondered what all those icebergs were doing all over the place, and either I had the healthiest crew who'd ever sailed the seven seas or else they distrusted the look of me, because I never had a patient, not a single one. I'd nothing to do all day except drink whisky with the chief engineer and listen to his stories about Glasgow, because all chief engineers come from Glasgow. It was really as a public health measure, to prevent myself getting cirrhosis of the liver, that when we got to the Tropics I put up a typewriter in a shady corner of the deck and I started writing about my experiences at Barts as a medical student. I intended the book to be a cross between *War and Peace* and *Gray's Anatomy*, but somehow it didn't turn out like that at all.

Medical students seem heartless, or they make themselves seem so, but of course that's only half the story. I think it was best put by John Brown, a nineteenth-century doctor/writer living in Edinburgh, who wrote about medical students in his book *Rab and his Friends*.

## *Rab and His Friends*

JOHN BROWN

Don't think (medical students) heartless; they are neither better nor worse than you or I: they get over their professional horrors, and into their proper work; and in them pity as an *emotion* ending in itself or at best in tears and a long-drawn breath, lessens, while pity, as a *motive*, is quickened, and gains power and purpose. It is well for poor human nature that it is so.

I think that explains why many of us take up medicine.

It is perhaps appropriate that I should write *Doctor in the House* on the way to Canada because one of my favourite authors was Stephen Leacock. He was a very comic writer who was a Professor of Economics at McGill University and he also wrote serious books. I've also written serious books, I've recently written *The Private Life of Florence Nightingale*, so I can sympathise with Stephen Leacock when a lady told him she'd read all the way through his *Principles of Economics* roaring her head off at every page, but here is his most accurate description of how to be a doctor.

## *How to Be a Doctor*

STEPHEN LEACOCK

'What about diet, doctor?' says the patient, completely cowed.

The answer to this question varies very much. It depends on how the doctor is feeling and whether it is long since he had a meal himself. If it is late in the morning and the doctor is ravenously hungry, he says:

'Oh, eat plenty, don't be afraid of it; eat meat, vegetables, starch, glue, cement, anything you like.' But if the doctor has just had lunch and if his breathing is short-circuited with huckleberry pie, he says very firmly:

'No, I don't want you to eat anything at all: absolutely not a bite; it won't hurt you, a little self-denial in the matter of eating is the best thing in the world.'

'And what about drinking?' Again the doctor's answer varies. He may say:

'Oh, yes, you might drink a glass of lager now and then, or, if you prefer it, a gin and soda or a whisky and Apollinaris, and I think before going to bed I'd take a hot Scotch with a couple of lumps of white sugar and a bit of lemon-peel in it and a good grating of nutmeg on the top.' The doctor says this with real feeling, and his eye glistens with the pure love of his profession. But if, on the other hand, the doctor has spent the night before at a little gathering of medical friends, he is very apt to forbid the patient to touch alcohol in any shape, and to dismiss the subject with great severity.

I don't suppose any of you have read any of my books, at least I hope not because I think the only people who read my books are people who are ill in hospital. I know this for a fact because a lady told me at a literary lunch the other day, over the trifle – she was wearing a lovely hat which matched it – 'Oh,' she said, 'my husband did so enjoy your latest novel. Such a pity he died when he was half way through.' Well, I think she was quite right, the best part of the book was the ending. But if you haven't read any of my books, I do hope you've seen some of the 'Doctor' films; you can still see them on television if you stay up late enough at night. If you have seen them I shall be terribly hurt if you haven't noticed that I have a small part in each of them. In the first one I played the anaesthetist. That was type-casting because when I was a doctor at Barts I *was* an anaesthetist, and now I can reveal to you why I became an anaesthetist: I couldn't stand talking to my patients. For an anaesthetist, you see, it's easy; you come in: 'Good morning,' needle in, bang, out flat. If I had taken my career very seriously I would have become a pathologist and then the patients would have been even less trouble!

Of course I'm only one of very many doctors who've made the transition into writing. To mention just a few: Tobias Smollett, a naval surgeon, who wrote *Roderick Random*; Oliver Goldsmith; Oliver Wendell Holmes; John Keats – Guy's man I'm afraid – he died at the age of twenty-six from tuberculosis. Conan Doyle was a doctor who based his famous Sherlock Holmes on Dr Bell who taught him in Edinburgh; A. J. Cronin whom one knows; Robert Bridges, the poet – a Barts man I'm glad to say; and of course Somerset Maugham. Right to the end of his long life he remained, like myself, on the Medical Register, and, like myself, was presumably perfectly entitled to write prescriptions for dangerous drugs or deliver a baby, had the occasion arisen and had he happened to feel like it.

I've also found, apart from those writers, twelve medical pirates. I am referring of course to the sea-going and not the Harley Street variety, and ten medical murderers – those of course were the ones who were found out. These include Dr Palmer, who was one of the last men to be hanged in public in this country – he was certainly the last doctor to be hanged in this country in public – outside Stafford Gaol on a very wet morning in 1856. He had killed his family and thirteen other people with strychnine which must have been very painful, and I'm sorry to say that Dr Palmer was a Barts man. Of course here at Barts we're all rather sensitive about the good doctor's end, so we explain that he was attending an open air meeting in an important capacity when the platform unfortunately collapsed beneath his feet.

Well now I'm going to confess something to you. I see medicine these days only as a patient. I suffer from gout. It's a thankless disease to have; most diseases attract sympathy, gout attracts only derision. One of my nicest friends used to hit me on the back and say, 'Ah, gout. Got your nose too deep into the port, old boy, what?' And I'm afraid that port and gout are linked in the public mind as firmly and as erroneously as wet feet and a cold in the head, or sitting on stones gives you piles. The poet William Cowper in 1782 wrote quite slanderously:

> Pangs arthritic that infest the toe
> Of libertine excess.

It's a very literary disease, but it is due not to port, but to purines. A. P. Herbert wrote in *Punch*:

> At last the happy truth is out –
> Port wine is *not* the cause of gout;
> Far more responsible for pain
> Are kidneys, liver, sweetbread, brain –
> The clubman should by any means
> Avoid anchovies and sardines,
> And citizens of every sort
> Owe some apology to port!

I think I must also quote Sir Thomas Browne, the seventeenth-century physician and author, about gout:

What famous men, what emperors and learned persons have been severe examples of that disease, and that it is not a disease of fools, but of men of parts and senses.

Many modern doctors say the same, but only, I think, because they've got gout themselves.

*Reader: Dinsdale Landen*

*Full Selection:*
*The Pickwick Papers*, CHARLES DICKENS
*Rab and His Friends*, JOHN BROWN
*How to Be a Doctor*, STEPHEN LEACOCK
*The Diary of a Nobody*, GEORGE and WEEDON GROSSMITH
*1066 and All That*, SELLARS and YEATMAN
*England, Their England*, A. G. MACDONNEL
*Right Ho, Jeeves*, P. G. WODEHOUSE
*Pangs Arthritic*, WILLIAM COWPER
*At Last the Happy Truth Is Out*, A. P. HERBERT
*On Gout*, SIR THOMAS BROWNE
*Old Man's Wish*, WALTER POPE

# GENERAL SIR JOHN HACKETT

## 1971

*Sir John's programme tells a story of an escape, or to be more accurate two escapes. The first is from a hospital behind enemy lines during the last war, a long, painful, dangerous escape which involved his being kept in hiding while his wounds healed. The second escape was an escape of the mind from pain and boredom, an escape provided by literature. It is a tribute to Sir John's account of that second escape – 'It is a great pleasure to me to be allowed to talk about a chapter in my life, only a few months long, which unfolded before most of you were born' – that it seems as filled with drama and adventure as the first.*

In the Autumn of 1944 I was commanding a brigade of around a thousand parachute infantry and jumped with them in the First British Airborne Division in the battle near Arnhem by which we hoped to seize and hold the crossing of the lower Rhine. We had ammunition, food and everything else for two or three days, until ground forces should come up to us. They never came and after eight days of hard fighting the remnant of the First Airborne Division – two thousand men out of ten thousand – were withdrawn back across the river Rhine, leaving the badly wounded behind in the hands of the enemy.

I was one of these, with severe wounds in the stomach from a shell splinter and a bullet through the thigh. Only a surgical miracle, as I have heard it described, performed by one of our own surgeons, kept me alive. Ten days after that surgeon had taken the splinter out and sewn my insides together again, the

Dutch Underground smuggled me through the SS guard out of the hospital and brought me to a township a few miles from Arnhem along the Utrecht road. That was how I came into the care of four middle-aged sisters and the son and daughter of one of them, in a little house set back in its garden a few yards from the street, less than thirty yards away from a German military police billet next door.

That was the start of the adventure in poetry I now have it in mind to talk about.

It was into an attic bedroom in this small, old-fashioned house that I was carried, by now absolutely all in, one night in late October 1944, and put to bed under a sampler embroidered with a scene from the Sleeping Beauty with the text (in Dutch), 'And she slept for a hundred years'. I never read anything more welcome.

One of the four middle-aged sisters who were hiding me from the Germans, had been in England and had trained there to teach English. In a day or two, when I was a little restored, this one, Aunt Ann, brought me her books. They included the Authorised Version of the Bible, the Oxford editions of Wordsworth and of Scott's verse, a complete *Oxford Shakespeare* in one volume and a book called *One Thousand and One Gems of English Verse*, edited by one Charles McKay.

Books to read in English! This was providential! But reflection upon the situation in which I found myself induced no great inclination to look for reading which gave an echo to it. The world outside our house in Torenstraat was full of unseen menace. When I was able to move to the window and look out I could see soldiers of the enemy walking unsuspecting in the street, always armed and often ludicrously young. In the mornings I would sometimes hear them marching and listened while they sang. This was not as British infantry soldiers used to sing as they marched, full throated and cynical and sentimental at the same time, to a swinging rhythm. What these sang was threatening, crisp and cocky, the singing voices clipped off at the end of a phrase (tramp, tramp) with another couplet sung and switched off as suddenly (tramp, tramp) as the sounds moved round the corner and down the street.

My life in this house became one of reflection, recollection and further exploration. In my little iron bed in that attic room I read the whole of Wordsworth. There was time in plenty and little to distract me. The embarrassment of choice offered by a large library did not exist here and I simply read what I had. I was now able to discover for myself that Wordsworth was a great poet. To read, for example, those two very long poems, 'The Prelude' and 'The Excursion' as continuous pieces and no longer see them only as quarries from which examination papers were hewn was a revelation. I even did what I had never dreamt of doing before and read through those almost endless sonnet sequences, mostly about the Established Church. There were other small things I was glad to see again – the sonnet on the sonnet for example.

## *The Uses and Beauties of the Sonnet*

WILLIAM WORDSWORTH

Nuns fret not at their convent's narrow room;
And hermits are contented with their cells;
And students with their pensive citadels;
Maids at the wheel, the weaver at his loom,
Sit blithe and happy; bees that soar for bloom,
High as the highest peak of Furness Fells,
Will murmur by the hour in foxglove bells;
In truth, the prison, unto which we doom
Ourselves, no prison is: and hence to me,
In sundry moods, 'twas pastime to be bound
Within the Sonnet's scanty plot of ground:
Pleased if some souls (for such there needs must be)
Who have felt the weight of too much liberty,
Should find brief solace there, as I have found.

I doubt if many of you who are students think of yourselves as living in 'pensive citadels'. But in the enclosed and inward turning life I lived just then it was to me most apt. Beautiful words too in spite of so much sibilance. It had been Tennyson, I seemed to recall, who spoke of getting rid of too many S-sounds as 'kicking the geese out of the boat'. But 'pensive citadels' was lovely, to be lingered over and added to remembered sounds like 'pavement' and 'cellar door' as a source of quiet pleasure. I now found more within the ordered framework of the sonnet than ever before.

I could read things that pleased or helped me again and again, for there was no hurry. I could find, and enjoy, comparisons. There was Eliza Cook's 'The Old Arm Chair', for example, typical of a certain time and of a literary outlook prevalent then but not easy to share now.

### *The Old Arm Chair*

ELIZA COOK

I love it – I love it, and who shall dare
To chide me for loving that old arm chair!
I've treasured it long as a sainted prize –
I've bedewed it with tears, and embalmed it with sighs;
'Tis bound by a thousand bands to my heart,
Not a tie will break, not a link will start.
Would you learn the spell? a mother sat there;
And a sacred thing is that old arm chair.

In childhood's hour I lingered near
The hallowed seat with listening ear;
And gentle words that mother would give,
To fit me to die, and teach me to live.
She told me shame would never betide,
With truth for my creed and God for my guide;
She taught me to lisp my earliest prayer,
As I knelt beside that old arm chair.

I sat and watched her many a day,
When her eyes grew dim and her locks were grey,
And I almost worshipped her when she smiled
And turned from her Bible to bless her child.
Years rolled on, but the last one sped –
My idol was shattered – my earth star fled:
I learnt how much the heart can bear,
When I saw her die in that old arm chair.

'Tis past! 'tis past! but I gaze on it now
With quivering breath and throbbing brow:
'Twas there she nursed me – 'twas there she died,

And memory flows with lava tide –
Say it is folly, and deem me weak,
While the scalding tears run down my cheek.
But I love it – I love it, and cannot tear
My soul from my mother's old arm chair.

I compared that Victorian sentimentality with the truer sentiment of those lines of Cowper, on a mother's picture.

### *On the Receipt of a Mother's Picture*

WILLIAM COWPER

O that those lips had language! Life has pass'd
With me but roughly since I heard thee last.
Those lips are thine – thy own sweet smiles I see,
The same, that oft in childhood solac'd me;
Voice only fails, else how distinct they say,
'Grieve not, my child, chase all thy fears away!'
The meek intelligence of those dear eyes
(Blest be the art that can immortalise,
The art that baffles Time's tyrannic claim
To quench it) here shines on me still the same.

Faithful remembrancer of one so dear,
O welcome guest, though unexpected here!
Who bidd'st me honor with an artless song,
Affectionate, a mother lost so long,
I will obey, not willingly alone,
But gladly, as the precept were her own:
And, while that face renewed my filial grief,
Fancy shall weave a charm for my relief,
Shall steep me in Elysian reverie,
A momentary dream, that thou art she.

A young Dutch minister of the Reformed Church was brought to see me secretly. This was Dominie Blauw, brave pastor of a harassed flock, one of very few allowed by the ladies of this house to know that I was there. He lent me at my request St Matthew in Greek.

As autumn moved on towards winter the Dutch Underground was busy planning my escape. I had hoped to be at home in

England for Christmas, but in mid-December I could still scarcely walk. Such a liability for any party trying to make its hazardous way through the German lines would be intolerable and I made them leave me out of their plans. One party of escapers from the Airbornes did in fact get through. Another failed and after that German security tightened up so hard in that sensitive area just north of the lower Rhine near Arnhem that we could only hope for later opportunities elsewhere.

I could see out of the window from my bed the branches of a tree waving in the autumn winds. Its leaves had gone – all but one, which stayed a long time alone on the bare branch until one day I awoke and saw that it had gone too. This seemed to me a sign that I knew I must accept.

It was then that I rediscovered Milton.

## *On His Blindness*

JOHN MILTON

When I consider how my light is spent
Ere half my days in this dark world and wide,
And that one talent which is death to hide,
Lodg'd with me useless, though my Soul more bent
To serve therewith my Maker, and present
My true account, lest he returning chide;
Doth God exact day-labour, light deny'd,
I fondly ask; but patience to prevent
That murmur, soon replies, 'God doth not need
Either man's work or his own gifts; who best
Bear his mild yoke, they serve him best: his state
Is kingly: thousands at his bidding speed,
And post o'er land and ocean without rest;
They also serve who only stand and wait'.

I read that over and over again. I re-read 'Lycidas' and thought of many friends now gone. 'For Lycidas is dead, dead ere his prime, Young Lycidas and hath not left his peer.' I rediscovered old acquaintance in 'Il Penseroso' and the pleasures of Melancholy, and in 'L'Allegro', which banishes it in pretty round terms 'Hence loathèd Melancholy, of Cerberus and blackest midnight born, in

Stygian Cave forlorn, 'mongst horrid shapes and shrieks and sights unholy . . .

But I now began to develop a longing for one great whole work above all others. It all began with the 'Gems'. It was fed by what I read in any other books I had. It was nourished by recollection and reflection. What I wanted above all was *Paradise Lost*. I wanted the whole of it. The 'Gems' only contained parts – long enough to leave one tuned in to the rhythm and the language and the images but frustrated at having to stop.

After four months I got away, piloted on a borrowed bicycle by a young friend, John Snoek, through snowy landscapes like a winter scene of Brueghel, with faultlessly forged papers and on my coat a little button of a type well known there, proclaiming that I was hard of hearing. I journeyed from one underground hideout to another. We were taken over the lower Rhine where the swift winter stream flowed between broken ice piled high against the banks, by a ferryman in danger of his life for putting out a boat, but unable to resist the price John offered him – a priceless skein of darning wool saved from his mother's shop. Then again in hiding until we could find more boatmen and a canoe for a journey by night through the huge marshland of the river Waal and down towards its mouth to where the southern bank was at last in allied hands. I was soon in England and they put me into a hospital to be tidied up. But when the village near Arnhem where I had lived was at last free from the enemy, I was allowed out of hospital, and the RAF lent me a little aeroplane called an Oxford, which we filled with tea and boots and chocolate and darning wool and the set of books Dominie Blauw wanted for his Doctorate in Theology, and I set off again to land for the second time in Holland.

And there my adventure story must stop. For this *is* an adventure story, I suppose. It is also a story of a poetic adventure, an experience which, in the way that a man is the product of his experience, has long been part of me. Experiences such as these are not the trimmings of life: they are part of its essential fabric and of course you do not have to get knocked about in a war to find them.

Let me only recall as we finish that my wife gave me the coming home present she had learnt I wanted most. And as I took off for

Holland for the second time I was beginning to read the whole of that majestic book that deals with 'man's first disobedience and the fruit of that forbidden tree' in such a fashion as to 'assert eternal Providence and justify the ways of God to Men'.

*Readers: Sheila Allen, Julian Glover*

*Full Selection:*
*Ode on Intimations of Immortality from Recollections of Early Childhood,* WILLIAM WORDSWORTH
*The Uses and Beauties of the Sonnet,* WILLIAM WORDSWORTH
*Sonnet VIII,* WILLIAM SHAKESPEARE
*Sonnet X,* WILLIAM SHAKESPEARE
*King Lear,* WILLIAM SHAKESPEARE
*Quotes from the Bible*
*Vanity Fair,* WILLIAM MAKEPIECE THACKERAY
*The Rime of the Ancient Mariner,* SAMUEL TAYLOR COLERIDGE
*The Old Arm Chair,* ELIZA COOK
*On the Receipt of a Mother's Picture,* WILLIAM COWPER
*The Sailor's Journal,* CHARLES DIBDEN
*On His Blindness,* JOHN MILTON
*Paradise Lost,* JOHN MILTON

# *ROY HATTERSLEY*

## *1986*

*It seemed strange to be sitting in his office at the House of Commons with the Shadow Chancellor and Deputy Leader of the Labour Party and discussing not for one moment matters of urgent political debate. Indeed they were never even mentioned. Roy Hattersley was clearly more interested on this occasion in the delights of good writing. Modern British governments are not noted for their attachment to the arts, their interest, if any, boiling down in the end to a question of money and how not to spend it. It was a delight, therefore, to find such a senior politician plainly enthusiastic about literature both from the classics and from contemporary authors. We arranged to have lunch after the recording. On the day, politics did emerge briefly. Firstly the 'Daily Express' had just published an article purporting to total Hattersley's earnings and those of his wife. He was rather amused as it had apparently grossly over-estimated his and under-estimated his wife's! Then, alas, it had been decided to have Treasury matters discussed at question time so Roy was unable after all to join us for lunch. A pity as I would have enjoyed getting to know him better.*

I don't support the Cruft's Dog Show school of literacy criticism which suggests that you can choose the best poem in its class and then, by comparing the champion lyric, sonnet and ballad as if they were the best Alsatian, whippet and poodle, choose a champion of champions. But if I held such views the simple and beautiful Sonnet XVIII by William Shakespeare would probably get the big rosette.

> Shall I compare thee to a Summer's day?
> Thou art more lovely and more temperate:
> Rough winds do shake the darling buds of May,
> And Summer's lease hath all too short a date:
> Sometimes too hot the eye of heaven shines,
> And often is his gold complexion dimm'd;
> And every fair from fair sometime declines,
> By chance, or nature's changing course, untrimm'd;
> But thy eternal Summer shall not fade,
> Nor lose possession of that fair thou owest;
> Nor shall Death brag thou wander'st in his shade.
> When in eternal lines to time thou growest;
> So long as men can breathe, or eyes can see,
> So long lives this, and this gives life to thee.

If there were such an award for prose, Lytton Strachey on the death of Queen Victoria probably qualifies.

## *The Passing of Victoria*

GILES LYTTON STRACHEY

When, two days previously, the news of the approaching end had been made public, astonished grief had swept over the country. It appeared as if some monstrous reversal of the course of nature was about to take place. The vast majority of her subjects had never known a time when Queen Victoria had not been reigning over them. She had become an indissoluble part of their whole scheme of things, and that they were about to lose her appeared a scarcely possible thought. She herself, as she lay blind and silent, seemed to those who watched her to be divested of all thinking – to have glided already, unawares, into oblivion. Yet, perhaps, in the secret chambers of consciousness, she had her thoughts too. Perhaps her fading mind called up once more the shadows of the past to float before it, and retraced, for the last time, the vanished visions of that long history – passing back and back, through the cloud of years, to older and ever older memories – to the spring woods at Osborne, so full of primroses for Lord Beaconsfield – to Lord Palmerston's queer clothes and high demeanour, and Albert's face under the green lamp, and Albert's first stag at Balmoral, and Albert in his blue and silver uniform, and the Baron coming in through a doorway, and Lord M. dreaming at Windsor with the rooks cawing in the elm-trees, and the Archbishop of Canterbury on his knees in the dawn, and the old King's turkey-cock ejaculations, and Uncle Leopold's soft voice at Claremont, and Lehzen with the globes, and her mother's feathers sweeping down towards her, and a great old repeater-watch of her father's in its tortoise-shell case, and a yellow rug, and some friendly flounces of sprigged muslin, and the trees and the grass at Kensington.

*Readers: Joss Ackland, Elizabeth Bell*

*Full Selection:*
*Sonnet XVIII*, WILLIAM SHAKESPEARE
*Spring and Fall*, GERARD MANLEY HOPKINS
*Difficult Poetry*, T. S. ELIOT
*Chard Whitlow*, HENRY REED

*American Names*, STEPHEN VINCENT BENET
*The Good Companions*, J. B. PRIESTLEY
*Removal from Terry Street*, DOUGLAS DUNN
*Chant-Pagan*, RUDYARD KIPLING
*The Passing of Victoria*, GILES LYTTON STRACHEY
*Dockery and Son*, PHILIP LARKIN
*In Memory of Eva Gore-Booth*, W. B. YEATS
*Into My Heart*, A. E. HOUSMAN

# *P. D. JAMES*

## *1985*

*When recording 'With Great Pleasure' we tend to avoid studios, not because there is anything wrong with them – most programmes are made in them, after all – but because much of the atmosphere of the series is due to the fact that we record in places with which the presenters have some personal connection – the town where they grew up, say, or where they settled in later life. It is also an opportunity for Radio 4 to visit a community rather than remaining cosily on its own premises. P. D. James lives in London, so we presented the programme at the New End Theatre in Hampstead, unaware that it is situated close to the radio masts for a number of minicab firms. On listening to the tapes back in Bristol, it was rather a shock to hear instructions to pick people up from dubious addresses interspersed with a stream of private jokes, along with the readings of Roy Marsden, who plays Adam Dalgliesh in the Anglia Television series of Phyllis James's novels, and Sheila Mitchell. It was some considerable time before we were able to assemble the same team in front of a different audience at the BBC's Paris Studio in Lower Regent Street!*

I was educated within the State system and at one time, more than fifty years ago, I was at a school where we were required each week to learn by heart the Collect for the following Sunday. I'm not sure that it did much for my general behaviour, but how it enhanced my love of words! Today there is a risk that the majority of children will grow up ignorant of those two seminal influences in our culture, The King James Bible and the Book of Common Prayer. So here are just eighteen verses from Psalm 139 to show this deprived generation what they are missing. The psalms comprise the whole drama of humanity; birth and death, love and hate, prayer and praise, hope and fulfilment. In these verses the psalmist is contemplating the wonder of man's creation.

## *Psalm 139 Verses 1–18*

KING JAMES VERSION

O LORD, thou hast searched me, and known me.
Thou knowest my downsitting and mine uprising,
Thou understandest my thought afar off.
Thou compassest my path and my lying down,
And art acquainted with all my ways.
For there is not a word in my tongue,
But, lo, O LORD, thou knowest it altogether.
Thou hast beset me behind and before,
And laid thine hand upon me.
Such knowledge is too wonderful for me;
It is high, I cannot attain unto it.
Whither shall I go from thy spirit?
Or whither shall I flee from thy presence?
If I ascend up into heaven, thou art there:
If I make my bed in hell, behold, thou art there.
If I take the wings of the morning,
And dwell in the uttermost parts of the sea;
Even there shall thy hand lead me,
And thy right hand shall hold me.
If I say, Surely the darkness shall cover me;
Even the night shall be light about me.
Yea, the darkness hideth not from thee;
But the night shineth as the day:

The darkness and the light are both alike to thee.
For thou hast possessed my reins:
Thou hast covered me in my mother's womb.
I will praise thee; for I am fearfully and wonderfully made:
Marvellous are thy works;
And that my soul knoweth right well.
My substance was not hid from thee,
When I was made in secret,
And curiously wrought in the lowest parts of the earth.
Thine eyes did see my substance, yet being unperfect;
And in thy book all my members were written,
Which in continuance were fashioned,
When as yet there was none of them.
How precious also are thy thoughts unto me, O God!
How great is the sum of them!
If I should count them, they are more in number than the sand:
When I awake, I am still with thee.

Poetry has been a joy to me all my life and I was fortunate in the headmaster of my primary school in Ludlow in Shropshire who loved poetry and had the gift of conveying his enthusiasm to young children. We learned a great deal by heart and recited it in the sing-song dialect of the Welsh border. Before I was eight I had kept the bridge with Horatius, defended outposts of Empire with the Gatling jammed and the Colonel dead, stood alone on the burning deck and, between these unfashionable patriotic fervours had strolled down the Shropshire lanes with A. E. Housman. It left me with a catholic taste in verse and the conviction that poetry is meant to be fun as well as wise and inspiring.

A poem which would always find a place in my personal anthology is Matthew Arnold's 'Dover Beach'. Although he lived in an age of progress and optimism, the theme of the poem and its deep pessimism seem to me more modern than Victorian. But I have always loved it, perhaps because walking by the sea is one of my keenest pleasures and this lyrical elegy on the death of faith perfectly expresses the peace, the nostalgia, the melancholy and the sense of timelessness which I experience when I look on the sea at the fading of the day.

## *Dover Beach*

MATTHEW ARNOLD

The sea is calm to-night.
The tide is full, the moon lies fair
Upon the straits; – on the French coast the light
Gleams and is gone; the cliffs of England stand,
Glimmering and vast, out in the tranquil bay.
Come to the window, sweet is the night-air!
Only, from the long line of spray
Where the sea meets the moon-blanched land
Listen! you hear the grating roar
Of pebbles which the waves draw back, and fling,
At their return, up the high strand,
Begin, and cease, and then again begin,
With tremulous cadence slow, and bring
The eternal note of sadness in.

Sophocles long ago
Heard it on the Aegaean, and it brought
Into his mind the turbid ebb and flow
Of human misery; we
Find also in the sound a thought,
Hearing it by this distant northern sea.

The Sea of Faith
Was once, too, at the full, and round earth's shore
Lay like the folds of a bright girdle furled;
But now I only hear
Its melancholy, long, withdrawing roar,
Retreating to the breath
Of the night-wind down the vast edges drear
And naked shingles of the world.

Ah, love, let us be true
To one another! for the world, which seems
To lie before us like a land of dreams,
So various, so beautiful, so new,
Hath really neither joy, nor love, nor light,
Nor certitude, nor peace, nor help for pain;

And we are here as on a darkling plain
Swept with confused alarms of struggle and flight,
Where ignorant armies clash by night.

One of my leisure-time pleasures when I'm not planning murder and fabricating clues is exploring churches. Apart from their architectural interest, the commemorative tablets and the carved gravestones give a fascinating insight into the lives and deaths of our forefathers. Very sensibly, today we prefer cremation and we aren't much given to putting up tablets so our descendants will be denied these intimate records of social history.

These words are carved above the west door of Staunton Harold church in Leicestershire.

In the yeare 1653
When all things sacred were throughout ye nation
Either demolisht or profaned
Sir Robert Shirley, Barronet,
Founded this church;
Whose singular praise it is,
to haue done the best things in ye worst times,
and
hoped them in the most callamitous.

The righteous shall be had in everlasting remembrance.

Those were brave words to incise in stone during the Commonwealth; Cromwell, furious, retaliated by saying that anyone who could should provide the money to raise a regiment. Sir Robert, who had never made any secret of his loyalty to the King, refused. He was sent to the Tower and died there, aged twenty-seven.

One of my personal pleasures, and I suspect I share it with many writers, is rummaging around second-hand bookshops and market stalls. To the addict of the written word the mere handling of old books, the potent smell of paper and print, the dusty ambience of these treasure houses is an unfailing delight. And there is always the chance of a find. An out-of-print favourite, a beautifully produced copy of a classic, or an anthology which can introduce me to new poems and writers I've neglected. And then there are the marvellous oddities, the curious, bizarre or entertaining pieces which provide their moments of pleasure. It was in a long-out-of-print anthology that I discovered the following description of how the well conducted household should start the day.

## *A Good Wife Begins the Day –* from *The Philosophy of Housekeeping*

ISABELLA MARY BEETON

A MISTRESS should rise at latest 7 o'clock. This will appear dreadfully late to some notables, but will be found to be a good hour all the year round. The Mistress should take her cold bath, and perform a neat, careful, and pretty morning toilet. Having performed this careful toilet, she will be ready to descend at 8 o'clock, but before leaving her room will place two chairs at the end of the bed, and turn the whole of the bedclothes over them, and, except on very rainy mornings, will throw open the windows of her room. She should then fold her own and husband's night-dress, which have been airing during her toilet, and place them in their ornamental cover; she will put brushes, combs, hairpins, etc, in their proper places, and leave her toilet-table clear and tidy, and make the whole room as neat as possible. Key-basket in hand, she should descend to the breakfast-room, at once ring for the kettle or tea-urn, according to the season, and make the tea, coffee, cocoa, or chocolate, as the case may be. Her eyes should now glance over the table to see that everything required for the table is in its place, and that all is neatly arranged and ready for the family – flowers on the table, preserve and marmalade in cut-glass dishes . . . When it is possible to get the Master to enjoy an eight o'clock breakfast, household matters go charmingly. He is usually out of the house by nine, and by that hour the windows are wide open, every door set open (weather permitting), and a thorough draught of 'delicious air' is passed through the whole dwelling. AS SOON AS THE MISTRESS hears her husband's step, the bell should be rung for the hot dish; and should he be, as business men usually are, rather pressed for time, she should herself wait on him, cutting his bread, buttering his toast, etc. Also give standing orders that coat, hat, and umbrella shall be brushed and ready; and see that they are, by helping on the coat, handing the hat, and glancing at the umbrella.

In my part of London, setting every door open for a rush of delicious air would invite a rush of undelicious burglars. But at least the wives listening can ensure that their husband's night-dress is in its ornamental cover before feeding him his buttered toast.

My next poem, 'The Toys' by the nineteenth-century poet and critic Coventry Patmore, makes a direct appeal to the reader because the deeply felt emotion it describes is one most of us have known; the tenderness, the pity and the occasional blindness and irritations of parental love. And if the parallel drawn with divine love is obvious, it has seldom been expressed with more sincerity or grace.

## *The Toys*

COVENTRY PATMORE

My little Son, who looked from thoughtful eyes
And moved and spoke in quiet grown-up wise,
Having my law the seventh time disobeyed,
I struck him, and dismissed
With hard words and unkissed,
– His Mother, who was patient, being dead.
Then, fearing lest his grief should hinder sleep,
I visited his bed,
But found him slumbering deep,
With darkened eyelids, and their lashes yet
From his late sobbing wet.
And I, with moan,
Kissing away his tears, left others of my own;
For, on a table drawn beside his head,
He had put, within his reach,
A box of counters and a red-veined stone,
A piece of glass abraded by the beach,
And six or seven shells,
A bottle with bluebells,
And two French copper coins, ranged there with careful art,
To comfort his sad heart.

So when that night I prayed
To God, I wept, and said:
'Ah, when at last we lie with trancèd breath,

Not vexing Thee in death,
And Thou rememberest of what toys
We made our joys,
How weakly understood
Thy great commanded good,
Then, fatherly not less
Than I whom Thou hast moulded from the clay,
Thou'lt leave Thy wrath, and say,
"I will be sorry for their childishness".

*Readers: Roy Marsden, Sheila Mitchell*

*Full Selection:*
*Pride and Prejudice*, JANE AUSTEN
*Pslam 139*
*Afterwards*, THOMAS HARDY
*As I Walked Out One Evening*, W. H. AUDEN
*Thou Art Indeed Just, Lord*, GERARD MANLEY HOPKINS
*Dover Beach*, MATTHEW ARNOLD
*Epitaphs (Bath Abbey and Staunton Harold)*
*Pot Pourri from a Surrey Garden*, JOHN BETJEMAN
*The Explosion*, PHILIP LARKIN
*The Philosophy of Housekeeping*, ISABELLA MARY BEETON
*The Toys*, COVENTRY PATMORE
*My Last Duchess*, ROBERT BROWNING
*The Inquest*, W. H. DAVIES
*Strychnine in the Soup*, P. G. WODEHOUSE
*Sonnet CVXI*, WILLIAM SHAKESPEARE

# *DAME CELIA JOHNSON*

## *1982*

*This programme was recorded shortly before Dame Celia's death. The fact is worth mentioning because on the tape she sounds joyous and full of life. Indeed, when I was asked to choose four programmes particularly worthy of a further repeat during Christmas week 1985, hers was one of the ones that was especially recommended to me. I was happy to include it, both for the pleasure of hearing again not only Dame Celia's voice, but that of David Davis, the much-loved 'Uncle David' from 'Children's Hour', who, along with Rosalind Shanks and Dame Celia herself, was one of the readers. A small mystery was resolved after that broadcast: one item, apparently found 'by the friend of a friend of a friend of a friend in a parish magazine', author unknown, was introduced as 'The Lord Said Unto Noah'. It was enormously popular and dozens of letters arrived from listeners after each transmission asking where it was possible to obtain a copy. After the Christmas broadcast we received a 'phone call from Keith Waterhouse's assistant. It turned out that he had written it for his 'Daily Mirror' column under the title 'How Long, O Lord . . . ?' I am pleased to give due acknowledgement here.*

Let me tell you it's not at all easy – one starts to look for a poem, and before you know where you are, you're knee deep in anthologies and collected works and odd scraps of paper to be used as bookmarks. Looking for a poem you find on the way poems you'd forgotten, lots you'd never known, poems you used to like and now like less and, of course, the other way around. It's all very enjoyable, but you decide to decide tomorrow. The poems are bad enough, but prose is impossible. In the end, I almost used a pin. A pin, or a peg to hang things on. My peg to start with is with places that have delighted me.

I'm now going to Greece, to be bewitched by the dolphins and the purple seas and the purple past, mixed with the scent of the wild flowers and herbs, at the almost purple present.

## *The Old Ships*

JAMES ELROY FLECKER

I have seen old ships sail like swans asleep
Beyond the village which men still call Tyre,
With leaden age o'ercargoed, dipping deep
For Famagusta and the hidden sun
That rings black Cyprus with a lake of fire;
And all those ships were certainly so old
Who knows how oft with squat and noisy gun,
Questing brown slaves or Syrian oranges,
The pirates Genoese
Hell-raked them till they rolled
Blood, water, fruit and corpses up the hold.
But now through friendly seas they softly run,
Painted the mid-sea blue or shore-sea green,
Still patterned with the vine and grapes in gold.

But I have seen,
Pointing her shapely shadows from the dawn
And image tumbled on a rose-swept bay,
A drowsy ship of some yet older day;
And, wonder's breath indrawn,
Thought I – who knows – who knows – but in that same
(Fished up beyond Æaea, patched up new
– Stern painted brighter blue –)
That talkative, bald-headed seaman came
(Twelve patient comrades sweating at the oar)
From Troy's doom-crimson shore,
And with great lies about his wooden horse
Set the crew laughing, and forgot his course.

It was so old a ship – who knows – who knows?
– And yet so beautiful, I watched in vain
To see the mast burst open with a rose,
And the whole deck put on its leaves again.

I've always liked poems that tell stories, and the next poem does just that. I read 'The Queen's Marie' once when I was in Hong Kong to some Chinese schoolchildren. They gazed at me with black, beautiful, unwinking eyes, they must have been astounded, but I suppose it was only a proof if proof were needed, of the bewildering idiocy of grown-ups – why should I read them this?

## *The Queen's Marie*

TRAD.

Marie Hamilton's to the kirk gane,
  Wi' ribbons in her hair;
The King thought mair o' Marie Hamilton
  Than ony that were there.

Marie Hamilton's to the kirk gane,
  Wi' ribbons on her breast;
The King thought mair o' Marie Hamilton
  Than he listen'd to the priest.

Marie Hamilton's to the kirk gane
  Wi' gloves upon her hands;
The King thought mair o' Marie Hamilton
  Than the Queen and a' her lands.

She hadna been about the King's court
  A month, but barely ane,
Till she was beloved by a' the King's court,
  And the King the only man.

She hadna been about the King's court
A month, but barely three,
Till frae the King's court Marie Hamilton,
  Marie Hamilton durstna be.

The King is to the Abbey gane,
  To pu' the Abbey tree,
To scale the babe frae Marie's heart;
  But the thing it wadna be.

O she has row'd it in her apron,
  And set it on the sea –

'Gae sink ye or swim ye, bonny babe,
  Ye'se get nae mair o' me.'

Word is to the kitchen gane,
  And word is to the ha',
And word is to the noble room
  Amang the ladies a',
That Marie Hamilton's brought to bed,
  And the bonny babe's miss'd and awa'.

Scarcely had she lain down again,
  And scarcely fa'en asleep,
When up and started our gude Queen
  Just at her bed-feet;
Saying – Marie Hamilton, where's your babe?
  For I am sure I heard it greet.

'O no, O no, my noble Queen!
  Think no sic thing to be;
'Twas but a stitch into my side,
  And sair it troubles me!'

'Get up, get up, Marie Hamilton:
  Get up and follow me;
For I am going to Edinburgh town,
  A rich wedding for to see.'

O slowly, slowly rase she up,
  And slowly put she on;
And slowly rade she out the way
  Wi' mony a weary groan.

The Queen was clad in scarlet,
  Her merry maids all in green;
And every town that they cam to,
  They took Marie for the Queen.

'Ride hooly, hooly, gentlemen,
  Ride hooly now wi' me!
For never, I am sure, a wearier burd
  Rade in your companie.'

But little wist Marie Hamilton,
  When she rade on the brown,
That she was gaen to Edinburgh town,
  And a' to be put down.

'Why weep ye sae, ye burgess wives,
  Why look ye sae on me?
O I am going to Edinburgh town,
  A rich wedding to see.'

When she gaed up the tolbooth stairs,
  The corks frae her heels did flee;
And lang or e'er she cam down again,
  She was condemmed to die.

When she cam to the Netherbow port,
  She laugh'd loud laughters three;
But when she cam to the gallows foot
  The tears blinded her e'e.

'Yestreen the Queen had four Maries,
  The night she'll hae but three;
There was Marie Seaton, and Marie Beaton,
  And Marie Carmichael, and me.

No one really seems to know who wrote this next piece. Rumour has it that it was found by a friend of a friend of a friend of a friend in a parish magazine. But perhaps somebody may claim it.

## *How Long, O Lord . . . ?*

KEITH WATERHOUSE

And God said unto Noah, Make thee an ark of gopher wood; rooms shalt thou make in the ark, and the length of the ark shall be 300 cubits.

And of every living thing of all flesh, two of every sort shalt thou bring into the ark, to keep them alive with thee.

And Noah said, Sign here, and leavest Thou a deposit.

And the Lord signed there, and left He a deposit.

And Noah was 600 years old when the flood of waters was upon the Earth.

And the Lord said unto Noah, Where is the ark, which I commanded thee to build?

An Noah said unto the Lord, Verily, I have had three carpenters off ill.

The gopher wood supplier hath let me down – yea even though the gopher wood hath been on order for nigh upon 12 months. The damp-course specialist hath not turned up. What can I do, O Lord?

And God said unto Noah, I want that ark finished even after seven days and seven nights.

And Noah said, It will be so.

And it was not so.

And the Lord said unto Noah, What seemeth to be the trouble this time?

And Noah said unto the Lord, Mine sub-contractor hath gone bankrupt. The pitch which Thou commandest me to put on the outside and on the inside of the ark hath not arrived. The plumber hath gone on strike.

Noah rent his garments and said, The glazier departeth on holiday to Majorca – yea, even though I offerest him double time. Shem, my son, who helpeth me on the ark side of the business, hath formed a pop group with his brothers Ham and Japheth. Lord I am undone.

And God said in his wrath, Noah, do not thou mucketh Me about.

The end of all flesh is come before me for the Earth is filled with violence through them; and behold, I will destroy them with the Earth. How can I destroy them with the Earth if thou art incapable of completing the job that thou was contracted to do?

And Noah said, Lo, the contract will be fulfilled.

And Lo, it was not fulfilled.

And Noah said unto the Lord, The gopher wood is definitely in the warehouse. Verily, and the gopher wood supplier waiteth only upon his servant to find the invoices before he delivereth the gopher wood unto me.

And the Lord grew angry and said, Scrubbeth thou round the gopher wood. What about the animals?

Of fowls after their kind, and of cattle after their kind, of every creeping thing of the Earth after his kind, two of every sort have I ordered to come unto thee, to keep them alive.

Where for example are the giraffes?

And Noah said unto the Lord, They are expected today.

And the Lord said unto Noah, And where are the clean beasts, the male and the female; to keep their seed alive upon the face of all the Earth?

And Noah said, The van cometh on Tuesday; yea and yea, it will be so.

And the Lord said unto Noah, How about the unicorns?

And Noah wrung his hands and wept, saying, Lord, Lord, they are a discontinued line. Thou canst not get unicorns for love nor money.

And God said, Come thou, Noah, I have left with thee a deposit, and thou hast signed a contract.

Where are the monkeys, and the bears, and the hippopotami, and the elephants, and the zebras and the hartebeests, two of each kind, and of fowls also of the air by sevens, the male and the female?

And Noah said unto the Lord, They have been delivered unto the wrong address, but should arrive on Friday; all save the fowls of the air by sevens, for it hath just been told unto me that fowls of the air are sold only in half-dozens.

And God said unto Noah, Thou hast not made an ark of gopher wood, nor hast thou lined it with pitch within and without; and of every living thing of all flesh, two of every sort hast thou failed to bring into the ark. What sayest thou, Noah?

And Noah kissed the Earth and said, Lord, thou knowest in thy wisdom what it is like with delivery dates.

And the Lord in his wisdom said, Noah, my son, I knowest. Why else dost thou think I have caused a flood to descend upon the Earth?

*Readers: David Davis, Rosalind Shanks*

*Full Selection:*
*A Smuggler's Song*, RUDYARD KIPLING
*Tregardock*, JOHN BETJEMAN

*The Old Ships*, JAMES ELROY FLECKER
*My Aunt's Rhinoceros*, PETER FLEMING
*No Room in the Ark*, ALAN MOOREHEAD
*Future Work*, FLEUR ADCOCK
*Extract from Letters*, JANE AUSTEN
*Being but Men*, DYLAN THOMAS
*The Queen's Marie*, ANON
*Wee Bit Mousikie*, ANON
*The Cow Who Jumped Over The Moon*, DAME CELIA JOHNSON
*How Long, O Lord . . . ?*, KEITH WATERHOUSE
*The Bat*, RUTH PITTER
*Welsh Incident*, ROBERT GRAVES
*Tartary*, WALTER DE LA MARE
*Farewell*, WALTER DE LA MARE

# THE EARL OF LICHFIELD

## 1982

*The last item in this programme is another one that gave rise to a rush of letters from listeners. It seems not to have been published widely, so I am pleased to include it here. The impression of Lord Lichfield that comes across from his script is very different from that given by the barbed ramblings of the popular press. He is clearly a sensitive man with a deep feeling for and love of things English. These include the game of cricket, a blind spot of mine, and English humour. Recovering from appendicitis, when he was 15, he read 'The Cricket Match' and 'England Their England' by A.G. MacDonell. His mother had given him the book to cheer him up. He laughed so much while reading it that his stitches burst.*

An ancient and distant relation of mine once laid out a cricket pitch, and being rather a grand Duke he felt that it was only right and proper that the grandest cricketer in the land should come to open it for him, and so he chose Dr Grace. And there was a blacksmith, who on arriving at the crease bowled a perfectly accurate ball which struck the gallant and noble doctor on the knee but plumb. A great shout of 'How's that?' went up. Before the umpire could get his hands out of his pocket, Dr Grace walked down the wicket and said 'Young man, these thousand people have come to watch me bat, not you bowl.'

When I was asked by the producer of this programme, Brian Patten, to think about what I would like to include in the programme, I was lecturing on the QE2 just before she was requisitioned to go to the Falklands and I spent a few hours in the library there just before she went. I have chosen a number of things which come very much from my childhood and I make no apology for being patriotic and rather 'Boys' Own' about the whole thing.

This piece is a personal one and rather obscure. In 1740 Admiral Anson, who happened to be a great-great-great-great-great-great-great-uncle of mine, left Staffordshire and set off around the world to harass the Spaniards and to come back with any treasure to be found on an incredibly enriched galleon which sailed between Acapulco and Manila. He left England with eight ships in 1740 and finally arrived back in 1744. But on April 13th 1741, which I imagine must have been a Friday, there was recorded a piece about his attempting to round Cape Horn.

## *Log of The Centurion*

LEO HEAPS

Edward Legge of the Severn and George Murray of the Pearle turned back after several unsuccessful attempts to round the Cape and ran off before the gales to the River Plate, eventually reaching Rio de Janeiro.

Their crews were no more disabled than the crews of the other ships, and they would have been no worse off had they remained with the squadron. The presence of two more fighting ships in the Pacific might have changed the course of history for Britain. Anson at the time presumed the Severn and Pearle had been lost.

Their commanders' reasons for returning were irrefutable. It seemed that they simply could not go on. They had reached the end. In fact there was no plausible reason for anyone continuing beyond the Horn in the face of more certain destruction. Except that brave men differed. Under the ultimate test Anson had a will that could not be weakened by adversity. So had Saumarez. Those fine, slight differences in human nature, never quite apparent until the final crisis, now showed themselves among the men. Colonel Cracherode, colonel of a dying force of marines, also clung grimly to life. He was a battered veteran of a dozen wars and survived to lead his pitiful remnants against the Spaniards at Payta in Chile. After Anson himself, the character of Philip Saumarez dominated. Perhaps the quiet, tortured nature of the man had been inhibited too long in the rigid cast of the Navy, and at last Anson gave Saumarez the chance he wanted. In many ways the rounding of Cape Horn in the Tryall was the making of Saumarez.

For over a month the squadron attempted to gain the west coast of Patagonia and leave behind the bleak, wild isthmus of Tierra del Fuego. The isthmus projected like a curved beak on the extremity of South America, bent back by untold centuries of severe storms.

In the conflicting streams and winds the ships were flung about like small boats. One man on the Centurion broke a collar bone, several fractured their legs and arms, while two seamen were thrown overboard and lost. From March to May there were almost continuous storms on an unprecedented scale.

Water constantly flooded the decks of all the ships, especially the Tryall, straining ahead of the squadron with the seas cascading like waterfalls from the plunging bows. Towards the middle of April, 'there came a storm which both in its violence and continuation exceeded all that hitherto encountered'. It lasted three days. On the last day the quarter gallery of the Centurion near the poop was stoved in and water 'rushed into the ship like a deluge'. Shrouds broke and for days the Centurion lay under the bare poles, heaving and crashing helplessly into the seas until the storm gradually subsided.

Almost everyone was infected with the scurvy and badly demoralised. Forty men had been lost since they came through the Le Maire Straits and most of the crew unable to perform their duties. On each watch no more than seventy seamen could be mustered, while the marines were all either sick or dead.

What's extraordinary about that is that it was 241 years ago and yet we still had to sail down to the South Seas not so long ago in much the same way. He went on with that beleaguered ship. In fact out of 1,939 men only 101 arrived back in England. After putting out the Great Fire of Canton on their way back, he arrived home and produced 39 wagons of silver which were taken to the tower of London and then distributed according to rank and the residue that he had went to build the house that I live in, which is called Shugborough. But it does demonstrate that the kind of spirit that existed then is something that I'm afraid keeps going through my choices, but I make no apology for that.

I want to go on to something quite different. I've always thought that if people become famous too early they're likely to reach a sticky end – in fact it always worries me that perhaps I've had a bit too much publicity myself, and what will it be like next year? And hence I go on to Oscar Wilde, not the Wilde you might expect, not the prose, but 'The Ballad of Reading Gaol' which, of course, is late in Wilde's literary career, and somehow there's something very touching in this. The sentiment is that of 'Well, I'm pretty badly off, but there's always somebody worse around the corner.'

## *The Ballad of Reading Gaol*

OSCAR WILDE

He did not wear his scarlet coat,
  For blood and wine are red,
And blood and wine were on his hands
  When they found him with the dead,
The poor dead woman whom he loved,
  And murdered in her bed.

He walked amongst the Trial Men
  In a suit of shabby grey;
A cricket cap was on his head,

And his step seemed light and gay;
But I never saw a man who looked
So wistfully at the day.

I never saw a man who looked
With such a wistful eye
Upon that little tent of blue
Which prisoners call the sky,
And at every drifting cloud that went
With sails of silver by.

I walked, with other souls in pain,
Within another ring,
And was wondering if the man had done
A great or little thing,
When a voice behind me whispered low,
'That fellow's got to swing.'

Dear Christ! the very prison walls
Suddenly seemed to reel,
And the sky above my head became
Like a casque of scorching steel;
And, though I was a soul in pain,
My pain I could not feel.

I only knew what hunted thought
Quickened his step, and why
He looked upon the garish day
With such a wistful eye;
The man had killed the thing he loved,
And so he had to die.

Yet each man kills the thing he loves,
By each let this be heard,
Some do it with a bitter look,
Some with a flattering word.
The coward does it with a kiss,
The brave man with a sword!

Some kill their love when they are young,
And some when they are old;
Some strangle with the hands of Lust,

Some with the hands of Gold:
The kindest use a knife, because
The dead so soon grow cold.

Some love too little, some too long,
Some sell, and others buy;
Some do the deed with many tears,
And some without a sigh;
For each man kills the thing he loves,
Yet each man does not die.

This last piece was shown to me after the death of an exceedingly dear relation and I was asked to read it in an exceedingly beautiful church. It quite simply had one effect on me in that it provided me with a completely new feeling that I hadn't thought I would experience after somebody had died. It's by Henry Scott Holland.

Death is nothing at all, . . . I have only slipped away into the next room . . . I am I and you are you . . . whatever we were to each other that we are still. Call me by my old familiar name, speak to me in the easy way which you always used. Put no difference into your tone; wear no forced air of solemnity or sorrow. Laugh as we always laughed at the little jokes we enjoyed together. Play, smile, think of me, pray for me. Let my name be ever the household word it always was. Let it be spoken without effect, without the ghost of a shadow on it. Life means all that it ever meant. It is the same as it ever was; there is an absolutely unbroken continuity. What is this death but a negligible accident? Why should I be out of mind because I am out of sight? I am but waiting for you, for an interval, somewhere very near just around the corner . . . All is well.

*Readers: Robert Hardy, Frank Windsor*

*Full Selection:*
*Lord Lundy,* HILAIRE BELLOC
*Summoned by Bells,* JOHN BETJEMAN
*England, Their England,* A. G. MACDONELL

*Log of The Centurion*, LEO HEAPS
*The Ballad of Reading Gaol*, OSCAR WILDE
*Preface to the Doctor's Dilemma*, BERNARD SHAW
*The Second World War, Volume 2*, SIR WINSTON CHURCHILL
*Speech to Schoolchildren of Rotorua, 3 March 1958*, LORD COBHAM
*Forty Years On*, ALAN BENNETT
*Death is Nothing at All . . .*, HENRY SCOTT HOLLAND

# PROFESSOR SIR BERNARD LOVELL

## 1978

*The learned astronomer from Jodrell Bank is clearly in love with the firmament and like all good scientists has the soul of a poet. He calculated that every year nearly a ton of books, papers and letters thud on to his desk and that these comprised most of his prose reading. Whilst paying them due professional attention, he was clearly not impressed with the quality of language in which the findings were expressed. As an example of what he so disliked he quoted a typical present-day description of the awe-inspiring sight of the launch of a huge balloon full of scientific apparatus and its ascent to a great height which began: 'The balloon was launched at 1204 UT and reached a float altitude of 2.9g cm$^{-2}$ at approximately 1530 UT where it remained for 6.5h before cutdown.' – and a recent account of the evolution of the Universe: 'it is generally believed that in the physically realistic case, an incomplete causal geodisc terminates in a singularity which destroys everything which enters . . .' – including sense and meaning presumably. He compared such modern scientific expression unfavourably with that of the great scientists of the past. Who can blame him?*

Nowadays I suppose that a quarter of a century is a long time to work in the same place, but I've worked here at Jodrell Bank for even longer than that – since the end of the war in fact. First in ex-army trailers amongst the corn fields, then amongst the mud and cranes as the steelwork of the great telescope rose above the Cheshire plain. Twenty years ago the massive bowl of the telescope began to probe the sky as it is doing tonight, searching far into time and space for answers to the problems of the universe. It's an exciting and romantic place, especially at night when the telephones no longer ring, and the huge structure stands isolated in the floodlights against the dark of the sky, as it is outside on this dome now.

This Planetarium is very close to that telescope. Many thousands of people visit here every year to see the stars and planets projected on to the dome. Now it is full of my friends and colleagues; I hope I am not going to bore you like Walt Whitman's 'The Learned Astronomer'.

### *When I Heard the Learn'd Astronomer*

WALT WHITMAN

When I heard the learn'd astronomer,
When the proofs, the figures, were ranged
in columns before me,
When I was shown the charts and diagrams, to add,
divide, and measure them,
When I sitting heard the astronomer where he lectured
with much applause in the lecture room,
How soon unaccountable I became tired and sick,
Till rising and gliding out I wandere'd off by myself,
In the mystical moist night-air, and from time to time,
Look'd up in perfect silence at the stars.

I can't help contrasting modern scientific prose with that I read as a young student. Two years ago the Council of the Royal Society allocated to me the task of writing the biographical memoir of Lord Blackett. For over 40 years he had been a major influence in my life and work and naturally I wanted to do this job thoroughly. So I collected and read more than 130 scientific papers, books and other articles which he had written. His prose was always good and often magnificent. As a young man he was a lieutenant in the Royal Navy and his diaries contain a graphic account of the Battle of Jutland. In 1919 he decided to leave the Navy and joined Rutherford's team in the Cavendish Laboratory. Within a few years he had obtained results in nuclear physics of such importance that they are described in every textbook of physics.

I wish the young scientists today would read those original papers, written between 1920 and 1930 – the elegance and simplicity of the style in which he describes his work is memorable. Here is a part of his description of the apparatus which he used to study the disintegration of the nitrogen atom by alpha-particles. He is describing the problem of achieving a vacuum in his apparatus:

> So usually an apparatus of this type is made in sections, these being fitted together and made tight against a leakage of air into the apparatus by the use of a grease or cement. It is curious that the most universally successful vacuum cement available for many years should have been a material of common use for quite other purposes. At one time it might have been hard to find in an English laboratory an apparatus which did not use red Bank of England sealing-wax as a vacuum cement. If its pre-eminence is now being shaken, it is not by some refined product of laborious research but by ordinary plasticine. It is hardly possible to exaggerate the controlling importance of such simple technical matters, however trivial they may seem to be.

We've been part of the technical revolution of the age: the telescope records signals which had their origin in remote space billions of years ago and started on their journey to us long before our own Earth came into existence. Even so, we often feel as Milton did 300 years ago. In Book 7 of 'Paradise Lost', Raphael explained to Adam how the World was first created. At the beginning of Book 8, Adam makes further enquiries concerning the celestial motions.

## *Paradise Lost Book 8*

JOHN MILTON

When I behold this goodly Frame, this World
Of Heav'n and Earth consisting, and compute
Thir magnitudes, this Earth a spot, a graine,
An Atom, with the Firmanent compar'd
And all her numberd Starrs, that seem to rowle
Spaces incomprehensible (for such
Thir distance argues and thir swift return
Diurnal) meerly to officiate light
Round this opacous Earth, this punctual spot,
One day and night; in all thir vast survey
Useless besides, reasoning I oft admire,
How Nature wise and frugal could commit
Such disproportions, with superfluous hand
So many nobler Bodies to create.

In 1638, twenty-nine years before the publication of 'Paradise Lost', Milton had travelled to Italy. The country was still distracted by the trial and imprisonment of Galileo. In the Areopagitica – the address which Milton made to Parliament pleading for the freedom of the Press – he wrote:

## *Areopagitica*

JOHN MILTON

I have sat among their learned men and been counted happy to be born in such a place of philosophic freedom as they supposed England was, while they themselves did nothing but bemoan the servile conditions into which learning amongst them was brought; that this was it which had damped the glory of Italian wits, that nothing had been there written now these many years but flattery and fustian. There it was that I found and visited the famous Galileo, grown old, a prisoner of the Inquisition.

The intellectual stability of the Western World had been based on the belief that the Earth was fixed in space at the centre of the Universe. In order to explain the varying positions of the planets in the sky a complex system of motions of the heavenly bodies around the Earth in epicycles had been devised. Galileo's crime was that he was the first to look at the heavens through a small telescope and so to find the observational evidence that the earth was not fixed in space, but was in motion around the Sun.

A generation later Milton placed the argument about the movement of the Earth, and about the geometrical description of the motions of the heavenly bodies in epicycles, in the ethereal context of Plato's moving image of eternity. In this marvellous passage Raphael is continuing his explanation to Adam.

## *Paradise Lost Book 8*

JOHN MILTON

Hereafter, when they come to model Heav'n
And calculate the Starrs, how they will weild
The mightie frame, how build, unbuild, contrive
To save appeerances, how gird the Sphear
With Centric and Eccentric scribl'd o're,
Cycle and Epicycle, Orb in Orb:
Alreadie by thy reasoning this I guess,
Who art to lead thy ofspring, and supposest
That Bodies bright and greater should not serve
The less not bright, nor Heav'n such journies run,
Earth sitting still, when she alone receaves
The benefit: consider first, that Great
Or Bright inferrs not Excellence: the Earth
Though, in comparison of Heav'n, so small,
Nor glistering, may of solid good containe
More plenty then the Sun that barren shines,
Whose vertue on it self works no effect,
But in the fruitful Earth; there first receavd
His beams, unactive else, thir vigor find.
Yet not to Earth are those bright Luminaries
Officious, but to thee Earths habitant
And for the Heav'ns wide Circuit, let it speak
The Makers high magnificence, who built
So spacious, and his Line stretcht out so farr;
That Man may know he dwells not in his own;
An Edifice too large for him to fill
Lodg'd in a small partition, and the rest
Ordain'd for uses to his Lord best known.

The swiftness of those Circles attribute,
Though numberless, to his Omnipotence,
That to corporeal substances could adde
Speed almost Spiritual; mee thou thinkst not slow,
Who since the Morning hour set out from Heav'n
Where God resides, and ere mid-day arriv'd
In *Eden*, distance inexpressible
By numbers that have name. But this I urge,
Admitting Motion in the Heav'ns, to shew
Invalid that which thee to doubt it mov'd;
Not that I so affirm, though so it seem
To thee who hast thy dwelling here on Earth.
God to remove his wayes from human sense,
Plac'd Heav'n from Earth so farr, that earthly sight,
If it presume, might erre in things too high,
And no advantage gaine. What if the Sun
Be Center to the World, and other Starrs
By his attractive vertue and thir own
Incited, dance about him various rounds?
Thir wandring course now high, now low, then hid,
Progressive, retrograde, or standing still,
In six thou seest, and what if sev'nth to these
The Planet Earth, so steadfast though she seem,
Insensibly three different Motions move?

When I was a student I played so much cricket and practised the organ for such long periods that I nearly let down my teachers of science who thought I might have promise.

Since I was a member of three cricket teams – the University, my local village and the Bristol Optimists, this was quite a serious diversion and I suppose I must have played on nearly every cricket ground in Gloucestershire and Somerset. When I finally left the West Country for Manchester I was inconsolably nostalgic and so understood very well the essence of Francis Thompson's poem about Hornby and Barlow. He suffered the same experience – but in reverse. Francis Thompson wrote this poem about a cricket match played at Old Trafford 100 years ago when he was 19 years old – in July 1878, the first time that Lancashire had met Gloucestershire and the fame of W. G. Grace and his brothers

E.M. and G.F. was such that on the last day of that match it's recorded that 16,000 people crammed into Old Trafford and that at least 2,000 of them forced the gates without payment when the ground had been declared full. In Lancashire's second innings Hornby scored a century and Barlow 80.

All of this unexpectedly came to life for me one day last summer. The scene was at a lovely country house in the west of England; outside the dining room windows stretched a perfect small cricket ground. Suddenly I realised that I was enjoying a luncheon with a near relative of the famous Hornby of the Francis Thompson poem!

Incidentally, Francis Thompson was an unsuccessful medical student in the University of Manchester and lived in great poverty until his first book of poems was published (including 'The Hound of Heaven') five years after the events referred to in the poem which we are to hear now. After his failures in Manchester he moved to London in 1907. His nostalgia for Old Trafford was so great that when, late in his life, he was invited to Lord's to watch Middlesex play Lancashire he could not face the ordeal and produced instead this memorable lament.

## *At Lords*

FRANCIS THOMPSON

It is little I repair to the matches of the Southron folk,
Though my own red roses there may blow;
It is little I repair to the matches of the Southron folk,
Though the red roses crest the caps, I know.
For the field is full of shades as I near the shadowy coast,
And a ghostly batsman plays to the bowling of a ghost,
And I look through my tears on a soundless-clapping host,
As the run-stealers flicker to and fro,
To and fro: –
O my Hornby and my Barlow long ago!

It is Glo'ster coming North, the irresistible,
The Shire of the Graces, long ago!
It is Gloucestershire up North, the irresistible,
And new-risen Lancashire the foe!

A Shire so young that has scarce impressed its traces,
Ah, how shall it stand before all resistless Graces?
O, little red rose, their bats are as maces
To beat thee down, this summer long ago!

This day of seventy-eight they are come up North against thee,
This day of seventy-eight, long ago!
The champion of the centuries, he cometh up against thee,
With his brethren, every one a famous foe!
The long-whiskered Doctor, that laugheth rules to scorn,
While the bowler, pitched against him, bans the day that he was born;
And G. F. with his science makes the fairest length forlorn;
They are come from the West to work thee woe!

It is little I repair to the matches of the Southron folk,
Though my own red roses there may blow;
It is little I repair to the matches of the Southron folk,
Though the red roses crest the caps, I know.
For the field is full of shades as I near the shadowy coast,
And a ghostly batsman plays to the bowling of a ghost,
And I look through my tears on a soundless-clapping host,
As the run-stealers flicker to and fro,
To and fro: –
O my Hornby and my Barlow long ago!

*Readers: Patience Collier, Patrick Troughton*

*Full Selection:*
*When I heard the Learn'd Astronomer*, WALT WHITMAN
*Paradise Lost, Book 8*, JOHN MILTON
*Areopagitica*, JOHN MILTON
*The Garden*, VITA SACKVILLE-WEST
*The Land (Summer)*, VITA SACKVILLE-WEST
*The Land (Spring)*, VITA SACKVILLE-WEST
*At Lords*, FRANCIS THOMPSON
*The Hill*, H.A. VACHELL
*Autobiography*, NEVILLE CARDUS

*Song*, PERCY BYSSHE SHELLEY
*Fugue (Splendours and Miseries)*, SACHEVERELL SITWELL
*A Search for the Reported 400KeV-Ray Line from Crab Nebula*, LING, MAHONEY, WILLETT, JACOBIAN
*Black Holes in Closed Universes*, F. J. TIPLER
*The Craft of Experimental Physics*, P. M. S. BLACKETT
*March Hare*, JEAN KENWARD
*Kingdoms*, JEAN KENWARD
*Wild Duck*, JEAN KENWARD
*Bavarian Gentians*, D. H. LAWRENCE
*Jodrell Bank*, PATRIC DICKINSON

# KIT McMAHON

## 1985

*Normally people who are asked to present 'With Great Pleasure' are at least fairly well-known to the public at large. It's far from being an invariable rule as it is always stimulating to meet and to present to the general listener someone gifted and/or eminent in their field, who is not frequently to be seen or heard on the 'media'. I must admit, however, that when I was approached by Kit McMahon's assistant it was the first time I had seriously considered including a banker in the series, although the Deputy Governor of the Bank of England, as he was then, was obviously not without interest. On meeting him for the first time in his palatial office, I was struck by how far he had already thought the programme through and how quietly enthusiastic he was about the possibility of taking part. He did not strike me as being particularly extrovert, but it was an attractive personality none the less. He turned up at the recording a jolly, friendly and not totally organised man (he had forgotten his notes which comprised the script) whom it was easy to like.*

I read an awful lot as a child and adolescent, all kinds of books from rubbish to difficult classics, which I liked less than I pretended. Apart from comics and thrillers, the taste for which has stayed with me for the rest of my life, if I do look back at my later school days and try to think of passages which especially excited me I think I might come up with the following:

If a body is at rest or in a state of uniform motion it will remain so unless acted on by an external force.

or:

To every action there is an equal and opposite reaction.

Newton's first and third laws. The second I have to say is a little bit too complicated to read here.

I can still remember the excitement of being shown this great jump in thought that those laws represented. The wonderful realisation that you needed force not to make something move, but to accelerate it. And ever since I've found scientific laws fascinating for the way in which a statement, which is in some sense just a tautology, can illuminate the real world and stimulate great discovery and achievement. And I may say in passing that against this standard I find the so called laws of economics pretty poor things.

In due course, however, I came to like poetry. I'd like to show you a poem which explores migration. I include it not just because I like it and think it a moving poem, but as an act of piety. Its author, A. D. Hope, Alec Hope, taught me English Literature at Melbourne University; he was the first true, uncompromising artist I'd met and that is always an experience to be grateful for. He is, I think, a very distinguished poet, I believe one of the best to have written in this century, but, at least in England, he is very under-rated – under-rated because under-read. Most anthologists, having to limit their field somewhere, draw the line at the British Isles. You might find a Hope poem in an anthology of Commonwealth verse, but what a ghastly, nonsensical concept to be embedded in. Anyway, I hope that some people will like 'The Death of the Bird' enough to seek out his collected works.

## *The Death of the Bird*

A. D. HOPE

For every bird there is this last migration:
Once more the cooling year kindles her heart;
With a warm passage to the summer station
Love pricks the course in lights across the chart.

Year after year a speck on the map, divided
By a whole hemisphere, summons her to come;
Season after season, sure and safely guided,
Going away she is also coming home.

And being home, memory becomes a passion
With which she feeds her brood and straws her nest,
Aware of ghosts that haunt the heart's possession
And exiled love mourning within the breast.

The sands are green with a mirage of valleys;
The palm tree casts a shadow not its own;
Down the long architrave of temple or palace
Blows a cool air from moorland scraps of stone.

And day by day the whisper of love grows stronger;
That delicate voice, more urgent with despair,
Custom and fear constraining her no longer,
Drives her at last on the waste leagues of air.

A vanishing speck in those inane dominions,
Single and frail, uncertain of her place,
Alone in the bright host of her companions,
Lost in the blue unfriendliness of space.

She feels it close now, the appointed season:
The invisible thread is broken as she flies;
Suddenly, without warning, without reason,
The guiding spark of instinct winks and dies.

Try as she will, the trackless world delivers
No way, the wilderness of light no sign,
The immense and complex map of hills and rivers
Mocks her small wisdom with its vast design.

And darkness rises from the eastern valleys,
And the winds buffer her with their hungry breath,
And the great earth, with neither grief nor malice,
Receives the tiny burden of her death.

I came to England in 1951 and have spent the rest of my life here absorbed in the worlds of economics, finance and public affairs. Enjoyable though that's been, I have to say that searching back through it, it hasn't yielded me passages that I could remember with particular pleasure, at least that could be read out. For my selections, therefore, I shall be drawing on my private life and I would like now to move to three poems on the deepest and most private of emotions, love. I suppose there are more poems on love than on anything else, certainly more bad poems, but perhaps more good ones as well. It took me a long time to select the ones I would most like you to hear. Some I rejected because I think they are too well known, some because, though clearly great poetry, they didn't speak to me or my wife, so I turned for my first selection to the greatest love poet, indeed for me the greatest poet, Yeats. Here is one of his less known poems, certainly not his greatest, but one which seems to me to capture very simply something of the mysterious crash of falling in love.

## *Her Triumph*

W. B. YEATS

I did the dragon's will until you came
Because I had fancied love a casual
Improvisation, or a settled game
That followed if I let the kerchief fall:
Those deeds were best that gave the minute wings
And heavenly music if they gave it wit;
And then you stood among the dragon-wings.
I mocked, being crazy, but you mastered it
And broke the train and set my ankles free,
Saint George or else a pagan Perseus;
And now we stare astonished at the sea,
And a miraculous strange bird shrieks at us.

Next something quite different, about love gone hopelessly wrong. This poem I think is remarkable for its drama and for the amazing way that though it is narrated by one of the two people concerned, it is completely even-handed and objective in its pity for both of them. It is by poor, unhappy Charlotte Mew.

### *The Farmer's Bride*

CHARLOTTE MEW

Three Summers since I chose a maid,
Too young maybe – but more's to do
At harvest-time than bide and woo.
    When us was wed she turned afraid
Of love and me and all things human;
Like the shut of a winter's day.
Her smile went out, and twasn't a woman –
    More like a little frightened fay.
    One night, in the Fall, she runned away.

'Out 'mong the sheep, her be,' they said,
'Should properly have been abed;'
But sure enough she wasn't there
Lying awake with her wide brown stare.
So over seven-acre field and up-along across the down
We chased her, flying like a hare
Before our lanterns. To Church-Town
    All in a shiver and a scare
We caught her, fetched her home at last
    And turned the key upon her, fast.

She does the work about the house
As well as most, but like a mouse:
    Happy enough to chat and play
    With birds and rabbits and such as they,
    So long as men-folk keep away.
'Not near, not near!' her eyes beseech
When one of us comes within reach.
    The women say that beasts in stall
    Look round like children at her call.
    *I've* hardly heard her speak at all.

Shy as a leveret, swift as he,
Straight and slight as a young larch tree,
Sweet as the first wild violets, she,
To her wild self. But what to me?

The short days shorten and the oaks are brown,
The blue smoke rises to the low grey sky,
One leaf in the still air falls slowly down,
A magpie's spotted feathers lie
On the black earth spread white with rime,
The berries redden up to Christmas-time.
What's Christmas-time without there be
Some other in the house than we!

She sleeps up in the attic there
Alone, poor maid. 'Tis but a stair
Betwixt us. Oh! my God! the down,
The soft young down of her, the brown,
The brown of her – her eyes, her hair, her hair!

A third love poem has given a great deal of pleasure to my wife and myself. It celebrates a very good emotion indeed, an emotion perhaps under some threat as the sexual revolution going on around us marches inexorably forward, the straightforward emotion of sexual affection. It is by Sir John Harington who lived from 1560–1612 and is best known for a major work which I confess never to have opened. But he also wrote a number of *jeux d'esprit* and this is one of them.

## *The Author to His Wife, of a Woman's Eloquence*

JOHN HARRINGTON

My Mall, I mark that when you mean to prove me
To buy a velvet gown, or some rich border,
Thou callst me good sweet heart, thou swearst to
love me,
Thy locks, thy lips, thy looks, speak all in order,
Thou thinks't, and right thou thinks't, that these
do move me,
That all these severally thy suit do further:

But shall I tell thee what most thy suit
advances?
Thy fair smoothe words? no, no, thy fair
smoothe haunches.

In the last few years Norfolk has become an important part of my life, we spend most weekends and many holidays there, and I've chosen, therefore, two Norfolk pieces. The first is a little poem by Frances Cornford, the author, you may remember, of that splendid poem that begins: 'Oh fat white woman whom nobody loves, why do you walk through the fields in gloves, missing so much and so much?' This poem is called 'The Coast: Norfolk' and was written, I suppose, 70 or 80 years ago, but it seems to us still to catch the space and feel of that lovely, remote, windswept county.

## *The Coast: Norfolk*

FRANCES CORNFORD

As on the highway's quiet edge
He mows the grass beside the hedge,
The old man has for company
The distant, grey, salt-smelling sea,
A poppied field, a cow, and calf,
The finches on the telegraph.

Across his faded back a hoe,
He slowly, slowly scythes alone
In silence of the wind-soft air,
With ladies' bedstraw everywhere,
With whitened corn, and tarry poles,
And far-off gulls like risen souls.

My second piece on Norfolk is rather a swizz. It's a passage from Thomas Browne, 'Urne Burial'. I managed to include it under Norfolk because Sir Thomas Browne was a seventeenth-century doctor in Norwich with a wide-ranging curiosity and a mind well stocked with classical scholarship. He attracts me as a kind of mid-point between old scholasticism and the beginning of modern science with the Royal Society. In his very minor way he seems to exemplify Britain's greatest century, the seventeenth. He loved to investigate in an apparently scientific way problems scarcely amenable to that approach. For example, one of his essays devotes a good deal of time to trying, in the end unsuccessfully, to establish exactly what fruit it was that Eve gave Adam. This extract, a famous one, concerns some ancient burial urns which a friend of his had found dug up in Walsingham, which is very near us in Norfolk. Sir Thomas Browne muses a good deal on the urns themselves, who buried them there and why, and expresses the magnitude of his problem in the following words:

## *Urne Burial*

SIR THOMAS BROWNE

What song the Syrens sang, or what name Achilles assumed when he hid himself among women, though puzzling questions are not beyond all conjecture. What time the persons of these Ossuaries entered the famous Nations of the dead, and slept with Princes and Counsellors, might admit a wide solution. But who were the proprietaries of these bones, or what bodies these ashes made up, were a question above Antiquarism. Not to be resolved by man, nor easily perhaps by spirits, except we consult the Provincial Guardians, or tutelary Observators. Had they made as good provision for their names, as they have done for their Reliques, they had not so grossly erred in the art of perpetuation. But to subsist in bones, and be but Pyramidally extant, is a fallacy in duration. Vain ashes, which in the oblivion of names, person, times, and sexes, have found unto themselves a fruitlesse continuation, and only arise unto late posterity, as Emblemes of mortal vanities; Antidotes against pride, vainglory, and madding vices.

*Readers: Dinsdale Landen, Jane Lapotaire*

*Full Selection:*
*Treasure Island*, R. L. STEVENSON
*The Windhover*, GERARD MANLEY HOPKINS
*The Death of the Bird*, A. D. HOPE

*The Big Sleep*, RAYMOND CHANDLER
*Her Triumph*, W. B. YEATS
*The Farmer's Bride*, CHARLOTTE MEW
*My Mall*, JOHN HARRINGTON
*Ulysses*, JAMES JOYCE
*The Coast: Norfolk*, FRANCES CORNFORD
*Urne-Burial*, SIR THOMAS BROWNE
*Musée des Beaux Arts*, W. H. AUDEN
*Life with Picasso*, FRANCOISE GELOT
*A Song to David*, CHRISTOPHER SMART

# *JOHN MORTIMER*

## *1978*

*John Mortimer is the only person who has deliberately been commissioned twice to take part in 'With Great Pleasure'. One other person, also a famous writer, had been, but it was an accident. On that occasion, neither the producer, nor the writer, remembered that he had done one before! In Mortimer's case, however, the second programme was not in his own name, but was written around a non-existent American author as an April Fool joke. I do remember, however, about twenty years ago working as a 'spot' operator – opening and shutting doors, pouring tea and generally clattering around – on the re-make of Mortimer's radio play 'A Voyage Around My Father', the original tapes having been mislaid or wiped. Three or four years later when I was, briefly, an assistant producer in Television Centre, the BBC announced with a great fanfare a season of new plays by major playwrights specially written for television. One of them was called 'A Voyage Around My father' by John Mortimer. No one seemed too pleased when I pointed out that it had already been broadcast twice on radio! Certainly it wasn't felt necessary officiously to strive to tell the public. Later it was turned into a successful stage play and subsequently produced once more for television, this time by a commercial company with Laurence Olivier in the lead.*

My father was a very well-known divorce barrister. Instead of bed-time stories, 'Snow White' or whatever, he used to sit at the end of my bed and say, 'Today I managed to get costs against the co-respondent', or 'Today I managed to prove adultery by inclination and opportunity. An important part of the evidence was "footprints on the dashboard".' So early in my life it was decided that I should become a lawyer.

Legal anecdotes always seem to me rather cruel and although hilarious to judges and lawyers, those sentenced to death or long terms of imprisonment rarely join in the laughter. For example:

*Judge.* (to convicted murderer) Have you anything to say why sentence of death should not be passed against you?
*Murderer.* Damn all, my lord.
*Judge.* (to counsel) Mr Bleaks, did your client say something?
*Mr Bleaks.* Damn all, my Lord.
*Judge.* Funny, I could swear I heard him say something . . .

The main thing I have always found in the law is that the judge and the judged speak in different languages, coming as they do from different worlds. There used to be one exquisite judge at the Old Bailey – he always used to rise at 11.30 in the morning for a glass of Chablis and a nibble of Stilton, and he had to sentence a dead-drunk Irish labourer who'd assaulted the police, vomited down the stairs of Leicester Square Tube Station and appeared unshaven, red-eyed and staggering in the dock. This judge said, 'I'm going to take a most unusual course with you. A most merciful course. I'm going to place you on probation.'

'Oh, God bless you, your Honour. God bless your Royal Highness,' says the Irishman.

'But on one condition.'

'Anything, my Lord. Any condition, your Worship.'

'You're not to take another drink in your life.'

'Not a drop, I swear to your Holiness. Not a solitary drop.'

'And by that I mean absolutely *nothing*.' The judge leaned forward, smiling charmingly, 'Not even the *teeniest weeniest* little dry sherry before your dinner.'

So you see what I mean by the two different languages?

Far more interesting are the letters, diaries, the evidence of the accused. For instance, the Thompson/Bywaters case. Edith Thompson was an incurable romantic, a sort of Madame Bovary of Kensington Gardens. She fell in love with a young seaman, Bywaters, whom they say she induced to stab her husband to death. This is how she wrote to Frederick Bywaters:

### *Letter from Edith Thompson to Frederick Bywaters*

On Thursday I went to the Waldorf for tea and while waiting in the vestibule by myself a gentleman came up, raised his hat and said, 'Are you Romance?' It seems he had an appointment with a lady he's corresponded with through the personal column . . .

I'm so stiff and sore today I can hardly move . . . This time last year you were able to rub me gradually and take that stiffness away. Do you remember?

It was rather fun on Thursday at the Garden Party. They had swings and roundabouts and flipflaps, coconut shies, Aunt Sallies, Hoopla, and all that sort of thing. I went in for them all and shocked a lot of people I think. I didn't care though. I'd got rather a posh frock on, white Georgette with rows and rows of jade ribbon and very white fur and large white hat, but all that didn't deter me from going into a fried fish shop in Snaresbrook and buying fish and chips. Getting it home was the worst part – it absolutely smelt the bus out. I didn't mind – it was rather fun – I only wish you had been with me. I think two halves would have enjoyed themselves, better than one half by herself.

Goodbye for now darlingest pal to Peidi.

Edith Bywaters and her lover were both hanged in 1923. But her love letters are better written than most judicial pronouncements.

When I was quite young my father went blind. As we lived near here, in the house I live in today, he used to travel up to London from Henley Station each day, and my mother had to read out all the evidence in his divorce cases to him. The First Class carriage on the Great Western would fall horribly silent as my mother read out accounts of private detectives peering through binoculars into strange bedrooms and seeing male and female clothing scattered around. But his being blind had two advantages for me. I used to read poetry aloud to him every night . . . to settle him down for sleep . . . And then he insisted on my writing myself so that we wouldn't run out of things to read . . . One of his favourite poets was Browning and I loved to read this poem because it is very musical and fun to read and because it speaks of an old dead romance which is still touching in the way that the romance of Bywaters and Thompson now is, perhaps, to us.

## *A Toccata of Galuppi's*

ROBERT BROWNING

Oh, Galuppi, Baldassaro, this is very
sad to find!
I can hardly misconceive you; it would
prove me deaf and blind;
But although I take your meaning, 'tis
with such a heavy mind!

Here you come with your old music,
and here's all the good it brings.
What, they lived once thus in Venice
where the merchants were the
kings,
Where St Mark's is, where the Doges
used to wed the sea with rings?

Ay, because the sea's the street there;
and 'tis arched by . . . what you
call
. . . Shylock's bridge with houses on it,
where they kept the carnival:
I was never out of England – it's as if
I saw it all!

Did young people take their pleasure
when the sea was warm in May?
Balls and masks begun at midnight,

burning ever to mid-day
When they made up fresh adventures
for the morrow, do you say?

Was a lady such a lady, cheeks so
round and lips so red, –
On her neck the small face buoyant,
like a bell-flower on its bed,
O'er the breast's superb abundance
where a man might base his head?

Well (and it was graceful of them)
they'd break talk off and afford
– She, to bite her mask's black velvet –
he, to finger on his sword,
While you sat and played Toccatas,
stately at the clavichord?

What? Those lesser thirds so plaintive,
sixths diminished, sigh on
sigh,
Told them something? Those suspensions,
those solutions – 'Must we
die?'
Those commiserating sevenths – 'Life
might last! we can but try!'

'Were you happy?' – 'Yes.' 'And are
you still as happy?' – 'Yes. And
you?'
– 'Then, more kisses!' – 'Did *I* stop
them, when a million seemed so
few?'
Hark! the dominant's persistence, till
it must be answered to!

So an octave struck the answer. Oh,
they praised you, I dare say!
'Brave Galuppi! that was music! good
alike at grave and gay!
I can always leave off talking, when I
hear a master play.'

Then they left you for their pleasure:
  till in due time, one by one.
Some with lives that came to nothing,
  some with deeds as well undone.
Death came tacitly and took them
  where they never see the sun.

But when I sit down to reason, think
  to take my stand nor swerve,
While I triumph o'er a secret wrung
  from nature's close reserve,
In you come with your cold music, till
  I creep thro' every nerve.

Yes, you, like a ghostly cricket, creaking
  where a house was burned:
'Dust and ashes, dead and done with.
  Venice spent what Venice earned!
The soul, doubtless, is immortal –
  where a soul can be discerned.

As for Venice and its people, merely
  born to bloom and drop,
Here on earth they bore their fruitage,
  mirth and folly were the crop:
What of soul was left, I wonder, when
  the kissing had to stop?

'Dust and ashes!' So, you creak it,
  and I want the heart to scold.
Dear dead women, with such hair, too
  – what's become of all the gold
Used to hang and brush their bosoms?
  I feel chilly and grown old.

I have always loved, even adored, Lord Byron. We went to school together, at least his Turkish slippers were still in the library at Harrow and I lay on the tomb in the churchyard where he lay to write poetry. It's a place that now commands an excellent view of Ruislip and the gasworks. His Lordship's mixture of common sense and Romanticism, of conservatism and revolutionary fervour, of Puritanism and sensuality, are all exactly to my taste. Here he is observing an execution with true, lucid indifference and writing about it to John Murray:

## *Letter to John Murray*

LORD BYRON

Venice, May 30th 1817

The day before I left Rome I saw three robbers guillotined. The ceremony – including the 'masqued' priests; the half-naked executioners; the bandaged criminals; the black Christ and his banner; the scaffold; the soldiery; the slow procession and the quick rattle and heavy fall of the axe; the splash of the blood, and the ghastliness of the exposed heads – is altogether more impressive than the vulgar and ungentlemanly dirty 'new drop', and dog-like agony of infliction upon the sufferers of the English sentence. Two of these men behaved calmly enough, but the first of the three died with great terror and reluctance, which was very horrible. He would not lie down; then his neck was too large for the aperture, and the priest was obliged to drown his exclamations by still louder exhortations. The head was off before the eye could trace the blow; but from an attempt to draw back the head, notwithstanding it was held forward by the hair, the first head was cut off close to the ears; the other two were taken off more cleanly. It is better than the oriental way, and (I should think) than the axe of our ancestors. The pain seems little; and yet the effect to the spectator, and the preparation to the criminal, are very striking and chilling. The first turned me quite hot and thirsty, and make me shake so that I could hardly hold the opera-glass (I was close, but determined to see, as one should see every thing, once, with attention); the second and third (which shows how dreadfully soon things grow indifferent) I am ashamed to say, had no effect on me as a horror, though I would have saved them if I could.

It is some time since I heard from you – the 12th April I believe.
Yours Ever Truly,
B.

'My hand shook so that I could hardly hold the opera-glass', the perpetual attitude of the writer in the face of experience!

*Readers: Jane Asher, Isobel Dean*

*Full Selection:*
*As I walked Out One Evening,* W. H. AUDEN
*Letter from Edith Thompson to Frederick Bywaters*
*A Toccata of Galuppi's,* ROBERT BROWNING
*The Myth of Sisyphus,* ALBERT CAMUS
*The Letters of Lord Byron*
*So We'll Go No More A'Roving,* LORD BYRON
*Seduced Girl,* HEDYLOS trans. UNTERMAYER
*Mr Youse Needn't be So Spry,* E. E. CUMMINGS
*As You Like It, Act 3, Scene 2,* WILLIAM SHAKESPEARE
*French Lisette: A Ballad of Maida Vale*
*The Taming of The Shrew, Act 5, Scene 2,* WILLIAM SHAKESPEARE
*The Way of the World, Act 4, Scene 5,* WILLIAM CONGREVE
*Waiting for the Barbarians,* C. P. CAVAFY
*The Possessed,* DOSTOEVSKY
*No Time to Go,* E. E. CUMMINGS
*Afterwards,* THOMAS HARDY

# DR DAVID OWEN

## *1985*

*Unlike many politicians David Owen was in fact born in the area for which he is Member of Parliament, Plymouth, and it was there we went to record the programme. His love of the place and its people was clear. Love of the sea has also exerted a powerful influence on his personality and was evident throughout his selection for the programme. His linking material was ad-libbed but, unusually for a politician, he was a man of few words.*

Both my parents are Welsh. During the war my father was away fighting and of course Plymouth was savagely bombed so we went back to Wales and I spent some of my childhood there.

When I was quite small I developed a taste for going round graveyards and finding the rhymes on tombstones, such as this one from a Welsh cemetery:

> Here lies the body of Mary Jones
> Who died of eating cherry stones.
> Her name was Smith, it was not Jones,
> But Jones was put to rhyme with stones.

Another one I heard recently is:

> Here lies Solomon Peas under the trees and sod,
> But Peas is not here, only the pod;
> Peas shelled out and is gone to God.

We Devonians think Devon is the most beautiful county in England, but what is it that is so lovely? I think it's that part of Devon that lies between Dartmoor and the sea, and none lovelier than North Devon. This is an extract from a not very widely known book by Lawrence Whistler, *Initials in the Heart*, and it explains for me why Devon is an unmatched jewel.

## *Initials in the Heart*

LAWRENCE WHISTLER

Between the valleys of the stream and the river, the deep and the deeper, the Halsdon ridge rose to a green brow with a wood on top, a landmark for miles. We began to know it as the Top of the World, the hyperbolical family name for a humbler knoll of my boyhood. From here extended westwards a view which I came to know like a face and love like a third person. It was a large view, though not large by the standards of mountain country – a semicircle of hilly distance that flowed from fluent Dartmoor about fifteen miles to the south, along the last high ground towards Cornwall, over flat tops and leafy knobs, grooved lanes roughly pointed towards hamlets, scattered white farms, and minute church-towers on skylines, round to Torrington spire, dead north; unexpected; a far sharp thought in a spireless composition. Towards that point the river dwindled in perspective, through a shaggy serpentine channel, hardly glimpsed. Engulfed immediately below us, it was quite unseen – but deeply understood – in the wide sweeps of its valley, whose funnelling walls were largely covered with woods cascading out of sight. From the pastures above they looked like overgrown amphitheatres of prodigious size, especially when a low sun put half into shadow, emphasizing the swerve of the fringed lip.

To many it might seem a very pleasant sample of pastoral England, hardly more. To me it was perfection; for it was secret and candid at once, wind-swept yet rich.

I'd like to read you a poem which was written by my greatest friend, Clive Grimson, who has since died sadly.

*Once I Was Young*

CLIVE GRIMSON

Once I was young
And filled with winged ideas
With songs unsung to echo down the years
The old man smiled
We sang those self same songs
Once on a time
Convinced we could right all wrongs
Thinking them blind
I kept my faith unfurled
Made up my mind
Youth would convert the world
The years have passed and I am older
Now
Youth does not last
The blossom leaves the bough
Yet wiser now I know a wider truth
I have learned how Hope is the
Spirit's youth.

I'm almost an adopted Londoner, having lived there ever since I was a medical student. I'd like to introduce to you 'The

Physician's Prayer' by Sir Robert Hutchison, a famous physician at the London Hospital. I might add that it would not be a bad name for it to call it the 'Politician's Prayer'!

### *The Physician's Prayer*

SIR ROBERT HUTCHISON

From inability to let well alone, from too much zeal for the new and contempt for what is old, for putting knowledge before wisdom, science before art and cleverness before common sense, from treating patients as cases and for making the cure of the disease more grievous than the endurance of the same, good Lord deliver us.

*Readers: Jane Asher, Peter Barkworth*

*Full Selection:*
*Drake's Drum*, HENRY NEWBOLT
*A Story*, DYLAN THOMAS
*Lepanto*, G. K. CHESTERTON
*Thou Shalt Dwell in Silence . . .* , RABINDRANATH TAGORE
*Solitude* ELLA WHEELER WILCOX
*Initials in the Heart*, LAWRENCE WHISTLER
*Candles*, CAVAFY
*Once I Was Young*, CLIVE GRIMSON
*The Ballad of Reading Gaol*, OSCAR WILDE
*They Who Are Near to Me*, RABINDRANATH TAGORE
*The Physician's Prayer*, SIR ROBERT HUTCHISON
*Business Girls*, JOHN BETJEMAN
*Body Remember*, CAVAFY
*The Hedgehog and The Fox*, ISIAH BERLIN
*Limerick*, VICTOR GREY
*Song by The Subconscious, Self*, A. LANG
*Adonais*, P. B. SHELLEY
*The Mary Gloster*, RUDYARD KIPLING

# JACQUELINE DU PRÉ

## 1980

*About twenty years ago I was sent to a listening room in Broadcasting House to play back a tape of a concert which featured as soloist the then leader of the BBC Symphony Orchestra, Paul Beard. He was waiting when I arrived and I hurried to make everything ready. 'Don't rush,' he said. 'I'm expecting someone else.' At that moment Jacqueline du Pré breezed in, all good humour, long hair and youthful energy. I was so surprised and in awe that I could only blurt out 'Hello. I've just bought one of your records.'*

*'Oh really,' said Paul Beard. 'Was it any good?'*

*The conversation between them was full of such banter. The music, when they finally allowed me to play the tape, was exquisite. The regard they had for each other was evident in the quality of the listening. Eventually, the concert over, she had to leave, watched admiringly by both of us. Even though she hadn't played a note, it was as if she had taken the music with her.*

One day, when I was four, I was in the kitchen, bored to tears. We had an old-fashioned wireless and I climbed over the ironing board and switched it on. There was a programme – some sort of illustration of the instruments of the orchestra. I didn't like it 'till I heard the cello and I said, 'I want to play that sound.' And so I was given a cello.

I woke up and found this whopping creature beside my bed. Plucking it made a nice sound. I got out of bed and put it between my legs – I'd never seen anyone playing before. I loved it, kept going back to it. I had heard somewhere: 'A noise rose from the orchestra as the leader drew across the intestines of the timid cat, the tail of the noble horse.' I remember being desperately inspired by the idea of horse hair and catgut getting married to make that lovely sound – the bow is made of horse hair, white horse hair, and the strings are made of catgut – actually it's sheep's gut, but don't tell anyone.

We lived in Purley. However, I ran away when I was three. I was away from 7 a.m. to 7.30 p.m. and the Surrey police were alerted. It was panic stations. 'Where have you been?'

'I've been to sea, of course.'

Although how I could possibly have gone to the sea from Purley, I can't imagine. I think it was pretty beastly personally. I did it again when I was five – on my tricycle.

'Where have you been?'

'I've been to Brighton.'

Since I've been talking about the sea, this poem can remind us of the smell of the sea, one of the poems I remember hearing my sister Hilary reciting as part of her elocution lessons.

## *Cargoes*

JOHN MASEFIELD

Quinquireme of Nineveh from distant Ophir
Rowing home to haven in sunny Palestine,
With a cargo of ivory,
And apes and peacocks,
Sandalwood, cedarwood, and sweet white wine.

Stately Spanish galleon coming from the Isthmus,
Dipping through the Tropics by the palm-green shores,
With a cargo of diamonds,
Emeralds, amethysts,
Topazes, and cinnamon, and gold moidores.

Dirty British coaster with a salt-caked smoke stack
Butting through the Channel in the mad March days,
With a cargo of Tyne coal,
Road-rail, pig-lead,
Firewood, iron-ware, and cheap tin trays.

I went in for a competition when I was ten and won it, which meant that I had to practise at least four hours a day. (I cut it down to as few as I could because I couldn't stand practising!) It meant that I had to leave school – to me, in fact, it was a golden day. It did, however, mean that I didn't come into contact with other children.

My family moved to Portland Place where my father took up some accountancy work. Father had a stick insect – bless its heart. I couldn't find a way to love it, and I hated it. She was christened Amanda, Mandy for short, and lived in her own aquarium. When she died she was given a burial in Regent's Park, and the deeply religious service was conducted by my father. He still remembers the place which marks the spot where Amanda lies. Thank goodness stick insects didn't have a prolonged stay. I did have a budgie and I know that humming-birds took my fancy as well.

## *Humming-Bird*

D. H. LAWRENCE

I can imagine, in some other world
Primeval-dumb, far back
In that most awful stillness, that only gasped and
hummed,
Humming-birds raced down the avenues.

Before anything had a soul,
While life was a heave of Matter, half inanimate,
This little bit chipped off in brilliance
And went whizzing through the slow, vast, succulent
stems.

I believe there were no flowers then,
In the world where the humming-bird flashed ahead of
creation.
I believe he pierced the slow vegetable veins with his
long beak.

Probably he was big
As mosses, and little lizards, they say, were once big.
Probably he was a jabbing, terrifying monster.

We look at him through the wrong end of the long
telescope of Time,
Luckily for us.

It was fortunate that we lived near Regent's Park, because it meant that, when I was fed up with practising, I could escape and be as wild as I liked, surrounded by all the things I loved, like trees and flowers. Regent's Park has been full of daffodils while we have been preparing this programme. I told John Carson (*the reader, with Penelope Lee, of most of the items in this programme*) that Wordsworth's 'Daffodils' was one of my favourites. He couldn't pick any in the park and the shops were shut on the following evening when we met, so he offered me this sentimental verse instead – written by the most famous poet in the world, Anon.

'Thank you for the flowers you sent,' she said,
And sweetly smiled and coyly turned her head
'I'm sorry for the things I said last night.
I was wrong and you were right,
Please forgive me.'
So I forgave her. And as we wandered through the
moonlit hours
I thought, 'What bloody flowers?'

Everybody knows, I think, what it's like to have the giggles and they can be quite devastating when you are trying to do something very smooth and controlled, like playing 'The Swan'. Perhaps you can imagine how difficult it is to hold a legato line when your body is dancing a wild tango inside. I certainly giggled during other bits of 'Carnival of the Animals'.

## *The Fossils* from *The Carnival of the Animals*

OGDEN NASH

At midnight in the museum hall
The fossils gathered for a ball.
There were no drums or saxophones
But just the clatter of their bones,
A rolling, rattling, carefree circus
Of mammoth polkas and mazurkas.
Pterodactyls and brontosauruses

Sang ghostly prehistoric choruses
Amid the mastodonic wassail
I caught the eye of one small fossil.
Cheer up, sad world, he said, and winked –
It's kind of fun to be extinct.

Elgar is certainly not fossilised, especially in our hearts. I found in this book of things I'd written:

Elgar's photo now hangs on the wall – a document which tells so vividly of his unhappy life. A sick man who had through it a glowing heart in such a profusion of loveliness as expressed in so many of his works. How his face haunts me, and always will.

These are other short observations which I found in my book:

Never mind about present affliction – any moment may be the next!

I suppose all of us must learn to find independence in dependence.

If the sunshine beckons you, accept its invitation and love the gold quality of it.

Genius is one who, with an innate capacity, affects for good or evil, the life of others.

Don't let the sound of your own wheels drive you crazy.

A relationship is not that you would like it to be – or what you think it is. It defines *itself* by the actual quality of the interchange between the people involved.

This is called 'A Persian Apothegm'

He who knows not and knows not that he knows not
is a fool – shun him
He who knows not and knows that he knows not
can be taught – teach him
He who knows and knows not that he knows
is asleep – wake him
He who knows and knows that he knows
is a prophet – follow him

This is about the reading of 'Peter and the Wolf' from an actress friend:

Don't over emotionalise the wording, the music is there to illustrate the words.

It occurred to me that this is what I want to convey to my pupils – that the expression is inbuilt in the music and shape of the piece as well. Too much expressive indulgence will distort the musical structure.

I was always a lover, since childhood, of the winter elements – of snow as it graced the earth gently with its snowdrops leaving that pristine white carpet. Oh what a shame to spoil its velvet smoothness with a common footprint, but what a delicious excitement to create evidence of one's exploration into a virgin land. I remember the search for the single, magically designed snowflake, or of flinging myself into the snow, loving its texture, the cold against one's skin and the fun of constructing hard snowballs to throw at random to watch their passage through the air and then their splintering rebound on the chosen target.

Wind and rain also thrilled me, as the first would dance wildly through my hair, buffeting my cheeks, exciting them to warmth, and also induce beauteous scents, and the second with its pitter-patter which would invite the imagination to new worlds, would bathe flowers into which I could explore the moisture with my face embedded in them, and the thrill with the luscious scents the rain would invite into my world.

Written at 2 a.m. when my mind feels somewhat muddy and I have never been much of a mud lover!

When I went to receive a doctorate from London University presented by the Queen Mother, the oration was read by Professor John Barron. At the end he read the last verse of Wordsworth's 'The Solitary Reaper'.

*The Solitary Reaper*

WILLIAM WORDSWORTH

Whate'er the theme, the Maiden sang
As if her song could have no ending;

I saw her singing at her work,
And o'er the sickle bending;
I listen'd, motionless and still;
And, as I mounted up the hill,
The music in my heart I bore,
Long after it was heard no more.

*Readers: John Carson, Penelope Lee*

*Full Selection:*
*Romance,* W. J. TURNER
*Cargoes,* JOHN MASEFIELD
*Humming-Bird,* D. H. LAWRENCE
*Inversnaid,* GERARD MANLEY HOPKINS
*Thank You for the Flowers . . . ,* ANON
*Heaven,* RUPERT BROOKE
*Fish for Luncheon,* HERBERT FARJEON
*The Solitary Reaper,* WILLIAM WORDSWORTH
*The Fossils* from *Carnival of the Animals,* OGDEN NASH
*A Persian Apothegm*
*Love's Labour's Lost,* WILLIAM SHAKESPEARE
*To Autumn,* JOHN KEATS
*To the Gentlemen in Row D,* VIRGINIA GRAHAM
*The Listeners,* WALTER DE LA MARE
*The Tiger,* WILLIAM BLAKE
*Snake,* D. H. LAWRENCE
*Museum Piece,* RICHARD WILBUR
*The English Are So Nice!,* D. H. LAWRENCE
*Lies,* YEVGENY YEVTUSHENKO
*Vote for Love* and *God Bless Love,* complied by NANETTE NEWMAN
*Searching for Love,* D. H. LAWRENCE

# STEVE RACE

## 1971

*'With Great Pleasure' is one of those programmes that has a repeat broadcast within the week of its first transmission. Due to some administrative quirk, however, Steve's edition did not get its second airing. I am hoping to repair that omission in the near future, but in the meantime, it gives me great pleasure to include some of the script here. Steve has managed to combine the career of a successful musician with that of a successful broadcaster. Indeed, in my early days of playing the records in such programmes as 'Housewives Choice', which he used to present regularly along with many others, he struck me as one of the disconcertingly few people in broadcasting who really knew what he was doing. My estimation of the others has grown kinder with experience, but the professionalism, ease and clarity of expression which Steve displayed and continues to display remain a model that many broadcasters could strive to emulate.*

105 years ago a relative on my father's side received through the post a proposal of marriage. She was Mary Foster, of Middlemoor, Pateley Bridge in Yorkshire, and she was the local beauty. The letter of proposal she received *is* genuine: my family has the original. The letter certainly was (as the writer said) 'in desprit and yurnest'.

*Hopeful Proposal to a Young Lady of the Village,*
Dated November 29th, 1866

My Dear Miss,

I now take up my pen to write to you hoping these few

lines will find you well as it leaves me at present Thank God for it. You will perhaps be surprised that I should make so bold as to write to you who is such a lady and I hope you will not be vex at me for it. I hardly dare say what I want, I am so timid about ladies, and my heart trimmels like a hespin. But I once seed in a book that faint heart never won fair lady, so here goes.

I am a farmer in a small way and my age is rather more than forty years and my mother lives with me and keeps my house, and she has been very poorly lately and cannot stir about much and I think I should be more comfortabler with a wife.

I have had my eye on you a long time and I think you are a very nice young woman and one that would make me happy if only you think so. We keep a servant girl to milk three kye and do the work in the house, and she goes out a bit in the summer to gadder wickens and she snags a few of turnips in the back kend. I do a piece of work on the farm myself and attends Pately Market, and I sometimes show a few sheep and I feeds between 3 & 4 pigs agen Christmas, and the same is very useful in the house to make pies and cakes and so forth, and I sells the hams to help pay for the barley meal.

I have about 73 pund in Naisbro Bank and we have a nice little parlour downstairs with a blue carpet, and an oven on the side of the fireplace and the old woman on the other side smoking. The Golden Rules claimed up on the walls above the long settle, and you could sit all day in the easy chair and knit and mend my kytles and leggums, and you could make the tea ready agin I come in, and you could make butter for Pately Market, and I would drive you to church every Sunday in the spring cart, and I would do all that bees in my power to make you happy. So I hope to hear from you. I am in desprit and Yurnest, and will marry you at May Day, or if my mother dies afore I shall want you afore. If only you will accept of me, my dear, we could be very happy together.

I hope you will let me know your mind by return of post, and if you are favourable I will come up to scratch. So no more at present from your well-wisher and true love –

Simon Fallowfield

P.S. I hope you will say nothing about this. If you will not accept of me I have another very nice woman in my eye, and I think I shall marry her if you do not accept of me, but I thought you would suit me mother better, she being very crusty at times. So I tell you now before you come, she will be Maister.

No, she didn't marry him, but I hope some nice girl did.

Up in Weardale, County Durham, lie the bones of my ancestors. They came from Weardale and Teesdale for 300 years; before that, from South Yorkshire, back to 1386, when John Race, of Beverley, leased some land and put his name to a deed.

So it's not surprising that the Dales are in my blood. My father – a young man growing up in the Durham dales – used to tramp over the fells with a friend called Fred G. Bowles. That was about the turn of the century, and there's a family story that one sweltering hot day Fred Bowles shed first his coat, then eventually his trousers, slinging them over his shoulder and tramping on across the deserted moors; until at last they came to a little town and Fred discovered that his trousers must have slipped off his shoulder . . . Anyway, all he had was a jacket.

Fred G. Bowles was a fine, if now unremembered poet.

## *Resurrection*

FRED G. BOWLES

As the slow evening gathered in her grey
And one clear star its ancient pathway trod,
With long, low cadences of clear delay
The lark, descending, left his song with God.
And peace came, like a reverential soul,
With far-off tremors of a further world,
And through the silver mist of twilight, stole
Into the heart of all. And upward curled
The April moon, resurgent of the sun,
To the blue dust of the exalted dome
Of heaven; and the white wind-flowers, one by one,
Shook in light slumber on their hilly home.
It was so sweet to stoop, and feel around! –
Each blade of grass a breathing lyre of life
Whereon the wind, in arias of sound,
Told subtle music; how the great world, rife
With scent of violets and primrose-strewn,

Strained tender fingers from each dewy sod
To the dear Christ of chrysalis and moon.
And dusk, descending, left her soul with God.

There are some people – kindred spirits – whom one positively *hugs* across the centuries. For me, one of these is the Reverend Sydney Smith, born in 1771. He was a great humanitarian, the most famous wit of his day, and a darling man. Consider this letter he wrote to a little girl:

Lucy, dear child,
Mind your arithmetic. You know, in the first sum of yours I ever saw, there was a mistake. You had carried two (as a cab is licensed to do) and you ought, dear Lucy, to have carried one. Is this a trifle? What would life be, without arithmetic, but a scene of horrors? . . . I now give you my parting advice: don't marry anybody who has not a tolerable understanding and a thousand a year. God bless you, dear child.

Sydney Smith, though himself a Canon of St Paul's, found senior churchmen irresistibly funny. Describing the scene when the Church Commissioners were at last compelled by the Home Secretary of the day to yield some of their property to its rightful owners, he wrote:

The Commission was separated in an instant. London clenched his fist; Canterbury was hurried out by his chaplains and put in a warm bed; a solemn vacancy spread itself over the face of Gloucester; Lincoln was taken out in strong hysterics.

When Lady Grey wrote to Sidney Smith angrily demanding his support for declaring war against Denmark, he replied:

My Dear Lady Grey:
For God's sake do not drag me into another war! I am worn down and worn out with crusading and defending Europe and protecting mankind: I *must* think a little of myself. I am sorry for the Spaniards – I am sorry for the Greeks – I deplore the fate of the Jews – the people of the Sandwich Islands are groaning under the most detestable tyranny – Bagdad is oppressed – I do not

like the present state of the Delta – Tibet is not comfortable. Am I to fight for all these people? The world is bursting with sin and sorrow.

No war, dear Lady Grey! No eloquence; but apathy, selfishness, commonsense, arithmetic. I will go to war with the King of Denmark if he is impertinent to you, but for no other cause.

More than Jingoists, more than Bishops, Sidney Smith disdained Politicians. Here he's describing William Pitt, the parliamentary spellbinder of his day.

He was one of the most luminous, eloquent blunderers with which any people was ever afflicted. For 15 years I have found my income dwindling away under his eloquence, and regularly in every session of Parliament he has charmed every classical feeling and stript me of every guinea I possessed. At the close of every brilliant display, an expedition failed or a Kingdom fell. By the time that his style had gained the summit of perfection, Europe was degraded to the lowest abyss of misery. God send us a stammerer; a tongueless man!

John Evelyn was a civil servant; a gardener; a diarist. He was a family man, living in Surrey and later near Deptford, and he left a description of his small son which I find almost unbelievable, and most touching.

### *John Evelyn's Diary*
Entry for 27 January 1658

After six fits of a quartan ague with which it pleased God to visit him, died my dear son Richard, to our inexpressible grief and affliction, five years and three days old only, but at that tender age a prodigy for wit and understanding; for beauty of body a very angel; for endowment of mind of incredible and rare hopes. To give only a little taste of them, and thereby glory to God, he hath learnt all his catechism; at two years and a half old he could perfectly read any of the English, Latin, French or Gothic letters, pronouncing the first three languages exactly. He had before the fifth year not only skill to read most written hands, but to decline all nouns, conjugate the verbs regular and most of the irregular;

learnt 'Puerilis', got by heart almost the entire vocabulary of Latin and French primitives and words, could make congruous syntax, turn English into Latin and vice versa, construe and prove what he read, knew the government and use of relatives, verbs, substantives, ellipses and many figures and tropes, began himself to write legibly and had a strong passion for Greek.

The number of verses he could write was prodigious; he remembered the parts of plays, which he would also act. Seeing a Plautus in one's hand, he asked what book it was, and being told it was comedy and too difficult for him, he wept for sorrow. Strange was his apt and ingenious application of fables and morals, for he had read Aesop. He had a wonderful disposition for mathematics, having by heart divers propositions of Euclid that we read to him in play. As to his piety, astonishing were his applications of Scripture on occasion. He had learnt all his Catechism early, and understood the historical part of the Bible and New Testament to a wonder.

These, and like illuminations far exceeding his age and experience, considering the prettiness of his address and behaviour, cannot but leave impressions in me at the memory of him. He would of himself select the most pathetic psalms and chapters out of Job to read to his maid during his sickness, telling her, when she pitied him, that all God's children must suffer affliction. He declaimed against the vanities of the world before he had seen any. How thankfully he would receive admonition! – How soon be reconciled! How indifferent, yet continually cheerful! He would give grave advice to his brother John, bear with his impertinences, and say he was but a child. He was all life, all prettiness; far from morose, sullen or childish in anything he said or did.

The day before he died he called to me, and in a more serious manner than usual, told me that for all I loved him so dearly, I should give my house, land and all my fine things to his brother Jack.

Next morning, when he found himself ill, and I persuaded him to keep his hands in bed, he demanded whether he might pray to God with his hands unjoined. A little after, whilst in great agony, he asked whether he should not offend God by using his only name so often calling for ease.

But thus God, having dressed up a saint fit for himself, would no longer permit him with us, unworthy of the future fruits of this incomparable hopeful blossom. Such a child I never saw, for such a child I bless God, in whose bosom he is. Thou gavest him to us, thou hast taken him away from us: blessed be the name of the Lord!

In my opinion he was suffocated by the women and maids who attended him, and covered him too hot with blankets as he lay in his cradle, near an excessive hot fire in a closed room.

Here ends the joy of my life, and for which I go ever mourning to the grave.

*15 February*
The afflicting hand of God being still upon us, it pleased him also to take away from us this morning my youngest son, George, now seven weeks languishing at nurse and ending in a dropsy. God's holy will be done.

*Readers: Prunella Scales, Timothy West*

*Full Selection:*
*Painting as a Pastime*, SIR WINSTON CHURCHILL
*At Grass*, PHILIP LARKIN
*A Discreet Immorality*, JOHN SMITH
*Boswell's Life of Johnson*
*Remember*, CHRISTINA ROSSETTI
*Jack Mytton*, VIRGINIA WOOLF
*Resurrection*, FRED G. BOWLES
*Quotations from Sydney Smith*
*Why I Love England*, MALCOLM MUGGERIDGE
*Diary of John Evelyn*
*When You Are Old*, W. B. YEATS
*The Caraway Seed*, OGDEN NASH
*The Fly*, OGDEN NASH
*The Bat*, OGDEN NASH
*The Pizza*, OGDEN NASH
*Crossing the Border*, OGDEN NASH
*Civilisation, A Personal View*, KENNETH CLARK

# DIANA RIGG

## 1978

*This excellent and attractive actress took on the task of compiling her programme with gusto. The range of people and literary styles included was wide, from John Wilmot, Earl of Rochester, to Freud – no doubt the latter would have had something to say about the former, but his words were intercut with an amusing poem mischievously celebrating physical love, thereby rendering him, at a stroke as it were, pompous and puzzled. In fact Diana Rigg's especial pleasure was in storytelling, and it was that which led her to her profession. By storytelling she meant not just the tale being told, but the excitement of the words themselves, 'finding a private interpretation fed by the sounds and one's imagination'.*

Whilst going through my books for this programme I came across an old half-crown edition of antonyms and synonyms. Twenty-five years ago I underlined certain words, words which now remind me of the conflict and pain of being teen-aged – bewilder, envenomed, forswear, grapple, impotent, mortal, mutinous, secret, waggish, void. The void was always guaranteed to be filled.

### *Sonnets from the Portuguese*

ELIZABETH BARRETT BROWNING

I lived with visions for my company,
Instead of men and women, years ago,
And found them gentle mates, nor thought to know
A sweeter music than they played to me.

But soon their trailing purple was not free
Of this world's dust, – their lutes did silent grow,
And I myself grew faint and blind below
Their vanishing eyes. Then THOU didst come . . . to be,
Beloved, what they seemed. Their shining fronts,
Their songs, their splendours, (better, yet the same,
As river-water hallowed into fonts)
Met in thee, and from out thee overcame
My soul with satisfaction of all wants –
Because God's gifts put man's best dreams to shame.

But if you happen to be a lumpish fourteen-year old, a God's gift wasn't likely to appear, nor indeed if he had would one have known what to do with him. An older man was the classic answer, but perhaps the next poem was going a tidge too far.

### *A Song of a Young Lady to Her Ancient Lover*

JOHN WILMOT, EARL OF ROCHESTER

Ancient Person, for whom I
All the flattering youth defy;
Long be it e're thou grow old,
Aching, shaking, crazy, cold.
But still continue as thou art,
Ancient Person of my Heart.

On thy withered lips and dry,
Which like barren furrows lie;
Brooding kisses I will pour,
Shall thy youthful heart restore.
Such kind show'rs in autumn fall,
And a second spring recall:
Nor from thee will ever part,
Ancient Person of my Heart.

All a lover's wish can reach,
For thy joy my love shall teach:
And for thy pleasure shall improve
All that art can add to love.
Yet still I love thee without art,
Ancient Person of my Heart.

I was deeply shocked on reading this next poem. I still am but for different reasons. Its overt sexuality was gross when I compared it to the softer, more abstract visions of women I'd hitherto encountered and the symbolism which runs through it disturbed my prosaic consciousness.

## *Figs*

D. H. LAWRENCE

The proper way to eat a fig in society,
Is to split it in four, holding it by the stump,
And open it, so that it is a glittering, rosy, moist,
 honied, heavy-petalled four-petalled flower.
Then you throw away the skin
Which is just like a four-sepalled calyx,
After you have taken off the blossom with your lips.

But the vulgar way
Is just to put your mouth to the crack, and take out the
 flesh in one bite.

Every fruit has its secret.

The fig is a very secretive fruit.
As you see it standing growing, you feel at once it is
 symbolic:
And it seems male.
But when you come to know it better, you agree with
 the Romans, it is female.

The Italians vulgarly say, it stands for the female part;
 the fig fruit:
The fissure, the yoni,
The wonderful moist conductivity towards the centre.

Involved,
Inturned,
The flowering all inward and womb-fibrilled;
And but one orifice.

The fig, the horse-shoe, the squash blossom.
Symbols.

There was a flower that flowered inward, womb-ward;
Now there is a fruit like a ripe womb.

It was always a secret.
That's how it should be, the female should always be
secret.

There never was any standing aloft and unfolded on a
bough
Like other flowers, in a revelation of petals;
Silver-pink peach, Venetian green glass of medlars and
sorb-apples,
Shallow wine-cups on short, bulging stems
Openly pledging heaven:
Here's to the thorn in flower! Here is to utterance!
The brave, adventurous rosaceae.

Foiled upon itself, and secret unutterable,
The milky-sapped, sap that curdles milk and makes
ricotta,
Sap that smells strange on your fingers, that even goats
won't taste it;
Folded upon itself, enclosed like any Mohammedan
woman,
Its nakedness all within-walls, its flowering forever
unseen,
One small way of access only, and this close-curtained
from the light;

Fig, fruit of the female mystery, covert and inward,
Mediterranean fruit, with your covert nakedness,
Where everything happens invisible, flowering and
fertilization, and fruiting
In the inwardness of you, that eye will never see
Till it's finished, and you're over-ripe, and you burst to
give up your ghost.

Till the drop of ripeness exudes,
And the year is over.

And then the fig has kept her secret long enough.
So it explodes and you see through the fissure the scarlet.

And the fig is finished, the year is over.

That's how the fig dies, showing her crimson through
 the purple slit.
Like a wound, the exposure of her secret, on the open
 day.
Like a prostitute, the bursten fig, making a show of
 her secret.

That's how women die too.

The year is fallen over-ripe,
The year of our women.
The year of our women is fallen over-ripe.
The secret is laid bare.
And rottenness soon sets in.
The year of our women is fallen over-ripe.

When Eve once knew in her mind that she was naked
She quickly sewed fig-leaves, and sewed the same for
 man.
She'd been naked all her days before,
But till then, till that apple of knowledge, she hadn't
 had the fact on her mind.

She got the fact on her mind, and quickly sewed fig
 leaves.
And women have been sewing ever since.
But now they stitch to adorn the bursten fig, not to
 cover it.
They have their nakedness more than ever on their
 mind,
And they won't let us forget it.

Now the secret
Becomes an affirmation through moist, scarlet lips
That laugh at the Lord's indignation.

What then good Lord! cry the women.
We have kept our secret long enough.
We are a ripe fig.
Let us burst in affirmation.

They forget, ripe figs won't keep.
Ripe figs won't keep.
Honey-white figs of the north, black figs with scarlet
inside, of the south.
Ripe figs won't keep, won't keep in any clime.
What then, when women the world over have all
bursten into self-assertion?
And bursten figs won't keep?

Mr Lawrence must be gyrating in his grave at the self-assertion of women today and I can't help adding that it serves him right!

*Readers: Philip Voss, Diana Rigg*

*Full Selection:*
*You English Words*, JOHN MOORE
*The Birth of the Rune from the Finnish*
*Jabberwocky*, LEWIS CARROLL
*How the Whale got His Throat*, RUDYARD KIPLING
*Romance*, W. J. TURNER
*The Listeners*, WALTER DE LA MARE
*Sonnets from the Portuguese*, ELIZABETH BARRETT BROWNING
*A Song from a Young Lady to Her Ancient Lover*, JOHN WILMOT, EARL OF ROCHESTER
*Figs*, D. H. LAWRENCE
*When I was Young and Fair*, ELIZABETH I
*The Hollow Crown* comp. JOHN BARTON
*Compilation: Young Corydon and Phyllis/Freud*
*Check to Song*, OWEN MEREDITH
*Poet in the Making*, DYLAN THOMAS
*Poetry*, YEVGENY YEVTUSHENKO
*Lullaby*, W. H. AUDEN

# *HARRY SECOMBE*

## *1975*

*It is frequently said of comedians that they conceal personalities well on the dismal side of gloomy. My own, fairly limited, experience of working with them leads me to the conclusion that this is only occasionally true and that funny men who are otherwise depressed are bound to be remarked upon. The remainder have as wide a range of off-stage personalities as any other group. However, there are neuroses and insecurities peculiar to that occupation: the fear of not being funny in front of maybe hundreds of people who have paid to see them being just that; the nagging feeling that after years of being successful it is not quite right that they remain merely an object of laughter – even though the pleasure of the audience is obvious, there must be a wish occasionally to say something without having people doubling up. I've met Harry Secombe in a studio only once and he was most entertaining. He clearly enjoyed giving pleasure and appeared withal a warm and genuinely friendly person. It was no surprise to read his 'With Great Pleasure' script and find a sensitive and thoughtful person amongst the jokes.*

As Wales contains some of the wildest, highest and most beautiful country in the British Isles, it's not surprising that the Welsh love nature poetry, even when it's written by an Englishman.

A favourite scene in nature is a lake, under a grey sky with a chill wind rippling the water and rustling the reeds, and the wild ducks flying. The awful loneliness of such a scene at evening, especially in late autumn, is brought to mind by extracts from John Masefield's passion play in verse, 'Good Friday'. I've chosen this because it was my first appearance in a play ever – in the church hall, of course. I was 14 years old and made up as an old blind beggar, covered in grey crêpe hair, which made speech rather difficult. I'm afraid I haven't got that excuse today.

## *Good Friday*

JOHN MASEFIELD

The wild duck, stringing through the sky,
Are south away.
Their green necks glitter as they fly,
The lake is gray.
So still, so lone, the fowler never heeds.
The wind goes rustle, rustle, through the reeds.

There they find peace to have their own wild souls.
In that still lake,
Only the moonrise or the wind controls
The way they take,
Through the gray reeds, the cocking moor-hen's lair,
Rippling the pool, or over leagues of air.

Not thus, not thus are the wild souls of men.
No peace for those
Who step beyond the blindness of the pen
To where the skies unclose.
For them the spitting mob, the cross, the crown of thorns
The bull gone mad, the Saviour on his horns.

I first discovered Keats when I was about 14 – the time when people usually start writing that terrible adolescent romantic verse, and I was no exception. I thought in Keats that I'd found a kindred spirit, and in fact I was so affected by Keats' life and work that by the time I was 15 I was sure I had all the symptoms of TB. This poem is the first Keats poem I ever read.

## *Ode to Autumn*

JOHN KEATS

Season of mists and mellow fruitfulness,
  Close bosom-friend of the maturing sun;
Conspiring with him how to load and bless
  With fruit the vines that round the thatch-eaves run;

To bend with apples the moss'd cottage-trees,
 And fill all fruit with ripeness to the core;
  To swell the gourd, and plump the hazel shells
With a sweet kernel; to set budding more,
 And still more, later flowers for the bees,
 Until they think warm days will never cease,
  For Summer has o'er-brimm'd their clammy cells.

Who hath not seen thee oft amid thy store?
 Sometimes whoever seeks abroad may find
Thee sitting careless on a granary floor,
 Thy hair soft-lifted by the winnowing wind;
Or on a half-reap'd furrow sound asleep,
 Drowsed with the fume of poppies, while thy hook
  Spares the next swath and all its twined flowers:
And sometimes like a gleaner thou dost keep
 Steady thy laden head across a brook;
 Or by a cider-press, with patient look,
  Thou watchest the last oozings, hours by hours.

Where are the songs of Spring? Aye, where are they?
 Think not of them, thou hast thy music too, –
While barred clouds bloom the soft-dying day,
 And touch the stubble-plains with rosy hue;
Then in a wailful choir the small gnats mourn
 Among the river sallows, borne aloft
  Or sinking as the light wind lives or dies;
And full-grown lambs loud bleat from hilly bourn;
 Hedge-crickets sing; and now with treble soft
 The red-breast whistles from a garden croft;
  And gathering swallows twitter in the skies.

After a year or two as a clerk in the colliery office, I joined the Territorial Army – not strictly out of patriotism, I may say, but because all the other clerks in the office joined the same Territorial Regiment which meant that when they all went off together to camp for two weeks I was left to do all the work, so, being rather clever, I put my age on by two years and joined up myself: went off to camp gaily in August 1939 and returned home in April 1946. Some fool had declared war in between. They say that a soldier can find a Field-Marshal's baton in his knapsack – well I went to war with Palgrave's *Golden Treasury* in mine for certain reasons, I mean shrapnel and other things coming over I could always place it in a strategic position. Today I'd need *Encyclopedia Britannica*. But after the war I took to reading much of the poetry left by the authors of the First World War; having been in a war myself, I wanted to see what they thought about it: Siegfried Sassoon, Edmund Blunden, Robert Graves and especially the Welsh poet, Wilfred Owen, but of course it was Rupert Brooke who helped set the mood of romantic patriotism that was so popular during the early days of the First World War.

## *The Soldier*

RUPERT BROOKE

If I should die, think only this of me:
  That there's some corner of a foreign field
That is for ever England. There shall be
  In that rich earth a richer dust concealed;
A dust whom England bore, shaped, made aware,
  Gave, once, her flowers to love, her ways to roam,
A body of England's, breathing English air,
  Washed by the rivers, blest by suns of home.

And think, this heart, all evil shed away,
  A pulse in the eternal mind, no less
    Gives somewhere back the thoughts by England given;
Her sights and sounds; dreams happy as her day;
  And laughter, learnt of friends; and gentleness,
    In hearts at peace, under an English heaven.

Rupert Brooke did die abroad, from malaria, but it was a hero's death, he was bitten by a German mosquito. He was buried in some foreign field and never knew how the war had changed from romantic patriotism into bitter disillusion. Compare Brooke's 'Soldier' with Siegfried Sassoon's 'Suicide in the Trenches'.

## *Suicide in the Trenches*

SIEGFRIED SASSOON

I knew a simple soldier boy
Who grinned at life in empty joy,

Slept soundly through the lonesome dark,
And whistled early with the lark.

In winter trenches, cowed and glum,
With crumps and lice and lack of rum,
He put a bullet through his brain.
No one spoke of him again.

You smug-faced crowds with kindling eye
Who cheer when soldier lads march by,
Sneak home and pray you'll never know
The hell where youth and laughter go.

The Welsh poet, Wilfred Owen who was killed in battle in 1918 just before the Armistice, had said of his poems 'The subject is war and the pity of war' which is what attracts me to the writings of most of those First World War poets. They saw war for what it really was, mud, death, stink and filth, not a flag-waving, jingoist adventure as so many of the folks at home saw it. Here is Wilfred Owen's 'Dulce et Decorum Est' – How sweet to die for one's country – or is it?

## *Dulce et Decorum Est*

WILFRED OWEN

Bent double, like old beggars under sacks,
Knock-kneed, coughing like hags, we cursed through sludge,
Till on the haunting flares we turned our backs
And towards our distant rest began to trudge.
Men marched asleep. Many lost their boots
But limped on, blood-shod. All went lame; all blind;
Drunk with fatigue; deaf even to the hoots
Of tired, outstripped Five-Nines that dropped behind.

Gas! GAS! Quick, boys! – An ecstacy of fumbling,
Fitting the clumsy helmets just in time;
But someone still was yelling out and stumbling
And flound'ring like a man in fire or lime . . .
Dim, through the misty panes and thick green light,
As under a green sea, I saw him drowning.

In all my dreams, before my helpless sight,
He plunges at me, guttering, choking, drowning.

If in some smothering dreams you too could pace
Behind the wagon that we flung him in,
And watch the white eyes writhing in his face,
His hanging face, like a devil's sick of sin;
If you could hear, at every jolt, the blood
Come gargling from the froth-corrupted lungs,
Obscene as cancer, bitter as the cud
Of vile, incurable sores on innocent tongues, –
My friend, you would not tell with such high zest
To children ardent for some desperate glory,
The old Lie: Dulce et decorum est
Pro patria mori.

*Readers: Andrew Secombe, Harry Secombe*

*Full Selection:*
*The Days that Have Been,* W. H. DAVIES
*Portrait of the Artist as a Young Dog,* DYLAN THOMAS
*The Collier,* VERNON WATKINS
*Fern Hill,* DYLAN THOMAS
*Madly in All Directions,* WYNFORD VAUGHAN THOMAS
*Good Friday,* JOHN MASEFIELD
*Ode to Autumn,* JOHN KEATS
*The Soldier,* RUPERT BROOKE
*Suicide in the Trenches,* SIEGFRIED SASSOON
*Dulce et Decorum Est,* WILFRED OWEN
*The Return,* WILFRED GIBSON
*Raining,* WILFRED GIBSON
*The Death of the Queen,* WILLIAM MCGONAGALL
*Fear No More the Heat of the Sun* from *Cymbeline,* WILLIAM SHAKESPEARE
*The Calf,* OGDEN NASH
*Listen,* OGDEN NASH
*The Rabbits,* OGDEN NASH

*Faithless Nellie Gray*, THOMAS HOOD
*The Pickwick Papers*, CHARLES DICKENS
*In Focus*, JEREMY ROBSON
*The Children of Aberfan*, SPIKE MILLIGAN

# NED SHERRIN

## 1970

*It is current fashion to dismiss the sixties as a decade of frivolity and profligacy, a celebration of decoration with no substance. What that view overlooks is the possibility that it perhaps represented a great sigh of relief at escaping the fifties, the drab landscape of cities and ideas scarred in the aftermath of the war. Suddenly it seemed as if that it was not after all necessary to have forever to perpetuate a Dunkirk view of the world. Britten's 'War Requiem' in 1962 and the magnificent new Coventry Cathedral seemed to embody the spirit of reconciliation, an end to public mourning. If the decade was a wild party, for which we are now 'paying the price', then it was as necessary as the meal after a funeral, an acknowledgement that life must go on. It was also, I believe, symptomatic of a genuine change in social order; authority, in whatever form, no matter who held it, was no longer sacred, but constantly open to question – however much the holders of high office did (and do) try to evade accountability. In the midst of all the muddled thinking and the handing out of flowers by perfect strangers one to another it seemed for a while as if there was a spirit of greater democracy abroad, and few institutions have remained untouched by it. Some years before 'the media' became a singular noun, one of the television programmes that reflected this change was 'That Was the Week That Was', as savagely satirical for the time as a Scarfe cartoon is now. Its producer was Ned Sherrin and he, along with its stars, has remained a household name. Although the satirical edge has dulled a little with the years (the party's over) I am sure he would be amused that the title of one of the pieces he chose for 'With Great Pleasure' seems strangely topical – 'Of Hunting a Thatcher'.*

Sexey's school, where I was educated, provided me with an introduction to the theatre. We went first to Stratford to see Esmond Knight, who is now my next door neighbour in Chelsea, in Peter Brook's *Winter's Tale* with Paul Scofield and Claire Bloom in small parts, and then we used to go regularly to the Bristol Old Vic where I distinctly remember one of Gertrude's breasts popping out in front of Robert Eddison's Hamlet. This was a bonus – sex education thrown in – and the production had another surprise for us. We'd been doing a little private sex educating at school, handing round a 'dirty' book called *Cue for Passion*, and when poor Hamlet came to his 'motive and cue for passion' line the whole row of Sexey's schoolboys collapsed with guilty laughter. I often wonder when I see Robert Eddison in the King's Road, if he tried without success to recapture that mysterious laugh on subsequent performances. I don't think it would be a very good idea if I were to read any Shakespeare. It would be a practical rebuttal of my contention that the thing that surprised me at school was to find that Shakespeare was such good money's worth if you actually went to see the plays: and so Robin Phillips, who is now a film actor and a distinguished stage director, and who also started his career at the Bristol Old Vic School and in the Bristol Old Vic Company, will read one of the sonnets.

## *Sonnet II*

WILLIAM SHAKESPEARE

When forty winters shall besiege thy brow
And dig deep trenches in thy beauty's field,
Thy youth's proud livery, so gazed on now,
Will be a tatter'd weed, of small worth held:
Then being ask'd where all thy beauty lies,
Where all the treasure of thy lusty days,
To say, within thine own deep-sunken eyes,
Were an all-eating shame and thriftless praise.
How much more praise deserved thy beauty's use,

If thou could'st answer 'This fair child of mine
Shall sum my count and make my old excuse,'
Proving his beauty by succession thine!
This were to be new made when thou art old,
And see thy blood warm when thou feel'st it cold.

My mother has on her bookshelves a memorial edition of the works of Walter Raymond, a Somerset dialect novelist who died in 1931, and whose ashes are buried at Yeovil. He is now almost unknown outside Somerset and I have enjoyed introducing him to Christopher Fry and John Betjeman, and I was fiercely loyal to him as a boy, especially his two best books, the light and charming *Gentleman Upcott's Daughter* – a sort of Queen Camel-and-Sparkford Romeo and Juliet (which I dramatised for the first radio play I ever wrote for the BBC's West Region) and the brooding *Two Men o' Mendip*. For me, Walter Raymond was always better than Thomas Hardy (though I'm prepared to believe that is local pride). I haven't been able to find a passage from either book that stands easily by itself, but here is a charming little essay which evokes very vividly for me the Somerset of my childhood.

## *Of Hunting a Thatcher*

WALTER RAYMOND

So I had a cottage to thatch.

My landlord has been as good as his word, and the first load of reed was brought unexpectedly one morning soon after dawn on a 'long cart' that would otherwise have been passing empty on its way to the nearest town. How beautiful it looked, that pile of neat sheaves of wheaten reed, when first I saw it, with an easterly sunlight gilding one side and a deep purple brown shadow on the other! No sign of a cloud disturbed the serenity of a clear May sky, and it lay inside the garden hatch, beside the little brier-bush which smelt so sweet of a morning.

The villagers admired it as much as I. One said it was 'a very tidy lot o' reed', and another called it 'beaudivul', all ready for the thatcher when he should come.

I had selected a thatcher and written a line, but no word came in reply. This surprised nobody but myself. Only a week had elapsed, and in a country that never yields to the folly of hurry, what is a week? Besides, to be sure, no thatcher was ever out of a job. Thatchers were scarce. A man might go down on his bended knees to a thatcher and never get him to come.

The villagers took the liveliest interest in my doings; and man, woman, and child crowded at all hours to confer on my affairs. As yet I scarcely knew my neighbours. Only Mr Huckleston, the sexton, by reason of official position and force of character, stood out from the rest. He gazed at the reed and said, as though there might be a doubt of it: 'If you do really want a thatcher now, why don't ee take an' goo an' hunt vor un?'

The idea was charming.

All men are hunters – so much of the instinct of primitive man remains in each of us, that he who cannot traverse another continent to kill big game will sit in his easy chair and chase a rare postage stamp among the leaves of a catalogue.

I said I would start at once and obtain a thatcher by hunting.

Mr Huckleston was a little man, bald on the crown, but with long grey hair around his ears. He had run out without his hat, as the occasion required. He was solemn and precise, and his instructions were very minute.

'Wull,' said he, 'to thatcher's house is up six mile – but there, 'tidden his house, for he's a widder-man an' do bide wi' his married sister – an' 'tidden a step more, or not much more. 'Tis so straight's a gun-barrel all the way. When you do come up 'pon to o' the moor, you'll see a trackway to the right, but don't you take no notice o' he. You keep as you be a-gwaine. An' when you do come down by the beechen hedges, you'll see a lane turn off short to the left, but don't you take no notice o' he. And when you do come to the four cross-roads, don't you take no notice o' they, right or left, but keep on straight avore. The house is a stonen house, the first you do come to. An' if you do bear in mind what I have a-told ee, you can't make no mistake. An' there you had better to ax for Thatcher Tapp. An' then, if, as is likely, he do chance to be out, you'll hear.'

By close attention I managed to hit the way.

Over the broad moorland, where the wind rustling through the bare heather kept the air fresh and cool, even under the noonday sun; where larks sang overhead and pipits rose at every step, and, taking only a short flight, alighted again on the small patches of fine grass; where the curlews, just returned to their lonely nesting-ground by the moist places where rushes grow, whistled in alarm at the passing stranger. Truly, hunting a thatcher may lead a man amidst a thousand simple joys.

I found the stone house, but the thatcher was from home.

'He is away up to Littlemoor 'pon a job,' said the woman. 'He won't be home tonight. You could walk across an' catch un there.'

'How far is it?'

'May be five mile. May be six.'

'And did he get my letter?'

'He'll bear it in mind to see to it when he've a-got time to spare,' said she, with smiling, placid contentment.

But such an assurance gave me no comfort. That thatcher I must run down. I found the six miles came to eight in fact, for nobody here need make more than a guess at distance. I followed him to his place of work. He was thatching an old barn, or at least he had been. There was his thatcher's ladder stuck into the mossy old roof – there were his bat and hook, his reed and spars, but that thatcher himself was nowhere to be seen.

A man came slowly out of the 'barn's door'.

'I Thatcher Tapp? Dear no. He is but jus' gone. You could a'most catch un if you was to run. He's gone out by Littleford to hunt for a job. And 'tis on your road, too – or not so very much out.'

The scent was warm, and I went away, merrily. Not a soul, coming or going, was to be seen upon the lonely road. But at Littleford they all said boldly: 'What? Thatcher Tapp? There's no job for the man here. He ha'nt so mucha as showed his nose here.' Then, recognising the limitations of human knowledge, each one paused, shook his head solemnly, and added: 'Not's I know.'

So that thatcher was lost after all. There was nothing for it but to trudge home, quietly reflecting upon a remarkably good run.

When at last I reached my cottage I found a stranger sitting at ease upon the garden wall as if it belonged to him.

He stepped down in front of me and said: 'I be Thatcher Tapp. I've acomed about thik bit of a job. I've a-tookt a look round. 'Tis a tidy bit o' reed – beaudivul reed. I could come a-Monday.'

I could have embraced the man in my simple delight.

'Very well, then, Monday let it be,' I cried with alacrity.

But Monday came and no thatcher. Then Tuesday and Wednesday. On Thursday I determined to hunt again, and decided to draw Norton this time.

But all in vain. Two sons and a married daughter of the man who used to be there were still living in the place. The thatcher, however, was accounted amongst the extinct fauna of that delightful old town.

On my return I found Thatcher Tapp perched like a gigantic bird on the slope of my roof. He was busily at work. Already he had laid a golden strip upon the old sparrow-furrowed thatch.

The man's head was lifted above the ridge, and his sunburnt cheek glowed red against the blue sky. How tenderly he embraced the reed and laid it gently down to rest! How deftly he hammered in the spars with his bat, and trimmed the new thatch smooth with his thatcher's hook! The gable, the small square chimney, and the man made a picture wonderful in line and rich in colour. But all the primitive crafts are beautiful to watch.

Thus I hunted my thatcher.

How long will there be a thatcher to hunt?

*Readers: Robin Phillips, Ned Sherrin*

*Full Selection:*
*The Old Curiosity Shop*, CHARLES DICKENS
*Sonnet II*, WILLIAM SHAKESPEARE
*Of Hunting a Thatcher*, WALTER RAYMOND
*Cricket Prints*, FRANK WOOLLEY
*Review of Augustin Daly's Production of a Midsummer Night's Dream*, BERNARD SHAW
*Essay on Dame Edith Evans – 'E' –*, KENNETH TYNAN
*New Year's Eve Poem 1965*, PETER LEVI
*A Consumer Guide to Religion*, ROBERT GILLESPIE and CHARLES LEWSEN
*No Bed for Bacon*, CARYL BRAHMS and S. J. SIMON

# *NORMAN ST JOHN STEVAS*

## *1984*

*Norman St John Stevas, once dubbed 'the acceptable face of Toryism', is a lover of the grand manner: few people after all, however religious, keep a harp in their living room. He asked and was able to arrange to have his programme recorded in the painted room at Chatsworth – a wonderful setting, but not exactly low key. However, another aspect of his character is one of elegant simplicity; his filing system, for example, consists of Harrods' bags tidily ranged on the floor around the walls of his study. His selection of items for the programme neatly reflected the driving passions of his life, politics and the Roman Catholic religion, leavened with an almost mischievous sense of humour.*

The two great British contributions to world civilisation have been Parliamentary Government and English Literature. Now, one point at which these two interests meet, at least in my mind, is Mr Disraeli. The career of Disraeli can be summed up as a literary genius who applied that genius to politics. 'What,' asked Queen Victoria, 'What did Mr Disraeli really believe?' If she had wanted an answer she could have looked at the novels; there you find some very rich pickings. Fortunately for him, most of his colleagues in the Conservative party never read anything, so his secret was safe. His outstanding novels are, I think, *Coningsby* and *Sybil* – the latter the archetype of the social model. Disraeli knew about the poor, he knew their life much better than Dickens; he cared, he was concerned. The most famous dichotomy he made was between two nations. How relevant that is today, the divisions between north and south, between those in work and those out of it, the division summed up by the Bishop of Liverpool in that prophetic television broadcast between comfortable and suffering Britain. *Sybil* set out that contrast nearly a hundred and fifty years ago.

## *Sybil*

BENJAMIN DISRAELI

'Well, society may be in its infancy,' said Egremont, slightly smiling; 'but say what you like, our Queen reigns over the greatest nation that ever existed.'

'Which nation?' asked the younger stranger, 'for she reigns over two.'

The stranger paused; Egremont was silent, but looked enquiringly.

'Yes,' resumed the younger stranger after a moment's interval, 'Two nations; between whom there is no intercourse and no sympathy; who are as ignorant of each other's habits, thoughts, and feelings, as if they were dwellers in different zones, or inhabitants of different planets; who are formed by a different breeding, are fed by a different food, are ordered by different manners, and are not governed by the same laws.'

'You speak of . . .' said Egremont hesitatingly.

'THE RICH AND THE POOR.'

'At this moment a sudden flush of rosy light, suffusing the grey ruins, indicated that the sun had just fallen; and, through a vacant arch that overlooked them, alone in the resplendent sky, glittered the twilight star.

Poetry is a deep thing and an elevating thing, the most surely wise and instructive of all the human things. Gerard Manley Hopkins is a poet's poet, but he was also a man of the spirit: a Jesuit who put his religious obedience ahead even of his genius. Where poetry is distinguished from prose is partly in rhythm and rhyme, but most of all I think in the concentration of images – and nowhere are the images denser than in Hopkins' poetry.

My choice is 'God's Grandeur'. I heard it recited in Westminster Cathedral by Dame Sybil Thorndike at a service for peace in Ireland. It was attended by both the Lord Chancellor and the Speaker of the House of Commons. And I read it myself at my mother's funeral.

I had a wonderful mother; she was adventurous, intrepid, witty, with a wonderful sense of fun. I remember, during her last illness, when she was in hospital, the matron came into her room – and matrons were matrons in those days. She was starched up to the eyeballs. My mother woke up at this moment, raised her hand into the air, and to my horror I heard her utter the single word, 'Waitress!' She realised that all was not well, said, 'A slip of the mind.' And went back to sleep. She was indomitable and I see something of her in this poem.

### *God's Grandeur*

GERARD MANLEY HOPKINS

The world is charged with the grandeur of God.
   It will flame out, like shining from shook foil;
   It gathers to a greatness, like the ooze of oil
Crushed. Why do men then now not reck his rod?
Generations have trod, have trod, have trod;
   And all is seared with trade; bleared, smeared with toil;
   And wears man's smudge and shares man's smell: the soil
Is bare now, nor can foot feel, being shod.

And for all this, nature is never spent;
   There lives the dearest freshness deep down things;
And though the last lights off the black West went
   Oh, morning, at the brown brink eastward, springs –
Because the Holy Ghost over the bent
   World broods with warm breast and with ah! bright
      wings.

Most of us have a no clear visual ideal of God. We are left with the stern judge or the man with the beard or the angry old man. To create an antidote to all this pernicious nonsense we have Mother Julian of Norwich, her 'Revelations of Divine Love'. Across the centuries comes her message which she wrote down 600 years ago.

## *Revelations of Divine Love*
JULIAN OF NORWICH

It was at this time that our Lord showed me spiritually how intimately he loves us. I saw that he is everything that we know to be good and helpful. In his love he clothes us, enfolds and embraces us; that tender love completely surrounds us, never to leave us. As I saw it he is everything that is good.

And he showed me more, a little thing, the size of a hazel-nut, on the palm of my hand, round like a ball. I looked at it thoughtfully and wondered, 'What is this?' And the answer came, 'It is all that is made.' I marvelled that it continued to exist and did not suddenly disintegrate; it was so small. And again my mind supplied the answer, 'It exists, both now and forever, because God loves it.' In short, everything owes its existence to the love of God.

*Readers: Jill Balcon, Michael Hordern*

*Full Selection:*
*Sybil*, BENJAMIN DISRAELI
*Ballade of Illegal Ornaments*, HILAIRE BELLOC
*Mapp and Lucia*, E. F. BENSON
*God's Grandeur*, GERARD MANLEY HOPKINS
*The Prince*, MACHIAVELLI
*Anthem for Doomed Youth*, WILFRED OWEN
*Revelations of Divine Love*, JULIAN OF NORWICH
*The Green Carnation*, HITCHENS
*On Shakespeare*, WALTER BAGEHOT
*King Lear* Act 5, Scene 3, WILLIAM SHAKESPEARE
*Sense and Sensibility*, JANE AUSTEN
*The More Loving One*, AUDEN
*To Hope*, JOHN KEATS

# *DORIAN WILLIAMS*

## *1982*

*At the beginning of the programme Dorian Williams gently mocked the idea that just because his professional life is taken up with things horsey he has no interest in other things, like reading. By displaying a sensitive and deeply humorous personality he proved his point for those who should have known better, including, I must confess, myself, and, I suspect Brian Patten who produced the programme. It confirmed what I have discovered again and again – that whatever view of the person I may have formed before meeting and working on this programme, I very soon discover that it was a one-sided impression and that the presenters are always more complicated, more interesting and more likeable than their public face would suggest.*

This is really a wonderful opportunity for me to wear another hat because I find that most people think, and perhaps understandably, that I am entirely associated with horses – in fact I often say that whenever I am introduced to speak at some function people expect half a horse to get up. I'm never sure which half, but perhaps that doesn't matter. Anyway it is true that I come from a horsey background, my parents in fact were really more or less founders of the Pony Club and my father was very much associated with the beginning of the British Show Jumping Association. But although my background is horsey, I have always enjoyed reading and as a small child I loved being read to aloud. I particularly enjoyed learning by heart. I loved the great epics and when I learned at prep school some of those great epics by heart I was probably the only boy in the school that really enjoyed it, but I did. In fact, at the age of thirteen I think I knew just about the whole of John Masefield's 'Right Royal' by heart. I always preferred it to the more famous 'Reynard the Fox' and I still think that in addition to the thrill of the race – it is, in fact, a fictitious description of the Grand National – it had real poetry in it and something of the magic that John Masefield used to bring to his poems about the sea.

### *Right Royal*

JOHN MASEFIELD

And now, beyond question, the field began tailing,
For all had been tested and many were ailing,
The riders were weary, the horses were failing,
The blur of bright colours rolled over the railing,
With grunts of urged horses, and the oaths of hot men,
'Gerr on, you', 'Come on, now', agen and agen;
They spattered the mud on the willow tree's bole
And they charged at the danger; and the danger took toll.

For Monkery landed, but dwelt on the fence,
So the Counter Vair passed him in galloping thence.
Then Stormalong blundered, then bright Muscatel
Slipped badly on landing and stumbled and fell,
With his whip in the mud and his stirrups both gone,
Yet he kept in the saddle and made him go on.

As Charles leaped the Turn, all the field was tailed out
Like petals of roses that wind blows about,
Like petals of colour blown back and brought near,
Like poppies in wind-flaws when corn is in ear;
Fate held them or sped them, the race was beginning.
Charles said, 'I must ride, or I've no chance of winning.'

Charles Cottill was of course the hero, who despite a fall caught up and won on the post.

As a teenager I was attempting to write poetry myself, most of it, I'm afraid, showing all too clearly the influence of Will Ogilvy, that great hunting poet whose marvellous books such as *Scattered Scarlet*, *Galloping Shoes* and *Over the Grass* were always welcome at

Christmas. One day at school we were set to write a poem with the title of 'Tranquillity'. In the same house as myself was Terence Rattigan, with whom I was quite friendly, and in discussing the matter with him, because he was already proving himself an extremely talented writer, he suggested that I should write a poem about a cat – I am sure I would have preferred a dog or a horse, but perhaps a cat *is* rather more tranquil. All went well until the last two lines or possibly the whole of the last verse, which very obligingly Terry supplied: so at last he's getting due credit, and he was probably responsible for my poem appearing in the school magazine – my first appearance in print.

### *Tranquillity*

DORIAN WILLIAMS

The room was quaintly lit, the firelight flicking
  The gloom with lash of flame.
Over the hearth, the clock was slowly ticking
  A song without a name.

An old man lay, in seas of slumber drifting,
  Remote and free from care;
On softened face the glow, forever drifting,
  Trembled, and on his hair.

A cat dozed, purring, by the tranquil sleeper,
  Lay, purring, dimly seen,
While shadows mingled deeper yet and deeper;
  Her half-closed eyes shone green.

And now, in drowsy peace, the cat crept nearer
  Her master's slippered feet,
And still her crooning, for her far-off hearer
  Lay lost in failing heat.

The embers, dying, dropped, their death was creeping;
  The last red spark had leapt;
Yet still those placid dreamers went on sleeping,
  And slept and slept and slept.

When one is very young one loves the illogical, nonsense, rubbish, everything exaggerated and eccentric. In adolescence one becomes very logical and one can neither understand nor accept anything that is illogical or nonsensical. In adulthood once again appreciates the joy of the illogical and so it is I believe that small children love *Alice in Wonderland*, adolescents just cannot take it, but adults, if they are lucky return to it and then fully appreciate the remarkable genius of Lewis Carroll. Here is a short passage from *Through the Looking Glass* which is, perhaps particularly appropriate, as it is a passage where the White Knight finds it very easy to fall off – but greatly resents being told that he needs more practice – another common fault in riders!

## *The White Knight* from *Alice Through the Looking Glass*

LEWIS CARROLL

Whenever the horse stopped (which it did very often), he fell off in front; and, whenever it went on again (which it generally did rather suddenly), he fell off behind. Otherwise he kept on pretty well, except that he had a habit of now and then falling off sideways; and as he generally did this on the side on which Alice was walking, she soon found that it was the best plan not to walk *quite* close to the horse.

'I'm afraid you've not had much practice in riding,' she ventured to say, as she was helping him up from his fifth tumble.

The Knight looked very much surprised, and a little offended at the remark. 'What makes you say that?' he asked, as he scrambled back into the saddle, keeping hold of Alice's hair with one hand, to save himself from falling over on the other side.

'Because people don't fall off quite so often, when they've had much practice.'

'I've had plenty of practice,' the Knight said very gravely: 'plenty of practice!'

Alice could think of nothing better to say than 'Indeed?' but she said it as heartily as she could. They went on a little way in silence after this, the Knight with his eyes shut, muttering to himself, and Alice watching anxiously for the next tumble.

'The great art of riding,' the Knight suddenly began in a loud voice, waving his right arm as he spoke, 'is to keep –' Here the sentence ended as suddenly as it had begun, as the Knight fell heavily on the top of his head exactly in the path where Alice was walking. She was quite frightened this time, and said in an anxious tone, as she picked him up, 'I hope no bones are broken?'

'None to speak of,' the Knight said, as if he didn't mind breaking two or three of them. 'The great art of riding, as I was saying, is – to keep your balance properly. Like this, you know –'

He let go the bridle, and stretched out both his arms to show Alice what he meant, and this time he fell flat on his back, right under the horse's feet.

'Plenty of practice!' he went on repeating, all the time that Alice was getting him on his feet again. 'Plenty of practice!'

'It's too ridiculous!' cried Alice, losing all her patience this time. 'You ought to have a wooden horse on wheels, that you ought!'

'Does that kind go smoothly?' the Knight asked in a tone of great interest, clasping his arms round the horse's neck as he spoke, just in time to save himself from tumbling off again.

'Much more smoothly than a live horse,' Alice said, with a little scream of laughter, in spite of all she could do to prevent it.

'I'll get one,' the Knight said thoughtfully to himself. 'One or two – several.'

*Readers: Richard Johnson, Joyce Redman*

*Full Selection:*
*Horatius,* LORD MACAULAY
*Right Royal,* JOHN MASEFIELD
*Tranquillity,* DORIAN WILLIAMS
*Ode to a Nightingale,* JOHN KEATS
*Kilvert's Diary,* REV. FRANCIS KILVERT
*Alice Through the Looking Glass,* LEWIS CARROLL
*A Shropshire Lad,* A. E. HOUSMAN
*Bredon Hill,* A. E. HOUSMAN
*Handley Cross,* R. S. SURTEES
*Hunter Trials,* JOHN BETJEMAN
*Venus Observed,* CHRISTOPHER FRY
*Henry V,* WILLIAM SHAKESPEARE
*East Coker,* T. S. ELIOT

# *WITH GREAT PLEASURE*

*Volume II*

# CONTENTS

# ACKNOWLEDGEMENTS

*Every Day in Every Way* by KIT WRIGHT reprinted by permission of Tessa Sayle Agency
*Letter to Sandor Ferenczi* by SIGMUND FREUD reprinted by permission of Hogarth Press
*Selected Letters* and *The Ascent of Parnassus Made Easy* by DYLAN THOMAS reprinted by permission of David Higham Associates Ltd
*The Ghost* reprinted by permission of the Literary Trustees of WALTER DE LA MARE and the Society of Authors as their representative
*The Flight From Bootle* and *Blame the Vicar by* JOHN BETJEMAN reprinted by permission of John Murray (Publishers) Ltd
*Tarantella* by HILAIRE BELLOC reprinted by permission of A. D. Peters & Co. Ltd
*The Life of the Bee* by MAETERLINCK trans Alfred Sutro reprinted by permission of George Allen and Unwin
*Doggerel About Old Days, Memoirs of a Fox-Hunting Man* and *The General* by SIEGFRIED SASSOON reprinted by permission of George Sassoon
*Symptom Recital* by DOROTHY PARKER reprinted by permission of Laurence Pollinger Ltd
Extract by ATHENE SEYLER from *The RADA Graduate's Keepsake and Counsellor* reprinted by permission of RADA
Extract from the *Diary* of HUGH WALPOLE reprinted by permission of M. L. R. Ltd
Extract from *Duet for One* by TOM KEMPINSKI reprinted by permission of Anthony Sheil Associates Ltd
Extract from *One for the Road* by WILLY RUSSELL reprinted by permission of Margaret Ramsay Ltd
*On a Tide of Murder* by PHILIP NORMAN reprinted by permission of A. D. Peters & Co. Ltd
*We Need a Star* by MICHAEL BURNETT reproduced by permission of the author

*The Tower* by W. B. YEATS reproduced by permission of A. P. Watt Ltd on behalf of Michael Yeats and Macmillan London Ltd
*Funeral Blues* and *Miss Gee* by W. H. AUDEN reprinted by permission of Faber and Faber Ltd
*The Ruin* trans KEVIN CROSSLEY-HOLLAND reproduced by permission of Deborah Rogers Ltd
*The Eternal Order* by EDWARD GRUBB reprinted by permission of Heckford, Norton & Co.
*The Happy Hour* by SYLVIA LIND reprinted by permission of Victor Gollancz Ltd
*Close of Play* by ALAN MILLER reprinted by permission of Hodder & Stoughton Ltd
*Bagpipe Music* by LOUIS MACNEICE published by Faber and Faber Ltd and reproduced by permission of David Higham Associates Ltd
*The Oxford Hysteria of English Poetry* from 'Ride the Nightmare' by ADRIAN MITCHELL reprinted by permission of Jonathan Cape Ltd
Extract from *The Dog Beneath the Skin* by W. H. AUDEN & CHRISTOPHER ISHERWOOD reprinted by permission of Curtis Brown Ltd
*may i feel said he* by E. E. CUMMINGS reprinted by permission of Jonathan Cape Ltd
*Introduction to a Science of Mythology* by JUNG & KERENYI trans R. F. C. Hull reprinted by permission of Routledge & Kegan Paul plc
*Like Men Betrayed* by FREDERIC RAPHAEL reprinted by permission of A. P. Watt Ltd
*Plain Words* by ERNEST GOWERS reprinted by permission of HMSO
*Who Am I?* by DIETRICH BONHOEFFER reprinted by permission of SCM Press
*Code Poem for the French Resistance* by LEO MARKS reprinted by permission of Big Ben Music Ltd
Extract from *The People of Providence* by TONY PARKER reprinted by permission of Anthony Sheil Associates Ltd
*Dear Mr Eggnogge* THE SPITTING IMAGE BOOK © SUE TOWNSEND
*Imaginings* by ROBERT GITTINGS reprinted by permission of Secker and Warburg Ltd

# *FOREWORD*

From the beginning there was talk that Century Hutchinson might wish to publish a second volume based on Radio 4's 'With Great Pleasure'. For that very reason, when compiling Volume I, I had to discipline myself not just to think in terms of producing a 'best of' collection, but to put some of my favourite editions to one side. Fortunately most of the programmes from the first in 1970 to the one I recorded earlier this week have been entertaining, with many including unusual pieces which reveal much about the guest people chosen to offer their favourite poetry and prose to the assembled audience. Inevitably, with the passing of time and the fickleness of public interest, certain names had lost their lustre, a few programmes must have sounded better on the air than they read on the page and a few more just did not capture my imagination. As to the latter I merely claimed the anthologist's privilege of leaving out anything which did not give *me* pleasure. Some of those omitted from Volume I were friends of mine and here I could only carry out the anthologist's duty of presenting what I hoped was a balanced selection regardless of personal preference. I am happy to be able to include them now.

In the Foreword to our first volume I mentioned that we had just recorded an edition of 'With Great Pleasure' with Peter Pears. Sadly, since then he has died. He will be fondly remembered in his beloved Aldeburgh and by friends all over the world. To all of us his voice will remain familiar through his many recordings with Benjamin Britten. These, along with the festival he helped to create, will be his legacy. Nevertheless, it gives me some satisfaction to add to it in some small degree by including part of his programme here.

Reading through recent 'With Great Pleasure' scripts, I am pleased to note a decline of interest in 'The Old Vicarage, Grantchester'. No one has included it for at least two years now. John Betjeman is chosen as often as he ever was: it is rare for a programme not to contain a poem of his – often a presenter tries to squeeze in two or three. However, in the interests of variety I tend to discourage having more than one piece by any author. Thomas Hardy and Robert Browning would certainly feature in any 'With Great Pleasure' hit parade, whilst Jane Austen would probably top the charts as the most quoted novelist. Although all are included in this book, I have not been over zealous in obeisance. One of the things that makes the programme of such continuing interest to the listeners is the choice of unfamiliar and unexpected material. For that reason Jane Austen is represented here not by *Persuasion* or *Pride and Prejudice*, but a rarely-seen piece written when she was a young girl.

This time there is no unpublished fragment by Geoffrey Chaucer, but there *is* unpublished Alan Bleasdale, especially written for the programme. Perhaps even more heartwarming are a couple of poems presented as an act of friendship, one to Heather Couper by Michael Burnett, the other to Ian Wallace by Robert Gittings – and jolly good they are too. There is also a poem by W. H. Auden which he tried to suppress because he thought it too shocking.

So, if your taste inclines to the sentimental you will find items enough to moisten at least two hankies. There are also pieces of savagery and wit, which express a profound distaste for life. However there are many more whose essence is the joy of being alive. It is that which in the end makes 'With Great Pleasure' such a genuine pleasure for so many listeners. As broadcasts are by their nature here today and gone tomorrow, it is my pleasure to offer this more permanent reminder of such a popular series.

Alec Reid
April 1988

# DANNIE ABSE

## 1984

*Before I moved to Bristol from London, Dannie Abse and I regularly used to have lunch together at an Italian restaurant just around the corner from the Middlesex Hospital where he worked. He always ordered the same dish, a Pizza Napoli without the anchovy. 'After all,' he argued, 'if you come to a pizza place you really ought to order a pizza.' It was a form of gastronomic logic I was unable to follow, but it was the only part of being with him that was in any way routine. He is a witty and clever conversationalist, always ready to startle with a fresh idea. I didn't have the pleasure of producing his 'With Great Pleasure', but at the time of writing have just arranged for him to be the subject of some 'Time for Verse' programmes. It will be a happy opportunity to work with him again and lunch is already on the agenda. So, no doubt, is the Pizza Napoli without the anchovy.*

At the rehearsal of this programme I heard someone say, 'Is he a real doctor?' I should have worn a tie. I became a doctor because of my eldest brother Wilfred who, not long after he had qualified as a physician, returned to our house in Cardiff to find me uselessly pushing a saucer of milk towards our sick cat. Merlin lay motionless on the carpet, his eyes staring at nothing. Was Merlin dying? 'I wouldn't mind being a vet,' I said.

I was a fourteen-year-old schoolboy, who wanted to be a concert pianist, an assassin that did for Hitler, a crooner like Bing Crosby, a boxer like Tommy Farr, a jockey like Gordon Richards, a racing driver like Sir Malcolm Campbell, the best centre forward

Cardiff City ever had, the fastest wing-threequarter capped for Wales, the greatest opening bat in Glamorgan's history. Maybe, in my spare time, I could become a reasonable vet?

'Better to become a doctor,' Wilfred had replied, 'like me, like so many of your cousins – like Uncle Max, like Uncle Joe.'

So, unselfish, I gave up all my ambitions and became a mere doctor. I say mere, because I've known a few in my life. My Uncle Max, apart from believing in the efficacy of modern drugs, believes powerfully in the power of suggestion. So did Dr Coué – whose theories of auto-suggestion apparently became a craze during the 1920s. On his recommendation hordes of people woke up in the morning to intone, 'Every day, in every way, I grow better and better.' A poet acquaintance of mine, Christopher . . . Kit . . . Wright, obviously tried out Dr Coué's recommendation himself.

## *Every Day in Every Way*
### KIT WRIGHT

When I got up this morning
I thought the whole thing through:
Thought, Who's the hero, the man of the day?
Christopher, it's you.

With my left arm I raised my right arm
High above my head:
Said, Christopher, you're the greatest.
Then I went back to bed.

I wrapped my arms around me,
No use counting sheep.
I counted legions of myself
Walking on the deep.

The sun blazed on the miracle,
The blue ocean smiled:
We like the way you operate,
Frankly, we like your style.

Dreamed I was in a meadow,
Angels singing hymns,

Fighting the nymphs and shepherds
Off my holy limbs.

A girl leaned out with an apple,
Said, You can taste for free.
I never touch the stuff, dear,
I'm keeping myself for me.

Dreamed I was in heaven,
God said, Over to you,
Christopher, you're the greatest!
And Oh, it's true, it's true!

I like my face in the mirror,
I like my voice when I sing.
My girl says it's just infatuation –
I know it's the real thing.

Doctors can be fair game for satirists. But what about patients? Sometimes they can be incredible. I recall one chap who was all in a dither because his wife had just had a baby. To keep him quiet I suggested he went out to buy mother and child a present. He returned with flowers for his wife and a bar of chocolate for his newborn son. 'I don't think . . .' I began. 'Don't worry, doctor,' he interrupted me blithely, 'it's *milk* chocolate.' It was a very big bar. Ignorant he was, stingy he was not, unlike Jimmy MacDougal:

A bugler called Jimmy MacDougal
Found ingenious ways to be frugal.
He learned how to sneeze
In various keys
Thus saving the price of a bugle.

Two of the pleasures of the morning for me are buttered toast and letters. If one or two real letters don't lie on the mat in the morning I feel the day hasn't truly begun. I'm glad, though, that these days I don't receive letters from one who called himself 'The Master'. Some years ago, whenever I appeared in print, published a book, did a broadcast, I would receive, on a tatty scrap of paper, a letter signed 'The Master'. These anonymous letters were in no way abusive. On the contrary, they were usually appreciative and, moreover, literary, finely composed. They puzzled me very much. Naturally I looked at the postmark. They came from a small town west of London. But knowing that didn't help. I received The Master's letters, usually written on blue-lined paper, for the best part of a decade. Indeed, when I published something I began to *wait* for The Master's response. One Friday my wife happened on a letter in the *New Statesman* written by a novelist whom I shall now call 'Tony'. 'Didn't you used to know Tony a little when you were a student?' my wife asked. 'Look at the address he's writing from.' It was from that same small town west of London. Tony was older than me – he'd had several novels published when I first met him and was much better known than he is now. Anyway, I took a chance and wrote to him:

Dear Tony,
Thank you for all those constructive and interesting letters you've sent me over the years.
Best Wishes
Dannie

The reply came back immediately:

Dear Dannie,
You've found me out. I should have posted your letters in a different town.
The Master

The next letter I received from him was still, surprisingly, signed 'The Master'. It was still on a scrappy bit of paper, but now it was abusive, full of aggression and unpleasantness. Subsequent letters, following any publication of mine, were equally hostile and still signed 'The Master'. Then one day I received a warm letter and since then there's just been silence. . . .

I won't read you any of the scraps of paper 'The Master' once sent me. Instead I want to introduce you to some marvellous letters – all of them having, incidentally, a tangential medical interest. The first is an ironic comical one by Freud to his disciple Ferenczi, in which he warns him not to kiss his patients.

## *Sigmund Freud's Letter to Sandor Ferenczi Written on December 13, 1931*

I see that the differences between us come to a head in a technical detail which is well worth discussing. You have not made a secret of the fact that you kiss your patients and let them kiss you; I had also heard that from a patient of my own. Now when you decide to give a full account of your technique and its results you will have to choose between two ways: either you relate this or you conceal it. The latter, as you may well think, is dishonourable. What one does in one's technique one has to defend openly. Besides, both ways soon come together. Even if you don't say so yourself it will soon get known just as I knew it before you told me.

Now I am assuredly not one of those who from prudishness or from consideration of bourgeois convention would condemn little erotic gratifications of this kind. And I am also aware that in the time of the Nibelungs a kiss was a harmless greeting granted to every guest. I am further of the opinion that analysis is possible even in Soviet Russia where so far as the State is concerned there is full sexual freedom. But that does not alter the facts that we are not living in Russia and that with us a kiss signifies a certain erotic intimacy. We have hitherto in our technique held to the conclusion that patients are to be refused erotic gratifications. You know too that where more extensive gratifications are not to be had milder caresses very easily take over their role, in love affairs, on the stage, etc.

Now picture what will be the result of publishing your technique. There is no revolutionary who is not driven out of the field by a still more radical one. A number of independent thinkers in matters of technique will say to themselves: why stop at a kiss? Certainly one gets further when one adopts 'pawing' as well, which after all doesn't make a baby. And then bolder ones will come along who will go further to peeping and showing – and soon we shall have accepted in the technique of analysis the whole repertoire of demiviergerie and petting-parties, resulting in an enormous increase of patients in psycho-analysis among both analysts and patients. The new adherent, however, will easily claim too much of this interest for himself, the younger of our colleagues will find it hard to stop at the point they originally intended, and God the Father, Ferenczi, gazing at the lively scene he has created will perhaps say to himself: maybe after all I should have halted in my technique of motherly affection *before* the kiss. . . .

And the next letter I've chosen is by Dylan Thomas, in which he apologizes for not turning up to a British Medical Association dinner in his home town.

## *'Selected Letters'*
**DYLAN THOMAS**

I plead that the collected will of the Members of the Swansea Branch of the British Medical Association, working by a clinically white magic known only to their profession, drove me, soon after my inexcusable non-appearance at their Annual Dinner, into a bag of sickness and a cropper of accidents from which I have not yet full recovered. The first effect of this malevolent mass medical bedevilment I experienced a week after the Dinner when stopping, heavily disguised, at Swansea in order to learn how really execrated I was in the surgeries and theatres, the bolus-rooms and Celtic lazarets of a town I can approach now only in the deepest dark and where certain areas, particularly around the hospital, are forever taboo to me. I felt sudden and excruciating pains, and when I whimpered about them to a friend he said, 'Whatever you do, don't get ill in Swansea, it's more than your life is worth. Go in with a cough and they'll circumcise you.' So I knew what the position was and I took my pains home. But even at home, word of my unworthiness had reached the doctor's ears, and I was treated like a leper (fortunately, a wrong diagnosis). Ever since then I have felt unwell. A little later I had an attack of gout – undoubtedly the result of some Swansea specialist sticking a pin into a wax toe – and a little later still was set upon by invisible opponents in the bogled Laugharne dark and fell down and cracked my ribs.

*Readers: Siân Phillips, David Brierley*

*Full Selection:*
*Le Médecin Malgré Lui*, MOLIÈRE
*A Dangerous Remedy*, RHYS DAVIES
*Every Day in Every Way*, KIT WRIGHT
*Hope Against Hope*, NADEZHDA MANDELSTAM
*A Prince from Western Libya*, C. P. CAVAFY
*The Cabinet of Pictures*, ALLAN CUNNINGHAM
*Letter to Sandor Ferenczi Written on December 13, 1931*, SIGMUND FREUD
*A Letter*, LUDWIG VAN BEETHOVEN
*'Selected Letters'*, DYLAN THOMAS
*Poem in October*, DYLAN THOMAS
*After a Journey*, THOMAS HARDY
*The River Merchant's Wife: A Letter*, EZRA POUND
*Part of Plenty*, BERNARD SPENCER
*James Joyce's Hundredth Birthday: Side and Front Views*, RICHARD ELLMANN
*Please*, MICHAEL BURN

# *RICHARD ADAMS*

## *1987*

*'With Great Pleasure' makes some strange connections. When in 1980 Kingsley Amis recorded his edition he included Philip Larkin's 'Going, Going', and said: 'He wrote it on a commission from the Department of the Environment, if you can believe such a thing.' Over drinks after his recording Richard Adams let slip that he was the chap in the department who had commissioned the poem. For the record, the author*

*of* Watership Down *knows all the jokes of the 'you've read the book, you've seen the film, now eat the pie' variety.*

I was lucky to have a very happy childhood, and on top of everything else there is one particular respect in which I owe my parents a great debt. They read to me; without compulsion and purely for pleasure; but good stuff and plenty of it. As it seems in memory, neither my father nor my mother was ever too busy for this delightful form of companionship, and each of them appeared to enjoy it every bit as much as I did. While I was quite small – no more than three or four – it was usually my mother who read; before bedtime, as I sat on her knee by the poppling gas fire – I can hear it now – to look at the pictures and ask questions. In this way I made the acquaintance of Peter Rabbit, Pigling Bland and the other Beatrix Potter characters: the Jumblies, the Dong and the other denizens of Edward Lear's world, as depicted so splendidly by Leslie Brooke; together with a host of others less remembered today, such as Bobbity Flop (he was a rabbit, by the way, so I suppose he must have taken root quite deeply), Tony O'Dreams and Little Black Sambo. (No one could see anything the matter with him in those days.) Winnie the Pooh hadn't yet been written.

There was plenty of poetry in this bedtime fare, including Robert Louis Stevenson's *Child's Garden of Verses*, which I've loved ever since. But here, to begin this programme, is another favourite of my mother and myself, which I dare say a good many other infants have cut their literary teeth on during the last hundred years. It's by Eugene Field, an American who died in 1895 at the too-early age of forty-four.

## *Wynken, Blynken and Nod*

**EUGENE FIELD**

Wynken, Blynken, and Nod one night
Sailed off in a wooden shoe –
Sailed on a river of crystal light,
Into a sea of dew.
'Where are you going, and what do you wish?'
The old moon asked the three.

'We have come to fish for the herring fish
That live in this beautiful sea;
Nets of silver and gold have we!'
Said Wynken,
Blynken,
And Nod.

The old moon laughed and sang a song,
As they rocked in the wooden shoe,
And the wind that sped them all night long
Ruffled the waves of dew.
The little stars were the herring fish
That lived in that beautiful sea –
'Now cast your nets wherever you wish –
Never afeard are we';
So cried the stars to the fishermen three:
Wynken,
Blynken,
And Nod.

All night long their nets they threw
To the stars in the twinkling foam –
Then down from the skies came the wooden shoe,
Bringing the fishermen home;
'Twas all so pretty a sail it seemed
As if it could not be,
And some folks thought 'twas a dream they'd dreamed
Of sailing that beautiful sea –
But I shall name you the fishermen three:
Wynken,
Blynken,
And Nod.

Wynken and Blynken are two little eyes,
And Nod is a little head,
And the wooden shoe that sailed the skies
Is the wee one's trundle-bed.
So shut your eyes while mother sings
Of wonderful sights that be,
And you shall see the beautiful things

As you rock in the misty sea,
Where the old shoe rocked the fishermen three:
Wynken,
Blynken,
And Nod.

I wasn't quite nine when I went to boarding school, and here, lonely and homesick, I came, almost by accident, under the influence of two twentieth-century poets. I suppose many people might think at least one of these, Thomas Hardy, a rather depressing sort of poet for a little boy. However our form-master can't have thought so, because the very first poem I was ever required to learn by heart was Hardy's *When I Set Out for Lyonnesse*. Heaven only knows what the form-master thought it meant. I don't think he could possibly have known that it is Hardy's cryptic and deeply personal account of how, as a young architect in 1870, he travelled, on a winter's day, from Dorset to a North Cornwall vicarage on business, and there met and fell in love with Emma Gifford, the girl he was to marry. I wasn't to know that either, of course: yet the odd truth is that one doesn't need to. What I did grasp clearly and arrestingly was that the poet had made a lonely journey, begun in cold and darkness, to a strange and distant place whence he had returned with the gain of some magical, spiritual blessing. That was quite enough to strike home, whereas the mundane facts would have meant little to a nine-year-old.

## *When I Set Out for Lyonnesse*
THOMAS HARDY

When I set out for Lyonnesse
A hundred miles away,
The rime was on the spray,
And starlight lit my lonesomeness
When I set out for Lyonnesse
A hundred miles away.

What would bechance at Lyonnesse
While I should sojourn there
No prophet durst declare,

Nor did the wisest wizard guess
What would bechance at Lyonnesse
While I should sojourn there.

When I came back from Lyonnesse
With magic in my eyes,
All marked with mute surmise
My radiance rare and fathomless,
When I came back from Lyonnesse
With magic in my eyes!

The other poet was Walter de la Mare, whom later, when I was up at Oxford, I was more than glad to have the chance to meet and thank for all that his work had meant to me. Although de la Mare wrote a great deal of poetry which is ostensibly for children, he is none the less a disturbing poet, inasmuch as his work is shot through and through with a deep awareness of mankind's essential ignorance and insecurity. Life is a prelude to death, and of death we know nothing. In his world cold, ghosts, grief, pain and loss stand all about the little cocoon of bright warmth, which is everywhere pierced by a wild, numinous beauty, often the catalyst of tears and terror rather than delight. He is certainly no orthodox Christian. Yet as a child I was both fascinated and curiously comforted by de la Mare's multifoliate insistence that there exists some strange world beyond our own; a beautiful, if wild and frightening place, with which we have intermittent, tenuous and mysterious contact. Many years later, this idea was to emerge as one of the mainsprings of *Watership Down* – Fiver's gift of second sight – but also as the whole basis of *The Girl in a Swing*. Here is de la Mare at his most grief-stricken and disquieting.

### *The Ghost*

**WALTER DE LA MARE**

'Who knocks?'/'I, who was beautiful,
Beyond all dreams to restore,
I, from the roots of the dark thorn am hither.
And knock on the door.'

'Who speaks?'/'I – once was my speech
Sweet as the bird's on the air,

When echo lurks by the waters to heed;
'Tis I speak thee fair.'

'Dark is the hour!'/'Ay and cold.'
'Lone is my house.'/'Ah, but mine?'
'Sight, touch, lips, eyes yearned in vain.'
'Long dead these to thine . . .'

Silence. Still faint on the porch
Brake the flames of the stars.
In gloom groped a hope-wearied hand.
Over keys, bolts, and bars.

A face peered. All the grey night
In chaos of vacancy shone;
Nought but vast sorrow was there –
The sweet cheat gone.

At quite an early age, therefore, I had discovered – even though I couldn't have expressed it in words – that while true poetry, like life itself, is often transcendentally beautiful – indeed that is its nature and function – it is also frightening in its manifold reminders that we are not only mortal but ignorant of any ultimate truth. I don't mean that all poetry that is not frightening in this way is of no value. I would express my feeling, I think, in converse terms. Of course there is much true poetry that is not explicitly concerned with our mortality and ignorance – Shakespeare's sonnets, to look no further – but nevertheless any writing, verse or prose, which contrives to ignore or to suggest that we are anything else than mortal and insecure, is shallow and, in effect, mendacious.

By the age of fifteen I was wide open to capture by the sheer *sound* of poetry – the beauty of words and rhythms virtually for their own sake. I was a sitting duck, in fact, for Gerard Manley Hopkins, for T. S. Eliot and even for Edith Sitwell, whom I still admire up to a point. For me the meanings expressed by these poets were secondary to the glorious sound and rhythms of their words. At that time Hopkins' poetry had been in print for only sixteen or seventeen years, and had made an enormous impact on the whole poetic climate of the twenties and thirties. Here is one of his best poems – his elegiac sonnet on the death of one of his parishioners, the village blacksmith, Felix Randal. Incidentally, this was a favourite of George Orwell, who knew it by heart and used to say it over to himself while on night sentry duty during the Spanish Civil War.

## *Felix Randal*

### GERARD MANLEY HOPKINS

Felix Randal the farrier, O is he dead then? my duty all ended,
Who have watched his mould of man, big boned and
  hardy-handsome
Pining, pining, till time when reason rambled in it and some
Fatal four disorders, fleshed there, all contended?

Sickness broke him. Impatient, he cursed at first, but mended
Being anointed and all; though a heavenlier heart began some
Months earlier, since I had our sweet reprieve and ransom
Tendered to him. Ah well, God rest him all road ever he
  offended!

This seeing the sick endears them to us, us too it endears.
My tongue had taught thee comfort, touch had quenched thy
  tears,
Thy tears that touched my heart, child, Felix, poor Felix Randal;

How far from then forethought of, all thy more boisterous
  years,
When thou at the random grim forge, powerful amidst peers,
Didst fettle for the great grey drayhorse his bright and battering
  sandal!

Shakespeare, of course, is not really a human being at all. He is like a great mountain upon whose lower slopes we all live, including those who are not consciously aware of it. The mountain affects the weather and the climate. It is a landmark for those far out to sea. We drink from the streams that flow from its heights and pasture our flocks on its slopes. Some people have actually climbed quite a long way up it. I needn't strain the analogy any further; but I will say, loud and clear, that I am in no doubt that by far the greatest secular blessing that we in this country possess in common is that Shakespeare was an Englishman and wrote in English.

Here is Edgar's famous speech from *King Lear*. Edgar, his identity disguised, is setting out to convince his poor old father, the Earl of Gloucester, who has been blinded by his cruel enemies, that the two of them are in fact standing on the summit of Dover cliff. Right at the start, in a miraculous piece of onomatopoeia, Shakespeare sends the vowels hurtling down the cliff from top to bottom. Then the eye follows them.

## *King Lear*
**WILLIAM SHAKESPEARE**

Come on, sir; here's the place: stand still. How fearful
And dizzy 'tis to cast one's eye so low!
The crows and choughs that wing the midway air
Show scarce so gross as beetles; half way down
Hangs one that gathers samphire, dreadful trade!
Methinks he seems no bigger than his head.
The fishermen that walk upon the beach
Appear like mice, and yond tall anchoring bark
Diminish'd to her cock, her cock a buoy
Almost too small for sight. The murmuring surge
That on the unnumber'd idle pebbles chafes,
Cannot be heard so high. I'll look no more,
Lest my brain turn, and the deficient sight
Topple down headlong.

*Readers: Ronald Pickup, Cheri Lunghi*

*Full Selection:*
*Wynken, Blynken and Nod,* EUGENE FIELD
*When I Set Out for Lyonnesse,* THOMAS HARDY
*Friends Beyond,* THOMAS HARDY
*The Ghost,* WALTER DE LA MARE
*Dream Song,* WALTER DE LA MARE
*Felix Randal,* GERARD MANLEY HOPKINS
*The Shield of Achilles,* W. H. AUDEN
*Oliver Twist,* CHARLES DICKENS
*Mansfield Park,* JANE AUSTEN
*King Lear,* WILLIAM SHAKESPEARE
*Antony and Cleopatra,* WILLIAM SHAKESPEARE

# BERYL BAINBRIDGE

## 1981

*This fine novelist has recently shown herself to be an accomplished presenter, both on television and on Radio 4's 'Down Your Way'. The personality that comes across in those broadcasts is sympathetic, down to earth, curious, celebratory. Yet, she confessed in her 'With Great Pleasure' programme that she has 'a morbid taste in literature', perhaps because her father wept during the 'sad bits' whilst he read to her when she was a child. Indeed, he made a point of selecting the saddest and gloomiest passages from Dickens. If that was the influence, then it was certainly a powerful one: her selection is characterized by an ineffable tug of sadness.*

There was a market in Southport which used to have a stall of second-hand books – I don't know whether it's still there now, probably it is. But as a child I bought several books every week. I didn't always read them, but I liked owning them. One of them was *The Sorrows of Satan* by a woman called Marie Corelli. She was a remarkable writer and a remarkable woman. She used to punt up and down the river at Stratford-on-Avon in a Venetian gondola. In her lifetime she was totally disliked by the press. She was called vain and silly because she swore she was ten years younger than she actually was. But, you see, there was a very sad reason for this – which was only discovered a few years ago. She was illegitimate and her father married her mother when she was eleven years old.

If the critics made fun of her, the public adored her. This particular novel sold 100,000 copies on the first morning of publication. It has a tremendous plot: it's about the devil coming down to live on earth. In this passage Geoffrey, the hero, has discovered that his wife is no better than she ought to be. By this, Geoffrey means that she's taking an unhealthy interest in sex. She's too fond of reading naughty novels.

## *The Sorrows of Satan*

### MARIE CORELLI

I found Sybil in the garden, reclining in a basket-chair, her eyes fixed on the after-glow of the sunset, and in her hands a book – one of the loathliest of the prurient novels that have been lately written by women to degrade and shame their sex. With a sudden impulse of rage upon me which I could not resist, I snatched the volume from her and flung it into the lake below. She made no movement of either surprise or offence – she merely turned her eyes away from the glowing heavens, and looked at me with a little smile.

'The new fiction is detestable,' – I said hotly – 'Both in style and morality. Even as a question of literature I wonder at your condescending to read any of it. The woman whose dirty book I have just thrown away – and I feel no compunction for having done it – is destitute of grammar as well as decency.'

'Oh, but the critics don't notice that,' – she interrupted, with a delicate mockery vibrating in her voice – 'It is apparently not their business to assist in preserving the purity of the English language. What they fall into raptures over is the originality of the "sexual" theme, though I should have thought all such matters were as old as the hills. I never read reviews as a rule, but I did happen to come across one on the book you have just drowned – and in it the reviewer stated he had cried over it!'

She laughed again. My God.

What was the use of living on. Knowing that she whom I had loved, and whom I loved still in a way that was hateful to myself, was a thing viler and more shameless in character than the veriest poor drab of the street who sells herself for current coin – that the lovely body and angel-face were but an attractive disguise for the soul of a harpy – a vulture of vice, . . .

My thoughts went on and on in the never-ending circle and problem of incurable, unspeakable despair.

I went for two years to a boarding school in Hertfordshire. And at half-term my parents came up to London and stayed at the Regent Palace Hotel. I used to meet them in the tea room there. And I remember the palm trees and the orchestra, and the splendid occasion when my father punched a man on the nose because he winked at my mother. My father called him a 'lounge lizard'.

Ever since then I've been fascinated by hotels, and I particularly like this poem by John Betjeman.

## *The Flight from Bootle*

**JOHN BETJEMAN**

Lonely in the Regent Palace,
  Sipping her 'Banana Blush',
Lilian lost sight of Alice
  In the honey-coloured rush.

Settled down at last from Bootle,
  Alice whispered, 'Just a min,
While I pop upstairs and rootle
  For another safety pin.'

Dreamy from the band pavilion
  Drops of the *Immortal Hour*
Fell around the lonely Lilian
  Like an ineffectual shower.

Half an hour she sat and waited
  In the honey-coloured lounge,
Till she with herself debated,
  'Time for me to go and scrounge!'

Time enough! or not enough time!
  Lilian, you wait in vain;
Alice will not have a rough time,
  Nor be quite the same again.

We used to go over the holiday to the Herbert Arms Hotel, which was in Chirbury in Shropshire. With a bit of a stretch of the imagination you could call it a coaching inn. Next door to the hotel lived a man who fell in love with a land-girl. I wish I could say her name was Miranda, but it wasn't. Every night the man next door would lean out of his window waiting for the girl. In the bar downstairs in the Inn, people sang and stamped their feet. The girl jilted the man, and one night he took a shot gun and stalked the graveyard in the moonlight. He didn't shoot anybody, but when I first heard 'Tarantella' by Hilaire Belloc, it reminded me of him.

## *Tarantella*

**HILAIRE BELLOC**

Do you remember an Inn,
Miranda?
Do you remember an Inn?
And the tedding and the spreading
Of the straw for a bedding,
And the fleas that tease in the High Pyrenees,
And the wine that tasted of the tar?
And the cheers and the jeers of the young muleteers
(Under the vine of the dark verandah)?
Do you remember an Inn, Miranda,
Do you remember an Inn?
And the cheers and the jeers of the young muleteers
Who hadn't got a penny,
And who weren't paying any,
And the hammer at the doors and the Din?
And the Hip! Hop! Hap!
Of the clap
Of the hands to the twirl and the swirl
Of the girl gone chancing,
Glancing,
Dancing,
Backing and advancing,
Snapping of a clapper to the spin
Out and in –
And the Ting, Tong, Tang of the guitar!
Do you remember an Inn,
Miranda?
Do you remember an Inn?

Never more;
Miranda,
Never more.
Only the high peaks hoar:
And Aragon a torrent at the door.
No sound
In the walls of the Halls where falls
The tread
Of the feet of the dead to the ground.
No sound:
But the boom
Of the far Waterfall like Doom.

When I was a child, Shirley Temple appeared in a film called *The Bluebird*, based on a book by Maeterlinck – there wasn't a dry eye in the cinema. And not long afterwards – again in Southport, at the bookstall – I bought for tuppence something by Maeterlinck called *The Life of the Bee*. When I first read it I thought it had something to do with religion. I still read it. I think it's both sinister and awe-inspiring.

## *The Life of the Bee*
**MAETERLINCK**

Our hive, then, is preparing to swarm; making ready for the great immolation to the exacting gods of the race. In obedience to the order of the spirit – an order that to us may well seem incomprehensible, for it is utterly opposed to all our own instincts and feelings – 60 or 70,000 bees out of the 80 or 90,000 that form the whole population, will abandon the maternal city at the prescribed hour. They will not leave at a moment of despair; or desert with sudden and wild resolve, a home laid waste by famine, disease or war.

No: the exile has long been planned, and the favourable hour patiently waited. Were the hive poor, had it suffered from pillage or storm, had misfortune befallen the royal family, the bees would not forsake it. They leave it only when it has attained the apogee of its prosperity; at a time when, after the arduous labours of the spring, the immense palace of wax has its 120,000 well-arranged cells overflowing with new honey, and with the many-coloured flour, known as 'bees' bread', on which nymphs and larvae are fed.

Never is the hive more beautiful than on the eve of its heroic renouncement, in its unrivalled hour of fullest abundance and joy; serene, for all its apparent excitement and feverishness. Let us endeavour to picture it to ourselves – not as it appears to the bees, for we cannot tell in what magical, formidable fashion things may be reflected in the 6 or 7,000 facets of their lateral eyes and the triple cyclopean eye on their brow – but as it would seem to us, were we of their stature. From the height of a dome more colossal than that of St Peter's at Rome, waxen walls descend to the ground, balanced in the void and the darkness; gigantic and manifold, vertical and parallel geometric constructions, to which, for relative precision, audacity, and vastness, no human structure is comparable.

Each of these walls, whose substance still is immaculate and fragrant, of virginal, silvery freshness, contains thousands of cells stored with provisions sufficient to feed the whole population for several weeks. Here, lodged in transparent cells, are the pollens, love-ferment of every flower of spring, making brilliant splashes of red and yellow, of black and mauve.

Close by, sealed with a seal to be broken only in days of supreme distress, the honey of April is stored, most limpid and perfumed of all, in 20,000 reservoirs that form a long and magnificent embroidery of gold, whose borders hang stiff and rigid. Still lower the honey of May matures, in great open vats by whose side watchful cohorts maintain an incessant current of air. In the centre, and far from the light whose diamond rays steal in through the only opening, in the warmest part of the hive, there stands the abode of the future; here does it sleep, and wake. For this is the royal domain of the brood-cells, set apart for the queen and her acolytes; about 10,000 cells wherein the eggs repose, 15 or 16,000 chambers tenanted by larvae, 40,000 dwellings inhabited by white nymphs to whom thousands of nurses minister. And finally, in the holy of holies of these parts there are three, four, six or twelve sealed palaces, vast in size compared with the others, where the adolescent princesses lie who await their hour; wrapped in a kind of shroud, all of them motionless and pale, and fed in the darkness.

*Readers: Alan Dobie, Rosalind Shanks*

*Full Selection:*
*Little Gidding*, T. S. ELIOT
*The Sorrows of Satan*, MARIE CORELLI
*The Flight from Bootle*, JOHN BETJEMAN
*The Life of the Bee*, MAURICE MAETERLINCK
*Dover Beach*, MATTHEW ARNOLD
*Therese at the Hotel*, FRANÇOIS MAURIAC
*Tarantella*, HILAIRE BELLOC
*At the Villa Madeira*, GAVIN EWART
*The Body in the Library*, AGATHA CHRISTIE
*The Big Sleep*, RAYMOND CHANDLER
*Lolita*, VLADIMIR NABOKOV
*The Worst Journey in the World*, APSLEY CHERRY-GARRARD
*Dombey and Son*, CHARLES DICKENS

# PETER BARKWORTH

## 1986

*Peter Barkworth is, of course, a gifted actor – one of the few who make the words 'quality television' not seem like a contradiction in terms – but he is also a charming man. Once, during a read-through for someone else's 'With Great Pleasure', he was roughly rebuked by the presenter for not performing a poem in the way that he, the presenter, preferred. Not having been given any indication that he should read it in a particular manner, Peter Barkworth had, correctly, offered an interpretation of his own. He responded to what was little less than an insult with great courtesy, and complied with what was wanted. When, shortly afterwards, I offered him the opportunity to present an edition of his own, I imagined that he would, like most actors, choose to read half the items himself, but not a bit of it. Even his beloved Siegfried Sassoon was left in the admittedly safe hands of Alec McCowen whilst he confined himself to presenting a most entertaining selection.*

I think the writer I feel, and have always felt, most at home with is Siegfried Sassoon, maybe because he lived in Kent and loved it as much as I do, maybe because I've always felt specially drawn to the writers of his period – Wilfred Owen, Rupert Brooke, Robert Graves – and maybe because he wrote a lot about his childhood; and I first read his books when I was a schoolboy.

In this poem, 'Doggerel About Old Days', which he wrote in 1939, he looks back to when he was a young man of twenty-three, living a happy and comparatively carefree life, before the onslaught of the First World War.

## *Doggerel About Old Days*

SIEGFRIED SASSOON

Young people now – they don't know what the past was like.
*Then* one could find the main roads museful on one's bike.
Give *me* a moment and I'm back in Kent; I know
How safe and sound life struck me thirty years ago.

Passenger trains puffed on through landscapes then like Time;
And this year with its next year found an easy rhyme.
Uninterrupted cricket seasons were to come.
Beanfields were good to smell and bees would always hum
In trees that knew no threat of overhead invasion.
One liked the foreground future, needing no persuasion.

Kent was all sleepy villages through which I went
Carrying my cricket bag. In wintertime, content
To follow hounds across wet fields, I jogged home tired.
In 1909 the future was a thing desired.

I travelled on; the train was Time; Kent was the scene;
And where I was I felt that, as I'd always been,
I should continue unperturbed in storm and shine.
Will someone tell me where I am – in '39?

When I became a RADA student in 1946, we all had to learn at least two pieces a week for diction and voice production classes. We boomed out loads of Auden, Eliot and Dylan Thomas, who were all the rage then, so it was always a relief when someone found something different, like a girl did one day, surprising us all with this new poem by the newly-discovered Dorothy Parker.

### *Symptom Recital*

**DOROTHY PARKER**

I do not like my state of mind;
I'm bitter, querulous, unkind.
I hate my legs, I hate my hands,
I do not yearn for lovelier lands.
I dread the dawn's recurrent light;
I hate to go to bed at night.
I snoot at simple, earnest folk.
I cannot take the gentlest joke.
I find no peace in paint or type.
My world is but a lot of tripe.
I'm disillusioned, empty-breasted.
For what I think, I'd be arrested.
I am not sick. I am not well.
My quondam dreams are shot to hell.
My soul is crushed, my spirit sore;
I do not like me any more.
I cavil, quarrel, grumble, grouse.
I ponder on the narrow house.
I shudder at the thought of men . . .
I'm due to fall in love again.

Of course, all self-respecting drama students knew Hamlet's advice to the players off by heart too. I'm always amazed at how modern it sounds, and what good advice it has remained for actors and actresses over the years.

## *Hamlet's Advice to the Players*

**WILLIAM SHAKESPEARE**

Speak the speech, I pray you, as I pronounc'd it to you, trippingly on the tongue; but if you mouth it, as many of your players do, I had as lief the town-crier spoke my lines. Nor do not saw the air too much with your hand, thus, but use all gently: for in the very torrent, tempest, and, as I may say, the whirlwind of passion, you must acquire and beget a temperance that may give it smoothness. O! it offends me to the soul to hear a robustious periwig-pated fellow tear a passion to tatters, to very rags, to split the ears of the groundlings, who for the most part are capable of nothing but inexplicable dumb-shows, and noise: I would have such a fellow whipp'd for o'erdoing Termagant; it out-herods Herod: pray you, avoid it.

Be not too tame neither, but let your own discretion be your tutor: suit the action to the word, the word to the action; with this special observance, that you o'erstep not the modesty of nature; for any thing so overdone is from the purpose of playing, whose end, both at the first and now, was and is, to hold, as 'twere, the mirror up to nature; to show virtue her own feature, scorn her own image, and the very age and body of the time his form and pressure. Now, this overdone or come tardy off, though it make the unskilful laugh, cannot but make the judicious grieve; the censure of the which one must in your allowance o'erweigh a whole theatre of others. O! there be players that I have seen play, and heard others praise, and that highly, not to speak it profanely, that, neither having the accent of Christians nor the gait of Christian, pagan, nor man, have so strutted and bellowed that I have thought some of nature's journeymen had made them and not made them well, they imitated humanity so abominably.

O! reform it altogether. And let those that play your clowns speak no more than is set down for them; for there be of them that will themselves laugh, to set on some quantity of barren spectators to laugh too, though in the mean time some necessary question of the play be then to be considered; that's villainous, and shows a most pitiful ambition in the fool that uses it. Go, make you ready.

When we left RADA – I don't know if they do it now – we were all presented with a most curious little black book called *The RADA Graduate's Keepsake and Counsellor* which makes very odd reading nowadays because it's so old-fashioned – not at all like Hamlet's advice. Distinguished actors and actresses contributed to it, and there is this delightful bit about correct behaviour in the theatre from Athene Seyler.

## *The RADA Graduate's Keepsake and Counsellor*

**ATHENE SEYLER**

I would like to emphasise that it is not good manners to throw cigarette ends on the stage at rehearsals, and leave the floor littered with stamped-out ends. If smoking is allowed by a Producer (which it ought not to be), and no ash trays are provided, the company must dispose of its cigarette stubs outside the theatre. I, personally, deplore the habit of addressing everybody by their Christian names before any personal intimacy has been established; and think that, at rehearsals certainly, the junior members of a company should formally address the others. And, above all, no one should ever try to put the blame for missing an entrance on the Call Boy. Every actor when called, or even when he hears the general call of 'Overture' or the Act beginning, should reply by thanking the Call Boy, to show that he has been heard. If this were universally done, it would be in the nature of signing for a message, and would protect the defenceless Call Boy, who is – in any case – a courtesy provided by the Management and not a right of the Actor.

I don't quite know why I keep a diary, but I do, and have done so every day since January 1968. That's millions and millions of words, it seems. It helps relieve my feelings and gets things off my chest, but it's also nice to have an accurate record of events and opinions. Of course the length of each entry is always determined by how much time I've got to write it, because I always do it the following morning. Sometimes it's just 'Sorry diary, no time today', but at other times it's pages and pages, especially, of course, when I haven't been too happy about things. Hugh Walpole was very good about diaries in his.

## *Hugh Walpole's Diary*

19th June 1924. Two rules for every honest diarist: One – no self-consciousness. Two – no sense of shame. Three – no false modesty. Four – no sham bravery. Five – no fine writing. Six – no fear of indecencies. Seven – no scorn of trivialities. Eight – no self disgust. There are others but these will do.

Well, for a start: I am forty years of age, have published seventeen volumes of more or less merit (cf rule 3: no false modesty), I am single and shall always be so, in excellent health save for toothache and neuralgia, never constipated, always sleep well, owe some five hundred pounds, am owed four thousand.

Now as to my character: I am kind-hearted, but have to rouse myself to take trouble. I am very sensual, but pious and pure if that sensuality is gratified. I am very non-condemnatory unless I am attacked, when I at once accuse the attacker of every crime. I am very generous about large sums and inclined to be mean about small ones. I adore to be in love but am bored if someone is much in love with me. I am superficially both conceited and vain but at heart consider myself with a good deal of contempt.

6th January 1926: (Question this!) I am greatly interested in the question of a future life but until it is settled the thought of it influences my conduct but little.

28th October 1932: (It occupies me more and more). I adore beauty in all its forms. I hate to see others suffer. I am a great coward but can be roused to endurance. I have a sense of humour which I get only too little into my work.

I couldn't resist including here a speech from Tom Kempinski's marvellous play *Duet for One.* It's about a concert violinist who contracted multiple sclerosis and therefore couldn't play any more. She talks about it to a psychiatrist, Dr Feldmann, and tells him what music means to her.

## *Duet for One*
**TOM KEMPINSKI**

Well – music. Music. Music, Dr Feldmann, is the purest expression of humanity that there is. Because, you see, it's magic; but real magic, true mystery, not trickery. You can say it is sound, as speech is sound, as bird-song is sound, but it isn't. It's itself. A piece of music which expresses pain or sorrow, or loneliness, it sounds nothing like what a lonely man says or does, but expresses it, and even better than the person does. Magic. You see, there's no God, you know, Dr Feldmann, but I know where they got the idea; they got it from music. It is a kind of heaven. It's unearthly. It lifts you out of life to another place.

And later, at the end of the play, she says:

Look, Dr Feldmann, I played the violin, because when Mummy died, the real world, your world, the world of jobs, Daddy's world, it disappeared; shattered. So I had to build another world, what you'd call a fantasy world. My new world was filled with the pain and the sorrow and the despair of the loss and the awful unfamiliar changes. So I hung on to the only world I had: music. My violin. And I sang the song of the pain and the sorrow and the loss and the awful changes, to soothe myself. And I sang for dear life – literally for life, 'cos it was all I had. And suddenly the song turned to one of joy, because of the beauty of the music; and I was ecstatic that I had turned such sorrow to happiness, because the change was such a relief, such a wonderful pleasure. And now I can't play any more. And because the shock and the pain were so awful again at this new loss, I tried to pretend I could cross back over to the old world and stupid little plans, like being David's secretary. But I'm not there, Dr Feldmann. The violin isn't my work; it isn't a way of life. It's where I live. It's when I play that I actually live in the real world; mine, of course. So what can you do? What can you possibly do, when I can't cross over? It's not your fault. It's not that you haven't got the skill. It's just that I'm over here – and I can't sing. . . .

*Readers: Alec McCowen, Penelope Wilton*

*Full Seiection:*
*Doggerel About Old Days,* SIEGFRIED SASSOON
*Symptom Recital,* DOROTHY PARKER
*Hamlet's Advice to the Players,* WILLIAM SHAKESPEARE
*The RADA Graduate's Keepsake and Counsellor,* ATHENE SEYLER
*A Postillion Struck by Lightning,* DIRK BOGARDE
*The Waves,* VIRGINIA WOOLF
*Absence Makes the Heart Grow Heart Trouble,* OGDEN NASH
*A Love,* C. P. CAVAFY
*Extract from the Diaries of Hugh Walpole*
*Full Circle,* JANET BAKER
*Duet for One,* TOM KEMPINSKI
*Skimbleshanks – The Railway Cat,* T. S. ELIOT

# ALAN BLEASDALE

## 1983

*I think it's fair to say that Alan Bleasdale first became known to the public at large when his 'Boys from the Blackstuff' was shown on television. 'Gissa job', the bitter catchphrase uttered by its central character, Yosser Hughes, will linger in the British consciousness long after the circumstances which brought it into being will (hopefully) have become a distant memory. Bleasdale's personality, as it comes across from his 'With Great Pleasure', is one of a shy and sensitive, noisy extrovert. At the age of eighteen, 'full of football, fear, anxiety, Chandler, Brian Rix, Orwell and Heller, Hemingway and Greene, lust and Lenny Bruce', he used to take girls to poetry readings because it didn't cost too much and to show them that the footballing drunkard was also a sensitive soul who 'knew for a fact that 17th Century Bacon wasn't an old piece of pork'. If the last item seems a little dated now, with Reagan no longer President, and an arms agreement having just been signed, chilling as ever, it still serves as a reminder of a near miss, and a warning.*

The biggest problem I've had with compiling the pieces is the sense of abject disappointment I've had when I've gone back to books and plays that I used to love years ago, that I thought I must still love today. That I can't stand anymore. This programme could very easily have been called *With Great Disinterest*.

Another difficulty I had was trying to break into the most brilliant books and plays and just rob the best bit of them – like stealing the smile off the *Mona Lisa*. 'Hey, hey boys, I got the smile!' And ruined the picture.

I was advised to look for a theme: you know, childhood, birth, marriage, the nobility of pain, the consequence of suffering, the influence of Ian Botham on the contestants for the Nobel Peace Prize. So, I got all the pieces together, and I looked at what I had, *and* . . . I couldn't find one. I mean, I have enough problems finding themes in my own work, never mind anyone else's. The pieces I have chosen are the things that have touched me to tears or to terror, laughter as I've gone along. And perhaps that's a theme in itself.

The book that had the biggest influence on my whole life without any shadow of a doubt is the Catholic Catechism. The Catechism of the Christian Doctrine. It's the most frightening book in the whole world. When you don't know it. When you're seven years old. And when you had a teacher like I had at the start of the Juniors. It's a big year that – yer first confession, yer first Holy Communion, yer first inklings of mortality, yer first trip to Chester Zoo – and there's this sarcastic atheist in Catholic clothing stood at the front of the class with the kind of acid wit that would shrivel anything, especially a sensitive, shy, sweet little seven-year-old boy. You see, the first Tuesday in every month, the priest would come in to test us on the Catechism and the Ten Commandments . . . and the first Monday in every month, Dorothy Parker's bitter sister would be there, breathing fire and polo mints, testing us for our test. It went something like this:

TEACHER: Bleasdale.
BLEASDALE: Yes Miss.
TEACHER: You first. Do you know why you're first?
BLEASDALE: No Miss.
TEACHER: Because you're a congenital idiot, Bleasdale, and if you know the answers, I can be fairly certain that the rest of the class will.
BLEASDALE: Yes Miss. Thank you Miss.
TEACHER: Now then, let's see if we can improve on your previous attempt, shall we? I don't think Father McMahon was over enamoured with your religious knowledge on the last occasion, do you, boy?
BLEASDALE: No Miss.
TEACHER: I don't think anyone could be too impressed with your rendition of Our Father. Our Father, who art in Heaven, Harold be his name indeed. The Blessed Trinity, Bleasdale.
BLEASDALE: Er . . . yes Miss?
TEACHER: Who or what are they?
BLEASDALE: Er, God the Father.
TEACHER: Whose name is not Harold.
BLEASDALE: Er, God the Son . . . God the Father, God the Son and er. . . .
DONOVAN: (*whispers*) God the Holy Ghost, Bleasy.
BLEASDALE: God the Holy Ghost. Miss.
TEACHER: Very good, Donovan, your lips didn't move once, but don't go Educating Archie, thank you. . . . What are you, Bleasdale, tell me, what are you?
BLEASDALE: I'm a genital idiot, Miss.
TEACHER: Well, I suppose there's always a chance you can be run over by a bus before tomorrow's test – the seventh commandment, boy, the one between six and eight.
BLEASDALE: Thou shalt not . . . er, thou shalt not. . . .
TEACHER: . . . Thou is not capable of. . . .
BLEASDALE: Thou shalt not steal?
TEACHER: No.
BLEASDALE: Murder?

**TEACHER:** I'm considering it, child.
**BLEASDALE:** Er, cover thy neighbour's wife, er, in a field, with his ass. On a Sabbath, Miss.
**TEACHER:** You are doomed, boy, doomed.
**BLEASDALE:** Thank you, Miss.
**TEACHER:** What is the seventh commandment, Donovan?
**DONOVAN:** Thou shalt not commit adultery, Miss.
**TEACHER:** Very good, Donovan, very good.
**DONOVAN:** Er, what is adultery, Miss?
**TEACHER:** We teach you that in the seniors, Donovan. Now then, what's mortal sin?
**DONOVAN:** Mortal sin is a grievous sin against God, Miss.
**TEACHER:** Why is it called mortal sin?
**DONOVAN:** It is called mortal sin because it kills the soul and deserves Hell, Miss.
**TEACHER:** Is it a great evil to fall into mortal sin?
**DONOVAN:** It is the greatest of all evils to fall into mortal sin, Miss.
**TEACHER:** Where will they go who die in mortal sin?
**DONOVAN:** They who die in mortal sin will go to hell for all eternity, Miss.
**TEACHER:** Good. And how should you finish the day, Donovan?
**DONOVAN:** I should finish the day by kneeling down and saying my night prayers, Miss.
**TEACHER:** And after your night prayers what should you do?
**DONOVAN:** After my night prayers I should observe due modesty in going to bed, and then occupy myself with thoughts of death, Miss.

'Occupy myself with thoughts of death.' I did that alright. I was terrified out of my tiny mind, not least of all when one particular first Tuesday in the month, the regular priest failed to sober up in time, and Canon O'Reilly arrived at the classroom door. To be greeted with the same joyful rapture that the City of London greeted the Great Plague of 1665.

My abiding memory is of this unshaven hulk with a nose the colour of Lent, standing wild-eyed above me, smelling of incense and cigarettes, as I stared at the buttons of his fly and completely failed even to begin *The Apostles' Creed*. And then he bent down, squashing to death the two kids directly in front of me, and thirty years of Christian wisdom hurtled from deep within him: 'You boy, you, of one thing be certain; when you die, when you die you will go to eternal Hell!'

I had a nervous breakdown during playtime. I mean, what kind of a future could you believe in, if you were deprived of the consolation of Heaven when you kicked it? – when all it came down to at the end of the day, when the plugs were pulled, was standing there between Adolf Hitler and Attila the Hun, stoking coal, with forked ears, two lungfuls of soot, a tail between your legs, and Beelzebub as your foreman. On twenty-four-hour nights.

And to be quite honest, I still carry the scars of my Catholic education, the catechism and the commandments, and the way they were taught – death threats at seven – even now, more than thirty years later.

I first met Willy Russell in 1974, when I was in my late twenties and he, as he occasionally delights in reminding me, was somewhat younger. I'd just written this first novel that was about to be published, that I confidently expected to attract the attention of the Booker Prize Committee, and he was in the middle of struggling with a mere trifle, a little piece for the Everyman Theatre called *John, Paul, George, Ringo and Bert*.

In Liverpool I'm always asked how we get on with each other, and I can only reply that we're best friends and mortal enemies – somewhat similar to Liverpool and Everton footballers, who twice a year spend ninety minutes kicking lumps out of each other, and then go and get legless together all over the clubs in town.

Anyway, I give him my plays to read hot off the typewriter, and he gives me his. I knew, for example, that *Educating Rita* was going to be a smash hit, a huge success, that it would run and run, and run, and the prospect sickened me for weeks.

But it's alright. No, it is. Because while Willy spends half his time being congratulated on writing *Boys from the Blackstuff*, *The Muscle Market* and *Having a Ball*, I regularly have drinks bought for me because I wrote *Educating Rita*, *The Daughters of Albion* and *Our*

*Day Out*. I kid you not. To the point that last summer as I walked towards the Liverpool Playhouse, two girls went past me, and one said to the other, 'That's the feller what wrote Educating Willy.'

What I really think about Willy Russell is that at his finest no one else depicts better, or more comically and truthfully, humanity's inner emptiness, despair and desire for escape. In *One for the Road*, Dennis, on the edge of his thirtieth birthday and a complete crack-up, is being treated by his wife Pauline to a birthday dinner in their new house on a new estate full of the new middle classes. Dennis's mother and father are late. Pauline goes to answer the 'phone.

## *One for the Road*

### WILLY RUSSELL

If that's your mother, I'll answer it. . . . Mother, you were supposed to be coming early. . . . But I told you to get off at the first bus stop. . . . Dennis, they've got lost! They got off at the wrong bus stop again. . . . Mother, you've been to the bungalow God knows how many times. Why can't you or Dad remember where it is? . . . Oh no, they don't all look alike. . . . We do not have a number because we do not like to deface the facade of the bungalow. . . . Look, exactly where are you? . . . Right. Now listen, go out of William Tell Avenue, take the first right into Wagner Walk. Go along Wagner Walk, up Elgar Drive into Beethoven Close and you'll see Brahms Close. Go down there, turn into Mahler Crescent and we're three down from 'Rivendell'. . . . No, no number, just 'The Haven'. . . .

Like absolutely everyone, to a larger or lesser degree, I'm the normal confusions. Moralist and thief, generous and mean, an anarchist most likely to break the legs of anyone trying to take my property, an atheist most happy to pray at the least opportunity or need. And, of course, I hate violence. So much so that when I see it, I usually join in. Naturally, like any *Guardian* reader, I also find the thought of taking life the deepest of all offences and, consequently, capital punishment a horror in itself. And yet . . . and yet, there is a part of me that is still swinging and grunting from tree to tree.

About eighteen months ago, we five Bleasdales and those five Russells spent a weekend on a camp site in Anglesey. On the Saturday night we all went for a drink in this pub on the coast, the kind that cater for children – you know, they lock them in a secure room with a security guard on the door – no, there was a games room, an animal den and a sweet counter between the games room and the lounge. To cut a long story short, I was playing snooker with our eldest, my wife was with the youngest, and our daughter, the middle child, was with my wife. Well, that is, I thought she was with my wife . . . while my wife thought she was with me. And she had been with both of us, but not for over twenty minutes, when she'd gone to queue at the sweet counter.

The place was packed to bursting point. And I burst through it, more and more panic as the moments went by, and Willy and Ann and my wife, Julie, with that feeling that only parents can possibly describe, they too ran from room to room . . . and I ran into the road, through the car park and down to the beach . . . and then started running after cars as they left the pub. . . .

And I tell you now, if anyone had taken our daughter away and I had found him there and then that night, I would have killed him. I would have, as they say, torn him limb from limb. . . . Our daughter was found crying, still queueing at the very front of the sweet counter, well hidden and very squashed by the other bigger kids around her.

A week later I read an article by Philip Norman in the *Sunday Times*, and I wrote my first letter to a journalist. Because I recognized that horrifying feeling of total helplessness and rage that he wrote about.

He wrote in response to a tide of murder, to the Beiruts and Belfasts and the brutal batterings that barely make a paragraph now in even our local newspapers. He wrote in memory of growing up in the fifties, in what he calls 'the great hush that seemed to enfold the world' – and to the fact that in separate incidents two people very close to him had been attacked by an intruder and might have been killed.

Some of you, sitting comfortably, some distance from Anglesey, may disagree passionately with his conclusions, but by God I recognize the *feelings*.

## *On a Tide of Murder*

**PHILIP NORMAN**

Like most children, I was afraid of the dark. I imagined, lying in bed, that 'murderers' were coming up the stairs. In time, I was comforted to realise my own insignificance. Who would want to be bothered to murder me? Murderers, I saw thankfully, belonged to a distant, highly idiosyncratic class, like Christie, or Ruth Ellis, the 'Mews Murderess' whose execution took place just before our school Assembly. I know because a boy came up to me, looked at his watch and said, 'Well, that's the end of Ruth Ellis.' Obscurely but powerfully, I felt the night was safe again.

But now I know that it is my destiny, and yours, to live in a world grown infinitely more terrifying than childhood's worst nightmares. I know that, on the contrary, almost anybody can be bothered to murder me.

We speak of civilisations that 'toppled', of the 'fall' of Athens or Rome, of a 'Dark Age' dropped over Europe like a sack. We choose not to recognise that, wherever chaos and terror have triumphed, it was slowly, through the bewildered acquiescence of millions of people like ourselves. They too tried not to worry; to get on with life. They moved, as we are moving, unconsciously with the tide of murder, from disbelieving horror to dazed unshockability.

The special paradox of our Dark Age is that it should have grown in the tatters of an era when 'peace' and 'love' were words in serious widespread use. Today's urban terrorist wears the blue jeans and amulets of yesterday's smiling liberal. The Maze 'hunger strikers', those empty, almost ectoplasmic faces, wear their hair long the way young men did as a plea for tolerance and a declaration of non-violence. The contagion took root, not in Dallas in 1963 but in California in 1969. We are menaced not by the children of Marx, but of Manson.

Our blindness is increased by our gigantic power of sight, through television: by habituation to terrible sights and, equally, by the growing adeptness of those responsible in hiding their crimes within language of perverted blandness. It strikes no one as strange any more when three madmen, machine-gunning an airport lounge, call themselves a 'popular front', when a hostage is butchered by a 'people's court'; when those who use children to plant explosives term themselves 'freedom fighters'; when innocent shopping crowds are 'targets'; or when the Provisional IRA, after ambushing a milk float, claim 'responsibility'.

In the age of the bloody mind, I can feel my own mind growing as bloody as the next. When I read that a bomb-maker has blown himself up, I feel quiet satisfaction at Fate's occasional symmetry. And I have come to believe in the death penalty, as a deterrent to those many crimes based on pure cowardice, and to eradicate – as has been justly done before – self-evident, unmitigated evil. I remember the words of Dr Herrema, the Dutchman whose intellectual toughness all but mesmerised his Irish kidnappers. 'Don't you realise?' he asked them at one point, 'These conditions are worse than in Belsen.'

As a child, my biggest nightmare contained men wearing hoods, with holes out for their eyes and mouths. The Fifties melted them at dawn, into sun and sticky buds. The Eighties legitimise them, slow-marching in Ulster. They are death embodied – perhaps yours, perhaps mine. I myself fear death as much as in childhood. But I see now what people throughout history must have seen in their own terror times: that death can be something you choose. It is preferable to the suffering of my family, or to life in any world where the hooded ones hold power.

Here to end are the words of Ronald Reagan, at a press conference without his auto-cue, without anyone to translate into any kind of intelligent language, in other words, without help except himself. The question asked was: 'Could battlefield nuclear weapons be fired without the inevitable consequence of an intercontinental nuclear exchange between the Super Powers?'

## *President Reagan at a Press Conference*

Well, I would – if they realised that we, again – if we led them back to that stalemate only because that our retaliatory power, our seconds, or our strike at them after their first strike at us would be so destructive that they couldn't afford it. That would hold them off. . . . Yes.

*Readers: Julie Walters, Michael Angelis*

*Full Selection:*
*Catechism and Ten Commandments,* ALAN BLEASDALE
*Sad Aunt Marge,* ROGER McGOUGH
*Little Johnny's Confession,* BRIAN PATTEN
*Love from Arthur Rainbow,* ADRIAN HENRI
*One for the Road,* WILLY RUSSELL
*Educating Rita,* WILLY RUSSELL
*Flying Blind,* BILL MORRISON
*Lost and Found Advertisement,* PRIVATE EYE
*Hollywood Quotes*
*On a Tide of Murder,* PHILIP NORMAN
*Quotation,* LENNY BRUCE
*Press Conference,* PRESIDENT REAGAN

# *HEATHER COUPER*

## *1987*

*'Are you astronomy or media?' It was, I imagine, a not uncommon greeting between two strangers brought together at any gathering organized by Heather Couper and her partner Nigel Henbest. They have formed a company, 'Hencoup', with the express purpose of bringing a greater knowledge of astronomy to the world at large – no doubt they would argue to the world at small. As someone who has a tolerable acquaintance with black holes, but could positively identify a great bear only in a zoo, I find their conversation stimulating and enlightening. Heather endeared herself to me when she arrived for the rehearsal of her programme, recorded appropriately enough in the old Royal Observatory at Greenwich, and announced that she had just bought a copy of volume I*

*of this anthology. 'Naturally,' I said, 'I shall be including you in volume II.' 'Oh good,' she said. 'I mean, oh dear. What will you say about me?' At this point I ought to mention the subsidiary activity of their company, the fermenting of a wine known as 'Château Hencoup'. It is very . . . distinctive. Indeed I would have argued that it spoilt you for anything else, but at a subsequent meeting in a Covent Garden wine bar I was relieved to see everyone present managing a bucket or two of house white. 'Media,' I said, but by the end of the evening I am not at all sure that I would have known the answer to the question.*

Via a year working as a dogsbody at the Cambridge observatories I went off to the University of Leicester and started studying for a degree in astro-physics. Now, when one is at university one tends to take up other interests as well as one's subject and one of my really all-pervading interests changed from astronomy to gastronomy, which I'm still fascinated by. Perhaps that's one of the reasons why I live in Greenwich where there are so many good restaurants and wine bars! As well as an interest in gastronomy I did become interested in other food for thought, I should say, theatre, music and painting. I did become interested in music of a very early period, the sixteenth, seventeenth and eighteenth centuries. What I like particularly about Baroque music and indeed earlier Renaissance music is how people could get away with such completely undiluted emotion. You could wallow on about your inconstant love affairs until you were blue in the face and everybody thought it was fabulous: odes to this, that and the other and terrible things that would happen to your heart, you could cry about them to your heart's content.

I was equally drawn to the poetry of the time and for me nobody can sum up the poetry of the Renaissance era so beautifully as John Donne. As well as the angst of inconstancy to be found in such poems as 'Now That Thou Hast Lov'd Me One Whole Day' Donne also found permanence, some of his poems are extremely beautiful and they do talk about true love. I like in one poem in particular about permanence how he weaves in contemporary observations of what else was going on in the world that surrounded him, by which I mean the voyages of exploration, new techniques in map-making, explorations of new cities, even new financial means of dealing with merchants and so on. In the following poem you will see there are references towards the end of the work of the mappers by which he means the work of the astronomers. I love this poem very very deeply because it means a great deal to me and my own feelings on permanence.

## *The Good Morrow*

### JOHN DONNE

I wonder by my troth, what thou, and I
  Did, till we loved? were we not weaned till then,
But sucked on country pleasures, childishly?
  Or snorted we in the seven sleepers' den?
'Twas so; but this, all pleasure's fancies be.
If ever any beauty I did see,
Which I desired, and got, 'twas but a dream of thee.

And now good morrow to our waking souls,
  Which watch not one another out of fear;
For love, all love of other sights controls,
  And makes one little room, an every where.
Let sea-discoverers to new worlds have gone,
Let maps to others, worlds on worlds have shown,
Let us possess one world, each hath one and is one.

My face in thine eyes, thine in mine appears,
  And true plain hearts do in the faces rest,
Where can we find two better hemispheres
  Without sharp north, without declining west?
What ever dies, was not mixed equally;
If our two loves be one, or, thou and I
Love so alike, that none do slacken, none can die.

I am absolutely delighted to be in Christopher Wren's great Octagon Room in the original building of the Royal Observatory built in 1675. Sitting here I think of the great Astronomers Royal of Greenwich and I think in particular of the one whom I consider to be the greatest of them all, Edmund Halley. He was made Astronomer Royal in 1720, very near to the end of his life. He was an amazing person, he spent some of his life studying astronomy, but a great deal of his life adventuring, being a diplomat, being a bon viveur, being a classicist, a translator, an editor. I find one of the most exciting enterprises of my life was to have been very involved in communicating astronomy to the public when Halley's comet last visited earth on its seventy-six-year cycle. Every time I gave a talk about it or went on a radio programme people would say to me 'Why is Halley's name given to a comet that he didn't actually discover?' Well, Halley was the first person to make the prediction that a comet might not be, as it were, a flash in the pan but something which came back again and again. In his writings he makes it very clear that he has noted a comet which came by on several occasions and he predicts it's going to come back again. For that reason we honour that comet and Halley today.

## *Synopsis on the Astronomy of Comets (1705)*

EDMUND HALLEY

For having collected all the Observations of Comets I could, I framed a table, the result of a prodigious deal of Calculation, which, tho' but small in Bulk, will be no unnacceptable present to Astronomers. For those Numbers are capable of Representing all that has been yet observed about the Motion of Comets, by the Help only of the following General Table; in the making of which I spared no Labour, that it might come forth perfect, as a Thing consecrated to Posterity, and to last as long as Astronomy itself.

The principal use therefore of this Table of the Elements . . . is, that whenever a new Comet shall appear, we may be able to know, by comparing together the Elements, whether it be any of those which has appeared before, and consequently . . . to foretell its Return. There are many Things which make me believe that the Comet . . . of 1531 was the same as that described in the Year 1607 and which I myself have seen return, and observed in the year 1682. All the Elements agree, and nothing seems to contradict this my Opinion . . . HENCE I DARE VENTURE TO FORETELL, THAT IT WILL RETURN AGAIN IN THE YEAR 1758. And, if it should then return, we shall have no Reason to doubt but the rest must return too.

Good old Halley. He got it right. It did come back in 1758; he would have been 112 years old. He lived to the ripe old age of 85, by the way. I understand he died with a glass of red wine in his hand. I don't think he'd be at all affronted if I included a sample of the kind of things people were saying about Halley's comet when it came here on its last but one return in 1910.

## *Tails*

### JAMES RAVENSCROFT

Tim O'Mara was conversing with his old pal, Mike Muldoon,
About the Halley comet while they gazed upon the moon,
'A comet's sure a wonder' said O'Mara, looking wise,
'It is,' Muldoon assented, 'An' the greatest in th' skies!
An' think of all th' books an' things the high-brow fellys write
About the strange beoggerfee of that celestial sight!'
Said O'Mara: 'For live writin's stuff the comet'll never fail,
And think of all it is because thereon hangs a tale.'

## *A Line-O-Type or Two*

### THE CHICAGO TRIBUNE

At a special meeting of the Chicago General Committee for the reception of Halley's Comet, Prof. Graham Taylor read a report from his Oxford colleague, Prof. Turner, stating that we shall all be in the tail of the comet May 18 and if we wish to bottle some of the air that day we can hand a part of the comet down to our grandchildren. On behalf of the Committee the Treasurer was instructed to purchase fifty dozen quarts of champagne for May 18. These, after being emptied, will be filled with Halley's best.

## *The St James's Gazette for April 16*

In an essay on Halley's Comet, a Bavarian schoolboy wrote 'In this country the Comet has already caused a rise in the price of beer, but it may cause even greater misfortunes in other countries.'

## *Comet Mania*

### THE OBSERVATORY APRIL 1910

Oh, you Mistuh Comet,
  Travelin' th'oo de sky
You's got us all a-tremble
  As you comes a-brushin' by
We don' know what you's up to
  An' we don't know whah you's bin,
Nor whah you is a-gwineter.
  You's jes a-buttin' in!

Look here, Mistuh Comet,
  As on yoh way you ride,
You ain't much in partic'lar,
  An' mos'ly gassified.
You's like some folks I knows of
  Dat raises heaps o'fuss
Wifout a-bein' nuffin
  Except Mysterious.

After Halley's comet and all the great interest it generated I spend my time at the moment tramping around the world and everywhere I go I get asked all kinds of questions about astronomy. Of course the obvious one is 'What's a black hole?' The second most common is 'Why are we here? What's life in the universe doing on this planet?' It must be a question that can be replied to in so many different ways, religious, philosophical and scientific. But of course in *With Great Pleasure* the only possible way is poetic. I was delighted to be sent a poem from Michael Burnett of Dorset which sums up so beautifully why there is life on this planet.

## *We Need a Star*

### MICHAEL BURNETT

We need a star that's fairly bright;
(Not too dark nor yet too light)
Not too big or brilliant blue;
Nor too red or feeble too.
We need one most that's by itself.
(Did fate leave it on the shelf?)

Doubles or triples just won't do
They make their planets go askew;
One day's too cold, the next's too hot,
Life's prospects there aren't worth a lot.
Our ideal, then, is 'medium yellow'
(And certainly a single fellow.)

A planet next, and fairly small,
One too big won't do at all;
For ones too big have forces that
Will tend to make things rather flat.
Yet one *too* small's no good, I fear,
'Cos it can't hold no atmosphere.
So, like its star, its girth should fall
Between the outsize and the small.
Next, it needs an orbit so's
It won't get burnt and won't get froze.
And if all this seems quite enough
Its make-up needs the 'proper stuff'.

Our nice round world, with gentle spin,
Needs atmosphere that's fairly thin.
It needs above all this, for sure,
An ozone layer to shut the door
On tissue-rending ultra-V
And then, below this too, some sea.
(It needs the sea for life depends
On water, water without end.)
Clouds – then lightning; strike the placid
Sleep of that amino-acid.
Now, wait five thousand million years.
And lo! Old Patrick Moore appears!

*Readers: Timothy West, Kika Markham*

*Full Selection:*
*The Animal's Prayer*, ENID BLYTON
*Nature Notes*, ENID BLYTON
*Guide to the Stars*, PATRICK MOORE

*O Moon*, ATTRIBUTED TO A MAID IN THE SERVICE OF THE 17TH-CENTURY ASTRONOMER CHRISTIAAN HUYGHENS
*Middlesex*, JOHN BETJEMAN
*The Universe*, ISAAC ASIMOV
*Your Years of Toil*, GEORGE GAMOW
*Woman's Constancy*, JOHN DONNE
*The Good Morrow*, JOHN DONNE
*Great Central Railway – Sheffield Victoria to Banbury*, JOHN BETJEMAN
*King's England*, ARTHUR MEE
*Kilvert's Diary*, FRANCIS KILVERT
*Henry Moore's Sheep Sketchbook*, HENRY MOORE (with introduction by LORD CLARK)
*Ode to Autumn*, JOHN KEATS
*Synopsis on the Astronomy of Comets*, EDMUND HALLEY
*Tails*, JAMES RAVENSCROFT
*A Line-O-Type or Two*, CHICAGO TRIBUNE
*Essay on Halley's Comet*, ST JAMES'S GAZETTE
*The Comet*, THE OBSERVATORY
*We Need a Star*, MICHAEL BURNETT

# RICHARD CROSSMAN

## 1971

*For the first thirty years of his life the late Richard Crossman was devoted to literature. A writer, teacher and would-be poet he thought of almost nothing else. In common with many of his generation, the war changed everything. He emerged a man of action, to whom politics were everything and literature 'just something there as a background'. As a government minister his reading was largely a matter of whatever was delivered in those little red boxes. In consequence his choices were mainly from the 1920s and '30s which he had read when they first came out – chosen because 'they were all, in a sense, presentiments of the shape of things to come.'*

The first thing I remember my mother reading to me deeply influenced my life. It was *Bleak House* by Charles Dickens, a tremendous book about a terrible law case and the people involved in it. My father was a Chancery Lawyer, and I don't know whether my mother realized it, but the reading of it to me made one thing quite sure: I would never become a lawyer.

## *Bleak House*
### CHARLES DICKENS

London. Michaelmas Term lately over, and the Lord Chancellor sitting in Lincoln's Inn Hall. Implacable November weather. As much mud in the streets, as if the waters had but newly retired from the face of the earth, and it would not be wonderful to meet a Megalosaurus, forty feet long or so, waddling like an elephantine lizard up Holborn Hill.

Fog everywhere. Fog up the river, where it flows along green aits and meadows; fog down the river, where it rolls defiled among the tiers of shipping, and the waterside pollutions of the great (and dirty) city. Fog on the Essex marshes, fog on the Kentish heights. Fog creeping into the cabooses of collier brigs; fog lying out on the yards, and hovering in the riggings of great ships; fog drooping on the gunwales of barges and small boats. Chance people on the bridges peeping over the parapets into a nether sky of fog, with fog all round them, as if they were up in a balloon, and hanging in the misty clouds.

The raw afternoon is rawest, and the dense fog is densest, and the muddy streets are muddiest, near that leaden-headed old obstruction, appropriate ornament for the threshold of a leaden-headed old corporation: Temple Bar. And hard by Temple Bar, in Lincoln's Inn Hall, at the very heart of the fog, sits the Lord High Chancellor in his High Court of Chancery.

Of course, home isn't the place where the biggest impressions come. So I move on quickly to school. I went to Winchester. You may think of Winchester as a place of conventional Wykehamists, but as a matter of fact it was for me a place of rebellion. I learnt to rebel against everything my parents taught me. My clearest memories of Winchester are not what I was taught in the class. In my first year I was the little fag who looked after Anthony Asquith, the son of Lady Asquith and, later, the distinguished film director. Under him we had readings of plays every Saturday. I was the leading lady, you'll be surprised to hear, in all the Chekhov plays long before they were produced in London because Anthony Asquith was reading all the latest things. There was nothing we didn't read in those days together. And naturally my favourite poet, I needn't tell you, because I'd been brought up very religious, was Swinburne. So I have to ask you to excuse me for a passage from *A Hymn to Proserpine*, because it did in a way form a kind of challenge in my life.

## *Hymn to Proserpine*

**SWINBURNE**

Oh Gods, dethroned and deceased, cast forth, wiped in a day!
From your wrath is the world released, redeemed from your
  chains, men say.
New Gods are crowned in the city; their flowers have broken
  your rods;
They are merciful, clothed with pity, the young compassionate
  Gods.
But for me their new device is barren, the days are bare;
Things long past over suffice, and men forgotten that were.
Time and the Gods are at strife; ye dwell in the midst thereof,
Draining a little life from the barren breasts of love.
Thou hast conquered, O pale Galilean; the world has grown
  grey from thy breath;
We have drunken of things Lethean, and fed on the fullness of
  death.

I went to Oxford and wanted to become a poet. I began to read almost nothing but poetry and I used to take a paper called the *New Criterion* which was edited by T. S. Eliot. In one number I remember there came out the first poem which captured me. I knew that I had discovered a poem, I knew what this poem meant to me and meant to the author. You'll be puzzled – it's a poem about an old man feeling old. I was a boy of twenty, but I felt very old. I've got a good deal younger since, I think. But I felt desperately old, desperately part of the establishment.

## *The Tower*

**W. B. YEATS**

I

What shall I do with this absurdity –
O heart, O troubled heart – this caricature,
Decrepit age that has been tied to me
As to a dog's tail?

Never had I more
Excited, passionate, fantastical
Imagination, more an ear and eye
That more expected the impossible –
No, not in boyhood when with rod and fly,
Or the humbler worm, I climbed Ben Bulben's back
And had the livelong summer day to spend.

It seems that I must bid the Muse go pack,
Choose Plato and Plotinus for a friend
Until imagination, ear and eye,
Can be content with argument and deal
In abstract things; or be derided by
A sort of battered kettle at the heel.

III

It is time that I wrote my will;
I choose upstanding men,
That climb the streams until
The fountain leap, and at dawn
Drop their cast at the side
Of dripping stone; I declare
They shall inherit my pride. . . .
As at the loophole there,

The daws chatter and scream,
And drop twigs layer upon layer,
When they have mounted up,
The mother bird will rest
On their hollow top,
And so warm her wild nest.

I leave both faith and pride
To young upstanding men
Climbing the mountain side,
That under bursting dawn
They may drop a fly;
Being of that metal made
Till it was broken by
This sedentary trade,
Now shall I make my soul
Compelling it to study
In a learned school
Till the wreck of body
Slow decay of blood,
Testy delirium
Or dull decrepitude,
Or what worse evil come –
The death of friends, or death
Of every brilliant eye
That made a catch in the breath –
Seem but the clouds of the sky
When the horizon fades;
Or a bird's sleepy cry
Among the deepening shades.

Yeats, Eliot, Gerard Manley Hopkins and D. H. Lawrence were the great people in my life then, they were more real to me than anyone else. The other person was Wystan Auden. We were undergraduates together and at that time I was writing poems like Wystan Auden – I don't say they were as good, but you couldn't I don't think very much distinguish between them. The Auden of that period was very different from the portentous, famous poet he later became. In a way he was a divine fool with tremendous passion and a wonderful new idea of poetry. Here first is a love poem by him, a love poem about a boy.

## *Funeral Blues*

### W. H. AUDEN

Stop all the clocks, cut off the telephone,
Prevent the dog from barking with a juicy bone,
Silence the pianos and with muffled drum
Bring out the coffin, let the mourners come.

Let aeroplanes circle moaning overhead
Scribbling on the sky the message He Is Dead,
Put crepe bows round the white necks of the public doves
Let the traffic policemen wear black cotton gloves.

He was my North, my South, my East and West,
My working week and my Sunday rest,
My noon, my midnight, my talk, my song;
I thought that love would last forever: I was wrong.

The stars are not wanted now: put out every one,
Pack up the moon and dismantle the sun,
Pour away the ocean and sweep up the woods;
For nothing now can ever come to any good.

A sad poem, but now we'll take another bit of Auden. He was a great satirist in those days and I have to tell you that the next poem is one he's trying to have removed from his collected works because he thinks it's too shocking and too sharp. But it's a poem which reminds me of the mood of Oxford and of Berlin under the Weimar Republic.

## *Miss Gee*

### W. H. AUDEN

Let me tell you a little story
About Miss Edith Gee;
She lived in Clevedon Terrace
At number 83.

Miss Gee knelt down in the side-aisle,
She knelt down on her knees;
'Lead me not into temptation
But make me a good girl, please.'

She bicycled down to the doctor,
And rang the surgery bell;
'O, doctor, I've a pain inside me,
And I don't feel very well.'

Doctor Thomas looked her over,
And then he looked some more;
Walked over to his wash-basin,
Said, 'Why didn't you come before?'

Doctor Thomas sat over his dinner,
Though his wife was waiting to ring;
Rolling his bread into pellets,
Said 'Cancer's a funny thing.

'Nobody knows what the cause is,
Though some pretend they do;
It's like some hidden assassin
Waiting to strike at you.'

His wife she rang for the servant,
Said, 'Don't be so morbid, dear.'
He said; 'I saw Miss Gee this evening
And she's a goner, I fear.'

They took Miss Gee to the hospital,
She lay there a total wreck,
Lay in the ward for women
With the bedclothes right up to her neck.

They laid her on the table,
The students began to laugh;
And Mr Rose the surgeon
He cut Miss Gee in half.

Mr Rose he turned to his students,
Said, 'Gentlemen, if you please,

We seldom see a sarcoma
As far advanced as this.'

They took her off the table,
They wheeled away Miss Gee
Down to another department
Where they study Anatomy.

They hung her from the ceiling,
Yes, they hung up Miss Gee;
And a couple of Oxford Groupers
Carefully dissected her knee.

I told you it was a bit sharp and it reminds me of the sharpness of the Berlin Germany of that time. I went to live in Germany then for a year and almost the first week I was there I went to the Opera at Frankfurt-am-Main for the first night of a new opera by two men who were not very well known outside Germany at that time, Kurt Weill and Bertolt Brecht. The opera was *The Rise and Fall of the City of Mahagonny*, and at the end of the first act there were so many stink-bombs being thrown by the Nazis in the gallery that the performance had to be stopped. As I walked home a great Nazi procession came past me with torches. When I got home that night I had a book I was reading by D. H. Lawrence called *Fantasia of the Unconscious*. It's a book about psychoanalysis. I'd reached a chapter called 'Trees and Babies and Papas and Mammas' which I read that night. It really deeply shaped my life and it may influence you.

## *Fantasia of the Unconscious*

**D. H. LAWRENCE**

I listen again for noises, and I smell the damp moss. The looming trees, so straight. And I listen for their silence – big, tall-bodied trees, with a certain magnificent cruelty about them – or barbarity – I don't know why I should say cruelty. Their magnificent, strong, round bodies! It almost seems I can hear the slow, powerful sap drumming in their trunks. Great full-blooded trees, with strange tree-blood in them soundlessly drumming.

I come so well to understand tree-worship. All the old Aryans worshipped the tree. My ancestors. The tree of life. The tree of knowledge. Well, one is bound to sprout out some time or other, chip off the old Aryan block. I can so well understand tree-worship, and fear the deepest motive.

Naturally. This marvellous vast individual without a face, without lips or eyes or heart. This towering creature that never had a face. Here am I between his toes like a pea-bug, and him noiselessly over-reaching me, and I feel his great blood-jet surging. And he has no eyes. But he turns two ways: he thrusts himself tremendously down to the middle earth, where dead men sink in darkness, in the damp, dense undersoil; and he turns himself about in high air; whereas we have eyes on one side of our head only, and only grow upwards.

And I can so well understand the Romans, their terror of the bristling Hercynian wood. Yet when you look from a height down upon the rolling of the forest – this Black Forest – it is as suave as a rolling, oily sea. Inside only, is bristles horrifice. And it terrified the Romans.

The Romans and the Greeks found everything human. Everything had a face, and a human voice. Men spoke, and their fountains piped an answer.

But when the legions crossed the Rhine they found a vast impenetrable life which had no voice. They met the faceless silence of the Black Forest. This huge, huge wood did not answer when they called. Its silence was too crude and massive. And the soldiers shrank: shrank before the trees that had no faces, and no answer.

No wonder the soldiers were terrified. No wonder they thrilled with horror when, deep in the woods, they found the skulls and trophies of their dead comrades upon the trees. The trees had devoured them: silently, in mouthfuls, and left the white bones. Bones of the mindful Romans – and savage, preconscious trees, indomitable. The true German has something of the sap of trees in his veins even now: he is a tree soul, and his gods are not human. His instinct still is to nail skulls and trophies to the sacred tree, deep in the forest. The tree of life and death, tree of good and evil, tree of abstraction and of immense, mindless life.

*Readers: Denis Goucher, Denys Hawthorne*

*Full Selection:*
*Bleak House,* CHARLES DICKENS
*Hymn to Proserpine,* ALGERNON CHARLES SWINBURNE
*Plato Today,* R. H. S. CROSSMAN
*The Tower,* W. B. YEATS
*Funeral Blues,* W. H. AUDEN
*Miss Gee,* W. H. AUDEN
*Fantasia of the Unconscious,* D. H. LAWRENCE
*The Choice Before the Labour Party,* R. H. TAWNEY
*Sent to Coventry,* GEORGE HODGKINSON
*Romance,* W. J. TURNER
*2001: A Space Odyssey,* ARTHUR C. CLARKE

# PROFESSOR BARRY CUNLIFFE

## 1983

*Many of those invited to present 'With Great Pleasure' begin with an account of being read to on a mother's or a father's knee. Professor Cunliffe on the other hand makes no bones about the fact that his childhood was un-literary. He hardly read anything until the age of twelve, preferring to spend the time roaming the fields around his uncle's farm. One day he learned that next to the farm had been a Roman villa. From then on he spent hours and hours kicking over the mole hills in search of Roman pot shards, picking up the tessiary that made up the mosaic pavements. It was a gentle introduction to what was to become his lifelong passion, archaeology. Fortunately for the programme he later developed other passions, including reading and second-hand bookshops.*

I spend a very considerable part of each working year actually involved in excavation, two to three months, and for me each archaeological site takes on a character, and it's almost invariably the character of a woman. This is a very sexist thing to say, but I can't help feeling that the relationship of an excavation director to a site is rather like that of a man to a woman – the woman has to be cared for and cajoled into showing her secrets. It will probably ruin my chances of appearing on 'Woman's Hour', but nevertheless I do actually feel that. I feel it in particular about Bath, beneath the Pump Room, right in the heart of the temple dedicated to Sulis Minerva the goddess of Wisdom, the goddess of healing. Every excavation produces wonderful experiences and surprises, and one of the surprises, egg on the faces of all the archaeologists working on it, was when we discovered temple steps where we were not expecting to find them. I thought a cellar had cut them away – a trench was dug to put a sewer in – but the cellar hadn't cut them away: there they were. I had to explain it quickly, why we were wrong, and then to explain to the press how very much we wanted to preserve those steps, but we didn't have any money to do it; we'd probably just have to fill the hole in and roof it over, but if we could get the money we would be able to lay them open to the public. Within two days I received a letter:

## *Letter from Children of Twerton School*

Dear Professor Cunliffe,
The children in this school are trying to save some money to help keep the temple steps where people can see them. Some of us are giving money instead of buying sweets and comics. We have collected £1-75p in two days. We have some other ideas as well. How soon will you be needing our money? We hope you are successful in your digging and getting the money for the steps.
Yours sincerely
The Children of Twerton Church of England School
(Newton Road, Twerton, Bath: 12th February 1981)

It's quite the nicest letter I've ever received. Now there is a tail piece to that story: the money *was* raised, the children handed over their cheque, the steps were protected and the first members of the general public to see the steps were the children of that school.

In the 8th century AD, a Saxon poet stood more or less where we were excavating beneath the Pump Room and he looked around and he saw this great decaying Roman building. What he would have seen, I think, was the chamber in which the sacred spring was, where the King's bath now is. The walls were standing and the roof was still there, a tiled roof although the tiles were falling off. The portico had fallen down in a great tumble of rubble and he got to thinking, presumably, about the transience of life and the inconsequence of man. He wrote a poem and the remarkable thing is that a substantial part of that poem still survives.

## *The Ruin*
### Translated from Old English by
### KEVIN CROSSLEY-HOLLAND

Wondrous is this stone wall, wrecked by fate;
the city buildings crumble, the works of the giants decay.
Roofs have caved in, towers collapsed,
barred gates are broken, hoar frost clings to mortar,
houses are gaping, tottering and fallen,
undermined by age. The earth's embrace,
its fierce grip, holds the mighty craftsmen;
they are perished and gone. A hundred generations
have passed away since then. This wall, grey with lichen
and red of hue, outlives kingdom after kingdom,
withstands tempests; its tall gate succumbed.
The city still moulders, gashed by storms. . . .

A man's mind quickened with a plan;
subtle and strong-willed, he bound
the foundations with metal rods – a marvel.
Bright were the city halls, many the bath-houses,
lofty all the gables, great the martial clamour,
many a mead-hall was full of delights

until fate the mighty altered it. Slaughtered men
fell far and wide, the plague-days came,
death removed every brave man.
Their ramparts became abandoned places,
the city decayed; warriors and builders
fell to the earth. Thus these courts crumble,
and this redstone arch sheds tiles.

The place falls to ruin, shattered
into mounds of stone, where once many a man,
joyous and gold-bright, dressed in splendour,
proud and flush with wine, gleamed in his armour;
he gazed on his treasure – silver, precious stones,
jewellery and wealth, all that he owned –
and on this bright city in the broad kingdom.
Stone houses stood here; a hot spring
gushed in a wide stream; a stone wall
enclosed the bright interior; the baths
were there, the heated water; that was convenient.
They allowed the scalding water to pour
over the grey stone into the circular pool.

Apart from excavating, I also spend a very considerable amount of time travelling abroad and it's something I enormously enjoy. I also enjoy the peculiarity of foreigners. This has produced the most substantial and extremely amusing literature, and I'm always surprised at how often things noted in the past are still very much true today.

If you drive through any part of France you'll be extremely aware, I think, of the Frenchman's love of shooting any living thing that moves. I remember driving through one part of France on a Sunday morning and I was absolutely convinced that the birds were actually using the car as cover, to get from one bunch of shooters to another. Exactly the same preoccupation was beautifully noted by Tobias Smollett in 1766.

## *Travels Through France and Italy*
### TOBIAS SMOLLETT

In the character of the French, considered as a people, there are undoubtedly many circumstances truly ridiculous. You know the fashionable people, who go hunting, are equipped with their jack boots, bag wigs, swords and pistols: but I saw the other day a scene still more grotesque. On the road to Choissi, a fiacre, or hackney-coach, stopped, and out came five or six men, armed with musquets, who took post, each behind a separate tree. I asked our servant who they were, imagining they might be archers, or footpads of justice, in pursuit of some malefactor. But guess my surprise, when the fellow told me, they were gentlemen à la chasse (out hunting). They were in fact come out from Paris, in this equipage, to take the diversion of hare-hunting; that is, of shooting from behind a tree at the hares that chanced to pass. Indeed, if they had nothing more in view, but to destroy the game, this was a very effectual method; for the hares are in such plenty in this neighbourhood, that I have seen a dozen together, in the same field. I think this way of hunting, in a coach or chariot, might be properly adopted at London, in favour of those aldermen of the city, who are too unwieldy to follow the hounds a-horseback.

I think that's a fair comment on those who kill things and call it fun.

Now one of the very exciting things I always find about archaeology is that I have to deal with sites or individual monuments about which people have written in the past, and to look at those sites in relation to the words that have been written about them is a remarkable experience.

In Athens away from all the dreadful tourists' tat and trouble and away from all those filthy petrol fumes, in so far as you can actually get away from petrol fumes in Athens, tucked away in a side street there's a small archaeological excavation which very few people go to. It's now known as Karonikos. If you look there you can see the city wall of Athens a few blocks high running across and a gate. Leading to that gate are two roads, and alongside those roads is a cemetery, a cemetery of the ancient Athenians, and it was here that in the 5th century BC Pericles gathered together all the citizens of Athens and addressed them. It was a moving occasion, a funeral oration given for the young men who had died saving Athens from Spartan totalitarianism. One of the things that Pericles did was to emphasize the nature of democracy. It is, I think, one of the finest pieces of writing on the nature of democracy ever.

### *Quotation From Pericles*

Let me say that our system of government does not copy the institutions of our neighbours. It is more a case of our being a model to others than of our imitating anyone else. Our Constitution is called a democracy because power is in the hands not of the minority but of the whole people. When it is a question of settling private disputes everyone is equal before the law. When it is a question of putting one person before another in positions of public responsibility what counts is not membership of a particular class but the actual ability which a man possesses. No one so long as he has it in him to be of service to the State is kept in political obscurity because of poverty. We give our obedience to those whom we put in positions of authority and we obey the laws themselves. Especially those who offer the protection of the oppressed. Our love of what is beautiful doesn't lead to extravagance, our love of things of the mind doesn't make us soft. We regard wealth as something to be properly used rather than something to boast about. As for poverty, no one need be ashamed to admit it. You must yourselves realise the power of Athens and feast your eyes upon her from day to day and become her lovers. And when all her greatness shall break upon you, you must reflect that it was by courage, sense of duty and a keen feeling of honour in action that men were able to win all this.

I confess that the enjoyment of food and wine is another of my passions. I think Hilaire Belloc got his priorities absolutely correct when, addressing an after-dinner speech to some friends after they had had a very good meal indeed, he ended up by saying 'When that this too too solid flesh shall melt away and I am called before my Heavenly Father I shall say to him Sire, I don't remember the name of the village and I don't remember the name of the girl, but the wine was Chambertin.'

He actually said that at the Saintsbury Club – a meeting of this very famous club that was founded in honour of a remarkable man, George Saintsbury. He was Regius Professor of Rhetoric at Edinburgh University. Whether he was any good at rhetoric I've no idea, but he is extremely well-known for his legendary love of wine.

### *Notes on a Cellar Book*
**GEORGE SAINTSBURY**

It was really a wonderful wine. This was a Red Hermitage of 1846. When the last bottle was put on the table it showed not the slightest mark or presage of enfeeblement, but it was the manliest French wine I ever drank. You had to be careful of it in some ways; one of the best-known of all my friends had very remarkable experiences as a consequence of neglecting my warnings, and consuming whisky instead of brandy with his soda after it. But there is no good in any man, woman or wine that will allow liberties to be taken with them. To champagne before it, it had no objection; nor, as hinted just now, to brandy afterwards. But it was uncompromisingly Gallic in its patriotism.

*Readers: Angela Down, Peter Jeffrey*

*Full Selection:*
*Memories of Christmas,* DYLAN THOMAS
*Emily Writes Such a Good Letter,* STEVIE SMITH
*Lenten Thoughts of a High Anglican,* JOHN BETJEMAN
*The Return of the Native,* THOMAS HARDY
*Letter from Children of Twerton School*
*The Ruin,* trans. KEVIN CROSSLEY-HOLLAND
*Travels Through France and Italy,* TOBIAS SMOLLETT
*Senility,* LLYWARCH HEN
*Warning,* JENNY JOSEPH
*Let Me Die a Youngman's Death,* ROGER McGOUGH
*Rome in Africa,* SIMON RAVEN
*The Odyssey,* HOMER
*The Portable Swift,* JONATHAN SWIFT
*Quotation From Pericles*
*Notes on a Cellar Book,* GEORGE SAINTSBURY
*Coming Down from the Chung-Nan Mountain,* LI PO

# *MARGARET DRABBLE*

## *1979*

*'I loved tragedy and wasn't very good at seeing jokes.' That was Margaret Drabble's brisk summing-up of herself as a child, and perhaps more than most her edition of 'With Great Pleasure' harked back to her childhood. Indeed, it was recorded at her old school, The Mount, in York. Since her time there she has, of course, learnt to enjoy jokes, and she included many in her selection. However, through the good humour and the enjoyment of adult pleasures there is a hint of wistfulness for the state of childhood itself, as if the party had ended too soon, before the last round of 'pass the parcel', the cake unfinished and the going-home present uncertain.*

I read a great deal while I was at school, I read licitly in the classroom and illicitly in boiler rooms and in bed with a torch under the bedclothes, and I can honestly say that I remember even the set texts we did in English for O' level and A' level with the greatest pleasure. But my passion for reading pre-dated my arrival at The Mount. All our family were great readers when I was little, and we all still are. My mother never censored our reading in any way; she encouraged us to read anything in the house or that we could find in the Sheffield Public Library. One of my earliest favourites was a book called *The Golden Windows* by Laura Richards, which I think was a Sunday School prize of one of my parents. I loved these fables, but lost sight of them for years when the book disappeared during one of the family's removals. I was delighted to find a copy of this rather rare book in a second-hand bookshop in Salisbury one sunny day a few years ago, and when I reread the stories I found them even more touching than I'd done as a child. This is one that I'd remembered with great clarity, and of which I often think as I watch my own children, two of them now larger than me, striding forth into the world.

## *The Blind Mother*

### LAURA RICHARDS

A blind woman had a son, who was the joy of her life. Though she had no sight of her eyes, yet she was skilful of her hands; and it was her delight to make pretty clothes for her boy, soft and fine and full of delicate stitches.

By and by the boy came to her and said: 'Mother, give me some other clothes to wear. These are too small for me; they pinch and bind me. Moreover, they are baby clothes, and my play-fellows mock and laugh at me because of them.'

But the mother said: 'Nay, my darling; these are by far the best clothes for you. See how soft and warm they are! They are pretty too, I know, although I cannot see them. Be content, for you are my own darling little son, and so you must remain.'

When he found he could not persuade her, the boy held his peace; and he went out and looked about him, and found the hide of a wolf and the pelt of a fox, and huddled them round him over his baby frock, and so went among his mates. Only, when he came back to the room where his mother sat, he threw aside the skins, and came to her in his frock; and she kissed him, and felt the frills and silken stitches, and said rejoicing: 'You are my own darling little son, and the light of my life.'

By and by again there was a war in that country, and all the young men went out to meet the enemy. Some were clad in the armour of proof, others in leathern jacks and doublets; and with them went the son of the blind woman.

Then when the woman knew that her son was gone, she wept and lamented, and ran out into the street. There she met one who was returning from the field of battle, and she asked him how went the fight.

'Bravely', he replied. 'Our men did well, all save one who had no arms, and whom I saw beaten down and at sore odds with the enemy.'

'Oh! stranger,' cried the blind woman, 'was that one a boy,

who had wandered by mistake into that dreadful field, – a sweet child, with the prettiest clothes, all wrought with needlework?'

'Nay', said the stranger. 'It was a man, half-naked, huddled in the skins of beasts, with strange rags showing under the skins.'

'Oh!' said the woman. 'I wonder who that poor soul might be; and I wonder when my little darling son will come home to me again.'

And even while she spoke her son lay dead, and huddled round him was the hide of a wolf and the pelt of a fox, with the baby clothes fluttering from under them.

As I said, I often think of that when my own children set off in their battle dresses, boiler suits, badges and armour plating, and I think that perhaps that's why they dress like that and I mustn't, as my son says, stifle them too much.

One of the most lasting legacies of my Mount days is an intimate knowledge of the contents of the *Songs of Praise*, which I used to feel was a sign of misspent meetings for worship, as too good a knowledge of billiards is said to be a sign of a misspent youth. But in the long run I think it is time well-spent, and hymns circulate round my head on occasions appropriate and inappropriate. Unfortunately I couldn't sing, though I learnt to mouth the words excellently to deceive Miss Birch in hymn practice – this is still a useful accomplishment during 'God Save the Queen'. One of my favourites, 'The Eternal Order', by Edward Grubb, still sums up my theological position (I believe Edward Grubb was a Quaker, related to Sarah Grubb, a founder of Ackworth School – one of the first real live poets I ever met was a relative named Frederick).

## *The Eternal Order*

**EDWARD GRUBB**

Our God, to whom we turn
  When weary with illusion,
Whose stars serenely burn
  Above this earth's confusion,
Thine is the mighty plan,
  The steadfast order sure,

In which the world began,
  Endures, and shall endure.

Thou art thyself the Truth;
  Though we, who fain would find thee,
Have tried, with thoughts uncouth,
  In feeble words to bind thee,
It is because thou art
  We're driven to the quest;
Till truth from falsehood part
  Our souls can find no rest.

In my day we were taught Scripture by a teacher called Mrs Webster, whom I remember vividly and with much affection. She introduced us to arguments for and against the existence of God. 'And I rather think "The Eternal Order", she said, 'was an illustration of the ontological argument in favour of the existence of God.' And she said that was why I liked it. I remember that she was surprised and I think a little disturbed to find me at the age of sixteen deeply impressed by the pessimism of Thomas Hardy, who seemed to me to have all the answers to life's meaninglessness. 'But don't you think it's *exaggerated*?' she would cry, as I wept over *Jude the Obscure*, and now I see what she meant, but I still love Hardy, and this poem, 'The Darkling Thrush', seems to me to capture the essence of his peculiarly hopeful despair, as well as presenting us with one of his finest landscapes.

## *The Darkling Thrush*
**THOMAS HARDY**

I leant upon a coppice gate
    When Frost was spectre-gray,
And winter's dregs made desolate
    The weakening eye of day.
The tangled bine-stems scored the sky
    Like strings of broken lyres,
And all mankind that haunted nigh
    Had sought their household fires.

The land's sharp features seemed to be
    The Century's corpse outleant,

His crypt the cloudy canopy,
    The wind his death-lament.
The ancient pulse of germ and birth
    Was shrunken hard and dry,
And every spirit upon earth
    Seemed fervourless as I.

At once a voice arose among
    The bleak twigs overhead
In a full-hearted evensong
    Of joy illimited;
An aged thrush, frail, gaunt and small,
    In blast be-ruffled plume,
Had chosen thus to fling his soul
    Upon the growing gloom.

So little cause for carollings
    Of such ecstatic sound
Was written on terrestrial things
    Afar or nigh around,
That I could think there trembled through
    His happy good-night air
Some blessed Hope, whereof he knew
    And I was unaware.

It's amazing and rather frightening looking back to see what lasting and unexpected discoveries teachers can make for us and, as a teacher myself, I sometimes feel rather frightened about the influence I might be having and things I forget I've ever said come back to me in the most curious ways. The next poem was introduced to me by the then headmistress, Miss Garrick Smith, who found me crying on those stone steps which go up by the side of her study – I can't remember what I was crying about – and she took me into her study which at first rather terrified me than comforted me, and then she read me this wonderful Shakespeare sonnet which I now know by heart and which I often repeat to myself in times of stress.

## *Sonnet 29*

### WILLIAM SHAKESPEARE

When, in disgrace with fortune and men's eyes,
I all alone beweep my outcast state,
And trouble deaf heaven with my bootless cries,
And look upon myself, and curse my fate,
Wishing me like to one more rich in hope,
Featured like him, like him with friends possess'd,
Desiring this man's art, and that man's scope,
With what I most enjoy contented least;
Yet in these thoughts myself almost despising,
Haply I think on thee, and then my state,
Like to the lark at break of day arising
From sullen earth, sings hymns at heaven's gate:
For thy sweet love rememb'red such wealth brings
That then I scorn to change my state with kings.

What a comfort it is to reflect that even Shakespeare had moments when he desired other men's art and scope. And as for envying other men's features or other girls' features, I know that when I was a girl I'd willingly have changed my appearance with anybody in the school and used to envy everyone for the plain fact that they didn't look like me. I've got over that now, I think.

One of the great revelations of my early reading years was Emily Brontë. I came across *Wuthering Heights* when I was just the right age, about fourteen, and have loved it ever since. It is one of the great romantic novels, and it managed to communicate itself even to the most philistine of us in our fourth year. Emily Brontë has also written some of the great love poetry, which is one of literature's paradoxes – how can she have known about love, living as she did so cut off from the world? I think the metaphysical quality of her yearning gives the poetry a terrible intensity, which in its way is as comforting as Shakespeare's sonnet. I've never worked out why the expression of intense emotion, even of the most painful variety, should be consoling, but it is so.

## *The Appeal*

**EMILY BRONTË**

If grief for grief can touch thee,
  If answering woe for woe,
If any ruth can melt thee,
  Come to me now!

I cannot be more lonely,
  More drear I cannot be!
My worn heart throbs so wildly,
  'Twill break for thee.

And when the world despises,
  When Heaven repels my prayer,
Will not mine angel comfort?
  Mine idol hear?

Yes, by the tears I've poured thee,
  By all my hours of pain,
Oh, I shall surely win thee,
  Beloved, again!

Arnold Bennett has long been one of my more eccentric pleasures. At Cambridge he was dismissed in a footnote, but I knew there was more to him than that. I enjoy everything he wrote, and he wrote plenty, but the great novels, *Clayhanger* and *The Old Wives' Tale*, seem to me to stand with the best novels in our literature. There is something in my own family background that responds to Arnold Bennett because in fact my mother's family came from the Potteries and claimed to be related to the Bennetts. Mind you, Bennett is a very common name, there are a lot of Bennetts in the Potteries, but we like to think that we're related to them and I recognize in particular the kind of social background that is described in this children's birthday party from *The Old Wives' Tale*.

## *The Old Wives' Tale*

**ARNOLD BENNETT**

Cyril, while attending steadily to the demands of his body, was in a mood which approached the ideal. Proud and radiant, he combined urbanity with a certain fine condescension. His bright eyes, and his manner of scraping up jam with a spoon, said: 'I am the king of this party. This party is solely in my honour. I know that. We all know it. Still, I will pretend we are equals, you and I.' He talked about his picture-books to a young woman on his right named Jennie, aged four, pale, pretty, the belle in fact. The boy's attractiveness was indisputable; he could put on quite an aristocratic air. It was the most delicious sight to see them, Cyril and Jennie, so soft and delicate, so infantile on their piles of cushions and books, with their white socks and black shoes dangling far distant from the carpet; and yet so old, so self-contained!

And they were merely the epitome of the whole table. The whole table was bathed in the charm and mystery of young years, of helpless fragility, gentle forms, timid elegance, unshamed instincts, and waking souls. Constance and Samuel were very satisfied.

They both really did believe, at that moment, that Cyril was, in some subtle way which they both felt but could not define, superior to all other infants.

Someone, some officious relative of a visitor, began to pass a certain cake which had brown walls, a roof of coco-nut icing, and a yellow body studded with crimson globules. Not a conspicuously gorgeous cake, not a cake to which a catholic child would be likely to attach particular importance; a good average cake! Who could have guessed that it stood, in Cyril's esteem, as the cake of cakes? Now, by the hazard of destiny that cake found much favour, helped into popularity as it was by the blundering officious relative who, not dreaming what volcano she was treading on, urged its merits with simpering enthusiasm. One boy took two slices, a slice in each hand; he happened to be the visitor of whom the cake-distributor was a relative, and she protested; she expressed the shock she suffered. Whereupon both Constance and Samuel sprang forward and swore with angelic smiles that nothing could be more perfect than the propriety of that dear little fellow taking two slices of that cake. It was this hullaballoo that drew Cyril's attention to the evanescence of the cake of cakes. His face at once changed from calm pride to a dreadful anxiety. His eyes bulged out. His tiny mouth grew and grew, like a mouth in a nightmare. He was no longer human; he was a cake-eating tiger balked of his prey. Nobody noticed him. The officious fool of a woman persuaded Jennie to take the last slice of the cake, which was quite a thin slice.

Then every one simultaneously noticed Cyril, for he gave a yell. It was not the cry of a despairing soul who sees his beautiful iridescent dream shattered at his feet: it was the cry of the strong, masterful spirit, furious. He turned upon Jennie, sobbing and snatched her cake. Unaccustomed to such behaviour from hosts, and being besides a haughty put-you-in-your-place beauty of the future, Jennie defended her cake. After all, it was not she who had taken two slices at once. Cyril hit her in the eye, and then crammed most of the slice of cake into his enormous mouth. He could not swallow it, nor even masticate it, for his throat was rigid and tight. So the cake projected from his red lips, and big tears watered it. The most awful mess you can conceive! Jennie wept loudly, and one or two others joined her in sympathy, but the rest went on eating tranquilly, unmoved by the horror which transfixed their elders.

A host to snatch food from a guest! A host to strike a guest! A gentleman to strike a lady!

Constance whipped up Cyril from his chair and flew with him to his own room, where she smacked him on the arm and told him he was a very, very naughty boy and that she didn't know what his father would say. She took the food out of his disgusting mouth – or as much of it as she could get at – and she left him, on the bed. Miss Jennie was still in tears when, blushing scarlet and trying to smile, Constance returned to the drawing-room. Jennie would not be appeased. Miss Insull had promised to see Jennie home, and it was decided that she should go. Then all pretended, and said loudly, that what had happened was naught, that such things were always happening at children's parties.

But the attempt to keep up appearance was a failure.

The Methuselah of visitors, a gaping girl of nearly eight years, walked across the room to where Constance was standing, and said in a loud, confidential, fatuous voice:

'Cyril *has* been a rude boy, hasn't he, Mrs Povey?'

*Readers: Eleanor Bron, Edward Petherbridge*

*Full Selection:*
*The Blind Mother,* LAURA M. RICHARDS
*The Eternal Order,* EDWARD GRUBB
*Pride and Prejudice,* JANE AUSTEN
*The Darkling Thrush,* THOMAS HARDY
*Sonnet 29,* WILLIAM SHAKESPEARE
*The Appeal,* EMILY BRONTË
*The Mill on the Floss,* GEORGE ELIOT
*Anglo-Saxon Attitudes,* ANGUS WILSON
*The Prelude, Book VI,* WILLIAM WORDSWORTH
*Scoop,* EVELYN WAUGH
*Casanova's Chinese Restaurant,* ANTHONY POWELL
*Consolation,* W. B. YEATS
*Antony and Cleopatra,* WILLIAM SHAKESPEARE
*The Old Wives' Tale,* ARNOLD BENNETT
*Vacillation,* W. B. YEATS

# *NELL DUNN*

## *1983*

Up the Junction, Poor Cow *and* Steaming, *plays about apparently ordinary people displaying great vitality in the face of an unjust society, have made Nell Dunn's reputation as a writer secure – not that one suspects she would give even a passing thought to such a thing as her reputation. On the evidence of her edition of 'With Great Pleasure' she is more concerned with the idea of properly taking stock of oneself, of achieving a proper understanding in a world where habit and custom could become an excuse for morality: responsible behaviour may be more correctly defined by an irresponsible act because it is more true to the person committing it than any amount of habitual virtue.*

I had an exotic childhood. I travelled, and what I always longed for was ordinariness. I had a mother who was always singing arias from Richard Strauss or Verdi, who spoke about five languages, and knew everyone, when what I longed for was a mum in a pinny, with floury hands, who bustled around the kitchen. And yet, Athens and the Far East – yes, it sounds exciting – but how to get security and excitement, that is the question.

*Clarissa* by Samuel Richardson was written in 1748. Some call it the first English novel: written in the form of letters, it is about a young woman's fight to preserve her integrity and not to marry Mr Solmes – as Clarissa puts it, she cannot 'cajole, fawn upon and play the hypocrite with a man to whom I have an aversion'.

I feel it was Clarissa Harlow, and women like her, whose courage eventually won us the enormous freedom women enjoy today. We are not only free now to marry the men we love, but also free, if we don't wish to marry, to live with men and pay our own bills, to be independent women. Here then Clarissa, about to be trapped into politeness with her suitor, Mr Solmes, shows her boldness and proceeds to beg her mother to speak on her behalf to her father that she should not be forced to marry. It seems, even in the eighteenth century, the nicest families had problems.

## *Clarissa*

### SAMUEL RICHARDSON

My mother was angry enough without all that; and asked me to what purpose I came down, if I were still so untractable?

She had hardly spoken the words when Shorey came in to tell her that Mr Solmes was in the hall, and desired admittance.

Ugly creature! What, at the close of day, quite dark, had brought him hither? But, on second thoughts, I believe it was contrived, that he should be here at supper, to know the result of the conference between my mother and me, and that my father, on his return, might find us together.

I was hurrying away; but my mother commanded me (since I had come down only, as she said, to mock her) not to stir; and at the same time see if I could behave so to Mr Solmes, as might encourage her to make the favourable report to my father which I had besought her to make.

My sister triumphed. I was vexed to be caught, and to have such an angry and cutting rebuke given me, with an aspect more like the taunting sister than the indulgent mother, if I may presume to say so: for she herself seemed to enjoy the surprise upon me.

The man stalked in. His usual walk is by pauses, as if from the same vacuity of thought which made Dryden's clown whistle he was telling his steps, and first paid his clumsy respects to my mother; then to my sister; next to me as if I were already his wife, and therefore to be the last in his notice; and sitting down by me, told us in general what weather it was. Very cold he made it; but I was warm enough. Then addressing himself to me; and how do *you* find it, miss? was his question; and would have taken my hand.

I withdrew it, I believe with disdain enough. My mother frowned. My sister bit her lip.

I could not contain myself: I never was so bold in my life; for I went on with my plea as if Mr Solmes had not been there.

My mother coloured, and looked at him, at my sister, and at me. My sister's eyes were opener and bigger than I ever saw them before.

The man understood me. He hemmed, and removed from one chair to another.

I went on, supplicating for my mother's favourable report: Nothing but invincible dislike, said I –

What would the girl be at, interrupted my mother? Why Clary! Is this a subject! Is this! – is this! – is this a time – and again she looked upon Mr Solmes.

I am sorry, on reflection, that I put my mamma into so much confusion. To be sure it was very saucy in me.

I beg pardon, madam, said I. But my papa will soon return. And since I am not permitted to withdraw, it is not necessary, I humbly presume, that Mr Solmes's presence should deprive me of this opportunity to implore your favourable report; and at the same time, if he still visit on my account (looking at him) to convince him, that it cannot possibly be to any purpose –

Is the girl mad? said my mother, interrupting me.

My sister, with the affectation of a whisper to my mother: This is – this is *spite*, madam (very *spitefully* she spoke the word) because you commanded her to stay.

I only looked at her, and turning to my mother, Permit me, madam, said I, to repeat my request. I have no brother, no sister! If I lose my mamma's favour I am lost for ever!

Mr. Solmes removed to his first seat, and fell to knawing the head of his hazel; a carved head, almost as ugly as his own – I did not think the man was so *sensible.*

My sister rose, with a face all over scarlet, and stepping to the table, where lay a fan, she took it up, and although Mr. Solmes had observed that the weather was cold, fanned herself very violently.

My mother came to me, and angrily taking my hand, led me out of that parlour into my own; which, you know, is next to it. Is not this behaviour very bold, very provoking, think you, Clary?

*Clarissa* for me is a highly moral book. It tells us to think independently, feel independently, trust your own thoughts and feelings.

My father was a Master of Hounds, and *Memoirs of a Fox-Hunting Man* by Siegfried Sassoon was one of his favourite books. This extract is about a young boy's first hunt on his marvellous pony, Sheila, and I'd like to dedicate it to my own son, Gem, also a keen huntsman; and to my own childhood, whose happiest hours were spent with my sister and our beloved ponies in Savernake Forest on the Marlborough Downs.

## *Memoirs of a Fox-Hunting Man*
### SIEGFRIED SASSOON

'That's Mr Macdoggart,' said Dixon in a low voice, and my solemnity increased as the legendary figure vanished on its mysterious errand.

Meanwhile the huntsman was continuing his intermittent yaups as he moved along the other side to the wood. Suddenly his cheers of encouragement changed to a series of excited shoutings. 'Hoick-holler, hoick-holler, hoick-holler!' he yelled, and then blew his horn loudly; this was followed by an outbreak of vociferation from the hounds, and soon they were in full cry across the covert. I sat there petrified by my private feelings; Sheila showed no symptoms of agitation; she merely cocked her ears and listened.

And then, for the first time, I heard a sound which has thrilled generations of fox-hunters to their marrow. From the far side of the wood came the long shrill screech (for which it is impossible to find an adequate word) which signifies that one of the whips has viewed the fox quitting the covert. 'Gone away' it meant. But before I had formulated that haziest notion about it Lord Dumborough was galloping up the ride and the rest of them were pelting after him as though nothing could stop them. As I happened to be standing well inside the wood and Sheila took the affair into her own control, I was swept along with them, and we emerged on the other side among the leaders. I cannot claim that I felt either excitement or resolution as we bundled down a long slope of meadowland and dashed helter-skelter through an open gate at the bottom.

I knew nothing at all except that I was out of breath and that the air was rushing to meet me, but as I hung on to the reins I was aware that Mr Macdoggart was immediately in front of me. My attitude was an acquiescent one. I have always been inclined to accept life in the form in which it has imposed itself upon me, and on that particular occasion, no doubt, I just felt that I was 'in for it'. It did not so much as occur to me that in following Mr Macdoggart I was setting myself rather a high standard, and when he disappeared over the hedge I took it for granted that I must do the same. For a moment Sheila hesitated in her stride. (Dixon told me afterwards that I actually hit her as we approached the fence, but I couldn't remember having done so.) Then she collected herself and jumped the fence with a peculiar arching of her back. There was a considerable drop on the other side. Sheila had made no mistake, but as she landed I left the saddle and flew over her head. I had let go of the reins, but she stood stock-still while I sat on the wet ground.

I wanted to include a bit from the *Confessions* of Jean Jacques Rousseau, because it was my bible when I was about fifteen or sixteen. I learnt about intimacy from Rousseau – I mean I perhaps felt on more intimate terms with Rousseau then than with anybody I actually knew. I also learnt about the delicious foolishness of the human race.

## *Confessions*
### JEAN JACQUES ROUSSEAU

I entered the room of a courtesan as if it had been the sanctuary of love and beauty; in her person I thought I beheld its divinity. I should never have believed that, without respect and esteem, I should have experienced the emotions with which she inspired me. No sooner had I realised, in the preliminary familiarities, the value of her charms and caresses than, for fear of losing the fruit of them in advance, I was anxious to make haste and pluck it. Suddenly, in place of the flame which consumed me, I felt a deathly chill run through my veins; my legs trembled under me; and, feeling ready to faint, I sat down and cried like a child.

Who would guess the reason of my tears, and the thoughts which passed through my head at that moment? I said to myself: this object, which is at my disposal, is the masterpiece of nature and love; its mind and body, every part of it perfect; she is as good and generous as she is amiable and beautiful. The great ones of the world ought to be her slaves; sceptres ought to be laid at her feet. And yet she is a miserable street-walker, on sale to everybody; a merchant captain has the disposal of her; she comes and throws herself at my head, mine, although she knows that I am poor, while my real merits, being unknown to her, can have no value in her eyes. In this there is something incomprehensible. Either my heart deceives me, dazzles my senses, and makes me the dupe of a worthless slut, or some secret defect, with which I am unacquainted, must destroy the effect of her charms, and render her repulsive to those who would otherwise fight for the possession of her. I began to look for this defect with a singular intensity of mind, and it never occurred to me that the possible consequences of having anything to do with her might possibly have something to do with it. The freshness of her skin, her brilliant complexion, her dazzlingly white teeth, the sweetness of her breath, the general air of cleanliness about her whole person, so completely banished this idea from my mind, that, being still in doubt as to my condition since my visit to the padoana, I rather felt qualms of conscience as to whether I was in sufficiently good health for her, and I am quite convinced that I was not deceived in my confidence.

These well-timed reflections so agitated me that I shed tears. Zulietta, for whom this was certainly quite a novel sight, under the circumstances, was astounded for a moment; but, having walked round the room and looked in her glass, she understood, and my eyes convinced her, that dislike had nothing to do with this whimsical melancholy. It was an easy matter for her to drive it away, and to efface the slight feeling of shame; but, at the moment when I was ready to sink exhausted upon a bosom, which seemed to permit for the first time the contact of a man's hand and mouth, I perceived that she had only one nipple. I smote my forehead, looked attentively and thought I saw that this nipple was not formed like the other. I immediately began to rack my brains for the reason for such a defect, and, feeling convinced that it was connected with some remarkable natural imperfection, by brooding so long over this idea, I saw, as clear as daylight, that, in the place of the most charming person that I could picture to myself, I only held in my arms a kind of monster, the outcast of nature, of mankind and of love. I pushed my stupidity so far as to speak to her about this defect. At first she took it as a joke, and said and did things in her frolicsome humour, which were enough to make me die of love; but as I was unable to conceal from her that I still felt a certain amount of uneasiness, she at last blushed, adjusted her dress, got up, and, without saying a word, went and seated herself at the window. I wanted to sit by her side, but she moved, sat down on a couch, got up immediately afterwards, and, walking about the room and fanning herself, said to me in a cold and disdainful tone, 'Zanetto, lascia de donne, et studia la matematica.'

(Give up the ladies, and study mathematics.)

*Readers: Geoffrey Palmer, Caroline Blakiston*

*Full Selection:*
*The Unquiet Grave,* CYRIL CONNOLLY
*Louise,* STEVIE SMITH
*Howards End,* E. M. FORSTER
*Miss Lonelyhearts,* NATHANIEL WEST
*Layabout,* CHRISTOPHER LOGUE
*The Awakening,* KATE CHOPIN
*Swann's Way,* MARCEL PROUST
*If the Nightflights,* CHRISTOPHER LOGUE
*Clarissa,* SAMUEL RICHARDSON
*Memoirs of a Fox-Hunting Man,* SIEGFRIED SASSOON
*The Waterfall,* MARGARET DRABBLE
*Confessions,* JEAN JACQUES ROUSSEAU
*Child's Poem,* ANON

# JOYCE GRENFELL

## *1970*

*The telephone rang. 'We must invite Noël to tea,' said one woman to another, summoning in the mind a social landscape of old-world courtesy and cucumber sandwiches. 'The poor dear hasn't been well.' Even today we are in no doubt that 'Noël' could only have been Noël Coward. The woman thus telephoned was Joyce Grenfell, the caller the Queen Mother. I only met Joyce Grenfell once, in a studio in the late 1960s. She told me of the 'phone call, and the tea that followed it, not to name drop – the thought would never have occurred to her – but to express her pleasure in the warmth of the Queen Mother's personality and the way in which she had included her as co-host of the occasion. They must have made a glittering trio and to use the words 'common touch' in that context may appear rather strange, but certainly the two women must have had it. I have never in my rather neurotic occupation met anyone who had so little sense of self and so much enjoyment of life and of other people, whoever they may be, as Joyce Grenfell displayed during the few hours I spent in her company.*

I've taken the title 'With Great Pleasure' seriously. For me it means the lifting of the heart in amusement or nourishment – a kind of recognition of something that may be half forgotten or not yet fully acknowledged; there is more to be discovered in the book or poem that I go back to again and again.

I've deliberately left out the great names. The field is too wide and the choice too difficult (Shakespeare, for instance!), so I've made my selection a miniature one – smaller stars, but they go on giving me an increasing illumination and *pleasure*.

A few years ago I met a Brown Franciscan brother in the unlikely setting of the Picnic Races in a remote corner of Queensland in Australia who told me the best way to explain to people what redemption means is to get them to read Frances Hodgson Burnett's *The Secret Garden*.

It had never occurred to me. I've read the book over and over again since I first had it, aged nine I think. It's got all the ingredients for a good story and I still enjoy it. I've just read it *again*. It has a sad beginning, mystery, cries in the night – and a happy ending grown out of the emancipation and development of the two central characters, Mary Lennox and her cousin Colin, both about ten years old. Our heroine is a scraggy, spoilt, unattractive orphan who comes from India to live with an anti-social, unhappy, widowed uncle in his huge gloomy house in Yorkshire on the edge of the moor. Mary learns that there is a hidden 'secret garden' lost within the vast acres of the place. Forlornly skipping down one of the many long paths, she comes across a robin who apparently leads her to find an old key stuck in a clod of newly-turned earth in a flower bed.

## *The Secret Garden*

**FRANCES HODGSON BURNETT**

'You showed me where the key was yesterday,' she said. 'You ought to show me the door to-day; but I don't believe you know!' Mary had stepped close to the robin, and suddenly the gust of wind swung aside some loose ivy trails, and more suddenly still she jumped towards it and caught it in her hand. This she did because she had seen something under it – a round knob which had been covered by the leaves hanging over it. It was the knob of a door.

Mary's heart began to thump and her hands to shake a little in her delight and excitement. The robin kept singing and twittering away and tilting his head on one side, as if he were as excited as she was. What was this under her hands which was square and made of iron and which her fingers found a hole in?

It was the lock of the door which had been closed ten years, and she put her hand in her pocket, drew out the key, and found it fitted the keyhole. She put the key in and turned it. It took two hands to do it, but it did turn.

And then she took a long breath and looked behind her up the long walk to see if anyone was coming. No one was coming. She held back the swinging curtain of ivy and pushed back the door which opened slowly – slowly.

Then she slipped through it, and shut it behind her, and stood with her back against it, looking about her and breathing quite fast with excitement, and wonder, and delight. She was standing *inside* the secret garden.

Nannies, as they once were, played a very big part in the lives of those lucky enough to have been looked after by a good one. Nannies were reassuring, comfortable, kind, cosy and loving, *and always there*. At least mine was. Nannies had a special language, jokes worn thin with over use: 'hurry up now, you're all behind like a cow's tail' – 'come along now, up the stairs to Bedfordshire' – 'don't care was made to care'.

I had the best of all possible worlds, a mother whom I saw constantly (small house, that kind of mother) and a nanny for the in-between times whom we loved.

Priscilla Napier, who wrote *A Late Beginner*, has a wonderful ear for Nanny talk and an accurate eye for childish responses to it.

## *A Late Beginner*

**PRISCILLA NAPIER**

Religion was dangerous ground with Nanny. One could not, as with one's parents, say anything, any time. Nanny's lips had a way of folding up, forbiddingly. The first time I heard the word Alleluia I was so enchanted with it that I spent ten minutes leaping up and down on the armchair in the far corner of the drawing-room loudly pronouncing it.

'Don't do that,' Nanny said, when she found me. Her voice had an edge.

'Alleluia!' I said, leaping higher. The springs sent one up and up, the sensation was glorious. Alleluia! Alleluia! Alleluia! It was highly enjoyable; I wanted never to stop.

'I said don't do that', Nanny said again, more sharply. 'You'll break the springs.' But one could tell it wasn't that she minded.

'Alleluia! Alleluia!' I said, boring of it very slightly but drawing her on. 'All-el-uia-a-a!'

'That's a holy word,' Nanny said, 'Not to be bandied about in play. I would think you'd know better.' She took me by the arm quite brusquely and led me off to have my face washed although we both knew it was perfectly clean.

I found this love poem in Walter de la Mare's anthology called *Love*. It's a wonderful collection and it has a long introduction that makes the whole book one to go back and back to. This poem is by Sylvia Lind – I see it as set in East Anglia in August sixty or seventy years ago.

## *The Happy Hour*

**SYLVIA LIND**

H.L.A.L.; with penknife deep embedded,
  He carved the letters on the ancient stile.
Harry and Alice, rural lovers wedded,
  Stayed and were happy here a little while.

Along the dykes they walked, while the sun wested,

In the warm summer evening, and so it was
That Harry stood and carved, while Alice rested,
Amid the knapweed and the tall bleached grass.

Blue shone the tide, the swallows skimmed and darted,
White gulls passed slowly, redshanks made their cry;
The wheat was newly cut, the beans were carted,
And haystacks golden-rooved against the sky.

Pale gold the oaten stocks above the clover,
Too still the air to lift the thistledown,
Sometimes a curlew cried, sometimes a plover,
And evening fullness grew, and the sun shone,

And stretched long shadows on the yellow stubble;
While Harry set his oriflamme to prove
That, in a world called sad and full of trouble,
Two people once were happy, being in love.

I have always loved visual detail – the detail of a flower, the hair-line design in a white violet petal, a snail's trail, a feather, a shell, indeed a grain of sand – and for the same reason as Blake – to see all heaven in.

I'm drawn to the sense of leisure, time to embroider, time to sit or stand and stare that seems to have operated in the Victorian and Edwardian eras. That is why for my first love poem I have chosen one by Dante Gabriel Rossetti – I've deliberately gone for *contented* love poems rather than anguished ones. I like a little agony here and there, but I'm after a calmer scene now.

## *Your Hands Lie Open*

**DANTE GABRIEL ROSSETTI**

Your hands lie open in the long fresh grass, –
The finger-points look through like rosy blooms:
Your eyes smile peace. The pasture gleams and glooms
'Neath billowing skies that scatter and amass.
All round our nest, far as the eye can pass,
Are golden Kingcup-fields with silver edge
Where the cow-parsley skirts the hawthorn-hedge.
'Tis visible silence, still as the hour-glass.

Deep in the sun-searched growths the dragon-fly
Hangs like a blue thread loosened from the sky: –
So this winged hour is dropped to us from above.
Oh! clasp we to our hearts, for deathless dower,
This close-companioned inarticulate hour
When twofold silence was the song of love.

I have included a little anguish, and it too is both a portrait of an era and a poem about love.

## *The Gifts Returned*

**WALTER SAVAGE LANDOR**

'You must give back' her mother said
to a poor sobbing little maid,
'All the young man has given you,
Hard as it may now seem to do.'
''Tis done already, mother dear'
Said the sweet girl, 'So never fear.'
(M) 'Are you quite certain? Come, recount.
(There was not much) the whole amount.'
(G) The locket; the kid gloves.
(M) Go on.
(G) Of the kid gloves I found but one.
(M) Never mind that. What else? Proceed.
You gave back all his trash?
(G) Indeed.
(M) And was there nothing you would save?
(G) Everything I could give I gave.
(M) To the last tittle?
(G) Even to that.
(M) Freely?
(G) My heart went pit-a-pat
At giving up . . . . ah me, ah me
I cry so I can hardly see. . . . .
All the fond looks and words that passed
And all the kisses, to the last.

*Reader: Cecil Day Lewis*

*Full Selection:*
*Autobiography,* ENID BAGNOLD
*The Secret Garden,* FRANCES HODGSON BURNETT
*A Late Beginner,* PRISCILLA NAPIER
*Who Goes There?* CECIL DAY LEWIS
*In Memory of Basil, Marquis of Dufferin and Ava,* JOHN BETJEMAN
*Words Come Best From Those Least Given to Speech,* DORIS PEEL
*Spring Song,* VIRGINIA GRAHAM
*Emma,* JANE AUSTEN
*The Happy Hour,* SYLVIA LIND
*Your Hands Lie Open,* DANTE GABRIEL ROSSETTI
*The Gifts Returned,* WALTER SAVAGE LANDOR
*Persuasion,* JANE AUSTEN
*A South African Childhood,* VICTOR STIEBEL
*A Hard Frost,* CECIL DAY LEWIS
*The Great Sneeze,* PATRICK CAMPBELL
*The Gospel According to John,* THE NEW ENGLISH BIBLE
*The Second Book of Kings,* THE BIBLE, AUTHORISED VERSION

# JO GRIMOND

## *1978*

*When, at an age too early to vote, I used to watch with my parents the party political broadcasts, Jo Grimond was always the man who talked the most sense and whose party gathered the least votes. No doubt the one was the reason for the other. He was also Liberal Member of Parliament for Orkney, a place which seemed strangely romantic and far away to one born and bred south of Watford. Certainly it exerts a powerful influence on those who left it to seek fame and fortune elsewhere. For such a tiny island it seems also to have bred a disproportionate number of fine writers, many of whom stayed put.*

I was born in St Andrews in 1913 and St Andrews in those days was rather like Robert Louis Stevenson's Edinburgh. We too had a light outside our house and Larry the Lamplighter came to light it every evening. But it is Stevenson's *Windy Nights* which reminds me most of my childhood.

## *Windy Nights*

**ROBERT LOUIS STEVENSON**

Whenever the moon and stars are set,
Whenever the wind is high,
All night long in the dark and wet,
A man goes riding by.
Late in the night when the fires are out,
Why does he gallop and gallop about?

Whenever the trees are crying aloud,
And ships are tossed at sea,
By, on the highway, low and loud,
By at the gallop goes he.
By at the gallop he goes, and then
By he comes back at the gallop again.

From early days at school I was made to learn poetry by heart; I think it's a very excellent idea and especially if you're allowed to choose it yourself, as I was later on. I've always rather liked those didactic, well-turned, eighteenth-century writers like Gray and Burke, but in particular let's have a bit of Goldsmith on the village schoolmaster.

## *The Deserted Village*

**OLIVER GOLDSMITH**

Beside yon straggling fence that skirts the way,
With blossom'd furze unprofitably gay,
There, in his noisy mansion, skill'd to rule,

The village master taught his little school;
A man severe he was, and stern to view;
I knew him well, and every truant knew;
Well had the boding tremblers learn'd to trace
The day's disasters in his morning face;
Full well they laugh'd, with counterfeited glee,
At all his jokes, for many a joke had he;
Full well the busy whisper, circling round,
Convey'd the dismal tidings when he frown'd;
Yet he was kind; or if severe in aught,
The love he bore to learning was in fault;
The village all declar'd how much he knew;
'Twas certain he could write, and cypher too;
Lands he could measure, terms and tides presage,
And e'en the story ran that he could gauge.
In arguing too, the parson own'd his skill,
For e'en though vanquish'd, he could argue still;
While words of learned length and thund'ring sound
Amazed the gazing rustics rang'd around,
And still they gaz'd, and still the wonder grew,
That one small head could carry all he knew.

As I'm a politician I think we must have a piece of rhetoric. The bit I've chosen is a well known speech by that old rogue Lord Palmerston. Palmerston had behaved in a fairly monstrous manner to the Greeks in defence of a very shady character called Don Pacifico who was in fact a Portuguese, but had acquired British citizenship, and a vote of censure was passed in the House of Lords and a vote of censure was put down in the House of Commons and it was expected to be passed too. However Old Pam turned up in the middle of the night and spoke for four and a half hours till daybreak and he carried the day quite easily.

## *Don Pacifico Debate*
### LORD PALMERSTON

We have shown that liberty is compatible with order; that individual freedom is reconcilable with obedience to the law. We have shown the example of a nation, in which every class of society accepts with cheerfulness the lot which Providence has assigned to it; while at the same time every individual of each class is constantly striving to raise himself in the social scale – not by injustice and wrong, not by violence and illegality – but by persevering good conduct, and by the steady and energetic exertion of the moral and intellectual faculties with which his Creator has endowed him. To govern such a people as this is indeed an object worthy of the ambition of the noblest man who lives in the land; and therefore, I find no fault with those who may think any opportunity a fair one, for endeavouring to place themselves in so distinguished and honourable a position. But I contend that we have not in our foreign policy done anything to forfeit the confidence of the country. . . . I therefore fearlessly challenge the verdict which this House, as representing a political, a commercial, a constitutional country, is to give on the question now brought before it; whether the principles on which the foreign policy of Her Majesty's Government has been conducted, and the sense of duty which has led us to think ourselves bound to afford protection to our fellow subjects abroad, are proper and fitting guides for those who are charged with the government of England; and whether, as the Roman in days of old, held himself free from indignity, when we could say 'Civis Romanus sum' so also a British subject, in whatever land he may be, shall feel confident that the watchful eye and the strong arm of England will protect him against injustice and wrong.

Palmerston was a remarkable old man; when he was over seventy and Prime Minister he is alleged to have seduced a girl at an official government reception. The Tories had the very greatest difficulty in preventing her outraged husband from taking action against him, because, as they rightly guessed, had he done so he would have won the forthcoming General Election by an even bigger majority than in fact he achieved. Now, I'm not a great reader of historical letters – I think letters should be rather tuned to the matter in hand, they should be quick comments on what is going on at the time. I don't think they should be written for posterity, but I rather like this letter written about Lord John Russell who was a contemporary and ally of Palmerston's, two terrible old men who terrified Queen Victoria and the Prince Consort.

## *Letter From Sydney Smith About Lord John Russell*

There is not a better man in England than Lord John Russell; but his worst failure is that he is utterly ignorant of all moral fear; there is nothing he would not undertake. I believe he would perform the operation for the stone – build St Peter's – or assume (with or without ten minutes notice) the command of the Channel Fleet; and no one would discover by his manner that the patient had died – the Church tumbled down – and the Channel Fleet had been knocked to atoms. . . . Another peculiarity of the Russells is that they never alter their opinions; they are an excellent race, but they must be trepanned before they can be convinced.

Sydney Smith, believe it or not, was a clergyman and he made a lot of celebrated remarks. One of the best, I think, was about the Bishop of Exeter, about whom he said: 'Of course I must believe in the Apostolic Succession. How else can one account for the descent of the Bishop of Exeter from Judas Iscariot?'

Another letter I rather like is from the Duke of Wellington. The Duke was walking in the park one day when he met a boy who was crying. The Duke asked him why he was crying, to which the boy replied 'I have to go back to school tomorrow and my parents have told me I must get rid of my pet toad.'

'Give me your toad,' said the Duke, 'and I will look after it.'

So the boy went back to school and forgot all about his toad. A year later he received the following letter from the Duke of Wellington:

Field Marshal the Duke of Wellington presents his compliments to Mr So and So and requests that at his convenience he will be so good as to call and collect his toad.

Winter in Orkney is usually a time of wet and wind rather than snow and ice, in fact we tend to get our snow in the spring and 'The Lady of Shallott' may seem rather an odd choice to commemorate winter, but to me it does conjure up winter days.

## *The Lady of Shallott, Part IV*

**ALFRED LORD TENNYSON**

In the stormy east-wind straining,
The pale yellow woods were waning,
The broad stream in his banks complaining,
Heavily the low sky raining
    Over tower'd Camelot;
Down she came and found a boat
Beneath a willow left afloat,
And round about the prow she wrote
    The Lady of Shallott.

And down the river's dim expanse –
Like some bold seer in a trance,
Seeing all his own mischance –
With a glassy countenance
    Did she look to Camelot.
And at the closing of the day
She loosed the chain, and down she lay;
The broad stream bore her far away,
    The Lady of Shallott.

Lying, robed in snowy white
That loosely flew to left and right –
The leaves upon her falling light –
Thro' the noises of the night
    She floated down to Camelot.
And as the boat-head wound along
The willowy hills and fields among,
They heard her singing her last song,
    The Lady of Shallott.

– Heard a carol, mournful, holy,
Chanted loudly, chanted lowly,
Till her blood was frozen slowly,
And her eyes were darken'd wholly,
    Turn'd to tower'd Camelot;
For ere she reach'd upon the tide
The first house by the water-side,

Singing in her song she died,
　　　The Lady of Shallott.

Under tower and balcony,
By garden-wall and gallery,
A gleaming shape she floated by,
Dead-pale between the houses high,
　　　Silent into Camelot.
Out upon the wharfs they came,
Knight and burgher, lord and dame,
And round the prow they read her name,
　　　The Lady of Shallott.

Who is this? and what is here?
And in the lighted palace near
Died the sound of royal cheer;
And they cross'd themselves for fear,
　　　All the knights at Camelot:
But Lancelot mused a little space;
He said, 'She has a lovely face;
God in his mercy lend her grace,
　　　The Lady of Shallott.'

Let us end on a cheerful and rather eccentric note – 'The Owl and the Pussy-Cat' by Edward Lear, who must have been one of the nicest men who ever lived.

## *The Owl and the Pussy-Cat*

**EDWARD LEAR**

The Owl and the Pussy-Cat went to sea
　In a beautiful pea-green boat,
They took some honey, and plenty of money,
　Wrapped up in a five-pound note.
The Owl looked up to the stars above,
　And sang to a small guitar,
'O lovely Pussy! O Pussy, my love,
　　What a beautiful Pussy you are,
　　　　You are,
　　　　You are,
What a beautiful Pussy you are!'

Pussy said to the Owl, 'You elegant fowl!
How charmingly sweet you sing!
O let us be married! too long we have tarried:
But what shall we do for a ring?'
They sailed away, for a year and a day,
To the land where the Bong-tree grows
And there in a wood a Piggy-wig stood
With a ring at the end of his nose,
His nose,
His nose,
With a ring at the end of his nose.

'Dear Pig, are you willing to sell for one shilling
Your ring?' Said the Piggy, 'I will.'
So they took it away, and were married next day
By the Turkey who lives on the hill.
They dined on mince, and slices of quince,
Which they ate with a runcible spoon;
And hand in hand, on the edge of the sand,
They danced by the light of the moon,
The moon,
The moon,
They danced by the light of the moon.

*Readers: Alan Dobie, Diana Olsson, Howie Firth*

*Full Selection:*
*Genesis, V: 1–27,* THE BIBLE
*The Origin of Species,* CHARLES DARWIN
*Windy Nights,* ROBERT LOUIS STEVENSON
*Childhood,* EDWIN MUIR
*Matilda, Who Told Lies and Was Burned to Death,* HILAIRE BELLOC
*Stiff Upper Lip, Jeeves,* P. G. WODEHOUSE
*The Deserted Village,* OLIVER GOLDSMITH
*Sailing to Byzantium,* W. B. YEATS
*Don Pacifico Debate,* LORD PALMERSTON
*A Letter,* SYDNEY SMITH
*A Letter,* DUKE OF WELLINGTON

*A Shropshire Lad,* A. E. HOUSMAN
*The Mower to the Slow-Worms,* ANDREW MARVELL
*In Memoriam,* ALFRED LORD TENNYSON
*The Lady of Shallott, Part IV,* ALFRED LORD TENNYSON
*Da Sang O Da Papa Men,* ANON
*Orkney Crofter,* ROBERT RENDALL
*Hamnavoe,* GEORGE MACKAY BROWN
*The Sun Rising,* JOHN DONNE
*The Owl and the Pussy-Cat,* EDWARD LEAR

# EDWARD HEATH

## 1980

*There are probably few modern prime ministers who, whatever their virtues and shortcomings in public life, have had such diverse interests outside politics as Edward Heath. One cannot be certain, of course, but it is somehow difficult to imagine Margaret Thatcher, as she commands the duties of high office, seeking the consolations of great music or fine literature. Heath, on the other hand, as well as being a keen reader, enjoys making music and sailing, gregarious occupations both. Nevertheless, he remains essentially a private man and little that is personal was revealed during the recording. He does, however, and this is perhaps another way in which he differs from our current PM, display a well-developed sense of humour.*

I went in to the City to be trained as a merchant banker. On the day I arrived there I was taken by one of the senior members into his room and he pointed, just above his fireplace, to a piece of poetry (almost) which was written there; and he said, 'Young man, just read this.' And what I read was this piece written in the sixteenth century.

### *The Heir of Adventure*
**NICOLAS BRETON**

A worthy Merchant is the Heir of Adventure, whose hopes hang much upon the winds.
Upon a Wooden horse he rides through the World, and in a Merry gale makes a path through the seas.
He is a discoverer of countries and a finder-out of commodities, resolute in his attempts and royal in his Expenses.
He is the life of traffic and the Maintenance of trade, the Sailors' Master and the Soldiers' friend.
He is the Exercise of the Exchange, the honour of Credit, the observation of time, and the understanding of thrift.
His Study is Number, his Care his accounts, his Comfort his Conscience, and his Wealth his good Name.
He fears not Scylla and sails close by Charybdis, and having beaten out a Storm rides at rest in a harbour.
By his sea gain he makes his land purchase, and by the Knowledge of trade finds the Key of his treasure.
Out of his travels he makes his discourses, and from his Eye-observations brings the Model of Architecture.
He plants the Earth with foreign fruits, and knows at home what is good abroad.
He is Neat in apparel, Modest in demeanor, dainty in diet, and Civil in his Carriage.
In sum, he is the pillar of a City, the Enricher of a Country, the furnisher of a Court, and the Worthy Servant of a King.

'That,' he said, 'should guide you all your life in business.' I very soon went into politics.

And the next piece is taken from one of the greatest of our political writers, Edmund Burke. It's an essay, written in 1770, with a title which is perhaps not entirely unusual.

## *Thoughts on the Cause of the Present Discontents, 1770*

**EDMUND BURKE**

I remember an old scholastic aphorism, which says, 'that the man who lives wholly detached from others must be either an angel or a devil'. When I see in any of these detached gentlemen of our times the angelic purity, power, and beneficence, I shall admit them to be angels. In the meantime we are born only to be men. We shall do enough if we form ourselves to be good ones. It is therefore our business carefully to cultivate in our minds, to rear to the most perfect vigour and maturity, every sort of generous and honest feeling, that belongs to our nature. To bring the dispositions that are lovely in private life into the service and conduct of the commonwealth; so to be patriots as not to forget we are gentlemen. To cultivate friendships, and to incur enmities. To have both strong, but both selected; in the one, to be placable; in the other immovable. To model our principles to our duties and our situation. To be fully persuaded that all virtue which is impracticable is spurious; and rather to run the risk of falling into faults in a course which leads us to act with effect and energy, than to loiter out our days without blame and without use. Public life is a situation of power and energy; he trespasses against his duty who sleeps upon his watch, as well as he that goes over to the enemy.

George Borrow is a man who is not very often read today. He wrote at the beginning of the nineteenth century. *Lavengro*, the story of a scholar, a gypsy and a priest, appealed to me when I first read it as a young boy. I chose the next piece from it, because although to begin with it deals with death, in the second part it shows the real joy of living and the desire of people to live.

## *Lavengro*

**GEORGE BORROW**

I now wandered along the heath till I came to a place where, beside a thick furze, sat a man, his eyes fixed intently on the red ball of the setting sun.

'That's not you, Jasper?'

'Indeed, brother!'

'I've not seen you for years.'
'How should you, brother?'
'What brings you here?'
'The fight, brother.'
'Where are the tents?'
'On the old spot, brother.'
'Any news since we parted?'
'Two deaths, brother.'
'Who are dead, Jasper?'
'Father and mother, brother.'
'Where did they die?'
'Where they were sent, brother.'
'And Mrs. Herne?'
'She's alive, brother.'
'Where is she now?'
'In Yorkshire, brother.'

'What is your opinion of death, Mr. Petulengro?' said I, as I sat down beside him.

'My opinion of death, brother, is much the same as that in the old song of Pharaoh, which I have heard my grandam sing: –

"Cana marel o manus chivios andé puv,
Ta rovel pa leste o chavo ta romi".

When a man dies he is cast into the earth, and his wife and child sorrow over him. If he has neither wife nor child, then his father and mother, I suppose; and if he is quite alone in the world, why, then, he is cast into the earth, and there is the end of the matter.'

'And do you think that is the end of man?'

'There's an end of him, brother, more's the pity.'

'Why do you say so?'

'Life is sweet, brother.'

'Do you think so?'

'Think so! There's night and day, brother, both sweet things; sun, moon and stars, brother, all sweet things; there's likewise a wind on the heath. Life is very sweet, brother; who would wish to die?'

'I would wish to die. . . .'

'You talk like a Gorgio – which is the same as talking like a fool.

Were you a Rommany Chal, you would talk wiser. Wish to die, indeed! A Rommany Chal would wish to live for ever!'

'In sickness, Jasper?'

'There's the sun and stars, brother.'

'In blindness, Jasper?'

'There's the wind on the heath, brother; if I could only feel that, I would gladly live for ever. Dosta, we'll now go to the tents and put on the gloves; and I'll try to make you feel what a sweet thing it is to be alive, brother!'

Naturally you will be expecting something from me about the sea. I have chosen Walt Whitman's 'A Song for All Seas, All Ships'. These were the words which Ralph Vaughan Williams used for the Sea Symphony, his first major work:

## *A Song for All Seas, All Ships*

**WALT WHITMAN**

Behold, the sea itself,
And on its limitless, heaving breast, the ships;
See, where their white sails, bellying in the wind, speckle the
  green and blue,
See, the steamers coming and going, steaming in or out of port,
See, dusky and undulating, the long pennants of smoke.
Behold, the sea itself,
And on its limitless, heaving breast, the ships.

Verse now of a different kind: the vigour and rhythm of Kipling's 'Mine Sweepers', which for me has a particular attraction because it is about the Foreland and about the Channel. So much of my life has been spent near the Foreland and sailing in the Channel.

## *Mine Sweepers*

**RUDYARD KIPLING**

Dawn off the Foreland – the young flood making
  Jumbled and short and steep –
Black in the hollows and bright where it's breaking –
  Awkward water to sweep.
  'Mines reported in the fairway,
  'Warn all traffic and detain.

'Sent up Unity, Claribel, Assyrian, Stormcock,
and Golden Gain.'

Noon off the Foreland – the first ebb making
Lumpy and strong in the bight.
Boom after boom, and the golf-hut shaking
And the jackdaws wild with fright!
'Mines located in the fairway,
'Boats now working up the chain,
'Sweepers – Unity, Claribel, Assyrian, Stormcock,
and Golden Gain.'

Dusk off the Foreland – the last light going
And the traffic crowding through,
And five damned trawlers with their syreens blowing
Heading the whole review!
'Sweep completed in the fairway.
'No more mines remain.
'Sent back Unity, Claribel, Assyrian, Stormcock,
and Golden Gain.'

I have chosen items of prose and poetry which have not only given me pleasure, but also reflect the various interests which I have in life. It's quite natural, I think, to include the Bible, because it has great influence on one in one's early life – it certainly did on me. But much, much more than that, it contains some of the most beautiful English prose, and indeed some would say poetry, in the psalms. I've chosen a piece from Ecclesiastes. I did so because it emphasizes the importance of time in life – the importance of timing. It is true of everything which one does, and it's certainly true in politics.

## *Ecclesiastes, Chapter 3, Verses 1–15*

To every thing there is a season, and a time to every purpose under the heaven:
A time to be born, and a time to die; a time to plant, and a time to pluck up that which is planted;
A time to kill, and a time to heal; a time to break down, and a time to build up;

A time to weep, and a time to laugh; a time to mourn, and a time to dance;
A time to cast away stones, and a time to gather stones together; a time to embrace, and a time to refrain from embracing;
A time to get, and a time to lose; a time to keep, and a time to cast away;
A time to rend, and a time to sew; a time to keep silence, and a time to speak;
A time to love, and a time to hate; a time of war, and a time of peace.
What profit hath he that worketh in that wherein he laboureth?
I have seen the travail, which God hath given to the sons of men to be exercised in it.
He hath made every thing beautiful in his time: also he hath set the world in their heart, so that no man can find out the work that God maketh from the beginning to the end.
I know that there is no good in them, but for a man to rejoice, and to do good in his life.
And also that every man should eat and drink, and enjoy the good of all his labour, it is the gift of God.
I know that, whatsoever God doeth, it shall be for ever: nothing can be put to it, nor any thing taken from it: and God doeth it, that men should fear before him.
That which hath been is now; and that which is to be hath already been; and God requireth that which is past.

*Readers: Norman Rodway, Michael Williams*

*Full Selection:*
*The Heir of Adventure,* NICOLAS BRETON
*Thoughts on the Cause of the Present Discontents,* EDMUND BURKE
*On England,* STANLEY BALDWIN
*Memoirs of a Fox-Hunting Man,* SIEGFRIED SASSOON
*Collect for 4th Sunday after Easter,* THE PRAYER BOOK
*A Short History of the English People,* JOHN RICHARD GREEN
*Lavengro,* GEORGE BORROW
*Sonnet for the Madonna of the Cherries,* LORD WAVELL
*A Song for All Seas, All Ships,* WALT WHITMAN

*Mine Sweepers*, RUDYARD KIPLING
*Poet's Pub*, ERIC LINKLATER
*Pied Beauty*, GERARD MANLEY HOPKINS
*The Young Melbourne*, LORD DAVID CECIL
*Prelude to Victory*, BRIGADIER-GENERAL E. L. SPIERS
*Angel Pavement*, J. B. PRIESTLEY
*The Spanish Journey*, JULIUS MEIER-GRAEFE
*I Love All Beauteous Things*, ROBERT BRIDGES
*On His Books*, HILAIRE BELLOC
*My Early Life*, SIR WINSTON CHURCHILL
*Ecclesiastes, Chapter 3*, THE BIBLE

# *BRIAN JOHNSTON*

## *1985*

*'Oh, good Lord, I'm not a great reader, Dick Francis, that sort of thing,' was Brian Johnston's first response on being asked if he would like to present an edition of 'With Great Pleasure'. In the event he seemed to have rather underplayed himself, but even if he hadn't, it was hardly the point. As a cricket commentator and broadcaster he has been a friendly and entertaining presence on radio and television for many years. He is also, apparently, one of the most popular after-dinner speakers in the country. After a hilarious evening spent in his company I can well believe it. A sentimental man, easily moved to tears, he was visibly moved at the reading from Oscar Wilde's 'The Selfish Giant'.*

I've been lucky all my life. I had marvellous parents, brothers and sisters and I'm now very luckily possessed of a lovely wife and a family of five. And like me when I was a small boy, I think they loved *Alice in Wonderland* and *Through the Looking Glass*: it was like entering another world. I haven't chosen the Mad Hatter's tea party, although it makes me laugh, but instead here is Tweedledee telling Alice about the Walrus and the Carpenter – I think it is the first time I ever remember feeling really sorry for anyone, those poor little oysters being conned by two confidence tricksters.

## *The Walrus and the Carpenter*

**LEWIS CARROLL**

The sun was shining on the sea,
  Shining with all his might:
He did his very best to make
  The billows smooth and bright –
And this was odd, because it was
  The middle of the night.

The moon was shining sulkily,
  Because she thought the sun
Had got no business to be there
  After the day was done –
'It's very rude of him,' she said
  'To come and spoil the fun!'

The sea was wet as wet could be,
  The sands were dry as dry.
You could not see a cloud, because
  No cloud was in the sky:
No birds were flying overhead –
  There were no birds to fly.

The Walrus and the Carpenter
  Were walking close at hand:
They wept like anything to see
  Such quantities of sand:
'If this were only cleared away,'
  They said, 'it would be grand!'

'If seven maids with seven mops
  Swept it for half a year,
Do you suppose,' the Walrus said,

'That they could get it clear?'
'I doubt it,' said the Carpenter,
And shed a bitter tear.

'O Oysters, come and walk with us!'
The Walrus did beseech.
'A pleasant walk, a pleasant talk,
Along the briny beach:
We cannot do with more than four,
To give a hand to each.'

The eldest Oyster looked at him,
But never a word he said:
The eldest Oyster winked his eye,
And shook his heavy head –
Meaning to say he did not choose
To leave the oyster-bed.

But four young Oysters hurried up,
All eager for the treat:
Their coats were brushed, their faces washed,
Their shoes were clean and neat –
And this was odd, because, you know,
They hadn't any feet.

Four other Oysters followed them,
And yet another four;
And thick and fast they came at last,
And more, and more, and more –
All hopping through the frothy waves,
And scrambling to the shore.

The Walrus and the Carpenter
Walked on a mile or so,
And then they rested on a rock
Conveniently low:
And all the little Oysters stood
And waited in a row.

'The time has come,' the Walrus said,
'To talk of many things:
Of shoes – and ships – and sealing wax –

Of cabbages – and kings –
And why the sea is boiling hot –
And whether pigs have wings.'

'But wait a bit,' the Oysters cried,
'Before we have our chat;
For some of us are out of breath,
And all of us are fat.'
'No hurry!' said the Carpenter.
They thanked him much for that.

'A loaf of bread,' the Walrus said,
'Is what we chiefly need:
Pepper and vinegar besides
Are very good indeed –
Now if you're ready, Oysters dear,
We can begin to feed.'

'But not on us!' the Oysters cried,
Turning a little blue.
'After such kindness, that would be
A dismal thing to do!'
'The night is fine,' the Walrus said.
'Do you admire the view?

'It was so kind of you to come!
And you are very nice!'
The Carpenter said nothing but
'Cut us another slice.
I wish you were not quite so deaf –
I've had to ask you twice!'

'It seems a shame,' the Walrus said,
'To play them such a trick.
After we've brought them out so far,
And made them trot so quick!'
The Carpenter said nothing but
'The butter's spread too thick!'

'I weep for you,' the Walrus said:
'I deeply sympathize.'
With sobs and tears he sorted out

Those of the largest size,
Holding his pocket-handkerchief
Before his streaming eyes.

'O Oysters,' said the Carpenter,
'You've had a pleasant run!
Shall we be trotting home again?'
But answer came there none –
And this was scarcely odd, because
They'd eaten every one!

As I grew up, I think like any boy, I was very keen on comics – things like *The Little Red Mag* or *Tiger Tim's Weekly* – but by the time I was eight I'd already begun to read Conan Doyle's stories of Sherlock Holmes. We were living in Hertfordshire at the time, in the depths of the country, and our garden backed on to a big field; as I read *The Hound of the Baskervilles* I imagined that this field was Dartmoor which was haunted by this terrifying hound. It had already killed Sir Hugo and Sir Charles Baskerville, whose family had lived at Baskerville Hall for several centuries. And now the present holder of the title, Sir Henry Baskerville, was persuaded by Sherlock Holmes to act as bait in order to catch the hound, so here we have Sherlock Holmes and Doctor Watson waiting with Inspector Lestrade in a swirling fog out on the moor. It still terrifies me.

## *The Hound of the Baskervilles*
### SIR ARTHUR CONAN DOYLE

A sound of quick steps broke the silence of the moor. Crouching among the stones, we stared intently at the silver-tipped bank in front of us. The steps grew louder, and through the fog, as through a curtain, there stepped the man whom we were awaiting. He looked round him in surprise as he emerged into the clear, starlit night. Then came swiftly along the path, passed close to where we lay, and went on up the long slope behind us. As he walked he glanced continually over either shoulder, like a man who is ill at ease.

'Hist!' cried Holmes, and I heard the sharp click of a cocking pistol. 'Look out! It's coming!'

There was a thin, crisp continuous patter from somewhere in the heart of that crawling bank. The cloud was within fifty yards of where we lay, and we glared at it, all three, uncertain what horror was about to break from the heart of it. I was at Holmes' elbow, and I glanced for an instant at his face. It was pale and exultant, his eyes shining brightly in the moonlight. But suddenly they started forward in a rigid, fixed stare, and his lips parted in amazement. At the same instant Lestrade gave a yell of terror and threw himself face downwards upon the ground. I sprang to my feet, my inert hand grasping my pistol, my mind paralysed by the dreadful shape which had sprung out upon us from the shadows of the fog.

A hound it was, an enormous coal-black hound, but not such a hound as mortal eyes have ever seen. Fire burst from its open mouth, its eyes glowed with a smouldering glare, its muzzle and hackles and dewlap were outlined in flickering flame. Never in the delirious dream of a disordered brain could anything more savage, more appalling, more hellish, be conceived than that dark form and savage face which broke upon us out of the wall of fog.

With long bounds the huge black creature was leaping down the track, following hard upon the footsteps of our friend. So paralysed were we by the apparition that we allowed him to pass before we had recovered our nerve. Then Holmes and I both fired together, and the creature gave a hideous howl, which showed that one at least had hit him. He did not pause, however, but bounded onwards. Far away on the path we saw Sir Henry looking back, his face white in the moonlight, his hands raised in horror, glaring helplessly at the frightful thing which was hunting him down.

But that cry of pain from the hound had blown all our fears to the winds. If he was vulnerable he was mortal, and if we could wound him we could kill him. Never have I seen a man run as Holmes ran that night. I am reckoned fleet of foot, but he outpaced me as much as I outpaced the little professional. . . .

In front of us as we flew up the track we heard scream after scream from Sir Henry and the deep roar of the hound. I was in time to see the beast spring upon its victim, hurl him to the ground and worry at his throat. But the next instant Holmes had emptied five barrels of his revolver into the creature's flank. With a last howl of agony and a vicious snap in the air it rolled upon its back, four feet pawing furiously, and then fell limp upon its side. I stooped, panting, and pressed my pistol to the dreadful, shimmering head, but it was useless to pull the trigger. The giant hound was dead.

Sir Henry lay insensible where he had fallen. We tore away his collar, and Holmes breathed a prayer of gratitude when we saw that there was no sign of a wound and that the rescue had been in time. Already our friend's eyelids shivered and he made a feeble effort to move. Lestrade thrust his brandy-flask between the baronet's teeth, and two frightened eyes were looking up at us.

'My God!' he whispered. 'What was it? What, in Heaven's name, was it?'

'It's dead, whatever it is,' said Holmes. 'We've laid the family ghost once and for ever.'

To end I've chosen a little masterpiece, a book which I keep by my bedside. I read it frequently: it's by Alan Miller and it's about a lovable old parson called Septimus. As a curate he'd once bowled a famous English cricketer called Ulysses, but his work as a parson in the slums had prevented him from playing any more cricket. The time is now 1948 and he's very ill with heart trouble, too ill to go and see the final test against Australia at the Oval, and he was very worried that England was going to be beaten again. On the night before the Test he went to bed early feeling ill and soon fell into a deep sleep and dreamt that he'd been selected to play for England as a mystery bowler.

## *Close of Play*

**ALAN MILLER**

After a firm handshake and a confident smile from Ulysses, Septimus – closely behind his captain, and with Bedser at his side – went out with the rest of the team. When the welcoming applause had subsided, he heard the buzz that went round the ground as the spectators became aware of his plump little figure and bald head. But he didn't mind – not a bit! He knew somehow that he wasn't going to let Ulysses and the Old Country down.

Very soon Morris and Barnes were at the wicket. They looked

determined and formidable. He expected them to. After all they were great batsmen with wonderful records! He trotted down to his place in the field. The buzz was louder here, since he was only a few yards from the boundary. But he had worked for years in a London slum; he knew these kindly Cockneys. They wouldn't make fun of him! And if he did well, how they would take him to their hearts – as indeed they had done, for other reasons, years ago. No, he could hear no jeering. One wag shouted 'Good luck to you, Daddy!' But he liked that! He knew it was meant sincerely. He was tempted to turn and smile his thanks; but the game was about to begin.

Bedser bowled the first over – hefty, energetic stuff. It was a maiden; and the batsman left three tempting outswingers alone. Then came the great moment! He walked up to the wicket, and Yardley, smiling, handed him the ball. 'Good luck, old man!' he said – and dash it, the great big chap seemed a bit upset!

He gave his sweater to the umpire – a contemporary! He grinned. Did he sense what was coming? The buzzing in the crowd sank almost to silence. Doubtless the 'knowalls' were wondering how a man of his age could bowl fast – for there had been but one over with the new ball. The side knew where to field for him: they had been carefully instructed. Barnes, looking very aggressive, took his guard. He surveyed the scene and then prepared to face this new England bowler who, for some reason, had been exhumed from the past.

Septimus took but four or five short steps in his run-up. Over went his arm, and the wizardry of those long fingers began. His first ball – a very slow one – was on its way!

Barnes watched it carefully: he was taking no chances. It was well pitched up to him on the line of the off stump. He played forward, but misjudged its length. It was a leg-break – a tremendous break too! When the ball was caught at second slip, the crowd went mad; but the bat had gone nowhere near it. Barnes looked at the pitch and prodded it with his bat. Yardley, at mid-off, smiled broadly. The next ball was of a different length and a shade faster. Barnes was in two minds about it, but decided to step back and play a push shot. He was just in time. The ball kept very low. He managed to stop it with the bottom of his bat. It travelled a foot.

Septimus sent down a simple full-toss which Barnes promptly hit for six. Yardley looked inquiringly at the bowler. He got a wink in reply. The next was also a full-toss, but of a different kind. This one wasn't ground bait! Barnes went for it, but the ball did something curious in the air. It seemed to swing a lot and it changed its expected trajectory towards the end of its flight. Barnes 'failed to connect' – failed by quite a great deal! It fell about eighteen inches from the wicket, broke in smartly, and the leg stump went back. The crowd yelled – loudly and long – and Barnes, not looking very pleased, departed.

Well, Septimus continued to astonish the crowd. He bowled Bradman for a duck and took five for twenty and Australia had to follow on and they collapsed. And then with one wicket to fall Sam Loxton hit a skier down to Septimus at long leg. . . .

Up and up it went. Surely a grand six. Septimus watched it fascinated, then suddenly he realised that it might not carry the distance. By Jove, it might be a catch. Johosaphat, he'd show them he could do more than bowl. He set off at full speed along the boundary cheered frantically by the friendly crowd, madly cheered, as if he were a potential Derby winner. But alas it seemed that he would never get there in time, it looked like coming down a yard from the fence. At roughly six feet from where he judged it must fall, he made a violent effort. He might just manage it. He dived forward, at full length, his arms outstretched, his hands ready to grasp the ball. And fell flat on his face.

The next morning his wife found Septimus, lying on the bedroom floor, with his arm flung out as if he'd died trying to grasp something in his right hand. If only he could have lived a little longer, she said wistfully, it's sad to think he missed the last test. Missed the last test? Set your heart at rest dear lady, he didn't miss the last test, he won it.

*Readers: Ian Carmichael, Julia Foster*

*Full Selection:*
*I Was There,* PETER TINNISWOOD
*The Walrus and the Carpenter,* LEWIS CARROLL

*The Hound of the Baskervilles,* SIR ARTHUR CONAN DOYLE
*The Road to Mandalay,* BILLY BENNETT
*England, Their England,* A. G. MACDONELL
*The Selfish Giant,* OSCAR WILDE
*Onwards to Victory,* SIR WINSTON CHURCHILL
*The Max Miller Blue Book,* MAX MILLER
*Leave It to Jeeves,* P. G. WODEHOUSE
*Close of Play,* ALAN MILLER

# GEORGE MACBETH

## 1987

*It has been my pleasure to know George MacBeth for many years, since the time when, as the BBC's poetry producer, he included a poem of mine in Radio 3's 'Poetry Now'. He is currently presenting 'Time for Verse' on Radio 4, which gives me the opportunity to produce him! I have always enjoyed his sly wit and sense of mischief: indelibly etched on my memory is seeing him, during a brief respite from a poetry-reading tour in the West Country, striding across muddy, windswept Dartmoor dressed for the city in pinstripe suit, polished shoes, and carrying a rolled umbrella. 'If you are properly dressed you can go anywhere,' he said. I don't know about that, but we all looked less than well turned out by the time we finally reached a friendly pub.*

You can't be a Scotsman and not admire Sir Walter Scott. Scott always thought of himself as a poet and he was very proud that for several years, in his own words, he had 'had the palm' before the rise of his admired younger contemporary and friend Lord Byron. We don't enough enjoy Scott's magnificent ballads and narrative poems nowadays. They stand the test of time very well, they contain genuine feeling and they move with a real surge of rhythm.

## *Lochinvar*

### SIR WALTER SCOTT

O Young Lochinvar is come out of the west,
Through all the wide Border his steed was the best;
And save his good broadsword he weapons had none,
He rode all unarm'd and he rode all alone,
So faithful in love, and so dauntless in war,
There never was knight like the young Lochinvar.

He staid not for brake, and he stopp'd not for stone,
He swam the Eske river where ford there was none;
But ere he alighted at Netherby gate,
The bride had consented, the gallant came late:
For a laggard in love, and a dastard in war,
Was to wed the fair Ellen of brave Lochinvar.

So boldly he enter'd the Netherby Hall,
Among bride's-men, and kinsmen, and brothers and all:
Then spoke the bride's father, his hand on his sword,
(For the poor craven bridegroom said never a word),
'O come ye in peace here, or come ye in war,
Or to dance at our bridal, young Lord Lochinvar?'

The bride kiss'd the goblet: the knight took it up,
He quaff'd off the wine, and he threw down the cup.
She look'd down to blush, and she look'd up to sigh,
With a smile on her lips and a tear in her eye.
He took her soft hand, ere her mother could bar, –
'Now tread we a measure!' said Young Lochinvar.

One touch to her hand, and one word in her ear,
When they reach'd the hall-door, and the charger stood near;
So light to the croupe the fair lady he swung,
So light to the saddle before her he sprung!
'She is won! we are gone, over bank, bush, and scaur;
They'll have fleet steeds that follow,' quoth Young Lochinvar.

There was mounting 'mong Graemes of the Netherby clan;
Forsters, Fenwicks, and Musgraves, they rode and they ran:
There was racing and chasing on Cannobie Lee,
But the lost bride of Netherby ne'er did they see.
So daring in love, and so dauntless in war,
Have ye e'er heard of gallant like Young Lochinvar?

I'm sure Sir Walter would agree with me that you can't be a Scotsman with my name and not admire Shakespeare – even if the famous play with the unlucky title did persecute my childhood with endless jokes. What bloody man is this? and so on. So to set the standard we all have to fight for, here we have the bloody lady, so to call her, in full spate from Act One, Scene Five.

## *Macbeth*

### WILLIAM SHAKESPEARE

*Inverness,* MACBETH'S *Castle*
*Enter* LADY MACBETH, *reading a letter*

'They met me in the day of success; and I have learn'd by the perfect'st report they have more in them than mortal knowledge. When I burn'd in desire to question them further, they made themselves air, into which they vanish'd. Whiles I stood rapt in the wonder of it, came missives from the King, who all-hailed me "Thane of Cawdor"; by which title, before, these weird sisters saluted me, and referr'd me to the coming on of time with "Hail, king that shalt be!" This have I thought good to deliver thee, my dearest partner of greatness, that thou mightest not lose the dues of rejoicing by being ignorant of what greatness is promis'd thee. Lay it to thy heart, and farewell.'

Glamis thou art, and Cawdor; and shalt be
What thou art promised. Yet I do fear thy nature;
It is too full o' the milk of human kindness
To catch the nearest way. Thou wouldst be great;
Art not without ambition, but without
The illness should attend it; what thou wouldst highly,
That would thou holily; wouldst not play false,
And yet wouldst wrongly win; thou'dst have, great Glamis,
That which cries 'Thus thou must do, if thou have it';

And that which rather thou dost fear to do
Than wishest should be undone. Hie thee hither,
That I may pour my spirits in thine ear,
And chastise with the valour of my tongue
All that impedes thee from the golden round,
Which fate and metaphysical aid doth seem
To have thee crown'd withal. . . .

Come, you spirits
That tend on mortal thoughts! unsex me here,
And fill me from the crown to the toe top full
Of direst cruelty; make thick my blood,
Stop up the access and passage to remorse,
That no compunctious visitings of nature
Shake my fell purpose, nor keep peace between
The effect and it! Come to my woman's breasts,
And take my milk for gall, you murdering ministers,
Wherever in your sightless substances
You wait on nature's mischief! Come, thick night,
And pall thee in the dunnest smoke of hell,
That my keen knife see not the wound it makes,
Nor heaven peep through the blanket of the dark
To cry 'Hold, hold!'

When I went up to Oxford in the early fifties the vogue in literary circles was very much for a kind of rigidly corseted metaphysical poem which owed a good deal more to William Empson than Andrew Marvell. But I did very quickly start to gulp down a delicious diet of minor Caroline lyricists like Suckling and Carew and one or two more far-flung classically minded writers like the formidable Dr Johnson. Here is his magisterial and moral elegy on the life of a friend who was a doctor.

## *Lines on the Death of Mr Levett*

**SAMUEL JOHNSON**

Condemn'd to Hope's delusive mine,
As on we toil from day to day,
By sudden blast or slow decline,
Our social comforts drop away.

Well try'd through many a varying year,
  See LEVETT to the grave descend;
Officious, innocent, sincere,
  Of ev'ry friendless name the friend.

Yet still he fills Affection's eye,
  Obscurely wise, and coarsely kind,
Nor, letter'd arrogance, deny
  Thy praise to merit unrefin'd.

When fainting Nature call'd for aid,
  And hov'ring Death prepar'd the blow,
His vigorous remedy display'd
  The pow'r of art without the show.

In Misery's darkest caverns known,
  His ready help was ever nigh,
Where hopeless Anguish pours his groan,
  And lonely want retir'd to die.

No summons mock'd by chill delay,
  No petty gains disdain'd by pride;
The modest wants of ev'ry day
  The toil of ev'ry day supply'd.

His virtues walk'd their narrow round,
  Nor made a pause, nor left a void;
And sure th'Eternal Master found
  His single talent well employ'd.

The busy day, the peaceful night,
  Unfelt, uncounted, glided by;
His frame was firm, his powers were bright,
  Though now his eightieth year was nigh.

Then, with no throbs of fiery pain,
  No cold gradations of decay,
Death broke at once the vital chain,
  And freed his soul the nearest way.

Not many poets can achieve that sort of emotional intensity right on the brink of prose. I kept the Levett poem in mind when I was trying to write my own fledgling elegy for an elderly Sheffield cutler, who took me into his house when my mother died. But I couldn't live up to the Johnson standard. I couldn't live up to the Louis MacNeice one either when I joined the BBC in 1955 as a general trainee. But it was the fact of MacNeice being employed by the BBC that made me feel it would be an organization worth working for. I knew that he'd been able to write the best radio play ever – *The Dark Tower* – while employed by Features Department and I had a fantasy I could follow in his footsteps. But I ended up as a minor cultural functionary in Talks Department. Here, anyway, is MacNeice in another challenging vein, illustrating how a foreigner, an Ulsterman to boot, can catch the ironical swing and drive of the Scottish national instrument, as no one else has done.

## *Bagpipe Music*

**LOUIS MACNEICE**

It's no go the merrygoround, it's no go the rickshaw,
All we want is a limousine and a ticket for the peepshow.
Their knickers are made of crêpe-de-chine, their shoes are made
  of python,
Their halls are lined with tiger rugs and their walls with heads of
  bison.

John MacDonald found a corpse, put it under the sofa,
Waited till it came to life and hit it with a poker,
Sold its eyes for souvenirs, sold its blood for whisky,
Kept its bones for dumb-bells to use when he was fifty.

It's no go the Yogi-Man, it's no go Blavatsky,
All we want is a bank balance and a bit of skirt in a taxi.

Annie MacDougall went to milk, caught her foot in the heather,
Woke to hear a dance record playing of Old Vienna.
It's no go your maidenheads, it's no go your culture,
All we want is a Dunlop tyre and the devil mend the puncture.

The Laird o' Phelps spent Hogmanay declaring he was sober,
Counted his feet to prove the fact and found he had one foot
  over.
Mrs Carmichael had her fifth, looked at the job with repulsion,

Said to the midwife 'Take it away; I'm through with
 over-production'.

It's no go the gossip column, it's no go the Ceilidh,
All we want is a mother's help and a sugar-stick for the baby.

Willie Murray cut his thumb, couldn't count the damage,
Took the hide of an Ayrshire cow and used it for a bandage.
His brother caught three hundred cran when the seas were
 lavish,
Threw the bleeders back in the sea and went upon the parish.

It's no go the Herring Board, it's no go the Bible,
All we want is a packet of fags when our hands are idle.

It's no go the picture palace, it's no go the stadium,
It's no go the country cot with a pot of pink geraniums,
It's no go the Government grants, it's no go the elections,
Sit on your arse for fifty years and hang your hat on a pension.

It's no go my honey love, it's no go my poppet;
Work your hands from day to day, the winds will blow the
 profit.
The glass is falling hour by hour, the glass will fall for ever,
But if you break the bloody glass you won't hold up the
 weather.

The vernacular line, the kind of low style that took over after the death of Dylan Thomas, reaches a fine climax in the best of Adrian Mitchell, the doyen of poetry performers on the hustings, and a poet who once said that a poet should shake – when reading his own work aloud – like an engine shakes. Well, I think there's enough energy in the political Mitchell to need a belt across its bonnet like an old Morgan.

'Tell Me Lies About Vietnam' galvanized a generation, and then 'An Oxford Hysteria of English Poetry' set us all laughing all the way to the voting booth. It's a genuinely hilarious whistle-stop tour of the main landmarks in our great national heritage, those dusty volumes lining the library shelves and waiting to burst into flame at the spark of a new imagination. Well, here's an imagination that manages to incorporate a good deal of affection for the old lady, the Muse, under its abrasively witty surface.

## *The Oxford Hysteria of English Poetry*

**ADRIAN MITCHELL**

Back in the caveman days business was fair.
Used to turn up at Wookey Hole,
Plenty of action down the Hole
Nights when it wasn't raided.
They'd see my bear-gut harp
And the mess at the back of my eyes
And 'Right,' they'd say, 'make poetry.'
So I'd slam away at the three basic chords
And go into the act –
A story about sabre-toothed tigers with a comic hero;
A sexy one with an anti-wife-clubbing twist –
Good progressive stuff mainly,
Get ready for the Bronze Age, all that,
And soon it would be 'Bring out the woad!'
Yeah, woad. We used to get high on woad.

The Vikings only wanted sagas
Full of gigantic deadheads cutting off each other's vitals
Or Beowulf Versus the Bog People.
The Romans weren't much better,
Under all that armour you could tell they were soft
With their central heating
And poets with names like Horace.

Under the Normans the language began to clear,
Became a pleasure to write in,
Yes, write in, by now everyone was starting
To write down poems.
Well, it saved memorizing and improvising
And the peasants couldn't get hold of it.
Soon there were hundreds of us,
Most of us writing under the name of Geoffrey Chaucer.

Then suddenly we were knee-deep in sonnets.
Holinshed ran a headline:
BONANZA FOR BARDS.

It got fantastic –
Looning around from the bear-pit to the Globe,
All those freak-outs down the Mermaid,
Kit Marlowe coming on like Richard the Two,
A virgin Queen in a ginger wig
And English poetry in full whatsit –
Bloody fantastic, But I never found any time
To do any writing till Willy finally flipped –
Smoking too much of the special stuff
Sir Walter Raleigh was pushing.

Cromwell's time I spent on cultural committees.

Then Charles the Second swung down from the trees
And it was sexual medley time
And the only verses they wanted
Were epigrams on Chloe's breasts
But I only got published on the back of her left knee-cap.
Next came Pope and Dryden
So I went underground.
Don't mess with the mafia.

Then suddenly – WOOMF –
It was the Ro-man-tic Re-viv-al
And it didn't matter how you wrote,
All the public wanted was a hairy great image.
Before they'd even print you
You had to smoke opium, die of consumption,
Fall in love with your sister
Or drown in the Mediterranean (not at Brighton).
My publisher said: 'I'll have to remainder you
Unless you go and live in a lake or something
Like this bloke Wordsworth.'

After that there were about
A thousand years of Tennyson
Who got so bored with himself
That he changed his name
To Kipling at half-time.

Strange that Tennyson should be
Remembered for his poems really,
We always thought of him
As a golfer.

There hasn't been much time
For poetry since the 'twenties
What with leaving the Communist Church
To join the Catholic Party
And explaining why in the C.I.A. Monthly.
Finally I was given the Chair of Comparative Ambiguity
At Armpit University, Java.
It didn't keep me busy,
But it kept me quiet.
It seemed like poetry had been safely tucked up for the night.

*Readers: John Shedden, Rose McBain*

*Full Selection:*
*Lochinvar,* SIR WALTER SCOTT
*Macbeth,* WILLIAM SHAKESPEARE
*November Eyes,* JAMES ELROY FLECKER
*Lines on the Death of Mr Levett,* SAMUEL JOHNSON
*Bagpipe Music,* LOUIS MACNEICE
*Thistles,* TED HUGHES
*A Study of Reading Habits,* PHILIP LARKIN
*Indoor Games Near Newbury,* JOHN BETJEMAN
*Do Not Go Gentle Into That Good Night,* DYLAN THOMAS
*Mort aux Chats,* PETER PORTER
*Dirge,* KENNETH FEARING
*The Oxford Hysteria of English Poetry,* ADRIAN MITCHELL
*The Flower,* GEORGE HERBERT

# BERNARD MILES

## 1971

*What any presenter of 'With Great Pleasure' comes to realize, sooner or later, is that however urbane and well guarded his or her linking script may be, much of the essential personality is revealed by the choice of items. Sir Bernard came across as well balanced and 'all of a piece'. He claimed to be somewhat of a magpie in his reading, 'a bit here and a bit there' and confessed, as many have done, that making his selection took many hours, before delivering a script left over from a pile of his favourite passages 3 feet 6 inches high. He was clearly a warm and loving man, and his love of the sea and life on the water must have had no small a part to play in his drive to bring into being, on the banks of the Thames, the Mermaid Theatre.*

One of the chief joys of this occasion is that I am doing it with my wife – indeed I am giving her the whole fee – and we are going to kick off with a pair of love letters, or at any rate letters about love.

The first was written on April 6th, 1761 by the famous Madame du Barry, Mistress of Louis XV, to a boyfriend in the days when she was still on the lower rungs of the ladder, serving in a millinery shop.

### *A Letter*

**MADAME DU BARRY**

Yes, my dear friend, I have told you, and repeat it: I love you dearly. You certainly said the same thing to me, but on your side it is only impetuosity; directly after the first enjoyment, you would think of me no more. I begin to know the world. I will tell you what I suggest, now: pay attention. I don't want to remain a shopgirl, but a little more my own mistress, and would therefore like to find someone to keep me. If I did not love you, I would try to get money from you; I would say to you, You shall begin by renting a room for me and furnishing it; only as you told me that you were not rich, you can take me to your own place. It will not cost you any more rent, nor more for your table and the rest of your housekeeping. To keep me and my head-dress will be the only expense, and for those give me three or four hundred francs a month, and that will include everything. Thus we could both live happily, and you would never again have to complain about my refusal. If you love me, accept this proposal; but if you do not love me, then let each of us try his luck elsewhere. Good-bye, I embrace you heartily.

Still on the never cloying subject of sex, I now turn to a delicious letter written by a wise and worldly man, the great American Benjamin Franklin, to a young anonymous friend who had written asking his advice on a very delicate personal problem. The date is June 25th, 1745.

## *A Letter*

### BENJAMIN FRANKLIN

My dear Friend,
I know of no medicine fit to diminish the violent natural inclination you mention, and if I did, I think I should not communicate it to you. Marriage is the proper remedy. It is the man and woman united that make the complete human being. A single man is an incomplete animal. He resembles the odd half of a pair of scissors.

But if you will not take this counsel and persist in thinking a commerce with sex inevitable, then I repeat my further advice that in all your amours you should prefer older women to younger ones.

My reasons are these:

1. Because when women cease to be handsome they study to be good. They learn to do a thousand services, small and great,

and are the most tender and useful of friends when you are sick.

2. Because through more experience they are more prudent and discreet. And if the affair should happen to be known, considerate people might be rather inclined to excuse an older woman, who would kindly take care of a younger man, and prevent his ruining his health and fortune among mercenary ladies of pleasure.
3. Because in every animal that walks upright the deficiency of the fluids that fill the muscles appears first in the highest parts, the lower parts continuing to the last as plump as ever. So that covering all above with a basket, and regarding only what is below the girdle, it is impossible of two women to tell an old one from a young one. In the dark all cats are grey.
4. Because the compunction is less. The having made a young girl miserable may give you frequent bitter reflection; none of which can attend the making an older woman happy.
5. And lastly, They are so grateful!

Now another letter, a serious one. It was written by the great Thomas Henry Huxley, contemporary and fellow worker with Charles Darwin, to the Reverend Charles Kingsley. Huxley had a favourite son who died young. This letter was written a few days after the boy's body had been put into the earth, in September 1860. Let me just add a confession of my own. Although I find it almost impossible to be a formal Christian, I am incorrigibly religious. And this letter expresses more perfectly than ever I could my own humble position in this eternal argument.

## *A Letter*

### THOMAS HENRY HUXLEY

As I stood beside the coffin of my little son the other day, with my mind bent on anything but disputation, the officiating minister read, as a part of his duty, the words, 'If the dead rise not again, let us eat and drink, for to-morrow we die.' I cannot tell you how inexpressibly they shocked me. St. Paul had neither wife nor child, or he must have known that his alternative involved a blasphemy against all that was best and noblest in human nature.

I could have laughed with scorn. What! Because I am face to face with irreparable loss, because I have given back to the source from whence it came, the cause of a great happiness, still retaining through all my life the blessings which have sprung and will spring from that cause, I am to renounce my manhood, and, howling, grovel in bestiality? Why, the very apes know better, and if you shoot their young, the poor brutes grieve their grief out and do not immediately seek distraction in a gorge.

Kicked into the world a boy without guide or training, or with worse than none, I confess to my shame that few men have drunk deeper of all kinds of sin than I. Happily, my course was arrested in time – before I had earned absolute destruction – and for long years I have been slowly and painfully climbing, with many a fall, towards better things. And when I look back, what do I find to have been the agents of my redemption? The hope of immortality or of future reward? I can honestly say that for these fourteen years such a consideration has not entered my head. No, I can tell you exactly what has been at work. Sartor Resartus led me to know that a deep sense of religion was compatible with the entire absence of theology. Secondly, science and her methods gave me a resting-place independent of authority and tradition. Thirdly, love opened up to me a view of the sanctity of human nature, and impressed me with a deep sense of responsibility.

If in the supreme moment when I looked down into my boy's grave my sorrow was full of submission and without bitterness, it is because these agencies have worked upon me, and not because I have ever cared whether my poor personality shall remain distinct for ever from the All from whence it came and whither it goes.

And thus, my dear Kingsley, you will understand what my position is. I may be quite wrong, and in that case I know I shall have to pay the penalty for being wrong. But I can only say with Martin Luther, 'Gott helfe mir, Ich kann nichts anders'. 'God help me, I can do no other'.

Many years ago Josephine and I went to Florence and into the Medici Chapel where lie Michelangelo's great marble figures of Night and Morning. We were the only two people there, it was in the evening, the attendant had gone off, and in the warm evening light the two great female figures really seemed alive, soft and warm, and I went up to one of them and gave way to the temptation to lay my hand between her thighs, hoping . . . certainly for the moment captured by the sense that this was not marble at all, but living flesh.

Well now, in the many choosings and re-choosings I made whilst putting together this programme, what I was never tempted to omit was three poems of Emily Dickinson. She was another extraordinary American, a New Englander, writing in the middle of the last century and endowed with a real genius for capturing the essence of an idea or situation in the most sharp and piercing language.

## *The Snake*

**EMILY DICKINSON**

A narrow fellow on the grass
Occasionally rides;
You may have met him, – did you not,
His notice sudden is!
The grass divides as with a comb,
A spotted shaft is seen;
And then it closes at your feet
And opens further on.
He likes a boggy acre,
A floor too cool for corn.
Yet when a child, and barefoot,
I more than once, at noon,
Have passed, I thought, a whip-lash
Unbraiding in the sun
When stooping to secure it,
It wrinkled and was gone.
Several of nature's people
I know, and they know me;
I feel for them a transport
Of cordiality;
But never met this fellow,
Attended or alone,
Without a tighter breathing,
And zero at the bone.

The second poem communicates her delight in simply being alive:

### *Leaning Against the Sun*
**EMILY DICKINSON**

I taste a liquor never brewed,
From tankards scooped in pearl;
Not all the vats upon the Rhine
Yield such an alcohol!
Inebriate of air am I,
And debauchee of dew,
Reeling, through endless summer days,
From inns of molten blue.
When landlords turn the drunken bee
Out of the foxglove's door,
When butterflies renounce their drams,
I shall but drink the more!
Till seraphs swing their snowy hats,
And saints to windows run,
To see the little tippler
Leaning against the sun!

The third poem describes the aftermath of death.

### *The Bustle in a House*
**EMILY DICKINSON**

The bustle is a house,
  The morning after death
In solemnest of industries
  Enacted upon earth, –
The sweeping up the heart,
  And putting love away
We shall not want to use again
  Until eternity.

Now to a different kind of aftermath, an acute comment from a little known lady, Geraldine Jewsbury writing to Jane Carlyle in 1843. I'm sure you've been in love at one time or another and I'm sure, like me, you've all fallen out of love, and this letter expresses the amazing reappraisal that one goes through when it's all over and one's temperature is back to normal.

## *A Letter*

**GERALDINE JEWSBURY**

When people are in love, they are in a magnetic state, and are very much astonished at themselves when they come to their senses. The other night the man who caused me more good and evil feeling than I ever knew, before or since the three years his influence lasted, ———, called here. I am frightened when I think of the last year, and yet even that one is now like a tale I have read – has no more to do with me, my present me, than the woes of Dido! Well, as I said, that very man came in the other evening, and stayed some time; he is really the most prosy, boring, wearisome, commonplace person Nature has ever created. Once, and not so long ago, that hour would have gilded a week, and now it required an effort of politeness not to give an intelligible hint to shorten his visit.

Now to a very favourite theme, the sea. Here is a letter from a boy named Sam who served on the *Royal Sovereign* under Admiral Collingwood. He's writing home to his father in a Yorkshire village and he's just taken part in the battle of Trafalgar, one of the most desperate and bloody of all sea actions.

## *A Letter*

**SAM**

Honoured Father,
This comes to tell you I am alive and hearty except three fingers; but that's not much, it might have been my head. I told brother Tom I should like to see a greadly battle, and I have seen one, and we have peppered the Combined Fleet rarely and they fought us pretty tightish, for French and Spanish. Three of our mess are killed, and four more of us winged. But to tell you the truth of it, when the game began, I wished myself at Warnborough with my plough again; but when they had given us one duster, and I found myself snug and tight, I set to in good earnest, and thought

no more about being killed than if I were at Murrell Green Fair, and I was presently as busy and as black as a collier. How my fingers got knocked over-board I don't know but off they are, and I never missed them till I wanted them. You can see, by my writing, it was my left hand, so I can write to you and fight for my King and Country still. We have taken a rare parcel of ships, but the wind is so rough we cannot bring them home, else I should be rolling in money, so we are busy smashing 'em and blowing 'em up wholesale.

But our dear Admiral Nelson is killed. So we have paid pretty sharply for licking 'em. I never set eyes on him, for which I am both sorry and glad; for to be sure I should like to have seen him – but then all the men in our ship who have seen him are sicker than toads, they have done nothing but blast their eyes and cry ever since he was killed. God bless you! Chaps that fought like the devil, sit down and cry like a wench. I am still in Royal Sovereign, but Admiral [Collingwood] has left her, so she's like a horse without a bridle; he is in a frigate now so he can be here and there and everywhere, for he's as bold as a lion. For all he can cry! – I saw his tears with my own eyes, when the boat hailed us and said Lord Nelson was dead. So no more at present from your dutiful son.

Sam (Royal Sovereign) 1805

*Readers: Sir Bernard and Lady Miles*

*Full Selection:*
*A Letter,* MADAME DU BARRY
*A Letter,* BENJAMIN FRANKLIN
*Ah, Are You Digging on My Grave,* THOMAS HARDY
*A Letter,* THOMAS HENRY HUXLEY
*Epitaph,* CHURCHYARD AT BOLSOVER
*The Elgin Marbles,* BENJAMIN ROBERT HAYDON
*The Snake,* EMILY DICKINSON
*Leaning Against the Sun,* EMILY DICKINSON
*The Bustle in a House,* EMILY DICKINSON
*A Letter,* GERALDINE JEWSBURY
*A Letter,* SAILOR ON HMS 'ELGAR'

# DESMOND MORRIS

## 1979

*Desmond Morris assured us in his programme that all the pieces he chose were from his library shelves. He acknowledged the temptation to rush out to the nearest bookshop and buy an armful of impressive classics 'to try and convince people how widely read you are', but resisted it. Most of the excerpts came from books he had bought a long time ago. Being a full-time writer, he conceded, gives him little time to read for pleasure. Nonetheless he retains a keen appreciation of poetry and the process of writing it.*

It began for me when I was at boarding school and my botany master introduced me to the then modern poets. Auden and Isherwood became my firm favourites. I found their choice of images deeply impressive and they have lingered in my mind ever since.

### *The Dog Beneath the Skin*

W. H. AUDEN and CHRISTOPHER ISHERWOOD

A man and a dog are entering a city: They are approaching a
  centre of culture:
First the suburban dormitories spreading over fields,

Villas on vegetation like saxifrage on stone,
Isolated from each other like cases of fever
And uniform in design, uniform as nurses.
To each a lean-to shed, containing a well-oiled engine of escape.
Section these dwellings: expose the life of a people
Living by law and the length of a reference,
See love in its disguises and the losses of the heart,
Cats and old silver inspire heroic virtues
And psychic fields, accidentally generated, destroy whole families.
Extraordinary tasks are set: a ploughman's hand acquires the most exquisite calligraphy,
A scheme is prepared for draining the North sea, with the aid of books from the local library:
One has a vision in the bathroom after a family quarrel: he kneels on the cork mat:
A naturalist leaves in a cab in time for the Breaking of the meres.
A youth with boils lies face down in bed, his mother over him;
Tenderly she squeezes from his trembling body the last dregs of his childhood.

Writer, be glib: please them with scenes of theatrical bliss and horror,
Whose own slight gestures tell their doom with a subtlety quite foreign to the stage.
For who patiently tell, tell of their sorrow
Without let or variation of season, streaming up in parallel from the little houses
And unabsorbed by their ironic treasures
Exerts on the rigid dome of the unpierced sky its enormous pressures?

I was beginning to find the natural world almost overwhelming – there were so many species I wanted to study, and there just wasn't enough time. I began to concentrate on reptiles and amphibians – toads and snakes in particular. They were unpopular enough to appeal to my rebel spirit. I bought a small book of animal poems and in it I was delighted to find a section dealing with my favourite creatures, including this beautiful poem.

## *Snake*

**D. H. LAWRENCE**

A snake came to my water-trough
On a hot, hot day, and I in pyjamas for the heat,
To drink there.

In the deep, strange-scented shade of the great dark carob tree
I came down the steps with my pitcher
And must wait, must stand and wait, for there he was at the trough before me.

He reached down from a fissure in the earth-wall in the gloom
And trailed his yellow-brown slackness soft-bellied down, over the edge of the stone trough
And rested his throat upon the stone bottom,
And where the water had dripped from the tap, in a small clearness,
He sipped with his straight mouth,
Softly drank through his straight gums, into his slack long body,
Silently.

Someone was before me at my water-trough,
And I, like a second comer, waiting.

He lifted his head from his drinking, as cattle do,
And looked at me vaguely, as drinking cattle do,
And flickered his two-forked tongue from his lips, and mused a moment,
And stooped and drank a little more,
Being earth-brown, earth-golden from the burning bowels of the earth.
On the day of Sicilian July, with Etna smoking.

The voice of my education said to me
He must be killed,
For in Sicily the black, black snakes are innocent, the gold are venomous.

And voices in me said, If you were a man
You would take a stick and break him now, and finish him off.

But must I confess how I liked him,
How glad I was he had come like a guest in quiet, to drink at my water-trough
And depart peaceful, pacified, and thankless,
Into the burning bowels of this earth?

Was it cowardice, that I dared not kill him?
Was it perversity, that I longed to talk to him?
Was it humility, to feel so honoured?
I felt so honoured.

And yet those voices:
*'If you were not afraid, you would kill him!'*

And truly I was afraid, I was most afraid,
But even so, honoured still more
That he should seek my hospitality
From out the dark door of the secret earth.

He drank enough
And lifted his head, dreamily, as one who has drunken,
And flickered his tongue like a forked night on the air, so black,
Seeming to lick his lips,
And looked around like a god, unseeing, into the air,
And slowly turned his head,
And slowly, very slowly, as if thrice adream,
Proceeded to draw his slow length curving round
And climb again the broken bank of my wall-face.

And as he put his head into that dreadful hole,
And as he slowly drew up, snake-easing his shoulders, and entered farther,
A sort of horror, a sort of protest against his withdrawing into that horrid black hole,
Deliberately going into the blackness, and slowly drawing himself after,
Overcame me now his back was turned.

I looked around, I put down my pitcher,
I picked up a clumsy log
And threw it at the water-trough with a clatter.

I think it did not hit him,
But suddenly that part of him that was left behind convulsed in undignified haste,
Writhed like lightning, and was gone
Into the black hole, the earth-lipped fissure in the wall-front,
At which, in the intense still noon, I stared with fascination.

And immediately I regretted it.
I thought how paltry, how vulgar, what a mean act!
I despised myself and the voices of my accursed human education.

And I thought of the albatross,
And I wished he would come back, my snake.

For he seemed to me again like a king,
Like a king in exile, uncrowned in the underworld,
Now due to be crowned again.

And so, I missed my chance with one of the lords
Of life.
And I have something to expiate:
A pettiness.

I was quite oblivious of any Freudian undertones there might have been in that poem. To me it was simply a perfect comment on the clash between the joy of observing nature and the desire to interfere with it. It was a conflict that was very much present in my own life and it was only slowly, very slowly, that the urge to watch overpowered the juvenile excitement of hunting, catching and keeping animals. I spent more and more time just sitting, looking at animals in the wild and, as the years went by, there were times when I felt I even preferred their company to that of my own species. Walt Whitman seemed to echo these feelings in this famous, short poem.

### *Animals*

**WALT WHITMAN**

I think I could turn and live with animals,
they are so placid and self-contain'd,

I stand and look at them long and long.
They do not sweat and whine about their condition.
They do not lie awake in the dark and weep for their sins,
They do not make me sick discussing their duty to God.
Not one is dissatisfied, not one is demented
  with the mania of owning things,
Not one kneels to another nor to his kind
  that lived thousands of years ago.
Not one is respectable or unhappy over the whole earth.

Although I liked the idea behind that poem, I was a bit worried about how he could be so sure that animals were never unhappy, or dissatisfied. And I had seen racehorses steaming after a race, so that I knew that some of them could sweat. He seemed to have got some of his facts wrong, but his heart was in the right place, so I forgave him. But my own studies, when I eventually became a zoology student at university, were more and more concerned with the objective analysis of animal behaviour and less and less with animal poetry. Later at Oxford I came under the influence of the great ethologists Niko Tinbergen and Konrad Lorenz. Lorenz, I remember, told me that the only time animals made him laugh was when they were making *people* look ridiculous.

Every meeting with Konrad was full of laughter – in fact I think it's true that almost every great man I have encountered, no matter how serious in his public role, has always been full of humour in his private moments. I have found this true of scientists and artists alike. When I was lucky enough to meet Dylan Thomas, shortly before his last fatal trip to America, he was no exception. And for that reason, in choosing something from his writings, I have selected the one occasion on which he allowed himself to be outrageously funny in print. Tony Hubbard, a friend of mine from my army days, had started a small magazine called *Circus*. It didn't last long, but in its first two issues, in April and May 1950, he persuaded Dylan to contribute a double piece on 'How to be a Poet'. Dylan called it *The Ascent of Parnassus Made Easy, a Worldly Lecture in Two Parts.* Here are brief extracts from each part, in which he lampoons two imaginary poets.

## *The Ascent of Parnassus Made Easy*
### DYLAN THOMAS

I do not intend to ask, let alone to answer, the question, 'Is poetry a Good Thing?' but only, 'Can Poetry Be Made Good Business?'

I shall, to begin with, introduce to you, with such comments as may or may not be necessary, a few of the main types of poets who have made the social and financial grade.

First, though not in order of importance, is the poet who has emerged docketed 'lyrical', from the Civil Service. He can be divided, so far as his physical appearance goes, into two types. He is either thin, not to say of a shagged out appearance, with lips as fulsome, sensual, and inviting as a hen's ovipositor, bald from all too maculate birth, his eyes made small and reddened by reading books in French, a language he cannot understand, in an attic in the provinces while young and repellent, his voice like the noise of a mouse's nail on tinfoil, his nostrils transparent, his breath grey; or else he is jowled and bushy, with curved pipe and his nose full of dottle, the look of all Sussex in his stingo'd eyes, his burry tweeds smelling of the dogs he loathes, with a voice like a literate airedale's that has learnt its vowels by correspondence course, and an intimate friend of Chesterton's whom he never met. Dropped into the Civil Service at an age when many of our young poets now are running away to Broadcasting House, today's equivalent of the Sea, he is at first lost to sight in the mountains of red tape which, in future years, he is so mordantly, though with a wry and puckered smile, to dismiss in a paragraph in his *Around and About My Shelves*. After a few years, he begins to peer out from the forms and files in which he leads his ordered nibbling life, and picks up a cheese crumb here, a dropping there, in his ink-stained thumbs. And soon he learns that a poem in a Civil Service magazine is, if not a step up the ladder, at least a lick in the right direction. And he writes a poem. It is, of course, about Nature: it confesses a wish to escape from the humdrum routine and embrace the unsophisticated life of the farm labourer: he desires, though without scandal, to wake up with the birds: he expresses the opinion that a ploughshare, not a pen, best fits his little strength: a decorous pantheist, he is one with the rill, the rhyming mill, the rosy-bottomed milkmaid, the russet-cheeked rat-catcher, swains, swine, pipits, pippins. You can smell the country in his poem, the fields, the flowers, the armpits of Triptolemus, the barns, the byres, the hay and, most of all, the corn.

And now we must move to see for a moment a very different kind of poet, whom we shall call Cedric. To follow in Cedric's footsteps – (he'd love you to, and would never call a policeman unless it was that frightfully sinister sergeant you see sometimes in Mecklenburgh Square, just like an El Greco) – you must be born twilightly into the middle classes, go to one of the correct schools – (which, of course, you must loathe, for it is essential, from the first, to be misunderstood) – and arrive at the University with your reputation already established as a coming poet and looking, if possible, something between a Guards' officer and a fashionable photographer's doxy.

So here is Cedric, known already to the discerning few for his sensitive poems about golden limbs, sun-jewelled fronds, the ambrosia of the first shy kiss in the delicate-traceried caverns of the moon (really the school boot-cupboard), at the threshold of fame and the world laid out before him like a row of balletomanes. If this were the 'twenties', Cedric's first book of poems, published while he was still an undergraduate, might be called *Asps and Lutes*. It would be nostalgic for a life that never was. It would be world-weary. (He once saw the world, out of a train carriage window: it looked unreal.) It would be a carefully garish mixture, a cunningly evocative pudding full of plums pulled from the Sitwells and Sacheverell other people, a mildly cacophonous hothouse of exotic horticultural and comic-erotic bric-a-brac, from which I extract these typical lines:

> 'A cornucopia of phalluses
> Cascade on the vermillion palaces
> In arabesques and syrup
>   rigadoons;
> Quince-breasted Circes of the
>   zenanas
> Do catch this rain of cherry-
>   wigged bananas
> And saraband beneath the raspberry
>   moons.'

*Readers: Freddie Jones, Brenda Kaye*

*Full Selection:*
*The Dog Beneath the Skin*, W. H. AUDEN and CHRISTOPHER ISHERWOOD
*The Beast in Me*, JAMES THURBER
*Snake*, D. H. LAWRENCE
*Animals*, WALT WHITMAN
*The Ascent of Parnassus Made Easy*, DYLAN THOMAS
*Children's Letters to God*
*Discretion*, ROGER McGOUGH
*Men*, DOROTHY PARKER
*Guarantee*, PHILIP OAKES
*In His Own Write*, JOHN LENNON
*The Fate of Felicity Fark in the Land of the Media*, CLIVE JAMES
*A World on the Wane*, CLAUDE LÉVI-STRAUSS

# PETER NICHOLS

## 1983

*On the opening night of one of Peter Nichols' plays I found myself on the outside balcony of a theatre in Shaftesbury Avenue placing smiley lanterns on the balustrade. The evening had started uneventfully enough. I had been sent by 'Kaleidoscope' to interview the playwright, record a brief scene with Albert Finney and the other actors and watch the play. Nichols was charming, if nervous, whilst the cast were in high good humour. The producer was Michael Medwin and the idea of the lanterns was his. Thirty minutes before curtain-up he realized that there was no-one left to undertake this precarious task but him and me. Thus for the first time in the West End I had my face if not my name in lights!*

Ours was not a literary family and my staple reading as a boy was a set of Odhams Press editions of children's classics, which luckily included *Tales of Robin Hood, Stories from Grimm*, Hans Andersen and the *Arabian Nights, Gulliver's Travels* and *Robinson Crusoe*. Otherwise I remember only the *William* books by Richmal Crompton, an American publication called *Believe It Or Not* and Rudyard Kipling's *Just-So Stories*. I still have my copy of the last, a present from an uncle for my eighth birthday. I wish I'd kept *Believe It Or Not*, which was a sort of freak show in book form, a precursor of *The Guinness Book of Records*, but with more emphasis on savage tribes who played football with a skull or how many people could stand on each other's heads inside the Statue of Liberty.

So, nothing from my childhood but a poem *about* children. It's on the birth of Christ and it's by the sixteenth-century Jesuit, Robert Southwell, who was executed for his allegiance to the Pope in 1595. His devotional poems are eloquent assertions of faith over common sense. I wish I could believe that innocence and goodness will prevail, but all my observation of life tells me they won't. Southwell says they will in his poem.

## *This Little Babe*

**ROBERT SOUTHWELL**

This little babe so few days old
Is come to rifle Satan's fold;
All earth doth at his presence quake
Though he himself for cold do shake;
For in this weak, unarméd wise
The Gates of Hell he will surprise.

With tears he fights and wins the field,
His naked breast stands for a shield;
His battering shot are babeish cries,
His arrows looks weeping eyes,
His martial ensigns Cold and Need
And feeble flesh his warrior's steed.

His camp is pitchéd in a stall,
His bulwark but a broken wall;
The crib his trench, haystacks his stakes,

Of shepherds he his muster makes;
And thus, as sure his bow to wound,
The angels' trumps alarum sound.

My soul, with Christ join thou in fight;
Stick to the tents that he hath pight.
Within his crib is surest ward;
This little Babe will be thy guard.
If thou wilt foil thy foes with joy,
Then flit not from this heavenly Boy.

Does the poet's subsequent torture and death prove he was wrong? Does human history ever since? Well, I'm an atheist but can still be moved to tears by Handel's *Messiah*. My religious experience as a child can be quickly dealt with. For two weeks I was a chorister in our parish church of St Bartholomew. One day during morning service the organist suffered such noisy wind that I literally fainted with laughter. I woke up being carried from the church head down by the muscular vicar. After that I seldom entered a church again until I started looking at architecture in my aesthetic twenties.

Falling in love was another experience I somehow missed. Everyone around me in wartime England was pursuing somebody else as though sex had just been discovered. Which, in many cases, it probably had. The quondam – I like that word, it means previously – the quondam sober women of Ashley Down were hurling themselves at successive waves of American soldiers now billeted in the orphanage. And I hung out in the milk bars feeding the juke-boxes and hoping some of that blatant sexiness would rub off on me. It's hard to realize how prim the official culture was. Real life was bursting out all over, GIs of all shades from sallow to black were buying British womanhood with Lucky Strikes and nylons, but not a hint of it got on to the BBC and not much more into the papers. This is perhaps why people of my age are generally fond of erotic literature, soft porn and what was known in my family as 'language'. If I so much as said 'damn' my father told me not to use language. How else were we to communicate?

Barking? Humming? Whistling? It came as such a relief when, during the sixties, we could at last unbutton our lips and talk dirty. I was amazed to find there was a wealth of filth going back to the dawn of civilization. The British Museum's full of it. The Vatican has one of the best collections. But most of it – from Ovid to 'Eskimo Nell' we still can't read on the air.

Here's one, though, a mild and ingenious poem by e. e. cummings. It's about as rude as I can get on this so-called programme of pleasure.

### *may i feel said he*
### e. e. cummings

may i feel said he
(i'll squeal said she
just once said he)
it's fun said she

(may i touch said he
how much said she
a lot said he)
why not said she

(let's go said he
not too far said she
what's too far said he
where you are said she)

may i stay said he
(which way said she
like this said he
if you kiss said she

may i move said he
is it love said she)
if you're willing said he
(but you're killing said she

but it's life said he
but your wife said she
now said he)
ow said she

(tiptop said he
don't stop said she
oh no said he)
go slow said she
(cccome? said he
ummm said she)
you're divine! said he
(you are Mine said she)

My wife and I were both teachers when we married, but my wife's dowry was a pressure cooker and her superannuation, which we soon cashed to eke out my income as a professional playwright. I've been lucky enough to earn a living most of the time. We've not always been well off but never desperately poor either. In days gone by, of course, writers usually were – poets particularly. Samuel Johnson wrote of the seventeenth-century Samuel Butler: 'A man whose name can only perish with his language. The mode and place of his education are unknown, the events of his life are variously related and all that can be told with certainty is, that he was poor.' Some years after his death, a monument was raised to him in Westminster Abbey and here's an epigram by Samuel Wesley to celebrate that event.

## *Epigrams*

### SAMUEL WESLEY

While Butler, needy wretch, was yet alive
No generous patron would a dinner give.
See him when starved to death and turned to dust
Presented with a monumental bust.
The poet's fate is here in emblem shown,
He asked for bread and he received a stone.

Mind you, he'd not have earned that much more bread reciting verse on Radio 4 instead.

We began with birth and we end with death. Which is all any of us can be sure of. Even Falstaff. A prose passage which shows the superstar scripter Shakespeare not only describing the dying man but, by the tone of voice, the character and attitude of Mistress Quickly, who speaks it. One of their friends wishes he were with the dead knight whether he's in Heaven or in Hell.

## *King Henry V*

**WILLIAM SHAKESPEARE**

Nay, sure, he's not in hell: he's in Arthur's bosom, if ever man went to Arthur's bosom. A' made a finer end, and went away, an it had been any Christom child; a' parted even just between twelve and one, even at the turning o' the tide: for after I saw him fumble with the sheets, and play with flowers and smile upon his fingers' ends, I knew there was but one way; for his nose was as sharp as a pen, and a' babbled of green fields. *How now, Sir John?* quoth I: *what, man! be o'good cheer*. So a' cried out – *God, God, God!* three or four times. Now I, to comfort him, bid him a' should not think of God; I hoped there was no need to trouble himself with any such thoughts yet. So a' bade me lay more clothes on his feet: I put my hand into the bed and felt them, and they were as cold as any stone; then I felt to his knees, and so upward, and upward, and all was as cold as any stone.

I hope this selection has helped you understand, if not share, the sentiments of Logan Pearsall Smith whose last words were:

'People say that life is the thing but I prefer reading.'

*Readers: Eileen Atkins, Joe Melia*

*Full Selection:*
*This Little Babe,* ROBERT SOUTHWELL
*Sarah Byng,* HILAIRE BELLOC
*Great Expectations,* CHARLES DICKENS
*Critical Essays,* GEORGE ORWELL
*In Praise of the Good Old Flag,* BILLY BENNETT
*Weekend in the Country,* IRA GERSHWIN
*Symptom Recital,* DOROTHY PARKER
*may i feel said he,* e. e. cummings
*Epigram,* SAMUEL WESLEY
*For Sidney Bechet,* PHILIP LARKIN
*Poppy (John Companee),* PETER NICHOLS
*Election Fever,* ROGER WODDIS

*The Surgeon at 2 A.M.*, SYLVIA PLATH
*The Little Things You Do Together*, STEPHEN SONDHEIM
*King Henry V*, WILLIAM SHAKESPEARE
*Famous Sayings*, WOODY ALLEN, WILLIAM PITT, DOROTHY PARKER, LORD PALMERSTON, LOGAN PEARSALL SMITH

# *MARY O'HARA*

## *1986*

*Mary O'Hara's story is well known through her autobiography and innumerable interviews: leaving the convent to which she had retreated for many years after the death of her first husband, she returned to the world in order to resume a successful career as a singer. Her first broadcast at that time was produced by Madeau Stewart for Radio 3. As the studio manager I enjoyed the challenge of recording voice and harp in a way that gave proper clarity to both elements, and I enjoyed meeting this warm woman who had obviously suffered much, come to terms with it and was confident that she was now doing the right thing. I did not meet her again until the recording of 'With Great Pleasure' in March 1986. What I remember most is the laughter. Her good humour and pleasure in life were captivating. A minute before we were due on stage we were both convulsed over some line or other in the script. Later, over dinner, she, her new husband and Kate Binchy told Irish jokes as only the Irish can. It was a fine evening.*

Some people fall in love with *The Wind in the Willows* when they are small children. I was in my early twenties when I was first bowled over by it and it has remained a huge favourite with me ever since. The little otter has gone missing, and Rat and Mole set out in their boat determined to find him. And in so doing they have the following mysterious experience.

## *The Wind in the Willows*
### KENNETH GRAHAME

Breathless and transfixed the Mole stopped rowing as the liquid run of that glad piping broke on him like a wave, caught him up, and possessed him utterly. He saw the tears on his comrade's cheeks, and bowed his head and understood. For a space they hung there, brushed by the purple loosestrife that fringed the bank; then the clear imperious summons that marched hand-in-hand with the intoxicating melody imposed its will on Mole, and mechanically he bent to his oars again. And the light grew steadily stronger, but no birds sang as they were wont to do at the approach of dawn; and but for the heavenly music all was marvellously still.

On either side of them, as they glided onwards, the rich meadow-grass seemed that morning of a freshness and a greenness unsurpassable. Never had they noticed the roses so vivid, the willow-herb so riotous, the meadow-sweet so odorous and pervading. Then the murmur of the approaching weir began to hold the air, and they felt a consciousness that they were nearing the end, whatever it might be, that surely awaited their expedition.

A wide half-circle of foam and glinting lights and shining shoulders of green water, the great weir closed the backwater from bank to bank, troubled all the quiet surface with twirling eddies and floating foam-streaks, and deadened all other sounds with its solemn and soothing rumble. In midmost of the stream, embraced in the weir's shimmering armspread, a small island lay anchored, fringed close with willow and silver birch and alder. Reserved, shy, but full of significance, it hid whatever it might hold behind a veil, keeping it till the hour should come, and, with the hour, those who were called and chosen.

Slowly, but with no doubt or hesitation whatever, and in something of a solemn expectancy, the two animals passed through the broken, tumultuous water and moored their boat at the flowery margin of the island. In silence they landed and pushed through the blossom and scented herbage and undergrowth that led up to the level ground, till they stood on a little lawn of a marvellous green, set round with Nature's own orchard-trees – crab apple, wild cherry, and sloe.

'This is the place of my song-dream, the place the music played to me,' whispered the Rat, as if in a trance. 'Here, in this holy place, here if anywhere, surely we shall find Him!'

Then suddenly the Mole felt a great Awe fall upon him, an awe that turned his muscles to water, bowed his head, and rooted his feet to the ground. It was no panic terror – indeed he felt wonderfully at peace and happy – but it was an awe that smote and held him and, without seeing, he knew that it could only mean that some august Presence was very, very near. With difficulty he turned to look for his friend, and saw him at his side cowed, stricken, and trembling violently. And still there was utter silence in the populous bird-haunted branches around them; and still the light grew and grew.

Perhaps he would never have dared to raise his eyes, but that, though the piping was now hushed, the call and the summons seemed still dominant and imperious. He might not refuse, were Death himself waiting to strike him instantly, once he had looked with mortal eye on things rightly kept hidden. Trembling he obeyed, and raised his humble head; and then, in that utter clearness of the imminent dawn, while Nature, flushed with fullness of incredible colour, seemed to hold her breath for the event, he looked into the very eyes of his Friend and Helper; saw the backward sweep of the curved horns, gleaming in the growing daylight; saw the stern, hooked nose between the kindly eyes that were looking down on them humorously, while the bearded mouth broke into a half-smile at the corners; saw the rippling muscles on the arm that lay across the broad chest, the long supple hand still holding the pan-pipes only just fallen away from the parted lips; saw the splendid curves of the shaggy limbs disposed in majestic ease on the sward; saw, last of all, nestling between his very hooves, sleeping soundly in entire peace and contentment, the little, round, podgy, childish form of the baby otter. All this he saw, for one moment breathless and intense, vivid on the morning sky; and still, as he looked, he lived; and still, as he lived, he wondered.

'Rat!' he found breath to whisper, shaking. 'Are you afraid?'

'Afraid?' murmured the Rat, his eyes shining with unutterable love. 'Afraid! Of *Him*? O, never, never! And yet – and yet – O, Mole, I am afraid!'

Then the two animals, crouching to the earth, bowed their heads and did worship.

Sudden and magnificent, the sun's broad golden disc showed itself over the horizon facing them; and the first rays, shooting across the level water-meadows, took the animals full in the eyes and dazzled them. When they were able to look once more, the Vision had vanished, and the air was full of the carol of birds that hailed the dawn.

The ability to laugh, especially at oneself, and not take oneself, one's work, one's life too seriously is a recipe for sanity. George Bernard Shaw with typical Shavian wit wrote that seriousness is a small man's affectation of greatness. I think I know what he meant. Sometimes if I find myself getting depressed about something and need to see things in perspective I go back to a book by Hugo Rahner called *Man at Play*. It's quite a powerful antidote.

## *Man at Play*
### HUGO RAHNER

The 'grave-merry' man is really always two men in one: he is a man with an easy gaiety of spirit, one might almost say a man of spiritual elegance, a man who feels himself to be living in invincible security; but he is also a man of tragedy, a man of ridiculous masks of the game of life and has taken the measure of the cramping boundaries of our earthly existence.

And so, only one who can fuse these two contradictory elements into a spiritual unity is indeed a man who truly plays. If he is only the first of these two things, we must write him down as a frivolous person who has, precisely, played himself out. If he is only the second, then we must account him as one who cannot conquer despair. It is the synthesis of the two things that makes Homo Ludens, the 'grave-merry' man, the man with a gentle sense of humour who laughs despite his tears, and finds in all earthly mirth a sediment of insufficience. . . .

The man who truly plays is, therefore, first of all, a man in whom seriousness and gaiety are mingled; and, indeed, at the bottom of all play there lies a tremendous secret. All play – just as much as every task which we set ourselves to master with real earnestness of purpose – is an attempt to approximate to the Creator, who performs his work with the divine seriousness which its meaning and purpose demand, and yet with the spontaneity and effortless skill of the great artist he is, creating because he wills to create and not because he must. . . .

This happy mingling of the light-hearted and the serious is a flower that grows only midway betwixt heaven and earth – in the man who loves this bright and colourful world and yet can smile at it, who knows in his heart that it has proceeded from God but also knows its limits. Within those limits, and because of them, things knock into each other, thus producing comedy – but also tragedy. These may annoy us; we can react angrily or we can accept them with calm good humour. They can disconcert us and still, at the same time, delight us in our vision directed always towards the Logos in his 'co-fashioning' action, for it is in him that everything has its source and it is towards the vision of him that all our play ultimately tends.

Nowadays we are all very conscious of the necessity to preserve the balance of nature that's so threatened by so-called progress. Perhaps we could be forgiven for thinking that such laudable concern was invented by Greenpeace – certainly any stories that I read as a child wouldn't have prepared me for regarding the American Indian as a forerunner for Greenpeace.

## *Letter to the President of the United States in 1885*
**CHIEF SEATHL**

The Great Chief in Washington sends word that he wishes to buy our land. The Great Chief also sends us words of friendship and good will. This is kind of him, since we know he has little need for our friendship in return. But we will consider your offer, for we know that if we do not do so, the white man may come with guns and take our land. What Chief Seathl says, the Great Chief in Washington can count on as truly as our white brothers can count on the return of the seasons. My words are like the stars – they do not set.

How can you buy or sell the sky – the warmth of the land? The idea is strange to us. Yet we do not own the freshness of the air or the sparkle of the water. How can you buy them from us? We will decide in our time. Every part of this earth is sacred to my people. Every shining pine needle, every sandy shore, every mist in the dark woods, every clearing and humming insect is holy in the memory and experience of my people.

We know that the white man does not understand our ways. One portion of the land is the same to him as the next, for he is a stranger who comes in the night and takes from the land whatever he needs. The earth is not his brother, but his enemy, and when he has conquered it, he moves on. He leaves his fathers' graves behind and he does not care. He kidnaps the earth from his children. He does not care. His fathers' graves and his children's birthright are forgotten. His appetite will devour the earth and leave behind only a desert. The sight of your cities pains the eyes of the redman. But perhaps it is because the redman is a savage and does not understand. . . .

There is no quiet place in the white man's cities. No place to hear the leaves of spring or the rustle of insects' wings. But because perhaps I am a savage and do not understand the clatter only seems to insult the ears. And what is there to life if a man cannot hear the lovely cry of the whippoorwill or the argument of the frogs around a pond at night? The Indian prefers the soft sound of the wind darting over the face of the pond, and the smell of the wind itself cleansed by a mid-day rain, or scented with pinion pine. The air is precious to the redman. For all things share the same breath – the beasts, the trees, the man. The white man does not seem to notice the air he breathes. Like a man dying for many days, he is numb to the smell of his own stench. . . .

When the last redman has vanished from the earth, and the memory is only the shadow of a cloud moving across the prairie, these shores and forests will still hold the spirits of my people, for they love the earth as the newborn loves its mother's heartbeat.

If we sell you our land, love it as we've loved it. Care for it as we've cared for it. Hold in your mind the memory of the land, as it is when you take it. And with all your strength, with all your might, and with all your heart preserve it for your children, and love it as God loves us all. One thing we know – our God is the same God. This earth is precious to him. Even the white man cannot be exempt from the common destiny.

*Readers: Sion Probert, Kate Binchy*

*Full Selection:*
*The Wind in the Willows,* KENNETH GRAHAME
*The Rat,* GEORGE SCOTT MONCRIEFF
*Mother and Son,* LIAM O'FLAHERTY
*Reflection,* R. J. SELIG
*Man at Play,* HUGO RAHNER
*The Lost World of the Kalahari,* LAURENS VAN DER POST
*If I Should Go Before the Rest of You,* JOYCE GRENFELL
*And Were You Pleased,* LORD DUNSANY
*Under Milk Wood,* DYLAN THOMAS
*Letter to the President of the United States in 1885,* CHIEF SEATHL
*The Best of Myles,* FLANN O'BRIEN
*The Fellowship of the Ring,* J. R. R. TOLKIEN
*In God's Underground,* RICHARD WURMBRAND
*The Little Prince,* ANTOINE DE SAINTE-EXUPERY
*Gitanjali,* RABINDRANATH TAGORE

# *PETER PEARS*

## *1986*

*As a young photographic printer working in Television Centre in 1962 I remember rushing home from work to be in time to listen to the first performance of Benjamin Britten's* War Requiem. *As Peter Pears sang the opening line from Wilfred Owen, 'What passing-bells for these who die as cattle', it was as if the air were filled with a sense of reconciliation and of hope for the future. The war was finally over. That strange excitement remains with me to this day and twenty-four years after that evening it was a great thrill for me to have the opportunity of meeting Sir Peter. He was, of course, with Britten a familiar figure in Aldeburgh and the affection in which he was held by the audience as he sat on the stage, in his favourite armchair specially brought in for the occasion, was unmistakable. When he spoke it was as if his voice could scarcely refrain from song. It was his last broadcast.*

I have been a singer for fifty years and in the course of those years I have got to love certain music and not love other music quite so much. I started singing these pieces fifty years ago and I sang them across America and I've got very fond of them. They are from the best period of English music, the Elizabethan time. I think they're beautiful.

### *Four Madrigals of Six Parts*
**THOMAS WEELKES**

Thule, the period of cosmography,
Doth vaunt of Hecla, whose sulphurious fire
Doth melt the frozen clime and thaw the sky;
Trinacrian Aetna's flames ascend not higher.
These things seem wondrous, yet more wondrous I,
Whose heart with fear doth freeze, with love doth fry.

The Andalusian merchant, that returns
Laden with cochineal and China dishes,
Reports in Spain how strangely Fogo burns
Amidst an ocean full of flying fishes.
These things seem wondrous, yet more wondrous I
Whose heart with fear doth freeze, with love doth fry.

### *The First Set of Madrigals*
**ORLANDO GIBBONS**

The silver swan, who living had no note,
When death approached unlocked her silent throat;
Leaning her breast against the reedy shore,

Thus sung her first and last, and sung no more:
Farewell, all joys: O death, come close mine eyes;
More geese than swans now live, more fools than wise.

What is our life? a play of passion
Our mirth the music of division.
Our mothers' wombs the tiring-houses be,
Where we are dressed for this short comedy.
Heaven the judicious sharp spectator is,
That sits and marks still who doth act amiss.
Our graves that hide us from the searching sun
Are like drawn curtains when the play is done.
Thus march we, playing, to our latest rest,
Only we die in earnest, that's no jest.

*The Second Set of Madrigals*
JOHN WILBYE

Draw on, sweet Night, best friend unto those cares
That do arise from painful melancholy.
My life so ill through want of comfort fares,
That unto thee I consecrate it wholly.
Sweet night, draw on! My griefs when they be told
To shades and darkness, find some ease from paining.
And while thou all in silence dost enfold,
I then shall have best time for my complaining.

One of the great loves of my youth was Jane Austen and I had the idea that we might have had a whole first chapter of one of her great books because in her first chapter she always seems to put the stage absolutely right for the rest of the book: you are told what so-and-so is, how another is a terrible snob and so on, but that's rather long so we didn't choose that. I decided on more juvenile Jane Austen, from an old album not often seen.

## *The Adventures of Mr Harley*
JANE AUSTEN

A short but interesting Tale, is with all imaginable Respect inscribed to Mr Francis William Austen Midshipman on board his Majestys Ship the Perseverance by his Obedient Servant, THE AUTHOR

Mr Harley was one of many Children. Destined by his father for the Church & by his Mother for the Sea, desirous of pleasing both, he prevailed on Sir John to obtain for him a Chaplaincy on board a Man of War. He accordingly cut his Hair and sailed.

In half a year he returned & set off in the Stage Coach for Hogsworth Green, the seat of Emma. His fellow travellers were, A man without a Hat, Another with two, An old maid & a young Wife.

This last appeared about 17 with fine dark Eyes & an elegant Shape; in short Mr Harley soon found out, that she was his Emma & recollected he had married her a few weeks before he left England.

**FINIS**

One of the oddities about Jane Austen was that she was rather an admirer of our local poet, George Crabbe. It is difficult to see them getting on really because she obviously had a tremendous sense of humour, 'though kept under, but he I don't think had a sense of humour at all. One thing we do know about him is that he did not like Aldeburgh although he was born here and as one way, I think, of getting his own back on Aldeburgh he wrote this poem.

## *Marsh Flowers*

**GEORGE CRABBE**

Here the strong mallow strikes her slimy root, .
Here the dull nightshade hangs her deadly fruit;
On hills of dust the henbane's faded green,
And pencill'd flower of sickly scent is seen.
Here on its wiry stem, in rigid bloom
Grows the salt lavender that lacks perfume.

At the wall's base the fiery nettle springs
With fruit globose and fierce with poison'd stings;
In ev'ry chink delights the fern to grow,
With glossy leaf and tawny bloom below;
The few dull flowers that o'er the place are spread
Partake the nature of their fenny bed,
These with our seaweeds rolling up and down
Form the contracted Flora of our town.

*Readers: Peter Pears, Julia Lang*

*Full Selection:*
*Four Madrigals of Six Parts,* THOMAS WEELKES
*The First Set of Madrigals,* ORLANDO GIBBONS
*The Second Set of Madrigals,* JOHN WILBYE
*The Moth and the Star,* JAMES THURBER
*The Glass in the Field,* JAMES THURBER
*The Adventures of Mr Harley,* JANE AUSTEN
*Marsh Flowers,* GEORGE CRABBE
*Dunwich: Winter Visit Along,* JOHN MATHIAS
*Two Ladies,* JOHN MATHIAS
*An Angel in Blythburgh Church,* PETER PORTER
*O Lurcher-Loving Collier,* W. H. AUDEN
*XXVII,* W. H. AUDEN
*Graveyard in Norfolk,* SYLVIA TOWNSEND WARNER
*Gloriana Dying,* SYLVIA TOWNSEND WARNER
*December 31st St Silvester,* SYLVIA TOWNSEND WARNER

# *LAURENS VAN DER POST*

## *1978*

*Unlike 'Desert Island Discs', 'With Great Pleasure' never invites a presenter back for a second go. That at any rate is the theory. In fact two people have found themselves twice talking to Radio 4 listeners about their favourite poetry and prose: John Mortimer reappeared in another guise for an 'April Fool' edition, whilst Laurens van der Post had taken part some years previously for another producer. The second invitation was an accident, but was accepted nonetheless. For the more recent programme this farmer, soldier, explorer, writer and adviser to the heir to the throne acknowledged his 'enormous unrepayable debt to the written literature of the world' but decided to lay his emphasis on to the 'literature out of which all literature arose, the spoken, the unwritten literature of the world'.*

I was fortunate to be born into an Africa where one had an immense amount of this sort of literature around. It was always around us. I was fortunate also that I was in contact daily with people who thought that story-telling was not just for children, that it was just as much for the old, that somehow this was one of the most important mechanisms in life. Years later when I was exploring the Kalahari Desert I found the people there would tell me everything except their stories. They knew instinctively that the story was their most precious possession and that the most dangerous thing you could do was to let a stranger in on to their stories, because if a stranger got in on to the story he might mock it, he might take it away, and I realized that we have killed off scores of civilizations and peoples merely by taking away their story. It's a peril which confronts the world today, everywhere people's stories are being taken away from them and as a result they are losing a sense of meaning and losing their sense of direction. As a result of all this inherited sense of the importance of the story my childhood memories are crowded with stories, but there was one story to which I'd turn again and again because it seemed to me that all literature, even the most sophisticated and highly orchestrated kind, is concerned with the theme of this story; it's a story told to me by my old bushman nurse so far back that I can't even remember my exact age. It's *The Story of the Great White Bird* and she had a special tone in her voice when she told this story.

## *The Story of the Great White Bird*

**TRADITIONAL**

There was a hunter once and, because he was young and beautiful and utterly hunter, he was loved by everyone. He was the greatest provider of food for his people. Because, feeling himself to be utterly hunter and utterly loved, his arrows and his spears never failed to find their mark. Then one day he felt himself called in a dream to go hunting in the forest of Duk-A-Duk-Duk. This forest was called Duk-A-Duk-Duk because it was so thick and so dark that people, once in a forest feeling itself to be utterly dark, found their hearts going duk-a-duk on account of it.

So they watched him go early in the morning, not without fear. But knowing him to be so utterly hunter they told themselves that their fears were foolish. The sun, feeling itself to be hot, was fierce and strong, and towards noon the hunter, feeling himself to be thirsty, branched from the track of an animal he was stalking and followed the voices of the purple doves he knew would lead him to water. Soon he came to a clearing where there was a deep pool of water. The water was still and so full of the blue of the day that it was as if he was looking into another sky at his feet. He knelt down to drink, but just before his lips touched the water suddenly, dazzling and swift, on the surface there appeared the reflection of a great white shining bird. He looked up quickly but the sky was empty and for a moment he wondered whether he had not dreamt it all because of the strangeness, the size, the whiteness and speed of the bird. But once back in the forest, he found he could not go on hunting. He no longer saw the trees or spoor of the animals, but only this dazzling reflection of the great white bird.

He went back for the first time to his people without food. That night he hardly slept. Whether he closed his eyes or opened them, he saw only the reflection of the bird. He thought that by morning he would have done with the bird, but again wherever he hunted this memory of this reflection dazzled his eyes. So it went on day after day. And his people, knowing that something was eating his heart out of him, although they could not put a name to it, tried to show him how they loved him by singing and dancing to him. Yet by day he became more and more silent. He would not eat, he could not sleep and in the air he realised that he would never rest again until he saw the bird itself. His people did everything to persuade him not to go on what seemed so foolish a search. He only said: 'I have seen the reflection of the bird and now

I must find and see the bird itself, but when I have seen it I will return to tell you all.'

He went back into the forest of Duk-A-Duk-Duk. He stayed and watched for days by the pool but the bird did not come back. He went on through the forest, and over the great wasteland plain so far and wide and long that the heart of the bravest who tries to cross it will cry out within: 'Oh! mother, I am lost' and turn back. But he went on and after the desert and through more plain, and forests and valleys; over the months and the years he went among many strange peoples and countries. Everywhere he asked for news of the bird. But everywhere people would either say that they had never heard of such a bird and that it must be a story for old women, or 'Ah, yes, we have heard of someone who once said he had seen such a bird, but we've never seen it ourselves.' At one faraway place indeed there were people who said: 'What a pity you did not come last night, because the bird roosted very nearby here, on its way to the West.' Encouraged for once, he went on searching but still without success until at last he had become a very old man, who had almost lost all memory of the people who had loved him utterly and was feeling only 'now I shall have to die without seeing the bird that once made the blue water white.'

But when he was very, very near the end of his strength, he came to the foot of a very high mountain and met some people who lived around it. When he asked them for news of the bird they said at once: 'Ah yes, we know of the bird. It makes its home on top of the mountain and comes there every night to sleep.'

So, slowly, he started to climb the mountain. After days of climbing, one evening as the sun was just about to set, he came to the bottom of a great cliff that was the top of the mountain. The cliff was as high as it was sheer. He knew he would never be able to climb it – and lay down on the ground ready to die, accepting that he had failed and saying to himself: 'Now I shall never see the bird whose reflection made me look for it for so long.' But as he said that, a voice spoke on this light wind that always comes out of evening and commanded him to look up. He looked. High up in the sky – red as blood with the red of the reddest of red sunsets, he saw a white feather come fluttering down. He held out his hand and, amazed, he felt the feather settling into his trembling fingers. He grasped it firmly with the last of the strength that comes only to the dying, and with this one feather in his hand he died utterly content.

I was always moved by this story in some utterly incomprehensible way and asked my old nurse what the name of the bird was, and in a very sad voice she would say, 'The bird today has many names, for most people have forgotten what it was called in the beginning, but the people of the early race called it the Bird of Truth.'

There, of course, we have the secret of the story, indeed the secret of the meaning of art, why artists are important, because all art is a means of heightening through tension our perception of truth and widening our awareness of reality. And I had to learn very early on that all this unwritten literature always moved on two levels; there was the manifest level where it was an event in everyday reality, but there was another level where within the person who truly took the story inside himself, it acquired a deeper symbolic sort of significance. Take the feather, for instance: the feather is very important here because in a sense it represents the bird and the bird always has been the symbol, the image of what comes inspired, out of the blue, without our wishing it even, into our imagination. And that's why the African chief wears a feather in the band round his head to show that his head is full of inspired wisdom.

What is particularly outstanding and remarkable about this unwritten literature of Africa is how a kind of cosmic awareness comes into the imagination of man and enlarges it by a kind of star consciousness. If you're born, as I was, in this packed starry sky of the southern hemisphere, packed in a way, alas, the northern hemisphere is not, and where at night you can see the stars rising one after the other over the horizon, where you experience star-rise as well as moon-rise and sunrise, you can understand why. Many of the stories that you hear even now in the desert are star stories. They talk of a moment when the stars threw down their spears, literally; the morning star is described again and again as coming home with an arrow in his bow and a spear in his hand. One of the loveliest of all the star stories is of how the Milky Way came to be made: the Milky Way was the creation of a young, lonely, suffering girl of the stone-age people. She was isolated because she was for the first time becoming a woman and she was sour and bitter. As she looked out at the fire outside her hut dying down it was as if she were looking at her childhood, burned out, lying there in front of her. In the deepest moment of her bitterness suddenly she looked up and saw the stars and, reassured, said to herself 'I must join the stars'. She discovered the great secret that, if you can find a meaning in suffering, there is no suffering so great that you cannot endure it, and suddenly she found a meaning in her suffering and she found it in the following way: she went out, picked up the coals that were left in the fire and threw them high into the sky, and as she threw them she addressed the coals thus:

## *The Milky Way*
**TRADITIONAL**

The wood ashes which are here mixed together have to become utterly the Milky Way. They must lie white along in the sky that the stars may stand outside of their way, so that the Milky Way is utterly the Milky Way. Then the stars, turning back to fetch the break of day, can come to lie nicely beside the Milky Way. The stars become white when the sun comes out. But when the darkness comes, the stars grow red, while the Milky Way becomes white and gently glows, giving a little light for the people so that they who have been caught in the darkness may find their way home in the middle of the night. For the earth would not have been a little light if it had not been for the stars and the Milky Way.

In Africa, as in ancient Greece, the Milky Way is the feminine contribution to life. This great circle of light that goes right round the universe, and in which our solar system spins, is almost a magic circle. Somewhere it protects us as it protected the girl and as it was conveyed in her story. You'll understand why I was so moved one evening in the desert coming home to a little group of stone-age people. And suddenly against the star glimmer, there was no moon, it was very bright, I thought I saw a woman and I stood still and watched and then I saw she was holding up a child of about six weeks old to the stars and she was saying to the stars, 'Oh you who sit up there with your hearts full of light and full of plenty, please give my child also the heart of a star'.

Now what's so amazing in a masculine-dominated world like Africa, where the man has played an even more despotic role than he has in Europe, and that's saying a lot, is that so many of the truest voices to break through the male barrier have been women's voices. Because of the way in which the feminine spirit breaks through into a male-dominated imagination I would like to offer you the story of a noble Abyssinian, an Ethiopian woman who lived nearly nine hundred years ago. It's something to this day which I think if I were a Minister of Education I would make every boy learn by heart.

### *Introduction to a Science of Mythology*

**JUNG** and **KERENYI** trans **R. F. C. HULL**

How can a man know what a woman's life is? A woman's life is quite different from a man's. God ordered it so. A man is the same from the time of his circumcision to the time of his withering. He is the same before he has sought out a woman for the first time, and afterwards. But the day when a woman enjoys her first love cuts her in two. She becomes another woman on that day. The man is the same after his first love as he was before. The woman is from the day of her first love another. That continues all through life. The man spends a night by a woman and goes away. His life and body are always the same. The woman conceives. As a mother she is another person than the woman without child. She carries the fruit of the night nine months long in her body. Something grows. Something grows into her life that never again departs from it. She is a mother. She is and remains a mother even though her child die, though all her children die. For at one time she carried the child under her heart. And it does not go out of her heart ever again. Not even when it is dead. All this the man does not know, he knows nothing. He does not know the difference before love and after love, before motherhood and after motherhood. He can know nothing. Only a woman can know that and speak of that. That is why we won't be told what to do by our husbands. A woman can only do one thing. She can respect herself. She can keep herself decent. She must always be maiden and always be mother. Before every love she is a maiden, after every love she is a mother. In this you can see whether she is a good woman or not.

*Reader: Ingaret Giffard*

*Full Selection:*
*A Story Like the Wind,* LAURENS VAN DER POST
*The Story of the Great White Bird,* TRADITIONAL
*The Lost World of the Kalahari,* LAURENS VAN DER POST
*The Zebras,* ROY CAMPBELL
*Ula Masondo's Dream,* WILLIAM PLOMER
*The Milky Way,* TRADITIONAL
*Introduction to a Science of Mythology,* JUNG and KERENYI trans R. F. C. HULL
*Daisies in Namaqualand,* INGRID JONKER trans WILLIAM PLOMER
*The Taste of the Fruit,* WILLIAM PLOMER
*The Flaming Terrapin,* ROY CAMPBELL
*Out of Africa,* KAREN BLIXEN

# DENNIS POTTER

## 1976

*Television as a medium is often derided, and as a radio producer I have not been above taking an occasional swipe at my colleagues who are hooked on small moving pictures. The ratio of bullshit to talent amongst them used to strike me as being a little too weighted in favour of the former, but I suppose the truth is that real talent is rare in any endeavour and radio is not without its share of overweening competence. It is always a pleasure to salute the exceptions: Dennis Potter with his searching, questioning, absorbing plays and serials has for decades set a standard by which television drama in general must find itself judged.*

'Tell me what you like,' said Ruskin, 'and I'll tell you what you are.' Hm. Maybe. I am not too keen to be quite so easily locatable as this or that sort of person. Sometimes I want the printed word to console me, sometimes to amuse, or challenge, or even frighten me – so many demands – and then, of course, there are occasions when I get pleasure from the succulent adjectives on the side of a sauce bottle. And, ah! the cornflake packets of yesteryear – red words, green words, blue words filling the void between the spoon, the jug and the sugar bowl. No, you cannot diagnose me by what I have read and liked, only by what I have read and forgotten, or even by what I have read and then eaten.

At the junior school next to the churchyard there was a young woman who taught us six- and seven-year-olds with such sweet grace, and so wondrous a smile, such lovely eyes and such – naturally I fell in love for the very first time. Certain fairy tales at *her* lips were full of mysterious tensions and secrets I had to wait years and years to unravel. Here's an extract from one of Grimms' fairy tales which *almost* tells a child all he wants to know and was too afraid to ask.

## *Grimms' Fairy Tales*

After a couple of years had passed away, it happened that the King's son was riding through the wood, and came by the tower. There he heard a song so beautiful that he stood still and listened. It was Rapunzel, who, to pass the time of her loneliness away, was exercising her sweet voice. The King's son wished to ascend to her, and looked for a door in the tower, but he could not find one.

So he rode home, but the song had touched his heart so much that he went every day to the forest and listened to it, and as he thus stood one day behind a tree, he saw the Witch come up, and heard her call out –

'Rapunzel! Rapunzel! Let down your hair.'

Then Rapunzel let down her long and beautiful tresses, as fine as spun gold, and the Witch mounted up. 'Is that the ladder on which one must climb? Then I will try my luck too,' said the Prince; and the following day, as he felt quite lonely, he went to the tower, and said –

'Rapunzel! Rapunzel! Let down your hair.'

Then the tresses fell down and he climbed up.

Rapunzel was much frightened at first when a man came in, for she had never seen one before; but the King's son talked in a loving way to her, and told how his heart had been so moved by her singing. So Rapunzel lost her terror, and when he asked if she would have him for a husband, and she saw that he was young and handsome, she thought 'Any one may have me rather than the old woman,' so, saying 'Yes,' she put her hand within his . . .

The old woman found out nothing, until one day Rapunzel innocently said, 'Tell me, mother, how it happens you find it more difficult to come up to me than the young King's son who is with me in a moment!'

'Oh, you wicked child!' exclaimed the Witch; 'I thought I had separated you from all the world, and yet you have deceived me.' And, seizing Rapunzel's hair in a fury, snip, snap, she cut off all her beautiful tresses, and they fell upon the ground. Then she was so hard-hearted that she took the poor maiden into a great desert, and left her to die in great misery and grief.

The old Witch bound the shorn tresses fast above to the window-latch, and when the King's son came, and called out 'Rapunzel! Rapunzel! Let down your hair,' she let them down. The Prince mounted, but when he got to the top he found, not his dear Rapunzel but the Witch, who looked at him with furious and wicked eyes.

'Aha!' she exclaimed scornfully, '– the beautiful bird sits no longer in her nest, singing; the cat has taken her away, and will now scratch out your eyes. To you Rapunzel is lost, you will never see her again.'

The Prince lost his senses with grief at these words, and sprang out of the window of the tower in his bewilderment. His life he escaped with, but the thorns into which he fell put out his eyes. So he wandered, blind, in the forest, eating nothing but berries and roots, and doing nothing but weep and lament for the loss of his dear wife.

He wandered about thus, in great misery, for some few years, and at last arrived at the desert where Rapunzel, with her twins – a boy and a girl – which had been born, lived in great sorrow. Hearing a voice which he thought he knew, he followed in its direction; and, as he approached, Rapunzel recognized him, and fell upon his neck and wept. Two of her tears moistened his eyes, and they became clear again so that he could see as well as ever.

There was a time when I would not have liked to be told that that story came from Germany. I started school in 1940 and so much of my childhood was filled to the brim with the war. My patriotism was total. The villains in the shrunken comics said *Achtung!* and *Himmel!* and *Ach, so-o-o* and *Englander pig-dog!* We, of course, were gentlemen at arms, saints in khaki or airforce blue. A poem by Sir Henry Newbolt – written much earlier, of course – brings back the way a small boy saw the true nature of the struggle. I am still able to enjoy it as dum-di-dum twaddle – and you will surely recognize the opening line.

## *Vitae Lampada*

**SIR HENRY NEWBOLT**

There's a breathless hush in the Close tonight –
Ten to make and the match to win –
A bumping pitch and a blinding light,
An hour to play and the last man in.
And it's not for the sake of a ribboned coat,
Or the selfish hope of a season's fame,
But his Captain's hand on his shoulder smote –
'Play up! play up! and play the game!'

The sand of the desert is sodden red, –
Red with the wreck of a square that broke; –
The Gatling's jammed and the Colonel dead,
And the Regiment blind with dust and smoke.
The river of death has brimmed his banks,
And England's far, and Honour a name,
But the voice of a schoolboy rallies the ranks:
'Play up! play up! and play the game!'

This is the word that year by year
While in her place the School is set,
Every one of her sons must hear,
And none that hears it dare forget.
This they all with a joyful mind
Bear through life like a torch in flame,
And falling fling to the host behind –
'Play up! play up! and play the game!'

It's occasionally sneaky and diverting, if not very profound, to see conflict between writers, who can of course be exceptionally childish, as I'm often being told, in terms of the yah-boo melodramas of the playground. A few sentences will soon disclose a sanctimonious creep or one who is prepared to put out his tongue. When Wordsworth aloofly referred to William Hazlitt as a 'miscreant' and 'not a proper person to be admitted into respectable society' he was already half-way to providing a picture of a man who warms the heart. Hazlitt was not an easy or comfortable person to know, it seems, and he is still not a comfortable writer to meet on the page. He used himself and used up himself, a formidable essayist, an absolute master of English prose, a writer who set out to mock and scourge all and any examples of humbug, cant and time-serving which crossed his path.

I have great difficulty in choosing a suitable piece from Hazlitt, mostly because he is the writer I revere above all others for the trenchant pertinence of his opinions, for his wit and style and honesty, and for his brave, uncompromising spirit and insights. Hazlitt could quite properly claim that he never wrote a single line which betrayed a principle or disguised a feeling. To read him is to *know* him.

Hazlitt was – and *needed* to be – a master of invective. To show this necessary and exhilarating art at full pitch I have chosen the opening and closing paragraphs of his long open letter to William Gifford in 1819. Gifford was a powerful editor and critic, but a terrible reactionary, using his position to damn all new and liberal voices. He abused the young Keats, for example. Hazlitt went for him, neck and crop. There is no more lethal, and no more justly aimed, invective than this in the English language. This is just a fragment – imagine the rest.

## *A Letter to William Gifford*

**WILLIAM HAZLITT**

Sir, – you have an ugly trick of saying what is not true of anyone you do not like; and it will be the object of this letter to cure you of it. You say what you please of others: It is time you were told what *you* are. In doing this, give me leave to borrow the familiarity of your style: for the fidelity of the picture I shall be answerable.

There cannot be a greater nuisance than a dull, envious, pragmatical, low-bred man, who is placed as you are in the situation of the Editor of such work as the Quarterly Review. Conscious that his reputation stands on very slender and narrow grounds, he is naturally jealous of that of others. He insults over unsuccessful authors; he hates successful ones. He is angry at the faults of a work; more angry at its excellences. If an opinion is old, he treats it with supercilious indifference; if it is new it provokes his rage. He cavils at what he does not comprehend, and misrepresents what he knows to be true. Bound to go through the nauseous task of abusing all those who are not like himself and abject tools of power, his irritation increases with the number of obstacles he encounters, and the number of sacrifices he is obliged to make of commonsense and decency to his interest and self conceit. Every instance of prevarication he wilfully commits makes him more in love with hypocrisy, and every indulgence of his hired malignity makes him more disposed to repeat the insult and injury. Grown old in the service of corruption, he drivels onto the last with prostituted impotence and shameless effrontery; salves a meagre reputation for wit by venting the driblets of his spleen and impertinence on others; answers their arguments by confuting himself; mistakes habitual obtuseness of intellect for a particular acuteness, not to be imposed upon by shallow appearances; unprincipled rancour for zealous loyalty; and the irritable, discontented, vindictive, peevish effusions of bodily pain and mental imbecility for proofs of refinement of taste and strength of understanding.

Such, sir, is the picture of which you have sat for the outline.

I sometimes think of that glorious onslaught when I see one of the Post Office advertisements: 'Someone, somewhere, wants a letter from you'. It all depends.

*The Diary of a Nobody* by George and Weedon Grossmith – which first appeared in book form in 1892 – is the nicest, happiest, least malicious satire, and most endearing invention I have ever read. Time and time again I go back to this fictional diary of dear, naive Mr Pooter, the city clerk, who resides at The Laurels, Brickfield Terrace, Holloway, six rooms not counting the basement, ten steps up to the front door and a nice little back garden that runs down to the railway. 'After my work in the City, I like to be at home,' writes Mr Pooter. 'What is the good of a home, if you are never in it?' My sentiments exactly.

Anyway, here we are with Mr Pooter, his paint-pot enthusiasms, his dreadful jokes, his wife Carrie and his two friends, Mr Gowing and Mr Cummings:

## *The Diary of a Nobody*

### GEORGE and WEEDON GROSSMITH

*April 27* – Painted the bath red, and was delighted with the result. Sorry to say Carrie was not, in fact, we had a few words about it. She said I ought to have consulted her, and she had never heard of such a thing as a bath being painted red. I replied: 'It's merely a matter of taste.'

Fortunately further argument on the subject was stopped by a voice saying, 'May I come in?' It was only Cummings, who said, 'Your maid opened the door, and asked me to excuse her showing me in, as she was wringing out some socks.' I was delighted to see him, and suggested we should have a game of whist with a dummy, and by way of merriment said: '*You* can be the dummy.' Cummings (I thought rather ill-naturedly) replied: 'Funny as usual.' He said he couldn't stop, he only called to leave me the *Bicycle News*, as he had done with it.

Another ring at the bell; it was Gowing, who said he 'must apologize for coming so often, and that one of these days *we* must come round to *him*.' I said: 'A very extraordinary thing has struck me.' 'Something funny, as usual,' said Cummings. 'Yes,' I replied; 'I think even *you* will say so this time. It's concerning you both; for doesn't it seem odd that Gowing's always *coming* and Cummings always *going*?' Carrie, who had evidently quite forgotten about the bath, went into fits of laughter, and as for myself, I fairly doubled up in my chair, till it cracked beneath me. I think this was one of the best jokes I have ever made.

Then imagine my astonishment on perceiving both Cummings and Gowing perfectly silent, and without a smile on their faces. After rather an unpleasant pause, Cummings, who had opened a cigar-case, closed it up again and said, 'Yes – I think, after that, I *shall* be going, and I am sorry I fail to see the fun of your jokes.' Gowing said he didn't mind a joke when it wasn't rude, but a pun on a name, to his thinking, was certainly a little wanting in good taste. Cummings followed up by saying, if it had been said by anyone else but myself, he shouldn't have entered the house again. This rather unpleasantly terminated what might have been a cheerful evening. However, it was as well they went, for the charwoman had finished up the remains of the cold pork.

In conclusion, I want you, please, to listen to the final stretch of Bishop King's, Henry King's, *Exequy* for his dead wife, Anne, who died young in 1624. I *have* to say, though, that I can never read this poem, in my head or out loud, without feeling extremely moved. It is, surely, the most beautiful and moving elegy in our language, in which every rhyme at the end of every line pushes it gradually and inevitably to a consummation in which love finally vanquishes doubt, and calm hope subsumes grief. The poet awaits his own death, seeing each passing minute of his life on this earth as part of the journey towards his dead wife and the reunion beyond the grave when 'I shall at last sit down by Thee'. The power of the feeling and the lucid grace of the resignation, the confidence is such that I am aware when I read this poem, even in the face of bereavement, even in the anguish of doubt, that I am somehow being touched by *some*, at least, some of that inner clarity and faith.

## *Exequy*

### HENRY KING

Sleep on my love in thy cold bed
Never to be disquieted!
My last good night! Thou wilt not wake
Till I thy fate shall overtake:

Till age, or grief, or sickness must
Marry my body to that dust
It so much loves; and fill the room
My heart keeps empty in thy tomb.
Stay for me there; I will not fail
To meet thee in that hollow Vale.
And think not much of my delay;
I am already on the way,
And follow thee with all the speed
Desire can make, or sorrows breed.
Each minute is a short degree,
And ev'ry hour a step towards thee,
At night when I betake to rest,
Next Morn I rise nearer my West
Of life almost by eight hours sail,
Than when sleep breath'd his drowsie gale.

'Tis true, with shame and grief I yield,
Thou like the Van first took'st the field,
And gotten hast the victory
In thus adventuring to die
Before me, whose more years might crave
A just precedence in the grave.
But Hark! My pulse like a soft drum
Beats my approach, tells thee I come;
And slow howe'er my marches be,
I shall at last sit down by Thee.

The thought of this bids me go on,
And wait my dissolution
With hope and comfort. Dear (forgive
The crime) I am content to live
Divided, but with half a heart,
Till we shall meet and never part.

I think we should always be willing to be surprised by literature in whatever shell or carapace we inhabit. Words divide us off from all other creatures, but they ought not to be used, wilfully or wantonly, to divide us off from each other. In literature, at least, the atheist can speak to the Christian, and the revolutionary can address the conformist. Good writing seeks completeness, wholeness. Words strongly felt, words properly arranged, scraped out of other people's experiences and insights, *can* complete and nourish and disturb our own lives. Mind you, I don't over-value the emancipations of a liberal culture, and I know that some at least of the guards in the Nazi concentration camps went off duty from the gas chambers and then read Goethe or listened to Beethoven and then went back to work. Our first duty is to the *people*, not the words in front of us, to their hopes and their pains and their needs. If we bow down before narrow ideas, cruel greeds, heartless systems or vacant money machines, then all the great *and* lesser literature, all the great *and* occasional art, will not serve us one jot. The books around us, quiet libraries full of this or that endeavour or humour, even these small pieces this evening, are only open to us if we are open to them. (And never mind the succulent adjectives on the sauce bottle and the cornflake packets of yesteryear!)

*Reader: June Barrie*

*Full selection:*
*Psalm 35*, THE BIBLE
*Fairy Tales*, THE BROTHERS GRIMM
*Vitae Lampada*, SIR HENRY NEWBOLT
*Just William*, RICHMAL CROMPTON
*A Letter to William Gifford*, WILLIAM HAZLITT
*Ivanov*, ANTON CHEKHOV
*The Waste Land*, T. S. ELIOT
*The Mayor of Casterbridge*, THOMAS HARDY
*The Diary of a Nobody*, GEORGE and WEEDON GROSSMITH
*In Memoriam*, ALFRED LORD TENNYSON
*The Big Sleep*, RAYMOND CHANDLER
*Exequy*, HENRY KING

# FREDERIC RAPHAEL

## 1978

*Several years ago, before this and many of the other programmes included in this volume were produced by the late Brian Patten, I stepped into a lift in Television Centre, my nose buried in* Like Men Betrayed, *a novel by Frederic Raphael. 'Good heavens! Are you enjoying it?' came a voice from the other side of the lift. 'Yes, very much,' I said, and then looked up to find myself face to face with the author. Sometimes it's very easy to make someone's day. That was my only meeting to date with Frederic Raphael, although there is a degree of self-mockery in his 'With Great Pleasure' script which makes me think he would be agreeable company. When he talks about poetry he says 'Every prose writer has the uneasy feeling that, compared to a poet, he is a staid married man of lamentably bourgeois provenance who cannot aspire to the daring liberties of the true blade.' He is more waspish, however, on the subject of playwrights: 'It still seems to me that, considering the brevity of their work, they earn their fame and their fortune on singularly easy terms.' Fighting talk!*

I have been working recently on a new translation of the *Oresteia* of Aeschylus, for BBC television. I have had the good fortune to collaborate on this with a good scholar, Kenneth McLeish, and so have been saved from the danger of schoolboy howlers, to which all the years I spent studying the Classics never rendered me wholly immune. But there are other pitfalls for the translator, not least the danger of falling into translationese. A great Classical scholar, A. E. Housman, once wrote the perfect warning to translators, and incidentally one of the best parodies of the language.

## *A Fragment of a Greek Tragedy*

### A. E. HOUSMAN

CHORUS: O suitably-attired-in-leather-boots
Head of a traveller, wherefore seeking whom
Whence by what way how purposed art thou come
To this well-nightingaled vicinity?
My object in enquiring is to know.
But if you happen to be deaf and dumb
And do not understand a word I say,
Then wave your hand, to signify as much.
ALCMEON: I journeyed hither a Boeotian road,
CHORUS: Sailing on horseback, or with feet for oars?
ALCMEON: Plying with speed my partnership of legs.
CHORUS: Beneath a shining or a rainy Zeus?
ALCMEON: Mud's sister, not himself, adorns my shoes.
CHORUS: To learn your name would not displease me much.
ALCMEON: Not all that men desire do they obtain.
CHORUS: Might I then hear at what your presence shoots.
ALCMEON: A shepherd's questioned mouth informed me that—
CHORUS: What? for I know not yet what you will say—
ALCMEON: Nor will you ever, if you interrupt.
CHORUS: Proceed and I will hold my speechless tongue.
ALCMEON: —This house was Eriphyla's, no one's else.
CHORUS: Nor did he shame his throat with hateful lies.
ALCMEON: May I then enter, passing through the door?
CHORUS: Go, chase into the house a lucky foot.
And, O my son, be, on the one hand, good
And do not, on the other hand, be bad;
For that is very much the safest plan.
ALCMEON: I go into the house with heels and speed.

Malcolm Muggeridge is not a man with whom I have any illusions of shared opinions. Nothing that he has said seems to me more wildly silly than his assertion, in a review some years ago, that Lord Byron was the most odious man who ever lived, or words to that effect. I daresay that Professor Wilson Knight was going a bit far when he accused his Lordship of possessing a whole volume full of Christian Virtues, but not even writing two unproduced screenplays on Byron has jaded my affection for the author, and impersonator, of 'Childe Harold' and 'Don Juan' and, above all, the writer of some of the best letters in English. If you can read Byron's correspondence and not warm to the man, I doubt if you have much sense of the comedy of life or taste for vitality.

Here he is writing to his friend Douglas Kinnaird after hearing that the contemporary Lord Longfords and Malcolm Muggeridges had been shocked by the latest section of 'Don Juan'.

## *Letter to Douglas Kinnaird*

**LORD BYRON**

My dear Douglas – My late expenditure has arisen from living at a distance from Venice and being obliged to keep up two establishments, from frequent journeys – and buying some furniture and books as well as a horse or two – and not from any renewal of the EPICUREAN system as you suspect. I have been faithful to my honest liaison with Countess Guiccioli – and I can assure you that *She* has never cost me directly or indirectly a sixpence – indeed the circumstances of herself and family render this no merit. – I never offered her but one present – a broach of brilliants – and she sent it back to me with her *own hair* in it (I shall *not* say of *what part* but *that* is an Italian custom) and a note to say that she was not in the habit of receiving presents of that value – but hoped I would not consider her sending it back as an affront – nor the value diminished by the enclosure. – I have not had a whore this half-year – confining myself to the strictest adultery. – Why should you prevent Hanson from making a *peer* if he likes it – I think the '*Garretting*' would be by far the best parliamentary privilege – I know of. – Damn your delicacy. – It is a low commercial quality – and very unworthy a man who prefixes 'honourable' to his nomenclature. If you say I must sign the bonds – I suppose that I must – but it is very iniquitous to make me pay my debts – you have no idea of the pain it gives one. – Pray do three things – get my property out of the *funds* – get Rochdale sold – get me some information from Perry about *South America* – and 4thly ask Lady Noel not to live so very long. – As to Subscribing to Manchester –

if I do that – I will write a letter to Burdett – for publication – to accompany the Subscription – which shall be more radical than anything yet rooted – but I feel lazy. – I have thought of this for some time – but alas! the air of this accursed Italy enervates – and disenfranchises the thoughts of a man after nearly four years of respiration – to say nothing of emission. – As to 'Don Juan' – confess – confess you dog – and be candid – that it is the sublime of *that there* sort of writing – it may be bawdy – but is it not good English? – it may be profligate – but is it not *life*, is it not *the thing*? – Could any man have written it – who has not lived in the world? – and tooled in a post-chaise? in a hackney coach? in a Gondola? against a wall? in a court carriage? in a vis à vis? – on a table – and under it? – I have written about a hundred stanzas of a third Canto – but it is damned modest – the outcry has frightened me.

There are some kinds of literary art and subject matter which require, somehow, the certificate of experience. Siegfried Sassoon's war poems are rendered unanswerable in their ferocious disgust by our knowledge that Sassoon himself endured the hell of the front line. His gallantry was as remarkable as the dandyism which led him, after a display of courage that won him the MC, to sit in a captured trench reading a volume of poetry. Had Sassoon denounced the war from the comfort of a library, his poem *The General* would have been, perhaps, no more than a clever exercise in irony. As it is, the cold shivers which Housman associated with true poetry never fail to prickle on my neck when I hear these lines.

## *The General*

**SIEGFRIED SASSOON**

'Good-morning; good-morning!' the General said
When we met him last week on our way to the line.
Now the soldiers he smiled at are most of 'em dead,
And we're cursing his staff for incompetent swine.
'He's a cheery old card,' grunted Harry to Jack
As they slogged up to Arras with rifle and pack.

. . .

But he did for them both with his plan of attack.

Anthologies have a way of being mock-modest. There is something shameful about confessing that one sometimes uses one's mirror in order to look at, even admire, onself. As if mirrors would be as popular as they are if one could never glimpse oneself in them! I confess therefore with a sort of hangdog shamelessness that I am not above looking at my own work from time to time. Sometimes one wishes that one had not used a certain idea or experience, since one could manage it so much better now, but sometimes one is agreeably surprised to find that the memory of a given passage is less flattering than the text seems, on fresh inspection, to warrant. Forgive me then, as I have already decided to forgive myself, if to end with I choose a passage from a novel of mine, *Like Men Betrayed*, a novel of, I confess, a certain measured sobriety and of which one critic was cruelly kind enough to say that it showed not the smallest glimmer of a sense of humour. In a world where entertainment at all costs is what is so often demanded of writers, it gives me a certain pained pleasure to think that at least once I have been taken for one of those unsmiling souls to whom levity can never be attributed. Here, from that book, is a description of a Greek dance.

## *Like Men Betrayed*
### FREDERIC RAPHAEL

Artemis danced as lightly as the sea which makes curtains of sand in gentle scollops along the shore. His feet fretted the sand in the circle and invented nothing. He moved as regularly as the scansion of an old metre, each line and each caesura in its place. He danced with his hands held up, like a puppeteer, and drew the eyes of the others after him. . . .

He took Dmitri by the hands and drew him to his feet. Dmitri, clumsy Dmitri, whose whole life would be perhaps a parody of elegance to hide his disquiet at this kind of direct and physical challenge, he came up like a deck-chair in the hands of a child, falling this way and that in stilted commotion, until Artemis . . . controlled him and, offering him the end of a strangled napkin, drew him into silent conversation. They turned and rode on the swollen sand, turned inside and under each other and Artemis schooled Dmitri in elegance with a mastery the other might find more unforgivable than violence. He could match violence with power, but there was no matching this slim and humorous pedantry. Kosta began to hum and moan like a wire in the wind, the first promise of the storm, while Dmitri was exhausted by the soft precision expected from him. He gasped as if he were dodging walls, as if a court was tight about the dancing pair, tighter than the loose circle of sand, and some penalty was due if one touched the cold face of it.

Artemis defined Dmitri for Katerina that night. He defined the man's limits in front of the girl. He defined his own superiority and he abdicated his share of the world of Stratis and his thick millions. He danced Dmitri as a man and a partner might run down and bewilder a bull with alternate goads. Katerina was his partner, but a partner promised a separation. Artemis allowed Dmitri every chance to command the steps. He bowed and yielded, as a lover will sometimes hesitate in a caress to allow its rejection or will lie back and give his partner the chance to discover the frontier of her own temerity, to assault herself with his body, but Dmitri could only guffaw at such times and make a gross imitation of some grand gesture which he knew to be beyond him. . . . Now Dmitri drew Michael Shaw to his feet, glad to find someone incapable even of parody. And then Artemis was cruel; he broke the chain and left the two to confont the music alone. They stammered and Kosta laughed and raised the rhythm to double and quadruple time till there was something savage in his fingers, something indifferent and immodest. He flung down the last phrases like an insult and clapped his hand over the mouth of his guitar. And then Artemis was like a ghost. As they looked he was dancing again, but beyond them now, down by the sea, he was dancing with the sea, he was measuring himself against the sea, stepping on its skirt as it sipped the land, courting the sea as he had courted Katerina, so that finally she ran to him and the others smiled.

*Readers: Angela Down, Norman Rodway*

*Full Selection:*
*Cakes and Ale,* SOMERSET MAUGHAM

*The Portrait of a Lady,* HENRY JAMES
*Appointment in Samarra,* JOHN O' HARA
*The Trial,* FRANZ KAFKA
*Laughter in the Dark,* VLADIMIR NABOKOV
*His Toy, His Dream, His Rest,* JOHN BERRYMAN
*Private Lives,* NOËL COWARD
*It's Terrible! It's Ghastly! It Stinks!* EDMUND WILSON
*Maxims of the Duc de la Rochefoucauld,* trans CONSTANTINE FITZGIBBON
*A Fragment of a Greek Tragedy,* A. E. HOUSMAN
*Letter to Douglas Kinnaird,* LORD BYRON
*King Claudius,* C. P. CAVAFY
*Antichrist, Or The Reunion of Christendom: An Ode,* G. K. CHESTERTON
*The General,* SIEGFRIED SASSOON
*Courtroom Address,* JUDGE CYRIL SALMON
*Like Men Betrayed,* FREDERIC RAPHAEL

# DR ROBERT RUNCIE

## 1986

*Many important people like to surround themselves with the trappings of power – people rushing around after them, an expectation of lavish hospitality, that sort of thing. This Archbishop of Canterbury could hardly have been more different. He clearly did not want any BBC 'brass' in attendance (some would argue that that displayed no more than good sense!) nor did he wish to be especially well fed. He arrived in Broadcasting House reception accompanied only by a couple of close colleagues and joined the production team for sandwiches after the recording. In between he was delighted and flattered to be sharing a platform with Michael Hordern and Judi Dench.*

I have always enjoyed and envied *style*, not in the sense of high-flown sentiments and ornate wording, but style meaning a directness and sincerity of expression so that the writers convey to my mind as exactly as possible what they are feeling and saying. The following passage expresses what I feel about style with a light but sure touch. It is by Ernest Gowers. He was editor of the *Oxford English Dictionary*, so he should know what he is talking about here.

## *Plain Words*

**ERNEST GOWERS**

Why do so many writers prefer 'pudder' to simplicity? It seems to be a morbid condition contracted in early manhood. Children show no signs of it. Here, for example, is the response of a child of ten to an invitation to write an essay (its genuineness is guaranteed) on a beast and a bird:

'The bird that I am going to write about is the owl. The owl cannot see at all by day and at night is as blind as a bat.

I do not know much about the owl, so I will go on to the beast which I am to choose. It is the cow. The cow is a mammal. It has six sides – right, left, an upper and below. At the back it has a tail on which hangs a brush. With this it sends the flies away so that they do not fall into the milk. The head is for the purpose of growing horns and so that the mouth can be somewhere. The horns are to butt with, and the mouth is to moo with. Under the cow hangs the milk. It is arranged for milking. When people milk, the milk comes and there is never an end to the supply. How the cow does it I have not yet realised, but it makes more and more. The cow has a fine sense of smell; one can smell it far away. This is the reason for the fresh air in the country.

The man cow is called an ox. It is not a mammal. The cow does not eat much, but what it eats it eats twice, so that it gets enough. When it is hungry it moos, and when it says nothing it is because its inside is all full up with grass.'

My mother was a hairdresser on an ocean liner. I was brought up beside the Mersey in cosmopolitan Liverpool. Perhaps this accounts a little for my lifelong enjoyment of travel. And it is partly just being Scots. The Scots and the Greeks have always gone out into all lands. They have thrived on doing so. But they never forget their native and beloved hills.

I have travelled for its own sake, but far more for the appreciation of other people, and of natural beauty – and for the contemplation of works of Art.

Providence has been very kind to me: allowing me to visit, and learn to love, so many places – Samarkand and San Francisco, Delhi, Venice and Istanbul. All this grew out of my first love for the Greek world. It is to Greece first of all that I long to return.

To celebrate this I have chosen the first three stanzas of Lord Byron's poem 'The Isles of Greece'. This was really nationalist propaganda when Greece was struggling for independence in the 1820s, but it breathes an eternal spirit.

## *The Isles of Greece*

**LORD BYRON**

The isles of Greece! the isles of Greece
Where burning Sappho loved and sung,
Where grew the arts of war and peace,
Where Delos rose, and Phoebus sprung!
Eternal summer gilds them yet,
But all, except their sun, is set.

The Scian and the Teian muse,
The hero's harp, the lover's lute,
Have found the fame your shores refuse:
Their place of birth alone is mute
To sounds which echo further west
Than your sires' 'Islands of the Blest'.

The mountains look on Marathon –
And Marathon looks on the sea;
And musing there an hour alone,
I dream'd that Greece might still be free;
For standing on the Persian's grave,
I could not deem myself a slave.

When the clouds gather, I frequently turn to that worldly cleric, Sydney Smith. A conservative in religion, and a liberal in politics, he said that his life was like a razor – spent either in hot water or a scrape.

When I have to go to, and possibly speak at, a City dinner, I usually arm myself with the *Sayings of Sydney Smith*. He is so eminently quotable. He said of someone that their idea of heaven is that of eating pâté de fois gras to the sound of trumpets. I have a Swiss sister-in-law, and I tease her by repeating his remark that Switzerland is an inferior sort of Scotland. Then, who else would have said: 'I have only one illusion left and that is the Archbishop of Canterbury'?

He may now be better known for his bons mots than for his pastoral diligence, but there was that side of him too. The best of both can be found in this letter to Lady Morpeth, who had complained of low spirits. Like many funny people he suffered from melancholy himself.

## *Letter to Lady Georgiana Morpeth*

SYDNEY SMITH

Dear Georgiana,
Nobody has suffered more from low spirits than I have done, so I feel for you.

1. Live as well and drink as much wine as you dare.
2. Go into the shower bath with a small quantity of water at a temperature low enough to give you a slight sensation of cold – 75 or 80 degrees.
3. Amusing books.
4. Short views of human life not further than dinner or tea.
5. Be as busy as you can.
6. See as much as you can of those friends who respect and like you;
7. and of those acquaintances who amuse you.
8. Make no secret of low spirits to your friends but talk of them fully: they are always the worse for dignified concealment.
9. Attend to the effects tea and coffee produce upon you.
10. Compare your lot with that of other people.
11. Don't expect too much of human life, a sorry business at best.
12. Avoid poetry, dramatic representations (except comedy),

music, serious novels, melancholy sentimental people, and everything likely to excite feeling or emotion not ending in active benevolence.

13. Do good and endeavour to please everybody of every degree.
14. Be as much as you can in the open air without fatigue.
15. Make the room where you commonly sit gay and pleasant.
16. Struggle by little and little against idleness.
17. Don't be too severe upon yourself, or underrate yourself, but do yourself justice.
18. Keep good blazing fires.
19. Be firm and constant in the exercise of rational religion.
20. Believe me dear Lady Georgiana very truly yours, Sydney Smith.

I usually only spend working weekends, and any holidays I ever have, at Canterbury. Otherwise, unless overseas, I am at Lambeth. I love Lambeth, for there so much history encircles such a great volume of work being done to serve the worldwide Anglican Church of the present. But I love the setting also. Although my vantage point is not quite the same as Wordsworth's, only a few hundred yards separate it from Westminster Bridge. What he wrote in 1802 was entirely true for me this morning.

## *Upon Westminster Bridge*

**WILLIAM WORDSWORTH**

Earth has not anything to show more fair:
Dull would he be of soul who could pass by
A sight so touching in its majesty:
This City now doth, like a garment, wear
The beauty of the morning; silent, bare,
Ships, towers, domes, theatres, and temples lie
Open unto the fields, and to the sky;
All bright and glittering in the smokeless air.
Never did sun more beautifully steep
In his first splendour, valley, rock, or hill;
Ne'er saw I, never felt, a calm so deep!
The river glideth at his own sweet will:
Dear God! the very houses seem asleep;
And all that mighty heart is lying still!

Who am I? Perhaps my selection has revealed parts of an answer that I scarcely know myself.

Dietrich Bonhoeffer was a German pastor who died in a Nazi prison. He was one of the great prophetic voices of modern times. He saw Christianity in a new kind of balance – relying less on words and more on practical love. Here is his poem about identity, written in prison. It speaks to my condition. For we all worry about our identity, and the truth – for Bonhoeffer and for me – is that without God there is no answer.

## *Who Am I?*

**DIETRICH BONHOEFFER**

Who am I? They often tell me
I would step from my cell's confinement
calmly, cheerfully, firmly,
like a squire from his country house.

Who am I? They often tell me
I would talk to my warders
freely and friendly and clearly,
as though it were mine to command.

Who am I? They also tell me
I would bear the days of misfortune
equably, smilingly, proudly,
like one accustomed to win.

Am I then really all that which other men tell of?
Or am I only what I know of myself,
restless and longing and sick, like a bird in a cage,
struggling for breath, as though hands were compressing
my throat,
yearning for colours, for flowers, for the voices of birds,
thirsting for words of kindness, for neighbourliness,
trembling with anger at despotisms and petty humiliation,
tossing in expectation of great events,
powerlessly trembling for friends at an infinite distance,
weary and empty at praying, at thinking, at making,
faint, and ready to say farewell to it all?

Who am I? This or the other?
Am I one person today, and tomorrow another?
Am I both at once? A hypocrite before others,
And before myself a contemptibly woebegone weakling?
Or is something within me still like a beaten army,
fleeing in disorder from victory already achieved?

Who am I? They mock me, these lonely questions of mine.
Whoever I am, thou knowest, O God, I am thine.

*Readers: Michael Hordern, Judi Dench*

*Full Selection:*
*Plain Words,* ERNEST GOWERS
*Lochinvar,* SIR WALTER SCOTT
*The Merchant of Venice,* WILLIAM SHAKESPEARE
*The Question,* ALEXANDER McKEE
*Portraits of Places 1883,* HENRY JAMES
*Kneeling,* R. S. THOMAS
*The Strangers All Are Gone,* ANTHONY POWELL
*The Isles of Greece,* LORD BYRON
*The Story of Art,* E. H. GOMBRICH
*Ithaka,* C. P. CAVAFY
*Thursday, Christmas Eve,* FRANCIS KILVERT
*Letter to Lady Georgiana Morpeth,* SYDNEY SMITH
*In a Bath Teashop,* JOHN BETJEMAN
*Murder in the Cathedral,* T. S. ELIOT
*Upon Westminster Bridge,* WILLIAM WORDSWORTH
*Limbo,* ALDOUS HUXLEY
*Missed,* P. G. WODEHOUSE
*Who Am I?* DIETRICH BONHOEFFER
*Revelations of Divine Love,* DAME JULIAN OF NORWICH

# *JOHN TIMPSON*

## *1986*

*The first thing John Timpson said when asked to present an edition of 'With Great Pleasure' was 'Has Redhead done one?' He looked absolutely delighted when I told him that he had not. Their double act on the 'Today' programme made the early mornings just bearable. Latterly Timpson's chairing of 'Any Questions' was entertaining not just for his firm handling of the panellists, but for his lengthy and witty introductions to them. He left both jobs earlier than he need to spend more time in his beloved Norfolk.*

I suppose like many others of my generation, my first encounter with Literature – with a capital L – was the incomparable, and to most ten-year-olds quite incomprehensible, William Shakespeare. I had to learn all the standard speeches, I understood perhaps one line in three, and I'm not sure I understand them all now, but I find I can still render 'Once more unto the breach' and 'All the world's a stage' and 'Tomorrow and tomorrow and tomorrow' – I can still get right through to the last couplet without a falter, even though I often can't remember the names of people I met yesterday. Perhaps it's because we had a headmaster who insisted that we actually performed Shakespeare as well as just reciting it – something which I see has just been hailed as a breakthrough in modern teaching methods, but he did it mainly to get publicity. He liked to impress prospective parents by staging entertainments in the Speech Room at Harrow School – how he acquired the use of it I shall never know, because the only connection between Harrow School and our school in Harrow was the name of the borough – but of course the parents loved it.

My favourite role was the Duke of Clarence in *Richard III*, who was foully murdered in the Tower. It's the scene with the classic stage direction: 'Enter two murderers', and I remember dying magnificently centre stage as the second murderer cried 'Take that and that, and if that will not do, I'll drown you in the malmsey butt within.' It was great stuff and we hammed it up disgracefully – particularly Clarence's gruesome description of the nightmare he'd had before the murderers appeared.

## *Richard III*

**WILLIAM SHAKESPEARE**

Methought that I had broken from the Tower,
And was embark'd to cross to Burgundy;
And in my company my brother Gloster;
Who from my cabin tempted me to walk
Upon the hatches: thence we look'd toward England,
And cited up a thousand heavy times,
During the wars of York and Lancaster,
That had befall'n us. As we pac'd along
Upon the giddy footing of the hatches,
Methought that Gloster stumbled; and, in falling,
Struck me, that thought to stay him, overboard,
Into the tumbling billows of the main.
Lord, Lord! methought what pain it was to drown:
What dreadful noise of water in mine ears!
What sights of ugly death within mine eyes!
Methought I saw a thousand fearful wrecks;
Ten thousand men that fishes gnaw'd upon;
Wedges of gold, great anchors, heaps of pearl,
Inestimable stones, unvalu'd jewels,
All scattered in the bottom of the sea:
Some lay in dead men's skulls; and in those holes
Where eyes did once inhabit there were crept,
As 'twere in scorn of eyes, reflecting gems,
That woo'd the slimy bottom of the deep,
And mock'd the dead bones that lay scatter'd by.

But then, my dream was lengthen'd after life;
O, then began the tempest to my soul.
I pass'd, methought, the melancholy flood
With that grim ferryman which poets write of,
Unto the kingdom of perpetual night.
The first that there did greet my stranger soul
Was my great father-in-law, renowned Warwick;
Who cried aloud, 'What scourge for perjury
Can this dark monarchy afford false Clarence?'
And so he vanish'd: then came wandering by
A shadow like an angel, with bright hair
Dabbled in blood; and he shriek'd out aloud,
'Clarence is come, – false, fleeting, perjured Clarence,
That stabb'd me in the field by Tewkesbury; –
Seize on him! Furies, take him unto torment!'
With that, methought, a legion of foul fiends
Environ'd me, and howled in mine ears
Such hideous cries that, with the very noise,
I trembling wak'd, and for a season after
Could not believe but that I was in hell,
Such terrible impression made my dream.

I always look forward to getting back to those vast Norfolk skies and the rolling countryside which is not at all flat and boring as people think – we just say it is to discourage too many visitors, much assisted in that by the vagaries of the Eastern Region of British Rail and the inadequacies of the main roads. I often think it is no accident that the only motorway in East Anglia stops at Cambridge. The other special feature of Norfolk is of course the churches. John Betjeman loved Norfolk too – he called it one of the great architectural treasures of Europe because of the sheer profusion of country churches. Perhaps indeed they are too profuse – our own rector has seven churches to cope with, and that is by no means unusual. Betjeman published a little collection of his poems which may well have been inspired by those Norfolk churches. Here's one I know will appeal to all parsons, including our own.

## *Blame the Vicar*

**JOHN BETJEMAN**

When things go wrong it's rather tame
To find we are ourselves to blame,
It gets the trouble over quicker
To go and blame things on the Vicar.
The Vicar, after all, is paid
To keep us bright and undismayed.
The Vicar is more virtuous too
Than lay folks such as me and you.
He never swears, he never drinks,
He never *should* say what he thinks.
His collar is the wrong way round,
And that is why he's simply bound
To be the sort of person who
Has nothing very much to do
But take the blame for what goes wrong
And sing in tune at Evensong.
For what's a Vicar really for
Except to cheer us up? What's more,
He shouldn't ever, ever tell
If there is such a place as Hell,
For if there is it's certain he
Will go to it as well as we.
The Vicar should be all pretence
And never, never give offence.
To preach on Sunday is his task
And lend his mower when we ask
And organise our village fêtes
And sing at Christmas with the waits
And in his car to give us lifts
And when we quarrel, heal the rifts.
To keep his family alive
He should industriously strive
In that enormous house he gets,
And he should always pay his debts,
For he has quite six pounds a week,

And when we're rude he should be meek
And always turn the other cheek.
He should be neat and nicely dressed
With polished shoes and trousers pressed,
For we look up to him as higher
Than anyone, except the Squire.
 Dear People, who have read so far,
I know how really kind you are,
I hope that you are always seeing
Your Vicar as a human being,
Making allowances when he
Does things with which you don't agree.
But there are lots of people who
Are not so kind to him as you.
So in conclusion you shall hear
About a parish somewhere near,
Perhaps your own or maybe not,
And of the Vicars that it got.
 One parson came and people said,
'Alas! Our former Vicar's dead!
And this new man is far more "Low"
Than dear old Reverend so-and-so,
And far too earnest in his preaching,
We do not really like his teaching,
He seems to think we're simply fools
Who've never been to Sunday Schools.'
That Vicar left, and by and by
A new one came, 'He's much too "High",'
The people said, 'too like a saint,
His incense makes our Mavis faint.'
So now he's left and they're alone
Without a Vicar of their own.
The living's been amalgamated
With the one next door they've always hated.
 Dear readers, from this rhyme take warning,
And if you heard the bell this morning
Your Vicar went to pray for you,
A task the Prayer Book bids him do.
'Highness' or 'Lowness' do not matter,

You are the Church and must not scatter,
Cling to the Sacraments and pray
And God be with you every day.

For many years now we have had hanging up in our kitchen what I've always known as *The Old Nun's Prayer*, though there are various sources. It includes for instance the word 'Cocksureness' which you do not immediately associate with old nuns. But it's a prayer which combines humility with humour – the sort of thing Rabbi Lionel Blue would probably wish he'd written. It was this prayer that I suggested when I was asked a few years ago to contribute to an anthology called *A Way With Words*, in aid of sufferers from dysphasia, that very distressing disorder which affects the ability to utter and understand language. Many people whose careers and livelihoods depend on that contributed to the book. *The Old Nun's Prayer* does too, but not under my name – under Mrs Thatcher's. She too selected it, and it was only fitting that I should withdraw in her favour. We in the BBC are like that. But at least I can choose it now – and perhaps you'll see why it's an appropriate prayer, not just for Mrs Thatcher but for almost any politician.

### *An Old English Nun's Prayer*

Lord, Thou knowest better than I know myself that I am growing older and will some day be old. Keep me from the fatal habit of thinking I must say something on every subject and on every occasion.

Release me from craving to straighten out everybody's affairs. Make me thoughtful but not moody; helpful but not bossy. With my vast store of wisdom, it seems a pity not to use it all, but Thou knowest Lord that I want a few friends at the end.

Keep my mind from the recital of endless details; give me wings to get to the point. Seal my lips on aches and pains. They are increasing, and love of rehearsing them is becoming sweeter as the years go by. I dare not ask for grace enough to enjoy the tales of other's pains, but help me to endure them with patience.

I dare not ask for improved memory, but for a growing humility and a lessening cocksureness when my memory seems to clash with the memories of others. Teach me the glorious lesson that occasionally I may be mistaken.

Keep me reasonably sweet. I do not want to be a Saint – some of them are so hard to live with – but a sour old person is one of the crowning works of the devil. Give me the ability to see good things in unexpected places and talents in unexpected people. And give me, O Lord, the grace to tell them so.

AMEN

I particularly like that line 'Teach me that occasionally I can be mistaken.' I am sure Mrs Thatcher does too.

I mentioned that I withdrew my claim to that contribution and I had to find another in rather a hurry. As always on such occasions, the mind went blank. But it so happened I was browsing through the *Radio Times* – mainly to see if I'm still working next week – when I came upon a little verse by Leo Marks that has haunted me ever since. There is a romantic and moving story behind the verse, involving a wartime woman agent and a secret code – I won't go into it all because for me this little verse has a life of its own – it doesn't need a background or an explanation. It says in a few simple lines what I think many a husband would like to say to his wife, but after, say, thirty-five years of married life he might think it would sound too sloppy, unless it was some special occasion. Well, this for me is a special occasion.

## *Code Poem for the French Resistance*

**LEO MARKS**

The life that I have is all that I have,
And the life that I have is yours.
The love that I have of the life that I have
Is yours and yours and yours.

A sleep I shall have
A rest I shall have,
Yet death will be but a pause,
For the peace of my years in the long green grass
Will be yours and yours and yours.

*Readers: Carol Drinkwater, Anthony Hyde*

*Full Selection:*
*Richard III*, WILLIAM SHAKESPEARE
*William the Bad*, RICHMAL CROMPTON
*The Quiet American*, GRAHAM GREENE
*The Pickwick Papers*, CHARLES DICKENS
*Scoop*, EVELYN WAUGH
*The Boy John*, SIDNEY GRAPES
*Blame the Vicar*, JOHN BETJEMAN
*Ballad of the Bread Man*, CHARLES CAUSLEY
*An Old English Nun's Prayer*, ANON
*Code Poem for the French Resistance*, LEO MARKS

# SUE TOWNSEND

## *1987*

*'Daddy, what's a French letter?' Those words uttered by my ten-year-old son within the confines of St David's Cathedral created a degree of head-turning amongst the tour guide's disciples. 'I'll tell you in a minute,' I whispered, I hoped not too audibly, as I steered him tactfully behind a pillar. After a moment or two of perhaps overly detailed explanation he muttered firmly and a little bored 'You mean a condom?' 'Yes, I suppose I do,' I said. 'By the way, where did you hear the expression "French letter"? You don't hear it so often nowadays.' 'Oh,' he said, 'Adrian Mole.' After that there was nothing for it but to invite Sue Townsend on to the programme. She proved to be a funny, scatty and warm person who was clearly loved by the audience made up of her many friends in Leicester where she lives.*

*Jane Eyre* was the first book I read all the way through in one go. I didn't sleep at all. The birds started to sing; I read on. I washed with the book leaning against the taps. I walked to school still reading. I read in Maths and French and in the cloakroom. This extract describes a visit from Mr Brocklehurst, a clergyman who is Superintendent at Lowood School where Jane Eyre was sent when she was eight years old.

## *Jane Eyre*
**CHARLOTTE BRONTË**

'Miss Temple, Miss Temple, what – *what* is that girl with curled hair? Red hair, ma'am, curled – curled all over?' And extending his cane he pointed to the awful object, his hand shaking as he did so.

'It is Julia Severn,' replied Miss Temple very quietly.

'Julia Severn, ma'am! And why has she, or any other, curled hair? Why, in defiance of every precept and principle of this house, does she conform to the world so openly – here in an evangelical, charitable establishment – as to wear her hair one mass of curls?'

'Julia's hair curls naturally,' returned Miss Temple still more quietly.

'Naturally! Yes, but we are not to conform to nature. I wish these girls to be the children of Grace: and why that abundance? I have again and again intimated that I desire the hair to be arranged closely, modestly, plainly. Miss Temple, that girl's hair must be cut off entirely; I will send a barber tomorrow: and I see others who have far too much of that excrescence – that tall girl, tell her to turn round. Tell all the first form to rise up and direct their faces to the wall.'

Miss Temple passed her handkerchief over her lips, as if to smooth away the involuntary smile that curled them; she gave the order, however, and when the first class could take in what was required of them, they obeyed. Leaning a little back on my bench, I could see the looks and grimaces with which they commented on this manoeuvre: it was a pity Mr Brocklehurst could not see them too; he would perhaps have felt that, whatever he might do with the outside of the cup and platter, the inside was farther beyond his interference than he imagined.

He scrutinised the reverse of these living medals some five minutes, then pronounced sentence. These words fell like the knell of doom.

'All these top-knots must be cut off.'

Miss Temple seemed to remonstrate.

'Madam,' he pursued, 'I have a Master to serve whose kingdom is not of this world: my mission is to mortify in these girls the lusts of the flesh, to teach them to clothe themselves with shamefacedness and sobriety, not with braided hair and costly apparel; and each of the young persons before us has a string of hair twisted in plaits which vanity itself might have woven: these, I repeat, must be cut off.'

One of my many jobs, before I started writing for a living, was as a community warden in two tower blocks that had been filled up with retired people. I soon realized that the pathetic image that old people had was completely misleading. These are Percy Collins' words, he is real and he is seventy-six.

## *The People of Providence*
**TONY PARKER**

A nice woman my own age, an hour or two in bed together with someone like that, that's always been the thing for me. And so long as it's regular, once a week or so, I'm perfectly content. It doesn't have to be what they call the full thing every time either – I enjoy the love-making and kissing and cuddling as much, or more even sometimes, on its own.

I've never been with a prostitute. I don't somehow fancy that, it's got to be someone I know and like. There again you see I've been lucky, there's any number of ladies around who're my age, widows or single most of them: I don't think it's right to run the risk of perhaps someone's husband finding out and making trouble about it. Most of them seem to feel the same way I do. I usually say something like 'Well shall we try it and see how it goes, and if you don't like it we'll not go on with it.' But there's not many that don't. I think there's something about sex that's really nice, it's fun but it's more than that, it gives you a good warm feeling inside of you, you're being absolutely natural. It's giving somebody pleasure, it's you giving somebody pleasure. I think that's very nice and very good. So long as you don't get jealous about them and they don't get jealous about you, it's not doing harm to anyone as far as I can see.

I suppose there must be about twelve or so ladies that we're on that kind of terms together. Most of them like myself belong to the church – it's a good meeting place to come into contact with other people who're on their own. And if someone goes to church you know she's got what you call a level-headed approach to things; she's not going to be like somebody you might pick up casually in a pub. I don't like the sort of coarse jokes you sometimes hear women making in pubs. If I'm love-making with someone I prefer her to be a conventional sort of person like myself.

Sojourner Truth was a freed slave who travelled around the United States trying to free her people from slavery. She believed in equality for all, black and white and women with men. At one meeting where she was due to speak some clergymen said that women could never be equal because men had more intelligence, because Christ was a man and because of the sin of Eve. She made the following speech.

## *Ain't I a Woman?*

### SOJOURNER TRUTH

Well, children, where there is so much racket there must be something out of kilter. I think that 'twixt the negroes of the South and women of the North, all talking about rights, the white men will be in a fix pretty soon. But what's all this here talking about?

That man over there says that women need to be helped into carriages, and lifted over ditches, and to have the best place everywhere. Nobody ever helps me into carriages, or over mud-puddles, or gives me any best place! And ain't I a woman? Look at me! Look at my arm! I have ploughed and planted, and gathered into barns, and no man could head me! And ain't I a woman? I could work as much and eat as much as a man – when I could get it – and bear the lash as well! And ain't I a woman? I have borne thirteen children; and seen them most all sold off to slavery, and when I cried out with my mother's grief, none but Jesus heard me! And ain't I a woman?

Then they talk about this thing in the head; what's this they call it? (Intellect, someone whispers.) That's it, honey. What's that got to do with women's rights or negro's rights? If my cup won't hold but a pint, and yours holds a quart, wouldn't you be mean not to let me have my little half-measure full?

Then that little black man in black there, he says women can't have as much rights as men, 'cause Christ wasn't a woman! Where did your Christ come from? Where did your Christ come from? From God and a woman! Man had nothing to do with Him!

If the first woman God ever made was strong enough to turn the world upside down all alone, these women together ought to be able to turn it back, and get it right-side up again! And now they is asking to do it, the men better let them.

Obliged to you for hearing me, and now Old Sojourner ain't got nothing more to say.

Wouldn't you love to hear a politician tell the truth? Just once? The following letter is a guess at how the truth might sound from one particular politician.

## *Dear Mr Eggnogge*

**THE *SPITTING IMAGE* BOOK** 1987

Dear Ernest Eggnogge,
I've received some whining, snivelling, wipe my eyes, pass the Kleenex letters in my time, but yours truly takes the Huntley and Palmers. Quite frankly I don't give a toss that your old mother died of hypothermia last winter or that your zit-faced moronic teenaged lout of a son has not worked since leaving school. And the news that your wife has been waiting for six years to have her nasty infected womb removed left me cold. Haven't you got a sharp knife for God's sake?

You dare to say that I am 'out of touch with real people' and suggest I 'jump on a train and come up North'.

Firstly, Mr Eggnogge, I am married to a 'real person'. Secondly, I would rather spend the night with Guy the Gorilla (Yes, I know he's dead) than climb aboard one of those vile rattling contraptions and visit you all up there in slag heap land. We have nothing in common. I hate ferrets, dripping, pigeons, corner shops and fat, ugly, pale people who are unable to speak in complete sentences and who don't understand how the International Monetary Fund works.

Finally, at the end of your letter you bleat on about your dole payment calling it 'a pittance' and 'an affront to your dignity'. This last bit made me laugh quite a lot. What did you get for Christmas? A subscription to *New Society*?

Listen parasite, that's the point, don't you see? We don't need you and your sort anymore – get the message now? Take my advice, shovel the coal out of the bath, then fill it up and jump in and drown yourself.

(NB Note to private secretary: Tidy this up a bit will you?)

And this is the tidied up version that Ernest Eggnogge actually received:

Dear Mr Eggnogge,
The Prime Minister was most concerned to hear of your difficulties. She is looking into the various matters you raised in your letter.
Yours sincerely
Rupert Brown-Bear

I think we accept too meekly the rules that professional politicians lay down for us. They are no wiser than you or I. When the Nazi storm troopers first goose-stepped through Berlin the German people should have laughed them off the streets. Laughter can be a very powerful weapon. Though there comes a time when even laughter fails.

This was written by Pastor Niemoller, who was a prisoner of the Nazis.

## *First They Came for the Jews*

**PASTOR NIEMOLLER**

First they came for the Jews
And I did not speak out –
Because I was not a Jew.

Then they came for the Communists
And I did not speak out –
Because I was not a Communist.

Then they came for the Trade
Unionists and I did not speak out –
Because I was not a Trade Unionist.

Then they came for me –
And there was no one left
To speak out for me.

*Readers: Peter Jeffrey, Julia Hills*

*Full Selection:*
*Janet and John,* MABEL O'DONNELL and RONA MUNRO
*Just William's Luck,* RICHMAL CROMPTON
*Jane Eyre,* CHARLOTTE BRONTË
*Cargoes,* JOHN MASEFIELD
*Lucky Jim,* KINGSLEY AMIS
*Songs For a Coloured Singer,* ELIZABETH BISHOP
*Extracts from* Punch *and* Country Life
*The People of Providence,* TONY PARKER
*Consult Me For All You Want To Know,*
FLANN O'BRIEN
*Loot,* JOE ORTON
*Ain't I a Woman?,* SOJOURNER TRUTH
*Noël Coward Diaries,* NOËL COWARD
*Dear Mr Eggnogge,* THE *SPITTING IMAGE* BOOK
*First They Came for the Jews,* PASTOR NIEMOLLER

# JOHN UPDIKE

## 1980

*Death, terrors in childhood and a faint light glimmering in the darkness, John Updike in his programme pondered on these, and they have obviously been a refrain throughout all his life. As a child he saw the Bible as containing 'much dark matter. There was, to the small child, much hate, terror and abandonment in it.' He had not expected to find the hard face of God in the New Testament. He empathized with 'the timidity of the man who, entrusted with but one meagre talent, buried it in the ground for safe keeping.' He was shocked and tried to be illuminated 'dark as it was' – again that faint light. At the end he thanked the actors for their 'brilliant re-animation of the ghosts from my personal world of print'. John Updike somehow managed to combine an autobiography of his inner mind with a robustness much enjoyed by the audience.*

The first poem which made an impression on me is this one. It frightened me. People in Pennsylvania believed in goblins and James Whitcomb Riley, a popular nineteenth-century poet from Indiana, reinforced that belief powerfully. I think that Miss Tate of the third grade used to read this poem to us; through it and the alarming reassurance of its refrain I did receive my first impression of poetry as something potentially powerful, with the peculiar power of rhyme and meter.

### *Little Orphant Annie*
JAMES WHITCOMB RILEY

Little Orphant Annie's came to our house to stay,
An' wash the cups an' saucers up, an' brush the crumbs away,

An' shoo the chickens off the porch, an' dust the hearth an'
  sweep,
An' make the fire, an' bake the bread, an' earn her
  board-an'-keep;
An' all us other children, when the supper-things is done,
We set around the kitchen fire an' has the mostest fun
A-list'nin' to the witch-tales 'at Annie tells about,
An' the Gobble-uns 'at gits you
            Ef you
              Don't
                Watch
                  Out!

Wunst they wuz a little boy wouldn't say his prayers, –
An' when he went to bed at night, away up-stairs,
His mammy heerd him holler, an' his daddy heerd him bawl,
An' when they turn't the kivvers down, he wuzn't there at all!
An' they seeked him in the rafter-room, an' cubby-hole, an'
  press,
An' seeked him up the chimbly-flue, an' ever'-wheres, I guess;
But all they ever found wuz thist his pants an' roundabout: –
An' the Gobble-uns'll git you
            Ef you
              Don't
                Watch
                  Out!

An' one time a little girl 'ud allus laugh an' grin,
An' make fun of ever' one, an' all her blood-an'-kin;
An' wunst, when they was 'company', an' old folks wuz there,
She mocked 'em an' shocked 'em, an' said she didn't care!
An' thist as she kicked her heels, an' turn't to run an' hide,
They wuz two great big Black Things a-standin' by her side,
An' they snatched her through the ceilin' 'fore she knowed what
  she's about!
An' the Gobble-uns'll git you
            Ef you
              Don't
                Watch
                  Out!

An' little Orphant Annie says, when the blaze is blue,
An' the lamp-wick sputters, an' the wind goes woo-oo,
An' you hear the crickets quit, an' the moon is gray,
An' the lightning'-bugs in dew is all squenched away, –
You better mind yer parunts, an' yer teachers fond an' dear,
An' churish them 'at loves you, an' dry the orphant's tear,
An' he'p the pore an' needy ones 'at clusters all about,
Er the Gobble-uns'll git you
Ef you
Don't
Watch
Out!

The next selection is also alarming. One is admonished as a child to read the classics without being told that the grim vision of the great writer might overwhelm a child's sensibility. In the middle of *Tom Sawyer,* which is urged upon fifth-grade children, there is a long episode in which Tom and his platonic girl friend, Becky, go into a cave and wander deeper and deeper – they come to a realm where there are no more initials scratched on the wall, no more candle stubs can be found and they become lost and it's very well described and very well felt. They wind up in the deep dark, the candle goes out, Becky curls up in a little passive ball and waits for death to come while Tom crawls up one limestone tunnel after another in an apparently hopeless search for the way out. He does indeed see at the end of a tunnel a bit of light, crawls toward it and comes out on the banks of the Mississippi, five miles beyond where they entered. The sequel of this horrifying episode is that the town, being an activist welfare-minded town, puts an iron gate over the mouth of the cave to prevent anything like this happening again. Tom is conveniently sent to sleep by the author for long enough to permit this to happen because when he wakes up he tells them that Injun Joe, a town outlaw, is in that cave also. At one point in this terrifying adventure Tom glimpsed Injun Joe holding a candle, so the townsfolk rush to the mouth of the cave.

## *Tom Sawyer*

**MARK TWAIN**

When the cave door was unlocked, a sorrowful sight presented itself in the dim twilight of the place. Injun Joe lay stretched upon the ground, dead, with his face close to the crack of the door, as if his longing eyes had been fixed, to the latest moment, upon the light and the cheer of the free world outside. Tom was touched, for he knew by his own experience how this wretch had suffered. His pity was moved, but nevertheless he felt an abounding sense of relief and security, now, which revealed to him in a degree which he had not fully appreciated before how vast a weight of dread had been lying upon him since the day he lifted his voice against this bloody-minded outcast.

Injun Joe's bowie-knife lay close by, its blade broken in two. The great foundation-beam of the door had been chipped and hacked through, with tedious labor; useless labor, too, it was, for the native rock formed a sill outside it, and upon that stubborn material the knife had wrought no effect; the only damage done was to the knife itself. But if there had been no stony obstruction there the labor would have been useless still, for if the beam had been wholly cut away Injun Joe could not have squeezed his body under the door, and he knew it. So he had only hacked that place in order to be doing something – in order to pass the weary time – in order to employ his tortured faculties. Ordinarily one could find a dozen bits of candle stuck around in the crevices of this vestibule, left there by tourists; but there were none now. The prisoner had searched them out and eaten them. He had also contrived to catch a few bats, and these, also, he had eaten, leaving only their claws. The poor unfortunate had starved to death. In one place, near at hand, a stalagmite had been slowly growing up from the ground for ages, builded by the water-drip from a stalactite overhead. The captive had broken off the stalagmite, and upon the stump had placed a stone, wherein he had scooped a shallow hollow to catch the precious drop that fell once in every three minutes with the dreary regularity of a clock-tick – a dessertspoonful once in four and twenty hours. That drop was falling when the Pyramids were new; when Troy fell; when the foundations of Rome were laid; when Christ was crucified; when the Conqueror created the British Empire; when Columbus sailed; when the massacre at Lexington was 'news'. It is falling now; it will still be falling when all these things shall have sunk down the afternoon of history, and the twilight of tradition, and been swallowed up in the thick night of oblivion.

Has everything a purpose and a mission? Did this drop fall patiently during five thousand years to be ready for this flitting human insect's need? And has it another important object to accomplish ten thousand years to come? No matter. It is many and many a year since the hapless half-breed scooped out the stone to catch the priceless drops, but to this day the tourist stares longest at that pathetic stone and that slow-dripping water when he comes to see the wonders of McDougal's cave. Injun Joe's cup stands first in the list of the cavern's marvels.

I went to college and while there majored in what was called English Lit. and my speciality was the seventeenth century – strange to say – and my speciality within that was poetry. It wasn't just that Eliot had made the metaphysicals chic; perhaps the same mind that used to delight in mystery novels was able to enjoy conceits elaborately developed. I've picked to represent this mass of literature a poem by John Donne.

## *A Valediction: of Weeping*

**JOHN DONNE**

Let me pour forth
My tears before thy face, whilst I stay here,
For thy face coins them, and thy stamp they bear,
And by this mintage they are something worth,
For thus they be,
Pregnant of thee;
Fruits of much grief they are, emblems of more,
When a tear falls, that thou falls which it bore,
So thou and I are nothing then, when on a divers shore.

On a round ball
A workman hath copies by, can lay
An Europe, Afric, and an Asia,
And quickly make that, which was nothing, all,
So doth each tear,
Which thee doth wear,
A globe, yea world by that impression grow,
Till thy tears mixt with mine do overflow
This world, by waters sent from thee, my heaven dissolved so.

O more than Moon,
Draw not up seas to drown me in thy sphere,
Weep me not dead, in thine arms, but forbear
To touch the sea, what it may do too soon;
Let not the wind
Example find,
To do me more harm, than it purposeth;
Since thou and I sigh one another's breath,
Whoe'er sighs most, is cruellest, and hastes the other's death.

I discovered the English novelist, Henry Green, at about the same time as I was taking in Wallace Stevens, and I was so struck by their resemblance, one to another, that I wrote a poem about it.

They were both business men, both mandarins, both wrote a kind of exquisiteist prose and poetry and both inspired love in me. My poem was written, I think, when I was about twenty-five. 'An Imaginable Conference' it's called, with a subtitle 'Mr. Henry Green, Industrialist and Mr. Wallace Stevens, Vice-President of the Heartread Accident and Indemnity Company, meet in the Course of Business'.

## *An Imaginable Conference*

JOHN UPDIKE

Exchanging gentle grips the men retire
Prolonged by courteous bumbling at the door,
Retreat to where a rare room deep
Exists on an odd floor, subtly carpeted,
The walls wear charts like chequered vests
And blotters ape the green of cricket fields.
Glass multiplies the pausing men to twice infinity
An inkstand of blue marble has been carven
No young girl's wrist is more discreetly veined.
An office boy, misplaced and slack, intrudes
Apologies, speaking without commas,
'Oh sorry sirs I thought'
Which signifies what wimbly wambly stuff it is
We seem to be made of.
Beyond the room a gander's son pure rhetoric ferments

Imbroglios of bloom.
The stone is so.
The peer confers in murmurings
With words select and Sunday soft
No more is known but rumour goes
That as they hatched the deal
Vistas of lilac waited their shrewd lids.

*Readers: Eleanor Bron, Ed Bishop*

*Full Selection:*
*Genesis 37*, THE BIBLE
*St Matthew*, THE BIBLE
*Little Orphant Annie*, JAMES WHITCOMB RILEY
*Tom Sawyer*, MARK TWAIN
*The Owl Who Was God*, JAMES THURBER
*On the Vanity of Earthly Greatness*, ARTHUR GUITERMAN
*The Problem of the Green Capsule*, JOHN DICKSON CARR
*A Valediction: of Weeping*, JOHN DONNE
*Upon Julia's Clothes*, ROBERT HERRICK
*Upon Prew His Maid*, ROBERT HERRICK
*To Criticks*, ROBERT HERRICK
*Moby-Dick*, HERMAN MELVILLE
*Sunday Morning*, WALLACE STEVENS
*An Imaginable Conference*, JOHN UPDIKE
*Nothing*, HENRY GREEN
*Journals*, SØREN KIERKEGAARD
*On the Circuit*, W. H. AUDEN

# *IAN WALLACE*

## *1988*

*Ian Wallace is one of the nicest men in radio. I first worked with him over twenty years ago when I was a junior studio manager responsible for the spot effects – opening and shutting doors, rattling cups of tea, walking on gravel, etc. – for a series of 'Flying Doctor'. Not much of it remains with me save the memory of Bill Kerr on a ladder declaiming to a studio wall and of Ian Wallace playing the part, I think, of a Maori. In each episode of this masterpiece he had to sing a song in a ringing bass-baritone. After he had mellifluously thrown off a number called something like 'Tahiti Nooky' he confessed to me that he had learnt it the night before whilst watching television. Many years later I had the pleasure of producing him in a musical version of Oscar Wilde's* The Selfish Giant *and, more recently, his 'With Great Pleasure'. Backstage he sang to us a little, his voice every bit as good as it had been all those years ago.*

I'm sure you've noticed that when interviewers ask any victim over a certain age about their childhood reading very many will reply, 'I read everything I could lay my hands on,' almost as though they feared that this exciting new found skill would be snatched away before the eager curiosity of youth could be satisfied.

My childhood reading filled in hours totally devoid of television for the simple reason that it hadn't been invented. There was the crystal set, but it provided programmes chosen for us by Sir John Reith rather than by popular demand. Even so I was a torch under the bedclothes reader as well.

I was born in London, the only child of Scots parents exiled by the needs of my father's business and being not a very robust child was frequently confined to bed with chest colds or tonsillitis – an unlikely start for an opera singer, but there you are. On these occasions my mother, undoubtedly an actress manqué, would deploy the full range of her suppressed histrionic talent to make me forget the alarming symptoms of bronchial asthma. I can still remember the thrill of anticipation as she embarked on the first page of Robert Louis Stevenson's *Treasure Island*.

## *Treasure Island*

**ROBERT LOUIS STEVENSON**

Squire Trelawney, Dr. Livesey, and the rest of these gentlemen having asked me to write down the whole particulars about Treasure Island, from the beginning to the end, keeping nothing back but the bearings of the island, and that only because there is still treasure not yet lifted, I take up my pen in the year of grace 17—, and go back to the time when my father kept the Admiral Benbow inn, and the brown old seaman, with the sabre cut, first took up his lodging under our roof.

I remember him as if it were yesterday, as he came plodding to the inn door, his sea-chest following behind him in a hand-barrow; a tall, strong, heavy, nut-brown man; his tarry pigtail falling over the shoulders of his soiled blue coat; his hands ragged and scarred, with black, broken nails; and the sabre cut across one cheek, a dirty, livid white. I remember him looking round the cove and whistling to himself as he did so, and then breaking out in that old sea-song that he sang so often afterwards:

> 'Fifteen men on the dead man's chest –
> Yo-ho-ho, and a bottle of rum!'

in the high, old tottering voice that seemed to have been tuned and broken at the capstan bars. Then he rapped on the door with a bit of a stick like a handspike that he carried, and when my father appeared, called roughly for a glass of rum. This, when it was brought to him, he drank slowly, like a connoisseur, lingering on the taste, and still looking about him at the cliffs and up at our signboard.

'This is a handy cove!' says he, at length, 'and a pleasant sittyated grog-shop. Much company, – mate?'

My father told him no – very little company, the more was the pity.

'Well then,' said he, 'this is the berth for me. – Here you, matey,' he cried to the man who trundled the barrow; 'bring up alongside and help up my chest. I'll stay here a bit,' he continued. 'I'm a plain man; rum and bacon and eggs is what I want, and that head up there for to watch ships off. – What you mought call me? You mought call me captain. Oh, I see what you're at – there;' and he threw down three or four gold pieces on the threshold.

'You can tell me when I've worked through that,' says he, looking as fierce as a commander.

I had the good fortune to be sent to Charterhouse where we are this evening and where fifty years ago there was a collection of masters, so many of them characters in their own right that I could supply descriptions of at least twelve of them good enough for the police to issue identikit pictures. One, Frank Ives, introduced us to poetry, especially Victorian narrative verse and the romantics, reading for us with gusto and conviction. And this tough, wiry little man who also commanded the Officers' Training Corps was not embarrassed by his emotion even when, occasionally, he brushed away a tear. He was at his best where some histrionic effort was required as in Robert Browning's 'My Last Duchess'. The haughty, jealous, recently widowed Duke showing off one of his paintings to an emissary from a prospective new father-in-law was meat and drink to Frank.

## *My Last Duchess*
**ROBERT BROWNING**

That's my last Duchess painted on the wall,
Looking as if she were alive. I call
That piece a wonder, now: Frà Pandolf's hands
Worked busily a day, and there she stands.
Will't please you sit and look at her? I said
'Frà Pandolf' by design, for never read
Strangers like you that pictured countenance,

The depth and passion of its earnest glance,
But to myself they turned (since none puts by
The curtain I have drawn for you, but I)
And seemed as if they would ask me, if they durst,
How such a glance came there; so, not the first
Are you to turn and ask thus. Sir 'twas not
Her husband's presence only, called that spot
Of joy into the Duchess' cheek: perhaps
Frà Pandolf chanced to say 'Her mantle laps
Over my lady's wrist too much,' or 'Paint
Must never hope to reproduce the faint
Half-flush that dies along her throat:' such stuff
Was courtesy, she thought, and cause enough
For calling up that spot of joy. She had
A heart – how shall I say? – too soon made glad,
Too easily impressed; she liked whate'er
She looked on, and her looks went everywhere.
Sir, 'twas all one! My favour at her breast,
The dropping of the daylight in the West,
The bough of cherries some officious fool
Broke in the orchard for her, the white mule
She rode with round the terrace – all and each
Would draw from her alike the approving speech,
Or blush, at least. She thanked men, – good! but thanked
Somehow – I know not how – as if she ranked
My gift of a nine-hundred-years-old name
With anybody's gift. Who'd stoop to blame
This sort of trifling? Even had you skill
In speech – (which I have not) – to make your will
Quite clear to such an one, and say, 'Just this
Or that in you disgusts me; here you miss,
Or there exceed the mark' – and if she let
Herself be lessoned so, nor plainly set
Her wits to yours, forsooth, and made excuse,
– E'en then would be some stooping; and I choose
Never to stoop. Oh sir, she smiled, no doubt,
Whene'er I passed her; but who passed without
Much the same smile? This grew; I gave commands;
Then all smiles stopped together. There she stands

As if alive. Will 't please you rise? We'll meet
The company below, then. I repeat,
The Count your master's known munificence
Is ample warrant that no just pretence
Of mine for dowry will be disallowed;
Though his fair daughter's self, as I avowed
At starting, is my object. Nay we'll go
Together down, sir. Notice Neptune, though,
Taming a sea-horse, thought a rarity,
Which Claus of Innsbruck cast in bronze for me!

One Scots versifier has given me considerable pleasure, William McGonagall, whose doggerel sincerely chronicled nineteenth-century triumphs and disasters and has provided subsequent generations with the delight of unconscious humour. Here are a few verses from one of my favourites.

## *The Humble Heroine*

**WILLIAM MCGONAGALL**

'Twas at the Siege of Matagarda, during the Peninsular War,
That a Mrs. Reston for courage outshone any man there by far;
She was the wife of a Scottish soldier in Matagarda Fort,
And to attend her husband she there did resort.

And Captain Maclaine of the 94th did the whole of them
command,
And the courage the men displayed was really grand;
Because they held Matagarda for fifty-four days,
Against o'er whelming numbers of the French – therefore they
are worthy of praise.

There was one woman in the fort during those trying days,
A Mrs. Reston, who is worthy of great praise;
She acted like a ministering angel to the soldiers while there,
By helping them to fill sand-bags, it was her constant care.

Methinks I see a brave heroine carrying her child,
Whilst the bullets were falling around her, enough to drive her
wild;

And bending over it to protect it from danger,
Because to war's alarms it was a stranger.

And while the shells shrieked around, and their fragments did shatter,
She was serving the men at the guns with wine and water;
And while the shot whistled around, her courage wasn't slack,
Because to the soldiers she carried sand-bags on her back.

A little drummer boy was told to fetch water from the well,
But he was afraid because the bullets from the enemy around it fell;
And the Doctor cried to the boy, Why are you standing there?
And Mrs. Reston said, Doctor, the bairn is feared, I do declare.

And she said, Give me the pail, laddie, I'll fetch the water,
Not fearing that the shot would her brains scatter;
And without a moment's hesitation she took the pail,
Whilst the shot whirred thick around her, yet her courage didn't fail.

So the French were beaten and were glad to run,
And the British for defeating them golden opinions have won;
All through brave Captain Maclaine and his heroes bold,
Likewise Mrs. Reston, whose name should be written in letters of gold.

Having set out to be an actor it was a great surprise to find that those friends who counselled me to audition for an opera company were proved right. However, one of my early extra-operatic activities was to take part in a dramatized version of Hilaire Belloc's book *The Four Men* on a tour of Sussex towns and villages to celebrate the Festival of Britain. We opened in Chichester and I was billeted with the poet Robert Gittings and his wife Jo in a nearby village. I arrived late on a still summer evening and we sat silent by the open window until we were rewarded by their resident nightingale. That was thirty-five years ago when we were all a long way from that part of life when the shadowy coastline of mortality is faintly discernible on the far horizon. Robert sends his friends a poem every Christmas, but this one is for a season hopefully still remote.

## *Imaginings*

**ROBERT GITTINGS**

I go to all the places you once loved,
Everywhere lost. I see a smudge of red
Climbing the path ahead,
Reach it at burst of lung; it has not moved;
Only a picnic rag fluttering the bush,
Not your coat's scarlet. In the birdsong hush
I hear alone the tears I have to shed.

I go to all the valleys you once named,
Deep Combe, Half Moon, and silent Celtic Fields,
Names only. Nothing yields
Your voice to me, no whisper that exclaimed
As deer and fawn came trotting the long ride
With delicate printed track from side to side.
They go, and leave a grief that nothing shields,

The naked grief that keeps an open nerve
To casual promptings, sharp and unaware,
The cold form of the hare,
Empty reminders of the populous day
You made around you, and which shaped the way
We went through time in your unconscious care.

All these imaginings – if you should go
Before me! And if I should leave the first –
Each choice impossibly worst –
And you the one to take the upward, slow,
Trail through the woodland, O, I promise you,
With my pale, breathless, tenuous residue,
I shall be trying to reach you, though the heart burst.

*Readers: Michael Williams, Jill Baker*

*Full Selection:*
*Parliament Hill Fields*, JOHN BETJEMAN
*Treasure Island*, ROBERT LOUIS STEVENSON
*My Last Duchess*, ROBERT BROWNING

*94 Declared Cricket Reminiscences,* BEN TRAVERS
*Seaside Golf,* JOHN BETJEMAN
*Literary Lapses,* STEPHEN LEACOCK
*Argus,* ELEANOR FARJEON
*A Red, Red Rose,* ROBERT BURNS
*The Humble Heroine,* WILLIAM MCGONAGALL
*The Scotch Forcing Gardener,* J. G. TEMPLE
*Letter from Mozart to His Father*
*Imaginings,* ROBERT GITTINGS
*Advertisements,* ROY BROOKS
*Song To Be Sung by The Father of Infant Female Children,* OGDEN NASH
*Great Operatic Disasters,* HUGH VICKERS
*The Slow Train,* MICHAEL FLANDERS

# INDEX